# AI, Human Communication, and the Challenges of Digital Addiction

Mohd Noorulfakhri Yaacob
https://orcid.org/0000-0002-0938-7833
*Universiti Malaysia Perlis, Malaysia*

Syed Zulkarnain Syed Idrus
*Universiti Malaysia Perlis, Malaysia*

Wan Nor Ashiqin Wan Ali
https://orcid.org/0000-0003-2489-2843
*Universiti Malaysia Perlis, Malaysia*

Wan Ahmad Jaafar Bin Wan Yahaya
https://orcid.org/0000-0002-8605-0062
*Universiti Sains Malaysia, Malaysia*

Christophe Rosenberger
https://orcid.org/0000-0002-2042-9029
*Ecole Nationale Supérieure d'Ingénieurs de Caen, France*

IGI Global
Scientific Publishing
Publishing Tomorrow's Research Today

Vice President of Editorial Melissa Wagner
Director of Acquisitions Mikaela Felty
Director of Book Development Jocelynn Hessler
Production Manager Mike Brehm
Cover Design Jose Rosado

Published in the United States of America by
IGI Global Scientific Publishing
701 East Chocolate Avenue
Hershey, PA, 17033, USA
Tel: 717-533-8845 | Fax: 717-533-7115
Website: https://www.igi-global.com E-mail: cust@igi-global.com



Library of Congress Cataloging-in-Publication Data

Names: Yaacob, Mohd Noorulfakhri, 1981- editor | Syed Idrus, Syed Zulkarnain, 1976- editor | Wan Ali, Wan Nor Ashiqin, 1988- editor | Wan Yahaya, Wan Ahmad Jaafar Bin, 1968- editor | Rosenberger, Christophe, 1973- editor
Title: AI, human communication, and the challenges of digital addiction / edited by: Mohd Noorulfakhri Yaacob, Syed Zulkarnain Syed Idrus, Wan Nor Ashiqin Wan Ali, Wan Ahmad Jaafar Bin Wan Yahaya, Christophe Rosenberger.
Description: Hershey PA : IGI Global Scientific Publishing, [2026] | Includes bibliographical references. | Summary: "This book aims to examine the profound impact of artificial intelligence on human communication and to analyze the emerging challenges associated with digital addiction"-- Provided by publisher.
Identifiers: LCCN 2025033190 (print) | LCCN 2025033191 (ebook) | ISBN 9798337356068 hardcover | ISBN 9798337356075 paperback | ISBN 9798337356082 ebook
Subjects: LCSH: Artificial intelligence--Social aspects | Human-computer interaction | Internet addiction
Classification: LCC Q335 .A429 2026 (print) | LCC Q335 (ebook)
LC record available at https://lccn.loc.gov/2025033190
LC ebook record available at https://lccn.loc.gov/2025033191

British Cataloguing in Publication Data
A Cataloguing in Publication record for this book is available from the British Library.

# Table of Contents

# Detailed Table of Contents

The rise of digital addiction represents a significant and complex phenomenon of the 21st century, reflecting the growing entanglement between human behavior and digital technologies. With the advent and ubiquity of smartphones, social media platforms, streaming services, online gaming, and digital communication tools, individuals are spending unprecedented amounts of time connected to digital devices. While these technologies offer immense benefits—facilitating communication, productivity, education, and entertainment—they have also given rise to patterns of compulsive, excessive, and unhealthy usage that can significantly impair psychological well-being, social relationships, academic and occupational performance, and physical health. Digital addiction, often referred to by terms such as "internet addiction," "screen addiction," or "technology dependency," is increasingly recognized as a behavioral addiction that mirrors many characteristics of substance use disorders, including tolerance, withdrawal, loss of control, and continued use despite adverse consequences.



The introduction of artificial intelligence (AI) into the digital space has transformed the whole process of human communication but has made the development of digital addiction and technology addiction more rapid. This chapter looks into the role of AI-augmented design functions i.e. infinite scroll, algorithmic nudging, and dopamine-based feedback loop, in the development of compulsive digital behaviors. It also discusses critically the cognitive, emotional, and social effects of digital addiction caused by AI. The chapter focuses on the responsibility dilemma of tech platforms and the place of regulatory frameworks and acts through the prism of persuasive technology ethics, attention economics, and the role of public policy in reducing digital harm. It also observes counter-movements in digital well-being.

By highlighting the contradiction that AI is at the same time a cause and possible solution to digital dependence, the chapter reminds of a future where the design of technology materializes the psychological health, freedom of action, and autonomy of its users.



The chapter examines the potential effects of cutting-edge technologies like emotionally intelligent artificial in-telligence and immersive worlds like the metaverse. These developments blur the boundaries between virtual and real experiences, even as they present new opportunities for engagement and education. This necessitates a careful re-examination of what meaningful communication in a world full of digital devices means. The chapter essentially offers a comprehensive framework for comprehending and addressing the relationship be-tween communication, AI, and digital addiction. Researchers, designers, educators, parents, and legislators are all urged to work together to create a future in which technology enhances human well-being and the depth of relationships rather than detracts from them.



Artificial Intelligence (AI) has transformed human communication, reshaping emotional expression and behavior. While AI-driven tools like social media and digital assistants offer connectivity, they also fuel digital addiction, raising serious psychological and legal concerns. This chapter adopts an interdisciplinary lens, combining legal and psychological insights to explore how AI-mediated communication impairs autonomy and mental well-being. It examines behavioral triggers like dopamine loops and social validation, alongside legal frameworks such as India's IT Act, 2000, the Digital Personal Data Protection Act, 2023, and the EU's GDPR and DSA. The chapter highlights how algorithmic persuasion and platform design exploit cognitive vulnerabilities, calling for ethical AI design, stronger regulation, and stakeholder accountability. It advocates a rights-based framework to protect users and ensure AI enhances rather than undermines autonomy and resilience.

# Preface

## INTRODUCTION

In the twenty-first century, artificial intelligence (AI) rapidly transformed the landscape of human communication. From instant messaging platforms to sophisticated virtual assistants, AI-driven technologies have become deeply embedded in our daily interactions. These advancements have created extraordinary opportunities for connection, collaboration, and access to information. Yet, they have also brought forth profound challenges, most notably the erosion of meaningful human relationships and the escalating phenomenon of digital addiction.

*AI, Human Communication, and the Challenges of Digital Addiction* emerges from a shared concern among scholars, practitioners, and technologists about how our reliance on digital systems is reshaping the ways we connect with one another. This edited volume brings together interdisciplinary perspectives to explore the intricate interplay between AI and human communication, examining both the transformative benefits and the unintended consequences of our increasingly digital lives. It investigates how AI influences our conversations, social behaviors, and emotional bonds, while also addressing the psychological and societal implications of compulsive technology use.

Our goal as editors has been twofold: first, to provide a comprehensive and balanced understanding of how AI-driven tools are redefining communication in the digital era; and second, to offer practical insights for mitigating the negative effects of digital addiction. The chapters within this volume illuminate key mechanisms through which AI affects communication patterns and social dynamics, explore the cultural and ethical dimensions of digital engagement, and present evidence-based strategies for fostering healthier relationships with technology.

We envision this book as a resource for diverse academics, educators, mental health professionals, technology developers, policymakers, and individuals seeking to navigate the complex relationship between human connection and digital innovation. Each contribution offers not only analysis but also reflection and action: a call to design, use, and regulate technology in ways that enhance rather than diminish our shared humanity.

As we stand at the crossroads of technological advancement and human well-being, we invite readers to pause and reflect. The decisions we make today about how we communicate, connect, and coexist with AI will shape the emotional and ethical contours of our future. It is our hope that this book inspires thoughtful dialogue, responsible innovation, and a renewed commitment to ensuring that technology remains a tool for human flourishing.

## ORGANIZATION OF THE BOOK

### Chapter 1: The Evolution of Artificial Intelligence in Media: A Bibliometric Study

The opening chapter provides a foundational analysis of how artificial intelligence has transformed media production and journalism over the past two decades. Through a comprehensive bibliometric study covering research from 2000 to 2024, this chapter maps the intellectual structure, thematic evolution, and geographic distribution of scholarly inquiry into AI-driven media. By employing advanced analytical tools such as VOSviewer and Bibliometrix, it identifies key authors, institutions, and emerging research clusters that define this rapidly developing field. Importantly, the chapter highlights the ethical and technological challenges that accompany AI integration in news production, offering a data-driven perspective that grounds the subsequent discussions on communication and digital dependency.

### Chapter 2: AI in Communication and its Impact on Interpersonal and Group Interaction

Building on the historical trajectory of AI in communication, Chapter 2 explores how artificial intelligence from early chatbots like ELIZA and ALICE to today's advanced large language models has redefined human interaction. The chapter examines how AI mediates identity, emotion, and trust in both interpersonal and group contexts, while also interrogating the darker aspects of this transformation, including algorithmic echo chambers, surveillance, and digital addiction. By tracing the development of communication technologies through the lenses of natural language processing and machine learning, the chapter underscores the dual role of AI as both a disruptor and an enhancer of human connection, inviting readers to reflect on the ethical implications of empathy mediated through algorithms.

## Chapter 3: AI-Mediated Communication and Digital Dependency: Navigating Human Connection in the Algorithmic Age

In Chapter 3, the authors turn their attention to the algorithmic forces shaping communication in the digital era. This chapter critically examines how AI-mediated platforms such as chatbots, social algorithms, and recommendation systems are reshaping the contours of human relationships. While acknowledging the efficiency and personalization these systems provide, the chapter warns of the risks of digital dependency and emotional disengagement. Drawing from psychology, communication theory, and AI ethics, it calls for mindful design and conscious digital habits to sustain authentic connection in an age of algorithmic mediation.

## Chapter 4: Mechanisms and Manifestations of Digital Addiction with a Focus on Social Media, Messaging Platforms, and AI-Driven Applications

Chapter 4 provides a detailed exploration of the mechanisms underlying digital addiction. Through an interdisciplinary lens, it examines how the ubiquity of social media, gaming, streaming, and messaging platforms has produced new forms of compulsive digital engagement. By comparing digital dependency to behavioral addiction models, the chapter highlights psychological and physiological parallels such as tolerance, withdrawal, and loss of control. It presents a compelling analysis of how AI-driven personalization amplifies these addictive behaviors, emphasizing the need for public awareness, mental health interventions, and responsible technology design.

## Chapter 5: Scroll, Swipe, Repeat: Understanding Digital Dependency in the Age of AI

Focusing on the design ethics of digital environments, Chapter 5 examines how AI-powered features such as infinite scroll, algorithmic nudging, and reward feedback loops fuel compulsive user behavior. This chapter situates digital dependency within the frameworks of attention economics and persuasive technology ethics, calling attention to the moral responsibility of technology companies and policymakers. It also highlights emerging counter-movements promoting digital well-being and regulation. Ultimately, the authors challenge readers to consider how AI can simultaneously exacerbate and alleviate digital addiction, and how thoughtful design can restore autonomy, focus, and psychological health in an AI-mediated world.

### Chapter 6: AI-Driven Communication and Digital Addiction: A Psychological and Social Inquiry

Chapter 6 extends the discussion into the psychological and social dimensions of AI-driven communication, examining how technologies such as emotionally intelligent AI and immersive environments like the metaverse blur the lines between reality and simulation. The authors present a holistic framework for understanding how digital immersion affects empathy, identity, and social connectedness. By encouraging collaboration among researchers, educators, policymakers, and families, the chapter advocates for a future where technological innovation strengthens rather than undermines human well-being and emotional depth.

### Chapter 7: AI, Autonomy, and Addiction: A Legal-Psychological Analysis of Communication Technologies in the Digital Age

Chapter 7 introduces a critical interdisciplinary perspective, combining psychological insights with legal frameworks to assess how AI-mediated communication impacts autonomy and mental health. The authors analyze how algorithmic persuasion and behavioral design exploit cognitive vulnerabilities, contributing to compulsive use and diminished self-regulation. Drawing on key legislation such as India's IT Act (2000), the Digital Personal Data Protection Act (2023), and the European Union's GDPR and DSA, this chapter underscores the urgency of ethical AI governance. It advocates for a rights-based approach that prioritizes user agency, transparency, and mental resilience in the digital sphere.

### Chapter 8: SmartSpeak Health: An LLM-Driven Virtual Health Assistant with Personalized Recommendations and Geo-Based Specialist Routing

This chapter presents an innovative case study on AI's potential to enhance human well-being through responsible application. *SmartSpeak Health* introduces a large language model-powered virtual assistant that provides personalized healthcare guidance and location-based specialist recommendations. The system integrates natural language processing, retrieval-augmented generation (RAG), and geospatial APIs to create a responsive, context-aware communication interface between patients and providers. The chapter not only illustrates the transformative potential of AI in healthcare communication but also raises broader questions about trust, privacy, and human oversight in medical decision-making.

### Chapter 9: Ethical Considerations in the Design and Deployment of AI Communication Tools, Including Privacy, Consent, and Algorithmic Bias

The concluding chapter centers on the ethical imperatives underpinning AI-mediated communication. As AI systems increasingly shape social interaction, decision-making, and information access, this chapter examines the pressing issues of transparency, accountability, bias, consent, and human dignity. It highlights how virtual assistants, chatbots, recommendation engines, and generative media platforms mediate not only communication but also influence thought and behavior. The authors argue that ethics must serve as the cornerstone of AI design, ensuring that technological innovation aligns with human values and societal trust. This closing reflection provides a moral and philosophical anchor for the volume, urging stakeholders to develop AI systems that respect autonomy, equity, and shared responsibility.

## CONCLUSION

As editors of *AI, Human Communication, and the Challenges of Digital Addiction*, we are acutely aware that this book emerges at a pivotal moment in the evolution of human interaction. The chapters collected here represent a convergence of disciplines communication studies, psychology, sociology, law, technology, and ethics each offering a unique perspective on how artificial intelligence is transforming the ways we connect, communicate, and coexist. Together, they illuminate a paradox at the heart of our digital age: while AI expands the possibilities for human connection, it also deepens our dependence on the very systems that mediate those connections.

Across these pages, readers will encounter both the promise and the peril of AI-mediated communication. The contributors demonstrate how algorithms can personalize and enhance human experiences yet also reveal how these same mechanisms can manipulate attention, erode autonomy, and foster compulsive engagement. They show that digital addiction is not merely a matter of excessive screen time, but a reflection of deeper psychological, cultural, and structural shifts in how meaning, identity, and emotion are negotiated in the presence of intelligent machines.

This book does not aim to resolve all the tensions that arise at the intersection of technology and humanity. Rather, it invites readers to engage with them critically and compassionately. The future of communication will not be determined solely by the sophistication of AI systems, but by the ethical choices of those who design, regulate, and use them. Whether in newsrooms, classrooms, clinical settings, or online communities, the challenge before us is to cultivate awareness, responsibility, and resilience in our digital interactions.

Our hope is that this volume serves as both a mirror and a guide—a mirror reflecting the complexities of our relationship with AI, and a guide pointing toward more humane and intentional ways of living with technology. As we stand on the threshold of an era defined by intelligent systems, we are reminded that the essence of communication lies not in the tools we use, but in the empathy, understanding, and shared purpose that connect us as human beings.

# Chapter 1
# The Evolution of Artificial Intelligence in Media: A Bibliometric Study

**Ahmed Chebli Alami**
https://orcid.org/0009-0006-7358-327X
*Faculty of Science of Rabat, Morocco*

**Aya Loudiyi Lamghafri**
https://orcid.org/0009-0007-3653-6412
*Faculty of Science of Rabat, Morocco*

**Abdeslam El Harraj**
*Moroccan National Society for Television and Radio Broadcasting, Morocco*

**Soumia Ziti**
*Faculty of Science of Rabat, Morocco*

## ABSTRACT

*The production and distribution of news is quickly being restructured by artificial intelligence. With media companies increasingly using AI to provide faster and more personalized content, the field has emerged as a point of interest to academic study. Up to date, there is no bibliometric research that would survey the development of the field, its geographic dispersion, or thematic trends. The current analysis fills this gap as it considers the publications between 2000 and 2024, retrieving the data in Scopus, using VOSviewer to visualize it, and resorting to Bibliometrix to conduct quantitative analysis. The research assesses the productivity of research by the h-index and lists top authors, institutions, and countries. Moreover, the paper employs*

DOI: 10.4018/979-8-3373-5606-8.ch001

*co-occurrence networks and thematic mapping to point out emerging topics, ethical aspects, and technological challenges. Altogether, the results give a general picture that can inform future studies on AI-based journalism.*

## INTRODUCTION

In media research, the use of artificial intelligence (AI) has become an active and fast-growing research pathway. The technological breakthroughs of recent times have transformed the process of media production, consumption, and distribution, and AI has become one of the main drivers. Automated systems that aim to increase the level of audience engagement, create content without the involvement of a human intermediary, and make decisions based on data have made AI the key axis of innovation in the modern media practice. This growth can be traced in the corresponding increase of scholarly production, which indicates a greater awareness of the multidisciplinary and global importance of AI in designing current communication landscapes. These dynamics are especially well demonstrated in the sphere of journalism. In this industry, AI is used to automate the writing of news, personalize the content feeds, moderate the user comments, and optimize headlines to attract readers. Similar trends are witnessed in the field of film and entertainment where AI is used to analyze scripts, recreate scenes, and even create deepfake characters. Social media exploits AI to sort out allowable and banned contents, and to analyze user behavior in such a way that it can maximize attention and advertising revenues. Such a variety of applications confirms the widespread use of AI in the entire media life cycle. Despite this multiplication of academic research, a sufficiently broad picture of international tendencies, key actors, and new challenges has not been drawn. Important questions like, what are the prevailing themes and partnership networks that define this interdisciplinary area, and who are the most influential countries and organizations in this field are still unanswered. Such concerns are necessary to monitor the development of AI in media and to determine the geographic, thematic, and collaborative gaps that are present, so that the future of AI can be inclusive and ethically oriented.

The bibliometric analysis is a necessary descriptive instrument of the evaluation of the paths of knowledge production. This approach is adopted in the current research to explore the intersection of media, public relations, and artificial intelligence, and to outline its major trends, key players, and topic areas as well as to determine the key actors. Co-authorship network analysis shows that the field is global and interdisciplinary, and mapping of institutional collaboration proves its multidimensional nature. Thematic tendencies represented by the corpus are AI-based content production, automated journalism, and the ethical aspect of AI adoption in the media practice in general. These insights are complemented by a more detailed analysis of how the field is growing, how its publications are referenced and who is contributing to it on the basis of geography. By means of systematic data extraction and analysis, the study offers quantitative and visual data on the blistering maturation of the AI-enabled media research.

This paper builds on the current bibliometric research in the field of AI and media studies, expands the boundaries of the previous research, and provides practical recommendations on responsible progress to scholars, professionals, and policymakers. The discussion highlights the need to develop frameworks that would make AI systems built with the purpose of communicating to the general population transparent, accountable, and diverse. In addition, it emphasizes the necessity of long-term communication between academic domains and industry players to balance technological innovation and the best interest of the people. The article is structured as follows: the second section describes the bibliometric methodology, including data collection, filtration criteria, and data analysis; the third section offers key findings regarding the emerging research topics, collaboration patterns, and publication dynamics, and explains their meaning to the field; the fourth section explains limitations and future research proposals; and the fifth section concludes on the study contributions and implications of its findings on the integration of AI in the media and public-relations settings. Overall, this analytical study will help to explain the changing role of AI in media and to encourage more interdisciplinary cooperation in this fast-growing field.

## METHODOLOGY

### Data Source

The present bibliometric study is based on the information retrieved in the Scopus database, which was selected due to its high coverage of peer-reviewed literature in a wide range of academic fields. Not only does Scopus make available an unprecedented volume of scholarly articles, but it also offers very fine-grained metadata, such as citation counts, author affiliations, keywords, and subject classifications, that enable advanced analytical methods and long-term longitudinal monitoring of research trends. The wide coverage of publications in the database in the area of media studies and artificial intelligence (AI) was especially appropriate when it came to detecting and tracking multidisciplinary interaction and collaborative dynamics in these convergent areas.

A conscious and well-documented search strategy was followed to guarantee reproducibility and methodological transparency. An ensemble of keywords was created to form a carefully crafted list that would help in retrieving the documents that touched on AI applications in the field of media, journalism, communication, and public relations. The use of Boolean operators (AND, OR and NOT) was also intentional to expand or reduce the search space accordingly. The time frame was 2000 2024, thus allowing to observe the long-term trends of publishing, identify the historical changes in the orientation of research, and consider the recent trends. There were no restrictions based on discipline, language, or geographic origin, which enhanced inclusivity and generated a dataset that reflects the rest of the domain in order to conduct a robust analysis.

## Data Query and Filters

A thorough search was developed and conducted in Scopus to retrieve articles relevant to the intersection of artificial intelligence (AI) and news production, and the aim was to create a narrow but varied corpus that represents the interdisciplinary character of the discipline. There was a focus on publications on automated journalism, content production, and the general newsroom digitization.

The search question was intentionally crafted and it was comprehensive and specific based on the systematic selection of keywords, phrases and Boolean operators. The literature search was conducted by combining phrases that connected the terms of artificial intelligence, machine learning, news production, automated journalism, and media automation with the use of connectors AND and OR, which allowed including resources of communication studies, computer science, media studies, and information systems, and ensuring significant breadth and relevance.

The query was designed to be more precise than exhaustive, in order to make sure that both seminal and emergent works of several decades were included. The resulting set therefore contained peer-reviewed journal articles, conference papers, and book chapters that directly correspond with the research objectives.

The last search term was:

```
TITLE-ABS-KEY (
"news production" OR "news automation" OR "automated jour-
nalism"
OR "AI journalism" OR "journalism automation" OR "media pro-
duction"
OR "news content automation" OR "news generation" OR "jour-
nalism technology"
OR "digital journalism" OR "broadcast journalism" OR "news
dissemination"
```

OR "news storytelling" OR "journalism workflows" OR "AI media production"
OR "automated video production" OR "news video generation"
OR "virtual news presenters" OR "AI video production"
OR "newsroom automation" OR "automated news delivery"
OR "media workflow automation" OR "AI-driven journalism"
OR "content automation" OR "robot journalism" OR "automated content creation"
OR "data-driven journalism" OR "automated news writing"
OR "AI-generated content" OR "automated content synthesis"
OR "AI-powered media" OR "algorithmic journalism" OR "robotic reporting"
OR "automated article writing" OR "machine-generated journalism"
OR "digital storytelling" OR "AI-assisted reporting"
OR "automated broadcast" OR "virtual anchors" OR "AI-driven anchors"
OR "text-to-video news" OR "synthetic media production"
OR "generative media" OR "deepfake news anchors" OR "AI synthetic anchors"
OR "automated documentary production" OR "AI-powered video creation"
OR "neural media production" OR "automated podcast production"
OR "automated transcription services" OR "AI-assisted editing"
OR "journalistic automation" OR "automated newsroom workflows"
OR "text-to-speech journalism" OR "AI-powered news transcription"
OR "automated video editing" OR "virtual news hosts"
OR "real-time AI news generation" OR "speech synthesis in journalism"
OR "AI avatars for broadcasting" OR "interactive media production"
)
AND TITLE-ABS-KEY (
"artificial intelligence" OR "AI" OR "machine learning"
OR "deep learning" OR "natural language processing"
OR "neural networks" OR "automation" OR "AI tools"

```
OR "algorithmic content" OR "AI-powered production"
OR "content synthesis" OR "media synthesis"
)
AND NOT TITLE-ABS-KEY (
"detection" OR "fake news" OR "classification"
OR "sentiment analysis" OR "object detection"
OR "anomaly detection" OR "content moderation"
)
```

This query returned 1,013 articles after applying the following filters:

- Timespan: 2000-2024
- Language: English
- Document Type: Article, Conference Paper, Book Chapter

The current investigation limited the scope of its research to the academic literature of the last 25 years (2000-2024) and, therefore, was able to encompass both the initial and the latest trends in the field. This time interval was wisely chosen to align with the emergence of artificial intelligence in media-related studies and practice. The focus on the modern and relevant developments, coupled with the maintenance of enough historical context allowed the study to focus on the current trends and developments, as well as highlight the long-term trends, changes in research priorities, and the development of new technologies and methodologies. By using this filtering process, only the works that could be considered relevant and peer-reviewed were kept, which further supports the analytic rigor and credibility of the investigation. The high level of quality in the corpus was maintained by excluding older or non-peer-reviewed materials. The last compilation consisted of scholarly journal articles, conference proceedings, and review papers that met high academic standards. The resulting data set was strong and reliable, which provided a good foundation to bibliometric indicators like publication trends, citation analysis, and thematic mapping of artificial intelligence in media research.

*Figure 1. Research strategy workflow*

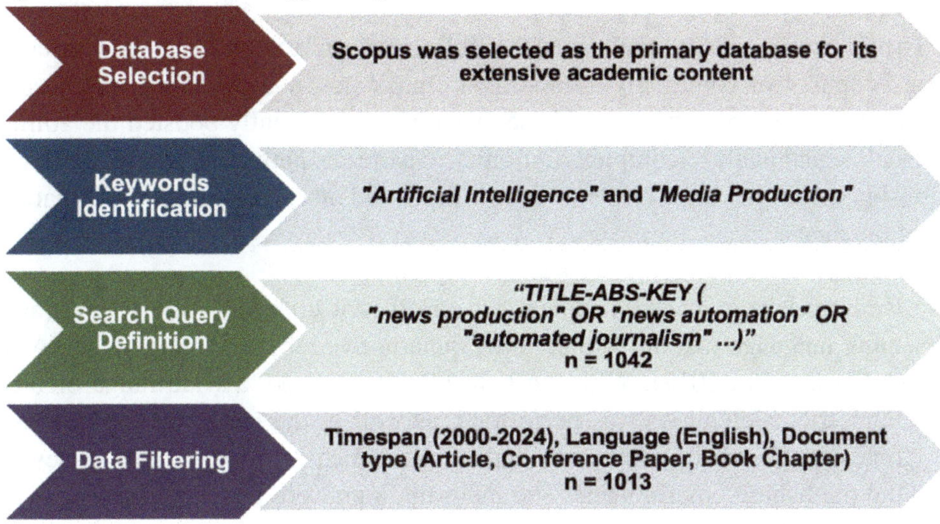


## Data Collection and Preprocessing

The current paper uses the dataset consisting of bibliographic records retrieved in Scopus database. The data is organized around a central set of items, namely title, names of authors, institutional affiliations, year of publication, number of citations and keywords. These variables form the analytical canvas of any bibliometric research, facilitating the study of publication trends, citation effect, and collaboration between institutions and between countries. The original data were exported as the CSV format, which is a commonly accepted architecture that supports statistical analysis as well as visualization methods.

Before the analysis, a preprocessing stage was introduced to improve the quality of data and reduce noise. The main procedures included the normalisation of the names of authors (combining heterogeneous forms of the same name), harmonisation of affiliated institutions, and the elimination of incomplete or irrelevant records that could not meet the inclusion criteria. Such steps were essential to the validity of co-authorship networks, institutional mapping, and collaboration metrics. Without such normalisation, the networks and metrics that would be obtained would be skewed thus affecting the reliability of the results. A consistent and uniformly structured dataset therefore supports valid and reliable bibliometric knowledge.

## Analytical Tools

To perform an in-depth analysis of the bibliometric information that was retrieved using Scopus, two commonly used software packages, namely, Bibliometrix and VOSviewer, were implemented. These programs significantly boosted the ability to visualize and analyze complex bibliometric patterns, networks, and research relationships, thus making it easier to extract more and more meaningful information out of the data set.

- Bibliometrix is an open-source, advanced tool created in the R programming language that aims to conduct quantitative bibliometric analysis (Aria & Cuccurullo, 2017). With the help of this package, a wide range of bibliometric calculations was performed, as well as the generation of descriptive statistics and performance indicators, which as a whole help to reveal the publishing environment. The main findings were the annual publication trends that defined the growth rates and changes in the research activity within the 20002024 period, and the country-wise publication distributions that highlighted the main countries in AI and media research. The measure of author productivity, that is, the h-index, the total number of citations, and the number of publications, were also computed, which provided an opportunity to gain a better understanding of influential scholars and their contribution to the field. Moreover, Bibliometrix facilitated the analysis of the frequency of keywords, thus, revealing both established and new research directions at the crossroad of AI and media studies. These analyses allowed one to map the historical development of research areas, and through it, it was possible to track the development and evolution of academic interest in different aspects of AI in media.
- VOSviewer (Van Eck & Waltman, 2010) was used as an addition to Bibliometrix to build and visualize co-authorship, co-citation and keyword networks. The simple graphical interface of VOSviewer generated co-authorship maps that shed light on collaborative patterns at the individual researcher, research group and institutional levels. This allowed outlining major actors and determining the centers of international scientific collaboration. Moreover, VOSviewer produced keyword co-occurrence maps which showed thematic clusters and the connections between research topics. The emergent maps identified the key research areas of automated journalism, AI-driven content personalization, ethical issues, and technological issues, thus helping scholars to identify the trends in the AI-driven media studies. Moreover, the software allowed visualizing the temporal and geographic overlaps, which gave an idea of how the patterns of collaboration and research interests

changed over time and space. The paper used these visual network analyses combined with bibliometric data to provide a multidimensional picture of the dynamic and interdisciplinary character of the AI research in the field of media and public relations.

The integrated application of the Bibliometrix and VOSviewer, therefore, formed a powerful set of tools that significantly expanded the bibliometric analysis of the project and allowed a comprehensive and subtle insight into research trends, collaboration networks, and thematic progress in AI-driven media studies.

## RESULTS

### Overview of Research Output

*Figure 2. Research output summary*

The body of literature exploring the topic of artificial intelligence in media has experienced a significant growth as there were 980 publications written by 2,630 distinct researchers in 581 unique sources in the period between 2000 and 2024. This growth trend is depicted in figure 2, which shows that there has been a growing academic interest in the transformative power of AI in fields like automated journalism, personalised content delivery, multimedia production, and audience analytics. The number of annual publications has been growing by an average of 25.04%, which highlights the growing rate of technological innovation as well as the growing academic interest in the study of AI-driven media processes. Cooperation is one of the key factors of this growth. The total percentage of international collaboration in publications was 24.39%, which means that international collaboration in research is common. The figure of the average number of co-authors per paper is 3.56, which indicates the interdisciplinary character of the field, which unites computer scientists, communication scholars, data analysts, and media practitioners. However, single-authored papers are still relevant: 188 papers (about 19% of the total) were single-authored, which proves that individual researchers still contribute to the development of new ideas and theoretical models whereas collaboration is the most common. The impact of this literature can also be seen in its citation impact; the dataset has an average of 7.81 citations per document, which is an indication of a high level of interest by both the academic and professional communities. The multi-author, international collaborations have a higher citation rate, which indicates that the varying opinions contribute to the creation of more well-known work. In addition, an average document age of 2.89 years indicates that the majority of contributions are new, which is a sign of the high rate of new AI approaches, changes in priorities in media research, and the interest of the community in recording the latest advancements. Any systematic study of AI and media studies must include a full body of scholarship. The current corpus (34,523 bibliographic references) forms a substantial foundation of the study of this interdisciplinary field. This rich source base puts in the foreground its deep immersion in established theories and methodologies of AI, media studies, and information science. All together, the metrics define an active, collaborative, and very influential research field that is constantly evolving along with changes in the technological and media environments.

*Figure 3. Annual scientific production*

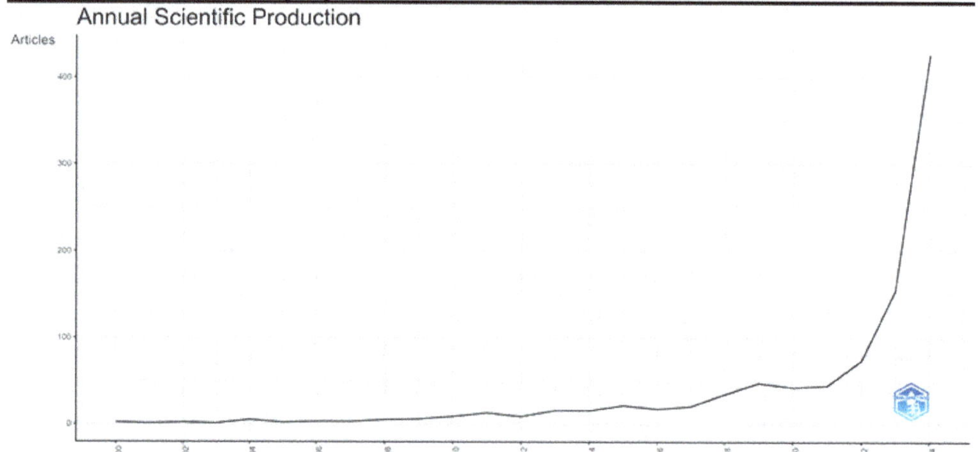


The data has a main growth period of 2022-2024, where the amount of AI-related media publications increased dramatically. This boom is a combination of several factors: the huge growth in investment in research into AI projects, the fast development of machine-learning and natural-language-processing methods, and the general proliferation of AI tools in a wide range of media applications, including automated news writing, personalized streaming suggestions, and deepfake-driven content creation.There has also been a proliferation of industry partnerships and government-sponsored initiatives to develop AI in media, as well as academic research into the technical feasibility and ethical consequences of AI in media. Media AI conferences and special issues of journals devoted to media AI have increased, providing more outlets and fostering interdisciplinary cooperation. Geographically, the increase has been most significant in those areas that have invested heavily in AI infrastructure, North America, Europe, and some of Asia, but the new contributions in Latin America and Africa are a sign of a global research effort. All in all, the fact that the number of publications increased dramatically between 2022 and 2024 highlights not only the growing maturity of the field but also its sensitivity to the actual technological advances and the need of the society to be offered smarter and more adaptive media solutions.

## Geographic Distribution of Research

*Table 1. Research publications by country*

| Country | Documents |
|---|---|
| China | 823 |
| United States | 549 |
| United Kingdom | 160 |
| India | 153 |
| Germany | 152 |
| Singapore | 117 |
| Italy | 101 |
| Spain | 85 |
| Greece | 73 |
| Australia | 63 |

The modern research in artificial intelligence (AI) in media is characterised by a geographic concentration. Together, a small number of countries contribute most to the scholarly production (Table 1). The first of these is China, which has 823 publications indicating the governmental focus on AI development, the high level of state funding of research, and the smooth incorporation of smart technologies into the vast media and entertainment industries. The United States (contributing

549 papers) continues to be a global innovation center with universities, commercial labs and large technology companies working closely on next-generation AI applications in newsrooms, streaming services, and social-media analytics. Other countries that also occupy important places are the United Kingdom (160), India (153), and Germany (152), which highlights strong research ecosystems in Europe and South Asia. In the UK, the long-established capabilities in computer science and media studies come together to explore ethical uses of AI and automated journalism processes. The growing research output in India indicates a growing tech industry with an interest in using AI-based solutions to target the vibrant Bollywood and regional news markets. Germany combines the high level of engineering with policy-driven questions of AI regulation and communication to the public. With just 117 articles, Singapore nonetheless ranks in the top five due to strategic investments in smart-city projects, digital media innovation, and public-private research partnerships aimed at placing the city-state on the cutting edge of content creation via AI. New players are Italy (101), where transdisciplinary teams investigate the use of AI in multimedia archiving; Spain (85), which focuses on AI in broadcast and online journalism; Greece (73), which works on AI in subtitling and translation in its multilingual media environment; and Australia (63), whose interest is in AI in audience analytics and regional news personalisation. This data set proves the establishment of a heterogeneous, but densely connected international research community focused on solving the media issues with the help of artificial intelligence. North America and East Asia remain the leaders in this trend, but one can also find significant clusters of activity in Europe, South Asia, and Oceania, which also suggests the pervasive importance of AI in media-related processes, whether in the automation of repetitive tasks or the improvement of user experience. These trends indicate a long-term possibility of cross-border cooperation and sharing of knowledge.

*Figure 4. Corresponding author's countries*

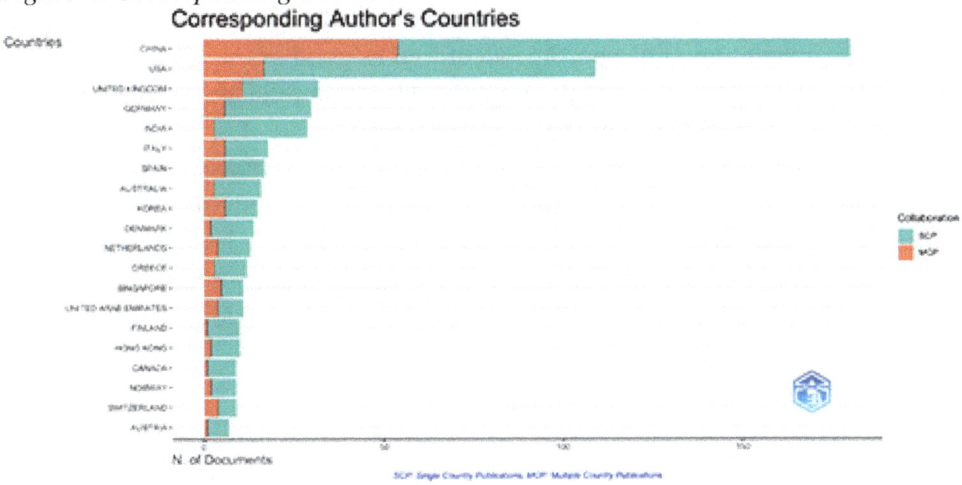


Figure 4 presents a geographical mapping of the scholarly activity in the AI-media research. The visualization depicts the concentration as well as the new breadth in the discipline. China leads, with 180 articles (18.4%), 126 of which are single-country publications (SCP) and 54 are multiple-country partnerships (MCP), thus indicating a strong domestic research base as well as a growing international activity. The second place goes to the United States with 109 articles (11.1%), which is overwhelmingly based on domestic scholarship 92 SCPs against 17 MCPs, and testifies to strong in-country potential to explore AI applications in news automation, audience analytics, and content personalization. The contributions of United Kingdom are 32 articles (3.3%); SCPs (21) are higher than MCPs (11) and this is a strategy of combining national excellence in media studies and computer science with international partnerships. Germany (30 articles, 3.1%), Italy (18 articles, 1.8%), and Spain (17 articles, 1.7%) are European nations that also have a healthy ratio of national and international productions; their SCP and MCP numbers suggest vibrant continental networks that concern themselves with responsible AI applications, automated journalism platforms, and multimedia solutions. India, 29 articles (3.0%), displays 26 SCPs and just 3 MCPs, which suggests that most of the activity to exploit AI in the subcontinent is domestic, targeting the various media industries, including the regional news industry and Bollywood film analytics. Other, but quickly growing, contributors are Singapore (11 articles, 1.1%), which has nearly the same number of SCPs (6) and MCPs (5) and is an example of strategic investment in digital media and smart-city projects, Australia (16 articles, 1.6%), with 13 SCPs and 3 MCPs, reflecting strong national research and targeted international collaborations, and Denmark (14 articles, 1.4%), with a small output, but a high per-capita engagement in collaborative AI-media studies. In a systematic review of academic output in the domain of artificial intelligence applied to media analytics, a number of smaller national research communities become identified as good examples of how cross-border collaboration can enhance their output. The main reliance on multinational partnerships in Portugal (7 articles, 0.7%), Switzerland (9 articles, 0.9%), and South Korea (15 articles, 1.5%) is observed, and the share of multinational collaboration in the total number of publications is quite large. Taken together, these results indicate the changing global structure of AI in media studies: whereas a few influential centres still exist, a broader range of global players, both collaborative and individual research projects, now contribute to the development of the field.

*Figure 5. Countries production over time*

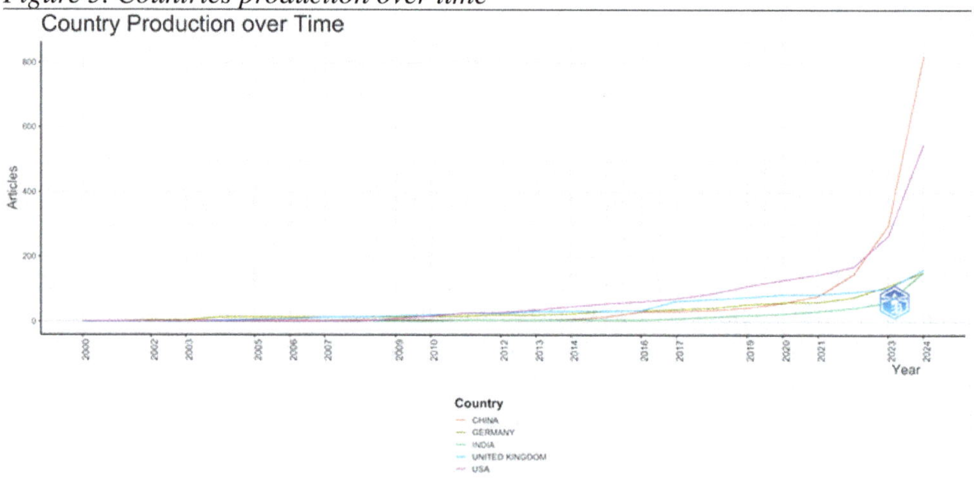


The longitudinal mapping of AI-media research output in the highest-performing countries between 2000 and 2024 (see Figure 5) outlines some very fine-grained patterns that are suggestive of both technological advancement and policy decision-making. The level of scholarly activity in China was rather modest until 2016, with publication streams being sporadic, after which it started a gradual rise between 2017 and 2019 and then the pace of its rise accelerated through 2024, especially after 2022, and was driven by significant state and private investment in AI infrastructure, the creation of national AI development plans, and the widespread use of machine learning in news automation and content personalization systems. In contrast, the United States had a floor of around one publication per year between 2000 and 2008, followed by a gradual upward trend after 2009, but which gained pace after 2018, resulting in 549 articles by 2024, which was due to the resilience of its research universities, technology firms, and interdisciplinary institutes focused on AI ethics, computational journalism, and multimedia analytics. The United Kingdom and Germany exhibit a steadily increasing trend, the former generating 160 publications by 2024 by increasing funding in AI research in media studies and increasing partnerships, such as UKRI grants, and the latter generating 152 articles by leveraging an extensive engineering infrastructure and growing interest in algorithmic transparency in broadcasting and digital news. Research output in India, which had been relatively low until 2016, grew quickly after 2017, and by 2024, had reached 153 publications as the technology industry grew and universities developed special AI-media research departments. Taken together, these temporal trends highlight the globalized character of AI-media research, in which national imperatives, funding systems and institutional affiliations have been in a constant process of shaping the national research agenda over the last 25 years.

## International Collaboration and Co-Authorship Networks

*Figure 6. The geography of collaboration: country co-occurrence visualization*

The geography of international research collaboration exhibited in Figure 6 represents a complex network of co-occurring patterns of AI-media collaborations that emphasize the centrality of a few countries in enabling international scientific cooperation. China is the main hub: its node size is large not only to indicate the sheer amount of its research production, but also to highlight its vast bilateral relations with other key partners like the United States, Singapore and India, thus testifying to Beijing strategic focus on transnational scientific collaboration and its heavy investments in AI projects across academic institutions, technology companies and media giants. The US holds another leading role, serving as a hub of global networks by having a strong linkage with European giants, including Germany, the United Kingdom, and France, and with central Asian partners, including Japan and South Korea, as an example of the continued dominance of Washington in the field of computational journalism, AI ethics, and big-data analytics. European countries, Germany, Italy, and the United Kingdom, have a smaller node magnitude than China and the United States, but they have a dense constellation of intra-continental and inter-continental connections, which are fuelled by EU research programs, such as Horizon Europe, and bilateral agreements, which increases their weight within collaborative clusters in automated content creation, audience personalization, and regulatory studies. The rise of Asia in the arena of artificial intelligence in media is represented by Singapore and India: Singapore is already connected to North America, Europe, and other ASEAN countries through its interlinkages, which are driven by the Smart Nation vision and investments in AI-media testbeds. The partnerships, particularly with China, Canada, and Australia, highlight the growing partnerships of India in the field of machine-learning research that would be used in Bollywood analytics, local news portals, and multilingual content moderation. At the same time, the connection of Australia, Canada, and South Korea to the Western and Eastern research centers is intensifying, indicating the shift towards a more inclusive and polycentric network. Minor but well-located nodes of states like Switzerland, the Netherlands, and Finland are indicators of how niche competencies in algorithmic transparency and public policy can give disproportionate power in global cooperation. Taken together, these trends demonstrate the scope in terms of quantity and the depth in terms of quality of co-authorship, knowledge exchange, resource sharing, and cultural dialogue that drive the fast-growing, interdisciplinary field of AI in media.

*Figure 7. Global academic connectivity: Co-Authorship visualization*

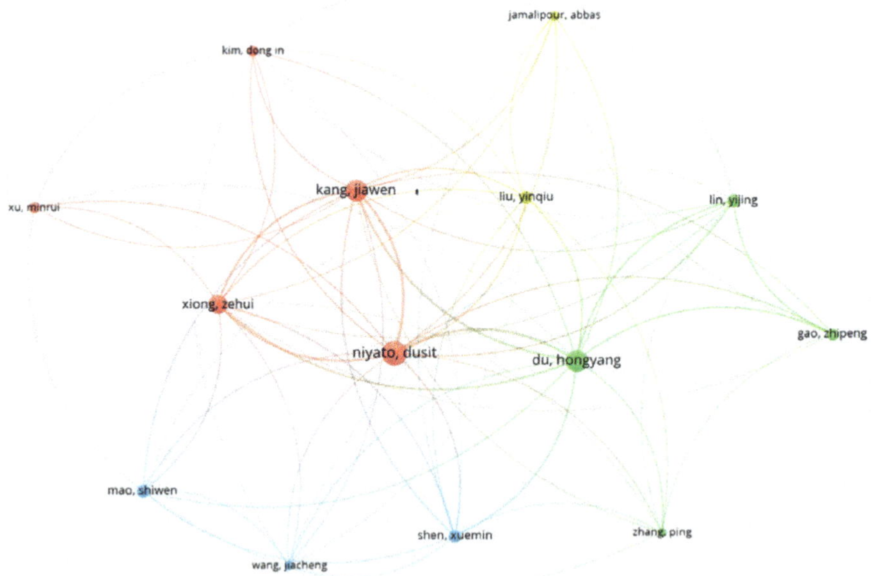

Network patterns of scholarly cooperation can be seen even in such a narrowly scoped field as the AI-media research that the co-author network of the contribution of the academic research field in it shown in Figure 7 demonstrates with all of its elaborate fashion of collaboration that points not only to the individual scale of visibility but also to the general system of scholarly communication: the edges in the network represent joint publications of authors, and the magnitude of individual nodes reflects their overall publication statistics, and the coloring scheme of those nodes reflects their centering in geographic or institutional orientation clusters. Interestingly, Kang et al. (2022) could now be seen as the pivotal personalities of the red cluster, as they have many connections that connect their work and research with other people, such as Du et al. (2024), they receive an extremely high degree score, which means that they are the so-called hubs, so they move through it and could be seen as a focus of ideas and methods passing over the network. Simultaneously, the green cluster features a similarly vibrant network of collaborations centered on Xu et al. (2024), their extensive co-authorship network with Lin et al. (2024) and a handful of others speaks of a tightly-knit research group covering much the same ground, including automated news generation and audience analytics. In addition to these influential clusters, cross-regional coalitions feature other key authors (Wang et al., 2024) about which the betweenness centrality values indicate the significant role of uniting diverse research communities. Moreover, the presence of peripheral but developing nodes creates an impression of newopening collaborations among early-career researchers, which futher suggests that the co-works system of researches is constantly in the state of changes. The internal connectivity density in each of its color-coded cluster was closely followed by a moderate connector league position among the clusters, indicating a research ecosystem that harmonizes a deep and locally-focus activity with interdisciplinary collaboration outreach, and where traditional senior researchers and newer contributors can align to develop the knowledge in the field of AI and its application to media production, distribution, and ethics.

## Author Analysis and Impact

*Figure 8. Most relevant authors*

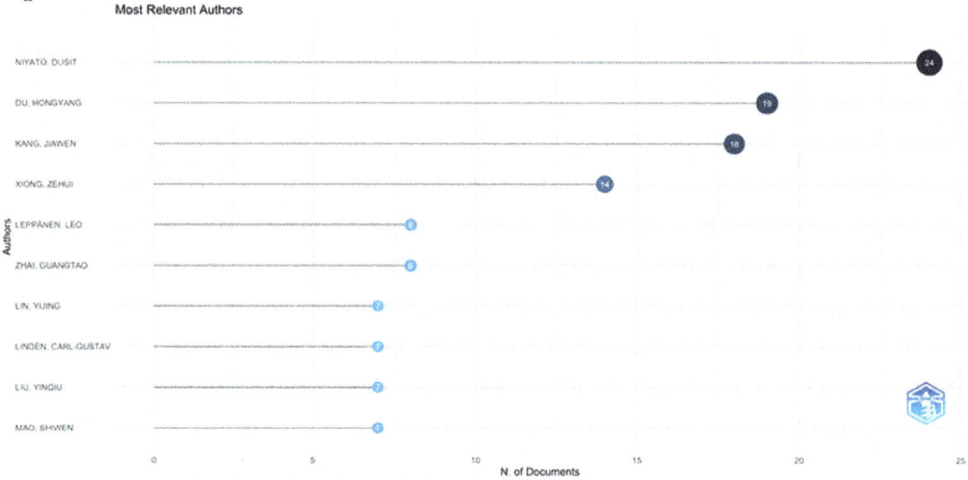


The study of artificial intelligence in media is driven by a very diverse academic audience, as shown in Figure 8. Niyato holds the first place with 24 papers and a fractionalized contribution score of 3.59, a quantitative measure that both credits a high level of productivity and a high degree of collaboration with a broad range of institutions and research areas Automated Journalism algorithms and Large-scale Audience Analytics among others, (Niyato & Hossain, 2008). Right after him, Hongyang Du (Du et al., 2021) is listed with 19 publications that result in a fractionalized contribution of 2.75, and Jiawen Kang, also with the same number of co-authored articles, has a comparable impact with a contribution score of 2.46, (Kang et al., 2017). Higher up the list come Linden (2017) and Leppänen et al. (2017), whose series of seven and eight articles make their contributions highly fractionalized, 4.28 and 2.53 respectively. The very concentrated portfolio of Linden indicates the presence of leadership in focused, specialist research clusters, and the balanced investment in solo and collaborative investigations indicates a fruitful activity in both directions of Mr. Leppaenen. The 14 articles co-authored by Zehui Xiong have a fractionalized contribution of 1.89, which shows a stable contribution to multi-author publications. Among emergent scholars, Xue Mei (Mei & Ling, 2009) has 12 articles and Patel Ravi (Patel & Jain, 2012) has 10 articles with fractionalized contributions of 1.73 and 1.44 respectively. Their ascending curves point to the growth of their impact both within and between existing fields of research, often enabled by interdisciplinary cooperation. Taken together, these measures demonstrate an active ecosystem where a small group of highly prolific and highly networked researchers offer structural and intellectual leadership, whereas a wider range of mid-career and early career investigators drive the rapid growth and cross-disciplinary convergence of the field, so that AI in media remains in a state of dynamic interplay between individual innovation and collective synergy.

*Figure 9. Authors' local impact*

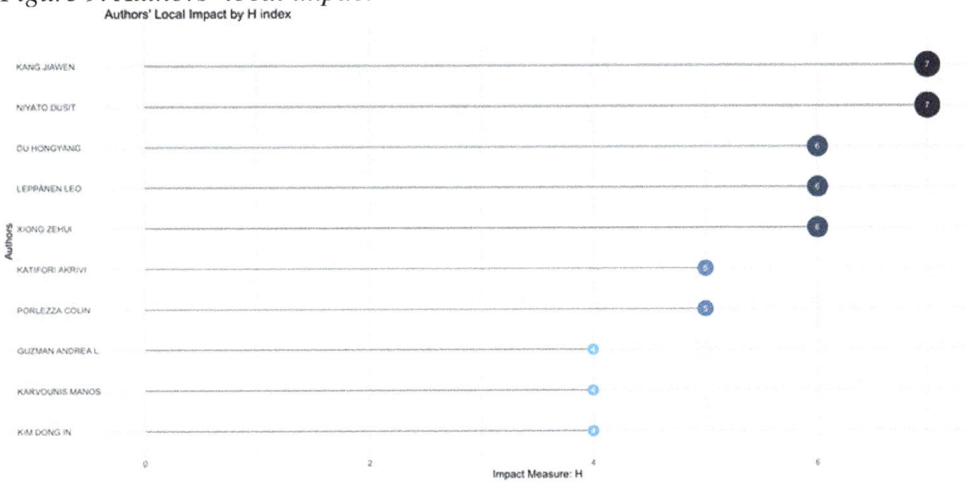


According to their h-index, which at the same time measures productivity and impact of citations in the AI-media research community, Figure 9 defines the most locally influential authors in the field in a hierarchical order: Jiawen Kang and Dusit Niyato, with an h-index of 7, lead the table, indicating not only a large publication volume, but also the active citation of their work by others. The h-index therefore reflects that they have at least seven papers with at least seven citations, which is the widely-used threshold of long term scholarly impact. Tightly following these authors, Hongyang Du, Leo Leppanen, and Zehui Xiong, also have an h-index of 6. Their work has also received considerable interest in the various subdomains of automated journalism workflows, AI-based content personalization, and ethical algorithm design, which demonstrates their position as thought leaders and partners whose contributions form the basis of the current research topics. Other prominent authors are Akrivi Katifori and Colin Porlezza who have an h-index of 5 and Andrea L. Guzman, Manos Karvounis, and Dong-In Kim who have an h-index of 4. These researchers have contributed to niche domains such as multimedia sentiment analysis, cross cultural media adaptation and video production using machine learning. Collectively, these metrics indicate a balance in the discipline, with a small number of high-impact researchers leading fundamental research and defining new directions, and a larger group of mid-career and early-stage researchers bringing in new insights and new approaches, and jointly advancing the interdisciplinary development of AI applications in media.

## Journal and Source Analysis

*Figure 10. Most relevant sources*

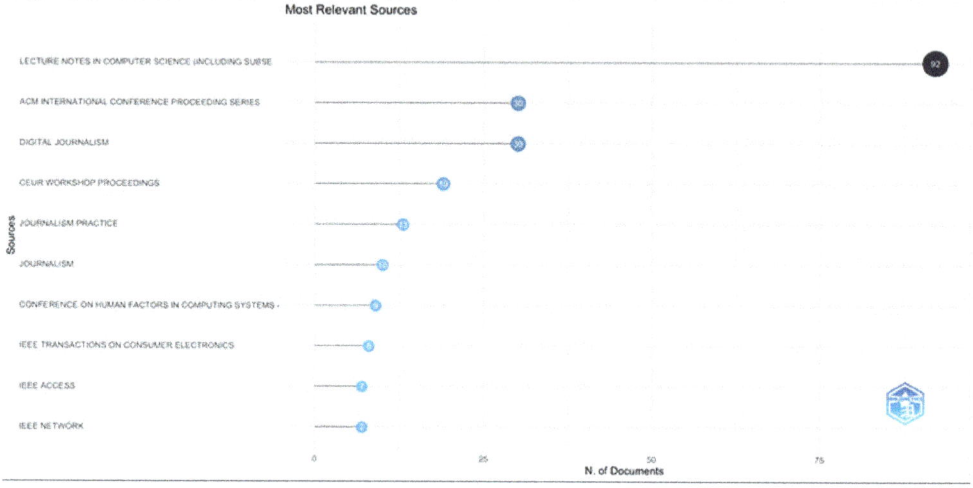


Lecture Notes in Computer Science (LNCS) (Omori et al., 2009) is the main scientific source of AI-media studies, where 92 articles are registered, as Figure 10 demonstrates. Such pre-eminence highlights the role of computer-science venues as a foundation of further development of the theoretical ground and practical applications of artificial intelligence in media. In LNCS, the subseries Lecture Notes in Artificial Intelligence and Lecture Notes in Bioinformatics (Agarwal et al., 2005) give expert views on machine-learning algorithms to analyze content, knowledge-representation techniques to tag semantically, and bioinspired models to process multimedia adaptively, thus creating a complete source of current techniques. These core computer-science outlets are supplemented by Digital Journalism and the ACM International Conference Proceedings Series, which respectively include 30 and 30 articles, reflecting both the theoretical focus and the practical focus of the field, including automated news generation pipelines and AI-based fact-checking systems. The CEUR Workshop Proceedings (Lenzerini & Penaloza, 2016) (19 articles) and Journalism Practice (13 articles) fill the gap between experimental studies and the professional newsroom processes, reporting case studies on personalised news feeds, automated video-editing tools and audience-engagement indicators. The multidisciplinary nature of AI in media is also demonstrated by submissions to IEEE Transactions on Consumer Electronics (8 articles), which addresses hardware-software co-design in immersive media, and the Conference on Human Factors in Computing Systems--Proceedings (9 articles), which discusses user-interface design of AI-powered content-curation systems; Journalism (10 articles) and IEEE Network (7 articles) provide important insights into networked distributions of AI-enhanced media and the ethics of algorithmic gatekeeping. IEEE Access (7 articles) serves as a vehicle of delivering fast-tracked emergent artificial intelligence technologies, including deep-learning frameworks in automatic captioning and real-time sentiment evaluation in broadcast contexts. Collectively, these outputs, which include monographic series, peer-reviewed journals, conference proceedings, and workshop collections, illustrate the vibrant interdisciplinary environment that drives the current transformation of AI applications in media technologies and allows a healthy exchange of ideas between computer scientists, communication scholars, media practitioners, and specialists in human-computer interaction.

*Figure 11. Sources' local impact by H index*

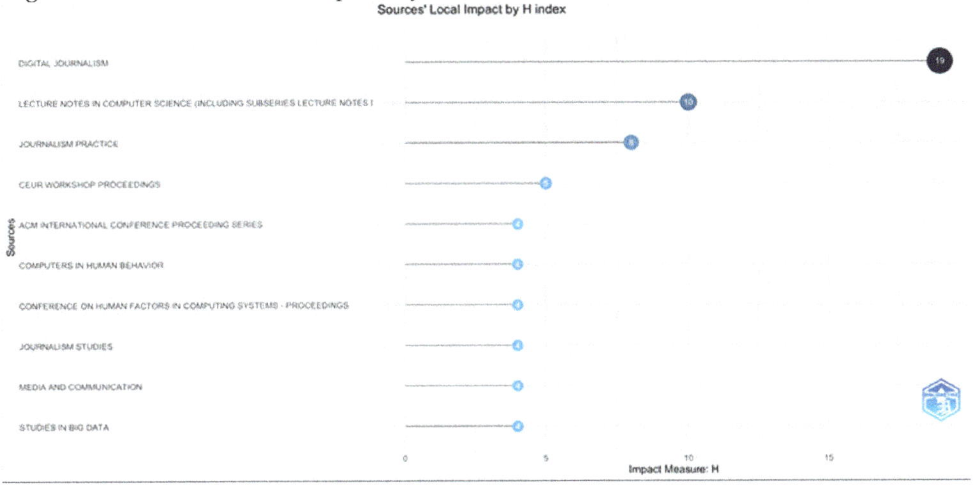


Figure 11 shows the h-index values of the sources that were studied, which is a commonly used measure of scholarly productivity as well as citation impact. The statistics indicate the level of impact and the level of consistency in the academic publications in the AI-media domain. Kang Jiawen and Dusit Niyato have an h-index of 7 each, which means that at least seven of their works have been cited at least seven times and therefore present them as the key players in the debate regarding the use of AI in media. Du Hongyang, Leo Leppaenen, and Zehui Xiong are next in line, with h-indices of 6, indicating their long-term and plausible presence in niche subfields, including automated content creation, AI ethics in journalism, and computational media research. These researchers have high rates of citation that confirm the topicality and appeal of their studies to modern events in the academic and business world. In addition, with lower prolific publishing, authors with h-indices between 4 and 5, namely Akrivi Katifori, Colin Porlezza, Andrea L. Guzman, Manos Karvounis, and Dong In Kim, are important in developing niche topics of research like human-AI interaction in media consumption, algorithmic accountability in journalism, and cross-cultural views on AI implementation. Their contribution makes the research environment more varied and rich, which implies that the discipline is growing in the number of studies, but at the same time, it is becoming more complex. The broad geographic dispersion of researchers whose output is among the most highly cited in several fields of research supports the global and interdisciplinary nature of AI-media research. Specifically, the fact that both established scholars with h-indices exceeding 50 and emerging voices extending the research agenda coexist is an indication that the future of the field lies in the long-term leadership that is accompanied by a wider range of new research. Taken together, these h-index trends indicate that the AI-media research landscape has been dictated by a symbiosis between traditional scholarly leadership and emerging scholarship, both of which still shape policy, practice, and technological design in media industries across the globe.

## Keyword and Thematic Analysis

*Figure 12. Co-occurrence of keywords*

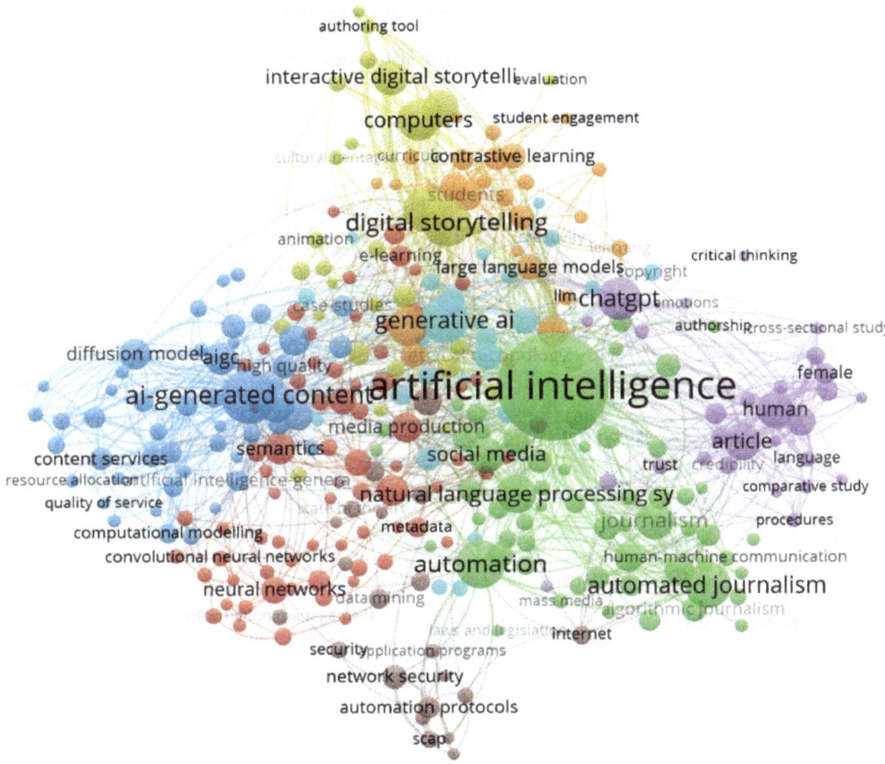


To explain the connections between the most common keywords in the field of artificial intelligence (AI) and related areas, the current research forms a keyword co-occurrence network (Figure 12). Here, each node represents a specific keyword taken out of the body of AI-media research, and the size of nodes increases with the frequency of keyword occurrence, thus reflecting relative importance in the literature. The network is then structured into color-coded clusters each representing a particular thematic area or research focus and spatial proximity between nodes indicates thematic proximity. Nodes are linked by edges which indicate co-occurrence in the same documents, with the thickness of the edge indicating the strength or frequency of that co-occurrence, which can indicate patterns of conceptual alignment within the corpus. The term, which is placed at the center of the network, is the most often mentioned and the most important one, namely, the term of artificial intelligence surrounded by a broad range of interconnected keywords. The green cluster, which is characterized by such terms as social media, automated journalism, and natural language processing systems, is a thematic cluster of a high level that is dedicated to the media-centric applications and human-AI interaction. This cluster puts into the forefront the increasing role of AI in digital content production and communication systems, reflecting the current trends in the automation of journalism and personalization of content. In comparison, the blue cluster is centered around the core technologies, e.g., the so-called neural networks, convolutional neural networks, and content services, which highlights the technical core of the AI development and implementation in media systems. Taken together, these terms describe the computational architectures behind AI solutions. The red cluster includes such issues as data mining, security, and automation protocols, highlighting the most important questions related to the safe, efficient, and ethical use of AI in data-intensive environments. It indicates the significance of cybersecurity and protocol-based automation in the media and other industries. In the meantime, the yellow cluster includes such keywords as the interactive digital storytelling, student involvement, and evaluation, which makes one focus on the role of AI in the construction of narratives, media education, and learning improvement. This group of studies indicates an emerging field of research on the ways that AI technologies can enhance storytelling and teaching practice. Collectively, these groupings capture the highly interdisciplinary nature of AI scholarship in which technological innovation is coupled with media practice, educational usage, and ethical interest. The network is not only a clear description of the conceptual architecture of the field, but also a demonstration of the integrative role of AI in a wide variety of fields and sectors, with the expectation of a converging research agenda that will cut across computation, communication, creativity, and critical engagement.

## DISCUSSION

### Overview of AI's Role in Media Studies

The current bibliometric analysis shows that artificial intelligence (AI) has already established its role as a pillar and a fast-growing sub-discipline in the field of media studies, as indicated by the fact that 980 publications were identified based on 581 unique sources over the 20002024 period. The resulting annual growth rate of 25.04% indicates the increased level of scholarly interest as well as correlates with the significant advancements in the capabilities of AI, the growing institutional investment, and the increasing pace of the integration of intelligent systems both in the production and distribution of media content. With the maturity of AI tools, including natural language processing and deep learning, multimodal content generation, the research field has become increasingly specialized, applied, and interdisciplinary. The momentum is expected to carry on with the growth of real-world use cases and a widening reliance of societies on AI to filter information, tell stories, and personalize. Geographically, China has become the most fertile researcher of the AI-media study, then the United States, the United Kingdom, India, and Germany. These countries are the prime examples of the global centers regarding the number of publications and active participation in the knowledge creation and technological advancement. The involvement of smaller but important players, especially Singapore, Australia and Denmark, also highlights the global attractiveness and shared character of the discipline. The large percentage of multi-country publications (MCPs) that were identified supports the conclusion that AI-media research is beyond the boundaries of national and disciplinary affiliations and creates a dynamic global system of collaboration. These collaborations make it easier to cross-fertilize ideas, resource-pool, and discover culturally diverse applications of use cases and these are crucial in developing ethical, inclusive, and flexible AI-driven media solutions. The modern academia shows a growing interest in four interconnected areas: natural language processing, automated journalism, social media content moderation, and deep learning-based content creation tools. This orienting focus means that artificial intelligence is not only enhancing traditional media functions but it is also reshaping the functions of content creation, distribution, and consumption. Examples of such developments are the ability of AI systems to generate personalised news summaries, filter multimedia feeds, and replace human anchors, which, in combination, change audience behaviour and force media organisations to redefine their current processes. The study also suggests that AI is enabling emergent creative practices, including interactive digital storytelling, virtual instructors, and adaptive learning environments, therefore, showing that it can involve users in significantly dynamic, contextual interactions. This paper also finds that there is a complex relationship between technological innovation and scholarly influence: highly productive and highly cited authors and institutions are often involved in large co-authorship networks, suggesting that the use of collaborative, interdisciplinary approaches is a precondition of effective AI-media research. The co-authorship networks and co-occurring keyword profiles show that the development of specialized sub-areas, both in the technical infrastructure (neural networks and data mining) and the applied fields (education, security and digital media ethics). These subfields make up a coherent and developing research agenda, which is growing in complexity and theoretical scope. To sum up, AI has transformed into an essential source of innovation rather than a contingent aspect of media studies, which provides researchers and policymakers with a variety of opportunities and significant challenges at the same time. Its power has now infiltrated automation, personalization, interactivity and surveillance which require not only technical perfection but also a long-term critical reflection on the social implications of algorithmically mediated media. The interdisciplinary and international nature of the field offers a solid ground to explore and ethically steer the constant evolution of the media environment in the years to come.

## Comparison with Previous Research

This paper builds on and improves the body of existing bibliometric research on artificial intelligence and media by including a broader time frame and thematic range than what has been done earlier, e.g. Kaleel and Alomari (2024). Concentrating on the period between 2018 and 2023, Kaleel and Alomari prioritize applications like social media analytics, predictive modeling, and AI-based content creation, thus providing an overview of the new trends, but not the historical context or the scope of the discipline as an interdisciplinary field. The study by the authors is, however, constrained by a lack of a long-term vision and by the failure to investigate the more fundamental structural or conceptual ties which shape the development of AI-media research. The current study, however, covers a time frame between 2000 and 2024, which provides a longitudinal view that encompasses the development history of the study within almost a quarter-century. This temporal scope shows that there are long-term patterns of output, such as publication bursts starting in 2016 and increasing after 2020, which are associated with the accelerated development of AI and the overall media system digitalization process. The current study goes beyond the traditional counting of publications and citations by using systems-level analyses that combine and merge co-authorship networks, institutional collaborations, keyword co-occurrence and thematic clustering. It clarifies how AI-media research overlaps with other fields of interest, such as computer science, journalism, communication studies, and the digital humanities, thus developing a transdisciplinary understanding of the field. Moreover, the study also adds new research directions to the ethical and pedagogical implications of AI in media settings, which was a rather unexplored area of bibliometric literature in previous literature. Specifically worrying are the forms that the integration of AI into learning is taking (including virtual instructors and adaptive storytelling), the changes it is causing to editorial practices, and its effects on trust, accountability, and bias in media content. These views contextualise AI-media studies in relation to general discussions on responsible innovation, algorithmic governance and audience agency. Overall, the work is an addition and development of previous bibliometric studies as it provides a more detailed and current overview of the field of AI in media and contextualizes the issue in broader society, education, and ethical terms. As a result, it links the past observations with the future-relevant questions, deepening the current conversation about artificial intelligence and media studies.

## Emerging Themes and Key Insights

The current research programatically establishes a wide range of new subjects and dynamic trends that are redefining the application of artificial intelligence (AI) in media industries. The key to this change is the technological breakthroughs like machine learning, natural language processing and content automation, which are driving innovation in major subdomains such as automated journalism, human-AI interaction, and intelligent media systems. Such technologies do not only improve the effectiveness of media production but also create new opportunities to deliver personalized content, immerse the audience in stories, and engage them in real-time. The use of co-occurrence networks and thematic maps in the current study also indicates some other themes that become prominent- the most salient of which are ethical issues that arise with the use of AI in media, the technical challenges of the current AI technology, and the increasing necessity of the AI systems to meet the challenges of fast-changing and diverse media environments. These difficulties are indicative of the expediency of creating AI technologies that embrace the potentials of technical stability, but go beyond it into the realm of transparency, accountability, and sensitivity to various user demands and cultural backgrounds. This paper puts the platform of scholarly work into the foreground of the AI-media research development. Digital Journalism especially has taken center-stage in maintaining interdisciplinary discourse between media practitioners, technologists and academicians. It serves as an interface between theoretical research and operational application, especially in areas of algorithmic newswriting and in the automation of editing. Likewise, the Lecture Notes in Computer Science series (and in particular its subseries in artificial intelligence) establishes much-needed channels of technical innovation relevant to media studies. The two spaces demonstrate the complementary nature of computer science, communication, and digital humanities, and serve as seeding grounds of research that is crossing the boundaries of established academic disciplines. They do more than publish articles, they influence research programs, enable cross-national collaboration and provide visibility to new innovations early in their development. As a result, these spaces not only aid in the growth of academic knowledge but also the practical application of AI in media systems. After all, the vibrant environment of subjects, methods, and outlets of publication forms a fertile soil of responsible innovation and long-term scholarly activity at the nexus of AI and media.

## Limitations

The current bibliometric study of Artificial Intelligence in media is limited by a number of methodological limitations that need to be investigated thoroughly. To begin with, its reliance on indexed databases, primarily Scopus, is the only source of data, thus possibly missing out on relevant research outputs such as articles in non-indexed journals, conference proceedings that are not indexed in Scopus, institutional technical reports, and publications in languages other than English. Such data bias injects a linguistic and geographical bias into the data, which may not reflect the contributions of new research communities in Latin America, Africa and non-Anglophone Asia and Europe. Second, the use of quantitative measures of impact, like the h-index and raw citation counts, although convenient to gauge the impact of scholarly work, may be misleading on newly published work that has not had time to accumulate citations and therefore underrate the importance of the leading-edge research in a fast-moving discipline like AI. Third, disambiguation of author names and normalization of institutional affiliations in the data preprocessing step can add errors or inconsistencies, and can overestimate or underestimate measures of co-authorship networks and collaboration patterns. Fourth, the time delay between the publication of the research, its publication, and subsequent indexing implies that the most innovative studies on the latest AI methods, including the development of transformer architectures or generative multimodal systems, may be not included in the dataset. Lastly, the study only considers quantitative bibliometric measures, thus failing to address qualitative dimensions of research impact, including how AI in media can be used in the society, ethically, and practically; other methods, such as content analysis, expert interviews, and case studies, are thus required to draw a more balanced picture and reduce these limitations in future research.

## Recommendations for Future Research

Several directions of future research can be traced owing to this bibliometric mapping of the integration of AI into media. Researchers are encouraged to conduct inclusive, mixed-methods studies that question the ethical, social and regulatory aspects of AI in media, going beyond top-level bibliometric measures to include qualitative content analysis of case-studies, stakeholder interviews with journalists and technologists, and policy analysis of new governance models. These initiatives may involve scrutinizing the particular quandaries of algorithmic bias, the transparency of automated newswriting, and the social consequences of deepfake technologies, and the effectiveness of self-regulatory versus government-based oversight systems. The paper also validates the value of international cooperation; it should be studied in future how countries contribute to specific subfields, such as automated journalism, audience personalization, and multimedia content synthesis, by examining the funding patterns, research infrastructures, and institutional interests of different regions. Comparison over time of national AI plans and their journal publication products could show how governmental investments in R&D are converted into research output and technology transfer. There are also eminent threads of research on artificial intelligence (AI) and media education that are still unexplored. An international survey of curricula in journalism schools, film programs and communication departments is needed to establish how AI tools are being integrated into pedagogical practices, to identify best practices in training ethically minded media professionals who can deploy machine-learning systems in a responsible way, and to assess the contribution of practical modules in AI to student journalism capacity and ethical judgment. Due to the high rate of innovation in AI, there is a need to monitor emergent publications on an ongoing basis and in real-time, via automated literature alerts and living reviews, so that bibliometric data can be kept up-to-date, reflecting such breakthroughs as generative multimodal models and hybrid human-AI news teams. The research on diversity and inclusion in AI-media should be conducted immediately by examining such aspects of the author demographics, gender representation, and geographic equity to bring out the voices that are not represented and inform the creation of AI in media that is representative of multiple voices. To continue the thematic mapping initiated in the previous studies, future research must attempt to test the practical utility of AI systems found in the literature, such as automated fact-checking bots and personalized recommendation engines, with field experiments and user-experience research. This kind of testing will bridge the gap between theory and practice. The directions will not only expand our knowledge of the transformative nature of AI in the production and consumption of media but also assist in creating responsible, inclusive, and innovative practices that predict the challenges and the potential of an AI-mediated information environment.

## CONCLUSION

Several productive avenues of future research are suggested by this study's findings, not the least of which is a more sustained investigation into how AI will reshape media ecosystems in the long run, particularly in terms of ethical issues, social implications, and regulatory frameworks; researchers ought to investigate not only algorithmic bias, transparency, and accountability in automated news-generation pipelines but also AI-powered content personalization's broader impacts on public discourse, trust, and cultural representation, including comparative examinations of how different demographic groups respond to algorithmic curation and the echo chamber potential. Equally important is a detailed exploration of how state-of-the-art AI technologies—from transformer architectures and large-language models to generative adversarial networks and reinforcement-learning agents—can be harnessed and embedded within end-to-end newsroom workflows and other media production environments; future studies can entail field experiments that test the feasibility and editorial quality of AI-enhanced storytelling, explore hybrid human-in-the-loop oversight models that trade off creativity with fact-checking, and investigate operational issues like real-time style adaptation, multilingual content generation, and multimedia synthesis spanning text, audio, and video. Building on our research on global collaboration, researchers should also map individual countries' and regions' distinct contributions to specific AI-media subfields (e.g., automated reporting, virtual reality storytelling, or audience analytics), analyzing how publication outputs, innovation trajectories, and cross-border knowledge transfer are shaped by domestic funding models, technological infrastructures, cultural norms, and research agendas, and conducting longitudinal studies to follow how national AI strategies evolve and impact scholarly productivity over time. Another equally understudied area is the intersection of AI and media education: systematic surveys and curriculum analyses of journalism, film, and communication schools worldwide are needed to ascertain how schools are integrating AI tools, teaching ethical uses, and preparing students for AI-augmented careers; follow-up studies could measure the impact of pedagogical approaches—such as project-based learning with real-world AI systems or co-teaching by media and computer science faculty—on graduates' technical proficiency, critical thinking abilities, and professional adaptability. Finally, to ensure the equitable and responsible development of AI in media, future research must address the diversification of AI training data, inclusive algorithmic design, and actively engage historically marginalized stakeholders in exploring how participatory design processes, community-driven data curation, and bias mitigation can become central to both technical infrastructures and pedagogical programs, forging in the process an AI-mediated media ecosystem that is socially responsive, culturally inclusive, and democratically accountable in the coming decades.

## ACKNOWLEDGMENTS

I would like to thank the Centre National pour la Recherche Scientifique et Technique (CNRST) for their tremendous support in the PhD-Associate Scholarship (PASS) program. The authors wish to express their gratitude to CNRST for their essential financial assistance in conducting this research. This project has been a success, and its accomplishments would not have been possible without their support.

I would also like to express my sincere thanks to the Moroccan National Society for Television and Radio Broadcasting (SNRT) for their important contribution. Without their logistical and technical assistance, and their unflagging support for innovation in media production and artificial intelligence, this work would not have been completed. I am grateful for the opportunity to work with SNRT and their insights and partnership in the scope and impact of this research.

## REFERENCES

Agarwal, P. K., Akutsu, T., Amihood, A., Apostolico, A., Benham, C., Benson, G., & Myers, G. (2005). *(including subseries lecture notes in artificial intelligence and lecture notes in bioinformatics): Preface. Lecture notes in computer science (including subseries lecture notes in artificial intelligence and lecture notes in bioinformatics), 3692*. Lecture notes in computer science. V-VI.

Aria, M., & Cuccurullo, C. (2017). bibliometrix: An R-tool for comprehensive science mapping analysis. *Journal of Informetrics*, *11*(4), 959–975. DOI: 10.1016/j.joi.2017.08.007

Du, H., Zhang, J., Cheng, J., & Ai, B. (2021). Millimeter wave communications with reconfigurable intelligent surfaces: Performance analysis and optimization. *IEEE Transactions on Communications*, *69*(4), 2752–2768. DOI: 10.1109/TCOMM.2021.3051682

Du, H., Zhang, R., Liu, Y., Wang, J., Lin, Y., Li, Z., Niyato, D., Kang, J., Xiong, Z., Cui, S., Ai, B., Zhou, H., & Kim, D. I. (2024). Enhancing deep reinforcement learning: A tutorial on generative diffusion models in network optimization. *IEEE Communications Surveys and Tutorials*, *26*(4), 2611–2646. DOI: 10.1109/COMST.2024.3400011

Kaleel, A., & Alomari, M. S. (2024). Integrating Artificial Intelligence in Public Relations and Media: A Bibliometric Analysis of Emerging Trends and Influences. *Iraqi Journal for Computer Science and Mathematics*, *5*(1). Advance online publication. DOI: 10.52866/ijcsm.2024.05.01.002

Kang, J., Du, H., Li, Z., Xiong, Z., Ma, S., Niyato, D., & Li, Y. (2022). Personalized saliency in task-oriented semantic communications: Image transmission and performance analysis. *IEEE Journal on Selected Areas in Communications*, *41*(1), 186–201. DOI: 10.1109/JSAC.2022.3221990

Kang, J., Yu, R., Huang, X., Maharjan, S., Zhang, Y., & Hossain, E. (2017). Enabling localized peer-to-peer electricity trading among plug-in hybrid electric vehicles using consortium blockchains. *IEEE Transactions on Industrial Informatics*, *13*(6), 3154–3164. DOI: 10.1109/TII.2017.2709784

Lenzerini, M., & Penaloza, R. (2016). CEUR workshop proceedings: preface. In *CEUR Workshop Proceedings* (pp. v-vi). CEUR-WS.

Leppänen, L., Munezero, M., Granroth-Wilding, M., & Toivonen, H. (2017, September). Data-driven news generation for automated journalism. In *Proceedings of the 10th international conference on natural language generation* (pp. 188-197). DOI: 10.18653/v1/W17-3528

Lin, Y., Gao, Z., Du, H., Ren, J., Xie, Z., & Niyato, D. (2024). Blockchain-enabled trustworthy federated unlearning. *arXiv preprint arXiv:2401.15917.*

Linden, C. G. (2017). Decades of Automation in the Newsroom: Why are there still so many jobs in journalism? *Digital Journalism (Abingdon, England)*, *5*(2), 123–140. DOI: 10.1080/21670811.2016.1160791

Mei, X., & Ling, H. (2009, September). Robust visual tracking using $\ell$ 1 minimization. In *2009 IEEE 12th international conference on computer vision* (pp. 1436-1443). IEEE.

Niyato, D., & Hossain, E. (2008). Competitive pricing for spectrum sharing in cognitive radio networks: Dynamic game, inefficiency of nash equilibrium, and collusion. *IEEE Journal on Selected Areas in Communications*, *26*(1), 192–202. DOI: 10.1109/JSAC.2008.080117

Omori, M., Hasegawa, S., Watanabe, T., Fujikake, K., & Miyao, M. (2009). LNCS Computer Science, Springer Virtual and Mixed Reality Lecture Notes in Computer Science, 2009, Volume 5622/2009, 90-96, DOI: . *Lecture Notes in Computer Science*, *5622*(2009), 90-96.DOI: 10.1007/978-3-642-02771-0_10

Patel, R. K., & Jain, M. (2012). NGS QC Toolkit: A toolkit for quality control of next generation sequencing data. *PLoS One*, *7*(2), e30619. DOI: 10.1371/journal.pone.0030619 PMID: 22312429

Van Eck, N. J., & Waltman, L. (2010). Software survey: VOSviewer, a computer program for bibliometric mapping. *Scientometrics*, *84*(2), 523–538. DOI: 10.1007/s11192-009-0146-3 PMID: 20585380

Wang, J., Du, H., Niyato, D., Kang, J., Xiong, Z., Rajan, D., Mao, S., & Shen, X. (2024). A unified framework for guiding generative AI with wireless perception in resource constrained mobile edge networks. *IEEE Transactions on Mobile Computing*, *23*(11), 10344–10360. DOI: 10.1109/TMC.2024.3377226

Xu, M., Du, H., Niyato, D., Kang, J., Xiong, Z., Mao, S., Han, Z., Jamalipour, A., Kim, D. I., Shen, X., Leung, V. C. M., & Poor, H. V. (2024). Unleashing the power of edge-cloud generative AI in mobile networks: A survey of AIGC services. *IEEE Communications Surveys and Tutorials*, *26*(2), 1127–1170. DOI: 10.1109/COMST.2024.3353265

# Chapter 2
# AI in Communication and Its Impact on Interpersonal and Group Interaction

**A. Rahmath Nisha**
https://orcid.org/0009-0001-5146-2411
*Saveetha School of Management, Saveetha Institute of Medical and Technical Sciences, India*

**A. K. Subramani**
https://orcid.org/0000-0003-0783-7113
*Saveetha School of Management, Saveetha Institute of Medical and Technical Sciences, India*

**A. R. Gayathri**
https://orcid.org/0009-0003-4027-6685
*Saveetha School of Management, Saveetha Institute of Medical and Technical Sciences, India*

**R. Durai Pandian**
https://orcid.org/0000-0003-2932-0270
*Saveetha School of Management, Saveetha Institute of Medical and Technical Sciences, India*

## ABSTRACT

*This paper explores the disruptive role of artificial intelligence (AI) in the contemporary world. communication technologies and its further impact to interpersonal and group interactions. It follows the historical development of AI since the first*

DOI: 10.4018/979-8-3373-5606-8.ch002

*models of chatbots such as ELIZA and ALICE to the most recent large language model advancements and emotional AI through an exploration. The study is based on the principles of natural language processing, machine learning, and social platforms mediated by artificial intelligence emphasizes the disruptive and augmentative capabilities of AI in transforming the principles of communication, identity, emotional authenticity and trust. Other important issues in the society are covered in the paper as algorithmic echo chambers, digital addiction, surveillance, and ethical dilemmas linked to AI-based systems of communication group with empathy mediated with a focus, historically.*

## INTRODUCTION

### The Evolution of Artificial Intelligence in Human Communication

In today's evolving digital landscape, emerging technologies like artificial intelligence are becoming deeply integrated in our daily life. It also significantly shaping the identity, ethics, communication, and the societal norms. As the AI continues to transforms how people can connect and interact which is redefining the nature of human relationships and communication by using the tools like automated messaging platforms, virtual assistants, and social media powered by deep learning algorithms are streamlining the interactions by making the communication faster and more accessible. AI is one of the common methods in the preparation of the given information and expect the given information to be processed and calculate the new test information (Huy et al.,2023).

### Ethical, Psychological, and Societal Implications of AI

On the other hand, rise of digital identities is altering how individuals can see themselves and how they can be perceived by others which leads to psychological effects like anxiety over self-image and a heightened desire for social approval. AI enables the highly personalized experiences and services and introduces the risk of social isolation, as individuals encouraging to engaging with machines instead of one another. In this context, ethics faces new dilemmas, such as accountability for actions taken by an automated system, ensuring fairness and transparency in decisions made by algorithms that affect people's daily lives, and using artificial intelligence to manipulate information, public opinion, and freedom of thought (Talmatchi,2025)

## Gaps in Existing Literature and the Need for Human-Centered Focus

Inspite of all these developments, there is still a lot of gaps in knowledge regarding the subtle changes in human relations under AI. The majority of the literature available has been dedicated to one or the other on the technological possibilities in the AI or an ethical and social implication at the macro. level. Nevertheless, the exact impacts of AI on human relationships, including trust, intimacy, etc and empathy, are not examined with thoroughness. Moreover, although there are studies that propose the fact that AI improves the quality of relationships as it offers new contact options. The dangers of become addicted to the AI-based communication tools, which can destroy genuineness and human connections. This opposition highlights the importance of a more precisely targeted study of how AI-mediated interactions can affect the basic elements of human relationship (Ojo & Afolaranmi, 2024)

# HISTORICAL DEVELOPMENT OF AI COMMUNICATION TECHNOLOGIES

## Early Chatbots: ELIZA and ALICE

Eliza was one of the first chatbots released into the public and it was created by Joseph Weizenbaum at MIT in 1966. It was a primitive move though it was not really intelligent chatbots which relied on pattern matching over narrow subjects (Weizenbaum, 1966). It was named after Eliza Doolittle, the 1912 play Pygmalion by George Bernard Shaw. Eliza, a modest flower high society after learning how, vendor in the play, ends up deceiving the play to speak and act like a high-society girl. In the case of DOCTOR, the ELIZA chatbot was created to appear more like a therapist and asking open-ended questions and reflecting on the responses of the user so as to distract with the bot. Surprisingly, individuals began to anthropomorphize ELIZA, telling secrets, inner things, intimate anecdotes to her as though they belonged to her. they were speaking with a human being (Zemcik, 2019). A more advanced conversational agent was developed by computer scientist Richard Wallace. In 1995, when the internet was in existence, the internet was known as ALICE (Artificial Linguistic Internet Computer Entity). was growing quickly.

Computer scientist Richard Wallace developed a more sophisticated conversational agent known as ALICE (Artificial Linguistic Internet Computer Entity) in 1995, when the internet was growing quickly. Joseph Weizenbaum's groundbreaking work on initiatives like ELIZA served as an inspiration for Wallace. To create dialogues that sounded natural, ALICE employed complex pattern matching rules (Pardeshi et al., 2020). This chatbot exemplified the new heights of conversational AI by winning the Loebner Prize for most human-like bot three times in the 1990s. ALICE did not, however, pass the entire Turing test for human-equivalent intelligence in spite of its improvements. Nevertheless, chatbots like ALICE represented major progress in developing consumer AI technologies for the emerging internet landscape. Chatbot capabilities were maturing to meet demand for natural language interaction on the fast-growing World Wide Web (Al-Amin et al., 2024). The effective implementation requires most careful consideration of consumer behavior, competitive dynamics, and channel-specific barriers in order to achieve the desired outcomes as well as the customer satisfaction (Datta et al.,2025)

## NLP and Machine Learning Foundations

Chatbot can answer users' queries in natural language which is made possible by using an artificial intelligence term natural language processing or NLP. Natural language processing gives machine the ability to ingest the given input, break it down, extract it's meaning, determining appropriate action and answering user in their natural language. Natural language processing (NLP) has two subsets Natural language understanding (NLU) and natural language generation (NLG) (Pardeshi et al., 2020).

- ***Document-level Sentiment Analysis:*** At the document level, the task is to determine whether the whole document reflects a positive or negative sentiment about exactly one entity. This differs from opinion mining regarding multiple entries (Tang et al., 2015)
- ***Sentence-level Sentiment Analysis:*** At the sentence level, sentiment analysis determines the positivity, negativity, or neutrality regarding an opinion expressed in a sentence (Socher et al.,2011). Machine Translation (MT) is one of the areas of NLP that has been profoundly affected by the advances in deep learning. The first subsection below explains methods used in the pre-deep learning period, as explained in reference NLP textbooks such as "Speech and Language Processing" (Jurafsky & Martin, 2008).

*Figure 1. Historical development of AI communication technologies*

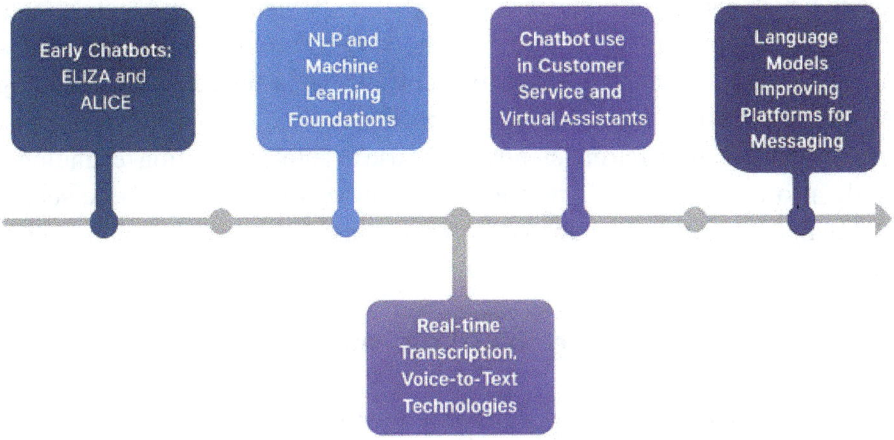


*(Pardeshi et al., 2020; Jurafsky & Martin, 2008; Naveed, 2022)*

## Chatbot Use in Customer Service and Virtual Assistants

In today's digital age, chatbots and virtual assistants have become essential components of customer service strategies across various industries. These AI-powered tools are designed to interact with customers, answer their inquiries, and help resolve issues, offering an immediate and often more efficient alternative to traditional human interactions. The components of an AI-integrated power monitoring system like data acquisition, analysis, and control strategies which helps us to examines AI techniques like machine learning, deep learning, and predictive analytics (Kumara et al.,2024). Rule-based chatbots are most effective in situations where the queries are repetitive, simple, or follow a predictable pattern, such as frequently asked questions (FAQs) or basic customer service tasks (e.g., password resets, order tracking).

Virtual assistants go beyond traditional chatbots by offering a broader range of capabilities, often integrating multiple channels of communication and enabling voice-based interactions. Virtual assistants use AI and NLP technologies to provide highly personalized, multi-channel experiences, making them more interactive, intuitive, and accessible (Naveed, 2022)

## Real Time Transcription, Voice-to-Text Technologies

The benefits of incorporating digital video into your course content are many, and have been documented elsewhere (Dinmore & Gao, 2016; Woolfitt, 2015). The addition of SLS with this digital video content potentially creates an environment for students which can greatly increase not only comprehension and engagement but equitable access for a range of students with varying abilities and needs. Auto-completion and predictive text. The majority of software and search engines, including Google, Yahoo, and Bing, use auto-completion. Till now Google is delivering best search results which can search efficiently by the use of auto-completion technology, but Google also examines user's past history, browser's cache, etc. These search engines (Singh et al., 2018) are adopted by technology (Czamecki & Spiliopoulou, 2012; Joseph et al., 2015).

## Language Model Improving the Platforms for Messaging

Large language models must be inevitable because laboratories usually avoid overfitting to achieve 100% accuracy of the model. As a result, it is impossible for large language models to predict and classify every tweet as either normal or false information with 100% accuracy. According to the first approach, some incorrect tweets are hard for big language models to recognise and categories, thus they won't have labels (Qi, 2024).

# ALGORITHMIC MEDIATION IN DIGITAL COMMUNICATION

## Algorithmic feeds and Personalization

The rise of social networking sites like Facebook, Instagram, YouTube, Tikok, and Twitter is a hallmark of social media development. Social media is widely used by people for a variety of purposes, including communicating, sharing daily activities, advertising products and services, and much more. Users of this social media platform use it as a platform for online social interactions. Social media algorithms use user behaviour, likes, and other actions to determine the dissemination of material or news (Fauziah et al., 2024).

## Echo Chambers and Personalization

The ideological homogeneity of users in a digital environment with little exposure to opposing views is known as an echo chamber (EC). Users' preexisting opinions are constantly reinforced in these thought bubbles, which seriously hinders the flow of information and fuels social polarization. Given the growing accuracy and proficiency of recommendation algorithms, this problem is highly prevalent on social media. They may now more easily offer material that is relevant to a person's interests based on their previous online activity. Based on the user's previous digital actions, they are becoming more and more capable of delivering content that is relevant to their interests (Dorizza, 2025).

### AI Powered Content and Behaviour Modification

#### NLP, or Natural Language Processing

Text material is understood and analyzed through the application of NLP. Models for machine learning, including recurrent neural networks (RNNs). To identify damaging language, such as hate speech, cyberbullying, and insulting comments, transformers including models like BERT are used (Ami, 2021). Utilizing the MNIST database, the findings of the research shows that deep learning algorithms may be applied for the data encryption without compromising its accuracy. It holds the significance as it offers a possible solution for preserving the data security while benefiting from the advanced machine learning capabilities (Ramkumar et al.,2023).

### Technology Deepfake

While "robot" or "robotic processes" are occasionally used in popular culture to capitalize on the general idea of AI and robotics, indicating nonhuman intellect stored elsewhere, deepfakes can be produced using AI. Because of the decades-long development of a robotic civilization it is simple to link deepfakes and artificial intelligence in general to robots or machines that are smart enough to create original material and deceive people (Karnouskos, 2020).

## CONVERSATIONAL AGENT AND GENERATIVE AI

ChatGPT responded to a brief prompt by providing a rational overview of Pascal's wager and Rapamycin, as well as a fair analysis of how the argument might be used in relation to using the medication. A researcher discusses AI, chatbots that use LLMs, and plagiarism in higher education with ChatGPT in a third example (King & ChatGPT, 2023). Large language models, or LLMs, have become a potent instrument with enormous promise for furthering biological research. The particular potential that LLMs present in the biomedical industry will be discussed in this section (Thapa & Adhikari, 2023).

## Virtual Companions, Influencers, and AI Avatars

As well-known digital influencers in the form of digital personas, such Imma (398K Instagram followers) and Lil Miquela (2.7M Instagram followers), Virtual influencers are already being used by all of the top brands to communicate with their customers and market their goods and services (Wilkens, 2023).

## Emotional AI and Affective Computing

Machines may now give sympathetic feedback based on profound contextual awareness thanks to affective computing. Building on the findings of sentiment analysis and recognition, robots and other agents can provide expressions and responses, expressing the emotional temperature to the user through body movements, emotional text responses, and facial expressions (Filippini et al., 2020; Spezialetti et al., 2020)

## Brain-Computer Interfaces (BCI) and VR/ AR Conversational Agents

Brain-computer interface (BCI) is a preventive communication device. dispatched to the exterior world through travelling via the normal output pathways of the brain of muscles and so forth peripheral nerves. As a case in point, the signals in an EEG-based BCI are coded by the EEG activity. A BCI provides its user with an alternative manner of engaging the external environment (Wolpaw, 2007). The objective of the virtual reality (VR) simulation is to generate the virtual environments which offer users a distinctive view on the way the real-world works (Kim et al., 2013; Whyte, 2007). The objective of enhancing the perception of a virtual prototype by a real person towards real objects achieved with AR technology. This maintains the flexibility of the virtual world and enhances its. connection to the actual world (Hou et al., 2013).

# THE IMPACT OF INTERPERSONAL CONVERSATION

## Mediated Empathy and Authenticity

Emojis are now a popular tool in text-based communication (Kelly, 2015). Seeking to reduce the vagueness of text in a simple form with an emotional touch. Emojis and emoticons have been developed considerably since the time they were invented in 1872 and are now a necessity signs of non-verbal communication with the digital world (Bai et al., 2019). In order to help people, organizations, and the larger community strike a balance between autonomy and uncertainty, strategic techniques must be used to solve the paradox of choice.in addition to streamlining complexity to provide precise instructions meant to minimize decision overlap and enhance decision-making effectiveness (Schneckenberg et al., 2023).

## Genuine Emotional Expression is Barred by AI

The general adoption of this technology is still significantly hampered by early users' psychological discomfort and lack of trust (Jung, 2025). The main beneficiaries of AI-based autonomous driving technology are elderly drivers and people with physical limitations.

### Changes to the Norms

When it comes to ending a relationship abruptly, most people believe that ghosting is improper (Freedman et al., 2022; Timmermans et al., 2021). Typically, impolite and discourteous behaviours include disregarding coworkers during talks or failing to welcome them, acting disrespectfully towards others, and breaking behavioural workplace norms (Cortina et al., 2017; Schilpzand et al., 2016).

### Love, Companionship and AI in Emotional Support

The idea of using the internet to promote mental health is not new; online interventions, like websites dedicated to psychoeducation, and internet-based mental healthcare therapies, like e-therapy, have been used for many years (Barak et al., 2008). Other names for chatbots, such as chatterbots, are AI communication interfaces that use automated methods to mimic human speech. A chatbot can translate speech into text, which it then analyses and utilizes to create a response, or it can interpret written language, including emojis, depending on the interface (Kretzschmar et al., 2019; Stiefel, 2018).

# PSYCHOLOGICAL AND BEHAVIORAL IMPACTS

## Anthropomorphism and Trust in AI

Cognitive trust is the assurance or readiness of a client to depend on the skill and dependability of a service provider. The confidence that one has in another person based on the emotions evoked by the other person's degree of concern and care is known as affective trust (Johnson-George et al.,1982; Rempel et al.,1985). Experimental research has shown that users often respond to computers and conversational agents as if they were social partners, mirroring human social norms in their evaluations of trust and warmth (Reeves & Nass, 1996). In other words, affective trust is driven by benevolence and honesty, but cognitive trust is influenced by competence and predictability (Dimitriadis & Kyrezis, 2010). Despite being aware that AI applications are not human, human users have a tendency to anthropomorphise them and establish social expectations around them (Nass & Moon, 2000).

## Expectations and Communication Style

### Reduced Spans for Attention

The impact of research on short attention spans on accessibility is one factor that emphasizes how crucial it is. In (Willcutt, 2012), making events more accessible for people with attention-related difficulties can be greatly aided by an understanding of and commitment to resolving short attention spans. As a result, this paper's emphasis on accessibility is extremely pertinent (Poláková & Klímová, 2019; Rothman, 2016).

### An Increase in Communication Based on Memes and Images

These memes are now widely used by internet users as a means of disseminating, replicating, and approving digital information. Generally speaking, images (memes) work best when they get widely shared. When paired with the written messages, the images' literal meanings created a far more powerful frame (Ademosu & Alade, 2019).

### Standardized Language Created by AI

One concept that upholds a hierarchy among linguistic variants is standard language ideology. It is an imposed "bias towards an abstracted, idealised, homogenous spoken language" with the aim of "Suppressing variation," according to Lippi-Green (1994). Actually, no actual community speaks "Standard" language; rather, it is an abstracted variant that can only be identified by comparing it to the speech of marginalized people, (Michaud & Colpitts, 2015).

## Overreliance on AI and Diminished Human Agency

According to the systematic study, ethical issues are the main factor driving the over-reliance on AI dialogue systems in research and education (Zhai et al., 2024). (Koos & Wachsmann, 2023) talked about the negative consequences of relying too much on the AI dialogue system, pointing out that it could hinder students' ability to improve their critical thinking and problem-solving abilities. Active listening and interpersonal communication abilities. Without passing judgement, a listener relays to the sender what they believe has been spoken (see section Active Listening). Face-to-face interactions provide instant response and low parallelism, making them a communication medium with high media synchronization. Compared to in-person conversations, instant messaging offers medium feedback and parallelism, which results in less media synchrony (Bauer & Figl, 2008)

## Privacy Boundaries: Personal vs. Professional Communication

The notion of communication privacy management, which was created by (Petronio, 2002), states that people learn or make privacy rules to help them. Rules are conceptual frameworks, sometimes subconscious, that dictate what information should be shared when, how, with whom, and under what circumstances. According to boundary theory (Ashforth et al., 2000), people draw borders between their homes and places of employment based on both time and place.

# GROUP DYNAMICS AND AI-MEDIATED INTERACTION

## Algorithmic Group Decision-Making and Mediation

There are many technological tools like group decision support systems that have been developed so as to make sure that there is fair participation in group discussion online (DeSanctis and Gallupe, 1987). Human facilitators are costly, lack scalability and require appropriate training, but they are able to interrupt group discussions with a lot of effectiveness under different settings. In order to promote teamwork, automatic feedback systems are also proposed by many researchers (Harper et al., 2007; Tausczik & Pennebaker, 2013). First, we rated urgency of the statement. We discovered that the reference to the time scheduling issues, the need to do something quickly, the importance of the caller, and the number of calls made by some particular caller or on a particular topic all increased the urgency rating of a message. We also rated messages in terms of how they were personal (Ringel & Hirschberg, 2002).

## AI and Collective Behavior in Online Communities

Artificial intelligence (AI) echo chambers are online spaces where users are continuously exposed to the same kind of data, viewpoints, or suggestions, which serves to reinforce preexisting attitudes while excluding opposing viewpoints. Concerns over the societal impact of AI echo chambers have been raised by their growing relevance in social media, news platforms, entertainment services, and even e-commerce (Goswami, 2025).

The intentional or unintentional elevation of particular content on digital networks is known as algorithmic amplification. Motivated by AI optimization techniques and engagement metrics (Matthews, 2024). One of the biggest social media sites in the world, Facebook, is a perfect example of how trend amplification and suppression interact (Matthews, 2024; Bradshaw & Howard, 2019)

Polarisation can take two forms: affective polarisation, which is the dislike of members of the outgroup, or ideological polarisation, which is the division of opinions on contentious matters (Barberá et al., 2018). Deepfakes are extremely lifelike yet phoney audio and video produced by artificial intelligence (AI). Deepfakes can be used to spread false information, damage people's reputations, or incite unrest by manipulating the media to show people saying or doing things they never did. Although artificial intelligence (AI) has revolutionized the dissemination of information, it has also facilitated the spread of misleading information, leading to serious sociopolitical and psychological consequences (Olanipekun, 2025).

Tools for workplace collaboration that explain the necessity of integrating AI into project management. As projects grow increasingly complex and dynamic, there is a growing need for sophisticated technologies to optimize project management procedures (Miissonier & Asgari, 2019). Applications of AI in project management go beyond chatbots and include a range of tools that enhance productivity and decision-making. (Joshi, 2024) Among the major technologies revolutionizing the planning, execution, and monitoring of projects are machine learning algorithms, predictive analytics, and natural language processing.

## AI Tools for Collaboration and Organizational Communication

ASR transcription Transcribing the speech recordings from each participant's device into the appropriate text is the first stage in the Smart Meeting process. Since labelling real-life data is expensive and time-consuming, DNN-based summarization models typically presuppose the availability of large-scale training data, which is nearly impossible in our situation (Song et al., 2021). When it comes to collaborative thinking, efficiency versus human creativity thinking abilities that can generate responses that are unique and different from those that have already been developed are known as creative or divergent thinking abilities. According to (Daud et al.,2012), creative thinking can improve talent and talent development, which is necessary in the twenty-first century. According to (Hillmayr et al.,2020), collaborative learning is very successful and frequently outperforms individual learning in terms of academic accomplishment.

In this case, sentiment analysis driven by artificial intelligence (AI) can be useful. AI-powered sentiment analysis systems can automate the processing of large amounts of textual data. This provides companies and helpful information on the opinions and feedback of customers (Taherdoost & Madanchian, 2023). Because more individuals than ever before freely express their thoughts and feelings on social media through surveys of customer happiness, product evaluations, and consumer feedback, among other channels. As a result, it has grown in interest as a subject of study in NLP (Gupta, 2018). Understanding human emotions is referred to as emotional intelligence. Understanding "Emotion" is a prerequisite to discussing the importance of emotional intelligence. Leaders need emotional intelligence, also known as emotional management skills, to optimize long-term success through a healthy balance of emotion and reason (Bhusan & Jain, 2024)

### AI-Supported Collaborative Platforms in Organizational Communication

In organizational contexts, collaborative AI systems have become integral to group communication and coordination. Tools such as Microsoft Teams, Slack, and Google Workspace now integrate AI assistants that automate summarization, action-item extraction, and real-time sentiment feedback. For instance, Slack's GPT integration supports context-aware recommendations and message drafting, while Microsoft Copilot within Teams uses large language models to synthesize meeting transcripts and suggest follow-up tasks (Koh, 2024).

## AI, EMOTIONAL MONITORING, AND DIGITAL DEPENDENCY

Recent studies show that sustained interaction with AI-driven communication tools can both foster and erode digital empathy, depending on perceived authenticity and responsiveness (Pataranutaporn et al., 2023). Surveys by Pew Research Center (2023) and Edelman Trust Barometer (2024) indicate a growing reliance on AI chat systems, with over 60% of users reporting emotional connection or empathy responses to conversational agents. However, this dependency correlates with a decline in human-to-human trust and relationship satisfaction (Morales-García et al., 2024).

## Emotional Tracking and Privacy Concerns

Techniques from the larger privacy-enhancing ecosystem and technology are applied to the emotional domain in privacy-preserving emotional recognition. The goal of emotional tracking is to identify affective states in a variety of scenarios, including retail settings, customer service, workplace monitoring, and personal gadgets, ranging from simple emotions to more complicated states (UMEANOZIE et al, 2025).

## Loss of Human Warmth in AI-Mediated Communication

The generation and understanding of human-generated language (henceforth referred to as human language) are influenced by AI-generated language (henceforth referred to as AI language). Although there are many characteristics that people look for in communication partners, warmth and competence have consistently emerged as two of the most crucial elements in the creation of an impression (McCroskey & McCain, 1974).

## Screen Time, Sleep Disruption, and Mental Health

People who spend more time online have higher mental workloads due to multitasking, higher levels of stress, and comparatively poorer quality and quantity of sleep, all of which are linked to declining health. Exposure to blue and intense light in the evening and at night from self-luminous devices may prevent melatonin from being produced, alter its timings of production and retention, and thus disturb the circadian rhythm (Lissak, 2018). Researchers have created and assessed several systems to assist users in managing, tracking, and establishing limits on their own use in order to help them restore their agency. Stand-alone timers (Hiniker et al., 2016), usage trackers (Kim et al., 2016), automated nudges to encourage the user to end an experience (Okeke et al., 2018), goal-setting tools to reduce usage (Ko et al., 2015; Lee et al., 2014)

## Self-Esteem, Validation, and AI Filter Dependency

Self-esteem is a psychological trait that enables individuals to evaluate themselves either favourably or unfavourably (Rosenberg, 1965). For mental health and quality of life, self-esteem must grow to a sufficient level (Boyd et al., 2014). One way to think of intelligence (AI) dependency is as a tendency or must rely too much on automated systems for tasks, validation, or decision-making (Morales-García et al., 2024)

## Beauty Filters and Body Image Distortion

Because AI has made the beauty industry more efficient and individualised, it has completely altered public perception. AI is assisting companies in personalising their goods and making more appealing makeup recommendations. When users are exposed to hyper-realistic filters that display idealised, frequently unachievable beauty standards, AI-based "virtual beauty" is contributing to an increase in body dissatisfaction. It is the duty of tech firms and social media sites to promote more genuine content by identifying, promoting, and even favoring unaltered photos and videos (Ilyas, 2024)

## Persuasive Design and Digital Addiction Mechanisms

Wearable technology for health and fitness is intended to give users instant feedback on their physical activity, which is linked to better physical health and wellbeing (Baker, 2017). Wearable technology-enabled feedback systems have shown promise in enhancing performance and communication. As a guide to propel such goal-directed behaviour, dopamine—a chemical essential to motivation and reward learning evolved. It made sure that the pursuit of pleasure was connected to work and long-term gain by rewarding behaviours that resulted in survival or successful reproduction (Termann, 2025).

*Table 1. Technology, emotions, and behavior: Simplified overview*

| Topic | Summary | References |
|---|---|---|
| Emotional Tracking & Privacy Concerns | Technology tracks emotions while keeping privacy. It is used in stores, workplaces, and personal devices. | UMEANOZIE et al., 2025 |
| Loss of Human Warmth in AI-Mediated Communication | AI can make communication feel less warm. Warmth and competence are important for impressions. | McCroskey & McCain, 1974 |
| Screen Time, Sleep Disruption & Mental Health | Spending too much time online causes stress and poor sleep. Tools like timers and trackers help manage screen time. | Lissak, 2018; Hiniker et al., 2016; Kim et al., 2016; Okeke et al., 2018; Ko et al., 2015; Lee et al., 2014 |
| Self-Esteem, Validation & AI Dependency | Self-esteem affects mental health. Some people rely too much on AI for validation and decisions. | Rosenberg, 1965; Boyd et al., 2014; Morales-García et al., 2024 |

continued on following page

*Table 1. Continued*

| Topic | Summary | References |
|---|---|---|
| Beauty Filters & Body Image Distortion | AI makes beauty products personalized. Filters can make people feel unhappy about their bodies. | Ilyas, 2024 |
| Persuasive Design & Digital Addiction Mechanisms | Wearables give instant feedback and motivate users. Technology can create addiction but also help reduce it. | Baker, 2017; Termann, 2025; Murillo-Munoz et al., 2018; Davazdahemami et al., 2016 |
| Chatbots as Companions & Illusion of Conversation | People can feel less lonely with human-like chatbots. Online chats can feel closer than face-to-face ones. | Pataranutaporn et al., 2023; Xia et al., 2025; Karapanos et al., 2016; Walther, 1996 |

According to (Murillo-Munoz et al.,2018), persuasive technology is a synthesis of technology and persuasion. Technology is inherently addictive due to its persuasion properties (Murillo-Munoz et al., 2018). Consequently, using the same quality, technology can be affirmatively persuaded by its designer to lessen addiction (Davazdahemami et al., 2016).

## Chatbots as Companions and the Illusion of Conversation

Depending on how the user interprets them, a chatbot's behaviour can also change into distinct patterns (Pataranutaporn et al., 2023). Users' psychosocial results can be influenced by how they view the chatbot; individuals who believe that chatbots possess more human-like attributes, such consciousness and agency, frequently report feeling less lonely and having better social health (Xia et al., 2025).

### The Conversation Illusion

Self-fulfilling prophecies allow perceivers to influence targets' actions, but the processes behind these effects were not explained. These bad experiences were frequently caused by WhatsApp's incompatibility with social communication norms. Some of the more notable examples are described here (Karapanos et al., 2016). Such findings echo Walther's (1996) hyper personal communication theory, which explains how mediated interactions when filtered and controlled can produce an *intensified sense of closeness*, even exceeding that of in-person relationships.

## ETHICAL, SOCIAL, AND GOVERNANCE PERSPECTIVES

### The Moral and Ethical Nature of AI Communication

Perhaps moral philosophy and ethics are missing. We plan to take advantage of the chance that new technologies frequently present to revisit and reevaluate some fundamental moral conceptions in an attempt to explicitly incorporate ethics and moral philosophy into this collection together with the other pertinent disciplines. Therefore, we shall address the intricate matter of AI and consent (Jones et al., 2018).

### Governmental and Organizational Responsibility

As the primary crisis communicators, local governments have a responsibility to play a vital role in enhancing the public's cognitive and informational capacity to handle emergencies pertaining to public safety.to foster a relationship between the public and local governments that is more trustworthy and long-lasting (Coombs, 2022) put public service providers in the forefront of citizen interaction, necessitating their adoption of new technology to optimise skilled and accountable communicators (Dong et al., 2023).

### Data-Driven Personalization and User Consent

An essential element of data-driven personalization is user consent. An individual's voluntary and informed consent to the gathering, use, and dissemination of their personal data is known as consent. Data-driven personalization is the process of creating experiences that are specifically designed for each individual using data analytics and machine learning. This strategy offers several advantages, such as: Better user experience: More user engagement and satisfaction can result from personalization. Enhanced effectiveness: Organisations can cut expenses and optimise their services by implementing personalization (Oladele, 2025).

### Transparency and Explainability in AI Systems

Depending on the application area, the machine learning model being used, and the kind of input and output data the model uses, there are several ways to establish algorithm transparency and interpretability. Understanding the modelling problem first, then defining a generative parametric model, fitting its parameters to the data, and interpreting the parameters is the simplest method (Schmidt et al., 2020). Medical students and clinical educators have vital roles to play. Second, even while both educators and students have a part to play, they cannot share equal responsibility for removing the broad barriers that is, understanding, awareness, agency, and motivation because doing so requires medical students to take on more responsibility. However, addressing others requires clinical educators to take on more responsibility (Abraham, 2023)

## Inclusion, Bias, and Non-Standard Communication Norms

It's critical to acknowledge algorithmic bias's complex nature. Historical, representational, measurement, aggregation, learning, evaluation, and deployment biases are among the stages of the machine learning life cycle when it appears (Suresh & Guttag, 2021). Existing research frequently ignores academic emotions like perplexity, irritation, and boredom in favour of focussing only on primary emotions like happiness, sorrow, rage, surprise, fear, and disgust. Each person has a unique speech pattern. If we include deeper variations in prior knowledge and mental maps in addition to grammatical and lexical aspects of speech Native speakers clearly make up a large portion of the wide range of personal speech variations (Mustajoki, 2010)

## Cultural and Linguistic Gaps in Global Communication

The impact of these cultural-linguistic gaps is exacerbated by the rapid nature of modern communication, as consumers and content creators struggle to maintain meaningful contact across culturally disparate contexts. Professionals in the media create content for consumers around the world. translators and cultural mediators who operate across linguistic divides. Global communication tactics being used by organisations (Rakhimovna, 2025)

## Safeguarding Vulnerable and Neurodiverse Groups

A useful method for researching the accountability and transparency of data integration and analysis platforms aiming to carry out government tasks is to compile public papers and establish a public interest repository. The origins of archives for the public interest and public good can be found in a number of places, such as Daniel Ellsberg's disclosure of the Pentagon Papers during the Vietnam War (Sheehan, 1971) and (Park et al.,1967) investigative studies on social control and scientific reporting (Frazier & Gaziano, 1979). A growing number of applications are being focused on by Explainable Artificial Intelligence (XAI) because of its many benefits, which include extremely transparent, reliable, and interpretable system development. Rich simulation infrastructure, intelligent machine communication, enhanced visualisation, improved service quality analysis, and production efficiency maximization are all guaranteed (Jagatheesaperumal et al., 2022). A general term for the neurological heterogeneity of the human brain that results in aberrant brain function, neurodiversity (ND) can impact emotion, memory, self-control, and learning capacity. Safety, security, and privacy criteria must all be followed by every safety-critical XR system. It is important to emphasize that (Sa/Se/Pr) may mean and measure differently depending on the industry in order to shed light on how XR developers handle this issue for ND individuals (Jones et al., 2023)

## TOWARD HUMAN-CENTERED AI COMMUNICATION

### AI as Augmentation vs Automation

We contend that in the field of management, augmentation and automation are inextricably linked. There is a paradoxical conflict between these two AI applications since they are dependent on one another in both space and time. Overemphasising automation or augmentation creates vicious cycles that impair an organization's effectiveness and have detrimental effects on society (Raisch & Krakowski, 2021).

### Designing Intentional and Empathetic Interfaces

Multi-level system interfaces might be completely different for each tier (for example, a hierarchical database data definition language is different from a database data manipulation language) or they can integrate the many levels of functionality into a single interface. (For instance, a spreadsheet enables the user to design the data's structure and enter data from a single interface) (Colman & Leung, 2000).

### Promoting Authentic Interaction over Algorithmic Engagement

While resolving crucial ethical issues to guarantee authenticity, including AI into consumer involvement procedures might improve personalization. encourages businesses to move away from only algorithm-centric tactics and encourage an authenticity-driven strategy to create real AI interactions (Nadeem, 2025).

*Figure 2. Human-centered AI communication*

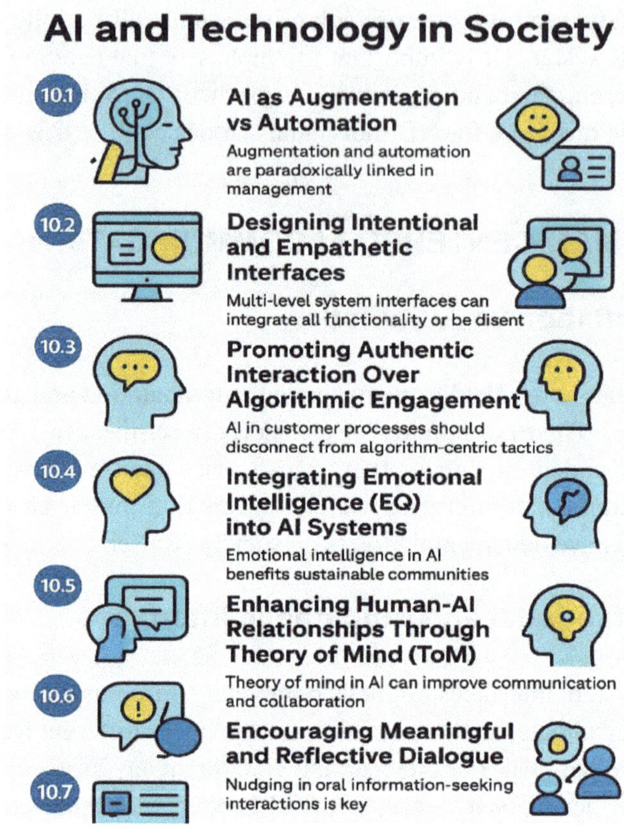


*(Nadeem, 2025; Colman & Leung, 2000; Raisch & Krakowski, 2021; Suresh & Guttag, 2021)*

## Integrating Emotional Intelligence (EQ) into AI Systems

We highlight AI's significance as a key component of contemporary dynamics by placing AI awareness and connection at the core of EQ. The Sustainable Development Goals (SDGs) of the UN, especially those pertaining to decent work, economic growth, excellent education, and less inequality, are in line with the sustainable integration of AI with EQ. We can build more fair, inclusive, and sustainable communities that use AI to benefit everyone by encouraging an inclusive approach to AI literacy and emotionally intelligent technology interactions (Cinar & Bilodeau, 2024)

## Enhancing Human-AI Relationships Through Theory of Mind (ToM)

ToM has a crucial function in communication, according to the Cognitive Science approach (Premack & Woodruff, 1978). ToM allows us to infer other people's thoughts from their words and actions serving as the basis for communication between people (Baron-Cohen, 1999). AI systems have enormous potential to improve human experiences, efficiency, and naturalness in a variety of human-AI interactions. In human-AI task collaborations, for example, AI systems with ToM-like capabilities can create readable robot motions based on expected human interpretations (Fukuchi et al.,2022), infer human intentions and plans to account for irrational human behaviours during collaborations (Kwon et al., 2020), and detect the knowledge state of human collaborators and provide additional information accordingly to complete the tasks (Lo et al., 2020)

## Promoting Digital Literacy and Responsible AI Use

Artificial intelligence (AI)-driven chatbots are made to follow conversations through text or voice interaction and deliver information in a conversational way (Labadze et al., 2023). According to recent research, educational chatbots and other generative AI technologies offer a lot of potential to support self-regulated learning (Chang et al., 2023). The use of Generative Pre-trained Transformer (ChatGPT) in the educational process is given particular consideration. (Stepanenko & Stupak.,2023) looked into the use of AI tools like ChatGPT to improve instruction, learning, and educational administration.

## Empowering Users to Regain Control Over Technology Habits

How individuals define themselves and achieve their purposes in the digital spaces or who do it- who bring among them, there is an immeasurable number of situations, interests, histories, talents, and abilities, etc. Aspirations are to be considered in case the society should be digital-inclusive. According to (Smith 2003), users are ethical beings who make their choices on what is good and otherwise bad, worthy and unworthy, just and unjust, and right and wrong. Words, photos, sounds, and all the meta-information related to document and interface structure are stored and transmitted by digital technology (Giannandrea, 2017).

## Hybrid Community Models and Collective Well-Being

Since the WiInf-Central community is relying on virtual and face-to-face interaction, we define it as a mixed community. Therefore, WiInf-Central community is not properly defined through existing definitions of virtual communities. With its exclusive membership, WiInf-Central provided a source of identity. According to this view, the efforts to build solid community boundaries (in restricting access to WiInf-Central) could be considered to be a means of fighting such emotions of loneliness and isolation as students can have during learning. Accordingly, we hypothesize a in a hybrid community high degree of dependency between virtual and face-to-face communications (Rohde et al., 2004).

## CONCLUSION

Artificial intelligence is rapidly reshaping the ways humans interact on both personal and collective levels. While AI technologies enhance efficiency, personalization, and accessibility in communication, they simultaneously pose risks to empathy, authenticity, and mental well-being. The rise of AI-mediated interactions challenges traditional norms of trust, intimacy, and emotional expression, blurring boundaries between human and machine communication. Issues such as deepfakes, echo chambers, and algorithmic manipulation further complicate the landscape, raising ethical and societal questions that demand attention. To navigate these challenges, a human-centered approach is essential—one that embraces emotional intelligence, promotes digital literacy, and safeguards user autonomy. By encouraging intentional design and regulatory accountability, society can harness AI's potential while preserving the core values of meaningful, empathetic human connection.

## REFERENCES


Abraham, R. M. (2023). Balancing responsibility-sharing in the simulated clinical skills setting: A strategy to remove barriers to feedback engagement as a new concept to promote a growth-enhancing process. *African Journal of Health Professions Education*, *15*(1), 2–6. DOI: 10.7196/AJHPE.2023.v15i1.1630

Ademosu, I., & Alade, M. O. (2019). Communicating via imagery: Speaking through online memes. *Journal of Communication and Media Research*, *11*(2), 34–46. http://dspace.run.edu.ng:8080/jspui/handle/123456789/214

Al-Amin, M., Ali, M. S., Salam, A., Khan, A., Ali, A., Ullah, A., . . . Chowdhury, S. K. (2024). History of generative Artificial Intelligence (AI) chatbots: past, present, and future development. *arXiv preprint arXiv:2402.05122.* https://doi.org//arXiv.2402.05122.DOI: 10.48550

Ami, R. (2021). AI in Automated Content Moderation on Social Media. *International Journal of Artificial Intelligence and Machine Learning*, *4*(3).

Ashforth, B. E., Kreiner, G. E., & Fugate, M. (2000). All in a day's work: Boundaries and micro role transitions. *Academy of Management Review*, *25*(3), 472–491. DOI: 10.2307/259305

Bai, Q., Dan, Q., Mu, Z., & Yang, M. (2019). A systematic review of emoji: Current research and future perspectives. *Frontiers in Psychology*, *10*, 476737. DOI: 10.3389/fpsyg.2019.02221 PMID: 31681068

Baker, D. A. (2017, May). Wearables and User Interface Design: Impacts on Belief in Free Will. *In International Conference on Human-Computer Interaction (pp.* 210-217*)*. Cham: Springer International Publishing.DOI: 10.1007/978-3-319-58750-9_30

Barak, A., Hen, L., Boniel-Nissim, M., & Shapira, N. A. (2008). A comprehensive review and a meta-analysis of the effectiveness of internet-based psychotherapeutic interventions. *Journal of Technology in Human Services*, *26*(2-4), 109–160. DOI: 10.1080/15228830802094429

Barberá, P., Tucker, J. A., Guess, A., Vaccari, C., Siegel, A., Sanovich, S., & Nyhan, B. (2018). Social media, political polarization, and political disinformation: A review of the scientific literature. DOI: 10.2139/ssrn.3144139

Baron-Cohen, S. (1999). *The evolution of a theory of mind* (pp. 261-277). na. DOI: 10.1093/acprof:oso/9780192632593.003.0013

Bauer, C., & Figl, K. (2008, October). Active listening" in written online communication-a case study in a course on "soft skills for computer scientists. *In 2008 38th Annual Frontiers in Education Conference (pp. F2C-1).* IEEE.DOI: 10.1109/FIE.2008.4720282

. Bhusan, B., & Jain, P. (2024). Artificial Intelligence as a Catalyst for Leadership Development: Enhancing Emotional Intelligence in Leaders. *International Journal of Innovations in Science, Engineering and Management, 263-269.*https://doi.org/.DOI: 10.69968/ijisem.2024v3si2263-269

Boyd, J. E., Otilingam, P. G., & DeForge, B. R. (2014). Brief version of the Internalized Stigma of Mental Illness (ISMI) scale: Psychometric properties and relationship to depression, self-esteem, recovery orientation, empowerment, and perceived devaluation and discrimination. *Psychiatric Rehabilitation Journal*, *37*(1), 17–23. DOI: 10.1037/prj0000035 PMID: 24660946

. Bradshaw, S., & Howard, P. N. (2019). The global disinformation order: 2019 global inventory of organised social media manipulation.

Chang, D. H., Lin, M. P. C., Hajian, S., & Wang, Q. Q. (2023). Educational design principles of using AI chatbot that supports self-regulated learning in education: Goal setting, feedback, and personalization. *Sustainability (Basel)*, *15*(17), 12921. DOI: 10.3390/su151712921

Cinar, A. B., & Bilodeau, S. (2024). Incorporating AI into the inner circle of emotional intelligence for sustainability. *Sustainability (Basel)*, *16*(15), 6648. DOI: 10.3390/su16156648

Colman, A. W., & Leung, Y. K. (2000). Using intentional models for the interface design of multi-level systems. *International Journal of Human-Computer Studies*, *52*(6), 1007–1029. DOI: 10.1006/ijhc.2000.0369

Coombs, W. T. (2022). Situational crisis communication theory (SCCT) refining and clarifying a cognitive-based theory of crisis communication. *The handbook of crisis communication, 193-204.*DOI: 10.1002/9781119678953.ch14

Cortina, L. M., Kabat-Farr, D., Magley, V. J., & Nelson, K. (2017). Researching rudeness: The past, present, and future of the science of incivility. *Journal of Occupational Health Psychology*, *22*(3), 299–313. DOI: 10.1037/ocp0000089

Czamecki, C., & Spiliopoulou, M. (2012). A holistic framework for the implementation of a next generattion network. *International Journal of Business Information Systems*, *9*(4), 385–401. DOI: 10.1504/IJBIS.2012.046291

Datta, A., Dey, B. K., Bhuniya, S., Sangal, I., Mandal, B., Sarkar, M., Guchhait, R., Sarkar, B., & Ganguly, B. (2025). Adaptation of e-commerce retailing to enhance customer satisfaction within a dynamical system under transfer of risk. *Journal of Retailing and Consumer Services*, *84*, 104129. DOI: 10.1016/j.jretconser.2024.104129

Daud, A. M., Omar, J., Turiman, P., & Osman, K. (2012). Creativity in science education. *Procedia: Social and Behavioral Sciences*, *59*, 467–474. DOI: 10.1016/j.sbspro.2012.09.302

Davazdahemami, B., Hammer, B., & Soror, A. (2016, January). Addiction to mobile phone or addiction through mobile phone*? In 2016 49th Hawaii international conference on system sciences (HICSS) (pp. 1467-1476).* IEEE.DOI: 10.1109/HICSS.2016.186

DeSanctis, G., & Gallupe, R. B. (1987). A foundation for the study of group decision support systems. *Management Science*, *33*(5), 589–609. DOI: 10.1287/mnsc.33.5.589

Dimitriadis, S., & Kyrezis, N. (2010). Linking trust to use intention for technology-enabled bank channels: The role of trusting intentions. *Psychology and Marketing*, *27*(8), 799–820. DOI: 10.1002/mar.20358

Dinmore, S., & Gao, J. (2016, November). Voice-to-Text Transcription of Lecture Recordings. In *Australian Society for Computers in Learning in Tertiary Education Conference (ASCILITE)*. DOI: 10.14742/apubs.2016.864

Dong, C., Zheng, Q., & Morehouse, J. (2023). What do we know about government public relations (GPR)? A systematic review of GPR in public relations literature. *Public Relations Review*, *49*(1), 102284. DOI: 10.1016/j.pubrev.2022.102284

. Dorizza, A. (2025). Exploring the impact of AI-based services on humans. A case study: echo chambers on social media.

Fauziah, J. L., Hanifah, H. F. B., & Sujatmoko, K. (2024). Autogeneration Social Media Content (TikTok, Instagram, Facebook, Twitter) Based on AI & RPA. *[CEPAT] Journal of Computer Engineering: Progress. Application and Technology*, *3*(01), 56–64. DOI: 10.25124/cepat.v3i01.7193

Filippini, C., Perpetuini, D., Cardone, D., Chiarelli, A. M., & Merla, A. (2020). Thermal infrared imaging-based affective computing and its application to facilitate human robot interaction: A review. *Applied Sciences (Basel, Switzerland)*, *10*(8), 2924. DOI: 10.3390/app10082924

Frazier, P., & Gaziano, C. (1979). Robert Ezra Park's theory of news, public opinion and social control. *Journalism & Communication Monographs*, •••, 64.

Freedman, G., Hales, A. H., Powell, D. N., Le, B., & Williams, K. D. (2022). The role of gender and safety concerns in romantic rejection decisions. *Journal of Experimental Social Psychology, 102*, 104368. DOI: 10.1016/j.jesp.2022.104368

Fukuchi, Y., Osawa, M., Yamakawa, H., Takahashi, T., & Imai, M. (2022). Conveying intention by motions with awareness of information asymmetry. *Frontiers in Robotics and AI, 9*, 783863. DOI: 10.3389/frobt.2022.783863 PMID: 35252364

Giannandrea, L. (2017). E-portfolio and Teacher Training. Building a Culture of Trust in School Contexts. *PG rossi, L. Giannandrea Eds. tEchnoLoGiEs and trust*, 89.

Goswami, G. (2025). AI Echo Chambers: How Algorithms Shape Reality, Influence Democracy, and Fuel Misinformation. *Authorea Preprints.*DOI: 10.36227/techrxiv.174059950.03385147/v1

. Gupta, S. (2018). Sentiment analysis: Concept, analysis and applications. *Towards data science,* 7(06).

Harper, F. M., Frankowski, D., Drenner, S., Ren, Y., Kiesler, S., Terveen, L., & Riedl, J. (2007, January). Talk amongst yourselves: inviting users to participate in online conversations. In *Proceedings of the 12th international conference on Intelligent user interfaces* (pp. 62-71). DOI: 10.1145/1216295.1216313

Hillmayr, D., Ziernwald, L., Reinhold, F., Hofer, S. I., & Reiss, K. M. (2020). The potential of digital tools to enhance mathematics and science learning in secondary schools: A context-specific meta-analysis. *Computers & Education, 153*, 103897. DOI: 10.1016/j.compedu.2020.103897

Hiniker, A., Hong, S., Kohno, T., & Kientz, J. A. (2016, May). MyTime: designing and evaluating an intervention for smartphone non-use. In *Proceedings of the 2016 CHI conference on human factors in computing systems* (pp. 4746-4757). DOI: 10.1145/2858036.2858403

Hou, L., Wang, X., Bernold, L., & Love, P. E. (2013). Using animated augmented reality to cognitively guide assembly. *Journal of Computing in Civil Engineering, 27*(5), 439–451. DOI: 10.1061/(ASCE)CP.1943-5487.0000184

Huy, P. Q., Shavkatovich, S. N., Abdul-Samad, Z., Agrawal, D. K., Ashifa, K. M., & Arumugam, M. (2023). Resource management projects in entrepreneurship and retain customer based on big data analysis and artificial intelligence. *The Journal of High Technology Management Research, 34*(2), 100471. DOI: 10.1016/j.hitech.2023.100471

Ilyas, Q. (2024). AI IN BEAUTY CONTENT: a theoretical study of ethical and psychological considerations surrounding ai-generated beauty content. https://urn.fi/URN:NBN:fi:amk-2024120432706

Jagatheesaperumal, S. K., Pham, Q. V., Ruby, R., Yang, Z., Xu, C., & Zhang, Z. (2022). Explainable AI over the Internet of Things (IoT): Overview, state-of-the-art and future directions. *IEEE Open Journal of the Communications Society*, *3*, 2106–2136. DOI: 10.1109/OJCOMS.2022.3215676

Johnson-George, C., & Swap, W. C. (1982). Measurement of specific interpersonal trust: Construction and validation of a scale to assess trust in a specific other. *Journal of Personality and Social Psychology*, *43*(6), 1306–1317. https://psycnet.apa.org/doi/10.1037/0022-3514.43.6.1306. DOI: 10.1037/0022-3514.43.6.1306

Jones, D., Ghasemi, S., Gračanin, D., & Azab, M. (2023, July). Privacy, safety, and security in extended reality: user experience challenges for neurodiverse users. In *International conference on human-computer interaction* (pp. 511-528). Cham: Springer Nature Switzerland.DOI: 10.1007/978-3-031-35822-7_33

Jones, M. L., Kaufman, E., & Edenberg, E. (2018). AI and the ethics of automating consent. *IEEE Security and Privacy*, *16*(3), 64–72. DOI: 10.1109/MSP.2018.2701155

Joseph, N. P. S., Mahmood, A. K., Yin, C. P., Wan, W. S., Yuen, P. K., & Heng, L. E. (2015). Barebone cloud IaaS: Revitalisation disruptive technology. *International Journal of Business Information Systems*, *18*(1), 107–126. DOI: 10.1504/IJBIS.2015.066130

Joshi, H. (2024). *Artificial intelligence in project management: A study of the role of ai-powered chatbots in project stakeholder engagement. Indian Journal of Software Engineering and Project Management*. IJSEPM., DOI: 10.54105/ijsepm.B9022.04010124

Jung, H. (2025). AI-Based UX Design Research for Mitigating Psychological Barriers in Early Autonomous Vehicle Users. *International Journal of Advanced Culture Technology*, *13*(1), 322–329. DOI: 10.17703/IJACT.2025.13.1.322

*. Jurafsky, D., & Martin, J. H. (2008). Speech and Language Processing: An introduction to speech recognition, computational linguistics and natural language processing*. Upper Saddle River, NJ: Prentice Hall.

Karapanos, E., Teixeira, P., & Gouveia, R. (2016). Need fulfillment and experiences on social media: A case on Facebook and WhatsApp. *Computers in Human Behavior*, *55*, 888–897. DOI: 10.1016/j.chb.2015.10.015

Karnouskos, S. (2020). Artificial intelligence in digital media: The era of deepfakes. *IEEE Transactions on Technology and Society, 1*(3), 138–147. DOI: 10.1109/TTS.2020.3001312

. Kelly, C. (2015). Do you know what I mean>:(: A linguistic study of the understanding of emoticons and emojis in text messages.

Kim, M. J., Wang, X., Love, P. E., Li, H., & Kang, S. C. (2013). Virtual reality for the built environment: A critical review of recent advances. [ITcon]. *Journal of Information Technology in Construction, 18*(14), 279–305. https://www.itcon.org/2013/14

Kim, Y. H., Jeon, J. H., Choe, E. K., Lee, B., Kim, K., & Seo, J. (2016, May). TimeAware: Leveraging framing effects to enhance personal productivity. *In Proceedings of the 2016 CHI Conference on Human Factors in Computing Systems* (pp. 272-283). DOI: 10.1145/2858036.2858428

King, M. R., & Chat, G. P. T. (2023). A conversation on artificial intelligence, chatbots, and plagiarism in higher education. *Cellular and Molecular Bioengineering, 16*(1), 1–2. DOI: 10.1007/s12195-022-00754-8 PMID: 36660590

Ko, M., Yang, S., Lee, J., Heizmann, C., Jeong, J., Lee, U., . . . Chung, K. M. (2015, February). NUGU: a group-based intervention app for improving self-regulation of limiting smartphone use. *In Proceedings of the 18th ACM conference on computer supported cooperative work & social computing* (pp. 1235-1245). DOI: 10.1145/2675133.2675244

Koh, M. (2024). Organizational Communication in the Digital Era: Examining the Impact of AI, Chatbots, and Covid-19. In Ndlela, M. N. (Ed.), *New Perspectives in Organizational Communication. Organizational Communication in the Digital Era: Examining the Impact of AI, Chatbots, and Covid-19 | SpringerLink.*, DOI: 10.1007/978-3-031-58307-0

Koos, S., & Wachsmann, S. (2023). Navigating the Impact of ChatGPT/GPT4 on Legal Academic Examinations: Challenges, Opportunities and Recommendations. *Media Iuris, 6*(2), 255–270. Advance online publication. DOI: 10.20473/mi.v6i2.45270

Kretzschmar, K., Tyroll, H., Pavarini, G., Manzini, A., & Singh, I. (2019). Can your phone be your therapist? Young people's ethical perspectives on the use of fully automated conversational agents (chatbots) in mental health support. *Biomedical Informatics Insights, 11*, 1178222619829083. DOI: 10.1177/1178222619829083 PMID: 30858710

Kumara, V., Sharma, D. M., Isaac, J. S., Saravanan, S., Suganthi, D., & Boopathi, S. (2024). An AI-integrated green power monitoring system: empowering small and medium enterprises. In *Convergence Strategies for Green Computing and Sustainable Development* (pp. 218–244). IGI Global Scientific Publishing., DOI: 10.4018/979-8-3693-0338-2.ch013

Kwon, M., Biyik, E., Talati, A., Bhasin, K., Losey, D. P., & Sadigh, D. (2020, March). When humans aren't optimal: Robots that collaborate with risk-aware humans. In *Proceedings of the 2020 ACM/IEEE international conference on human-robot interaction* (pp. 43-52). DOI: 10.1145/3319502.3374832

Labadze, L., Grigolia, M., & Machaidze, L. (2023). Role of AI chatbots in education: Systematic literature review. *International Journal of Educational Technology in Higher Education*, *20*(1), 56. DOI: 10.1186/s41239-023-00426-1

Lee, H., Ahn, H., Choi, S., & Choi, W. (2014). The SAMS: Smartphone addiction management system and verification. *Journal of Medical Systems*, *38*(1), 1. DOI: 10.1007/s10916-013-0001-1 PMID: 24395031

Lippi-Green, R. (1994). Accent, standard language ideology, and discriminatory pretext in the courts. *Language in Society*, *23*(2), 163–198. DOI: 10.1017/S0047404500017826

Lissak, G. (2018). Adverse physiological and psychological effects of screen time on children and adolescents: Literature review and case study. *Environmental Research*, *164*, 149–157. DOI: 10.1016/j.envres.2018.01.015 PMID: 29499467

Lo, S. Y., Short, E. S., & Thomaz, A. L. (2020, March). Planning with partner uncertainty modeling for efficient information revealing in teamwork. In *Proceedings of the 2020 ACM/IEEE International Conference on Human-Robot Interaction* (pp. 319-327). DOI: 10.1145/3319502.3374827

Matthews, A. (2024). Sculpting the social algorithm for radical futurity. *AI & Society*, *39*(1), 75–86. DOI: 10.1007/s00146-023-01760-8

. McCroskey, J. C., & McCain, T. A. (1974). The measurement of interpersonal attraction. .DOI: 10.1080/03637757409375845

Michaud, M., & Colpitts, B. D. (2015). English as a lingua franca: Globalization, ownership, and the diversification of English. *Kwansei Gakuin University Humanities Review*, *20*, 125–131.

Morales-García, W. C., Sairitupa-Sanchez, L. Z., Morales-García, S. B., & Morales-García, M. (2024, March). Development and validation of a scale for dependence on artificial intelligence in university students. *In Frontiers in Education (Vol. 9, p. 1323898).* Frontiers Media SA. DOI: 10.3389/feduc.2024.1323898

Murillo-Munoz, M. F., Vazquez-Briseno, M., Cota, C. X. N., & Nieto-Hipólito, J. I. (2018, February). A framework for design and development of persuasive mobile systems. In *2018 International Conference on Electronics, Communications and Computers (CONIELECOMP)* (pp. 59-66). IEEE.DOI: 10.1109/CONIELECOMP.2018.8327176

. Mustajoki, A. (2010). Types of non-standard communication encounters with special reference to Russian. *Language ideologies in transition multilingualism in Russia and Finland*, 35-55.

Nadeem, M. (2025). From Algorithms to Authenticity: Ensuring Ethical Customer Engagement in the Age of Artificial Intelligence. *International Journal of Business and Management, 20*(2), 13. https://ccsenet.org/journal/index.php/ijbm/issue/view/0/3194. DOI: 10.5539/ijbm.v20n2p13

Nass, C., & Moon, Y. (2000). Machines and mindlessness: Social responses to computers. *The Journal of Social Issues, 56*(1), 81–103. DOI: 10.1111/0022-4537.00153

Naveed, H. (2022). CHATBOTS AND VIRTUAL ASSISTANTS: THE FUTURE OF CUSTOMER SERVICE. *Computer Science Bulletin, 5*(01), 15–36.

Ojo, S. O., & Afolaranmi, A. O. (2024). The Effects of Artificial Intelligence (AI) on Human Interpersonal Connections. *Lead City Journal of Religions and Intercultural Communication, 2*(2), 162–174.

Okeke, F., Sobolev, M., Dell, N., & Estrin, D. (2018, September). Good vibrations: can a digital nudge reduce digital overload? In *Proceedings of the 20th international conference on human-computer interaction with mobile devices and services* (pp. 1-12). DOI: 10.1145/3229434.3229463

Oladele, S. (2025). Exploring User Consent Mechanisms in Data-Driven Personalization. https://www.researchgate.net/publication/388508656_Exploring_User_Consent_Mechanisms_in_Data-Driven_Personalization

Olanipekun, S. O.Samson Olufemi Olanipekun. (2025). Computational propaganda and misinformation: AI technologies as tools of media manipulation. *World Journal of Advanced Research and Reviews, 25*(1), 911–923. DOI: 10.30574/wjarr.2025.25.1.0131

Pardeshi, S., Ovhal, S., Shinde, P., Bansode, M., & Birajdar, A. (2020). A survey on Different Algorithms used in Chatbot. [IRJET]. *International Research Journal of Engineering and Technology*, *7*(5), 6092–6098.

Park, R. E., Turner, R. H., & Janowitz, M. (1967). *On social control and collective behavior: Selected papers*. No Title.

Pataranutaporn, P., Liu, R., Finn, E., & Maes, P. (2023). Influencing human–AI interaction by priming beliefs about AI can increase perceived trustworthiness, empathy and effectiveness. *Nature Machine Intelligence*, *5*(10), 1076–1086. DOI: 10.1038/s42256-023-00720-7

Petronio, S. (2002). *Boundaries of privacy: Dialectics of disclosure*. Suny Press. DOI: 10.1353/book4588

Poláková, P., & Klímová, B. (2019). Mobile technology and Generation Z in the English language classroom—A preliminary study. *Education Sciences*, *9*(3), 203. DOI: 10.3390/educsci9030203

Premack, D., & Woodruff, G. (1978). Does the chimpanzee have a theory of mind? *Behavioral and Brain Sciences*, *1*(4), 515–526. DOI: 10.1017/S0140525X00076512

Qi, J. (2024, January). The Impact of Large Language Models on Social Media Communication. In *Proceedings of the 2024 7th International Conference on Software Engineering and Information Management* (pp. 165-170). DOI: 10.1145/3647722.3647749

Raisch, S., & Krakowski, S. (2021). Artificial intelligence and management: The automation–augmentation paradox. *Academy of Management Review*, *46*(1), 192–210. DOI: 10.5465/amr.2018.0072

Rakhimovna, A. S. (2025). Cultural and Linguistic Gaps in Contemporary Media Communication. *Spanish Journal of Innovation and Integrity*, *38*, 193–197.

Ramkumar, G., Sujatha, V., & Raja, B., TamilSelvi, M., Balaji, A., & Kumar, A. K. (2023, November). An Experiment to Develop an Enhanced Medical Image Security by using Deep Learning Assisted Crypto Policy. In *2023 International Conference on Research Methodologies in Knowledge Management, Artificial Intelligence and Telecommunication Engineering (RMKMATE)* (pp. 1-8). IEEE.

Reeves, B., & Nass, C. (1996). The media equation: How people treat computers, television, and new media like real people and places. Cambridge University Press. The_Media_Equation_How_People_Treat_Comp20161127-17472-1s43e41-libre.pdf

Rempel, J. K., Holmes, J. G., & Zanna, M. P. (1985). Trust in close relationships. *Journal of Personality and Social Psychology, 49*(1), 95–112. https://psycnet.apa.org/doi/10.1037/0022-3514.49.1.95. DOI: 10.1037/0022-3514.49.1.95 PMID: 11474726

Ringel, M., & Hirschberg, J. (2002, April). Automated message prioritization: Making voicemail retrieval more efficient. *In CHI'02 Extended Abstracts on Human Factors in Computing Systems* (pp. 592-593). DOI: 10.1145/506443.506499

Rohde, M., Reinecke, L., Pape, B., & Janneck, M. (2004). Community-building with web-based systems–investigating a hybrid community of students. [CSCW]. *Computer Supported Cooperative Work, 13*(5), 471–499. DOI: 10.1007/s10606-004-5066-4

Rosenberg, M. (1965). *Society and the adolescent self-image* (Vol. 11). Princeton university press. DOI: 10.1515/9781400876136

Rothman, D. (2016, October). *A Tsunami of learners called Generation Z.* http://www.mdle.net/Journal/A_Tsunami_of_Learners_Called_Generation_Z.pdf

Schilpzand, P., De Pater, I. E., & Erez, A. (2016). Workplace incivility: A review of the literature and agenda for future research. *Journal of Organizational Behavior, 37*(S1), S57–S88. DOI: 10.1002/job.1976

Schmidt, P., Biessmann, F., & Teubner, T. (2020). Transparency and trust in artificial intelligence systems. *Journal of Decision Systems, 29*(4), 260–278. DOI: 10.1080/12460125.2020.1819094

Schneckenberg, D., Roth, S., & Velamuri, V. K. (2023). Deparadoxification and value focus in sharing ventures: Concealing paradoxes in strategic decision-making. *Journal of Business Research, 162*, 113883. DOI: 10.1016/j.jbusres.2023.113883

Sheehan, N. (1971, June 13). Vietnam archive: Pentagon study traces 3 decades of growing US involvement. The New York Times,6. https://www.nytimes.com/1971/06/13/archives/vietnamarchive-pentagon-study-traces-3-decades-of-growing-u-s.html

Singh, V., Singh, A., Jain, D., Kumar, V., & Verma, P. (2018). Patterns affecting structural properties of social networking site 'Twitter'. *International Journal of Business Information Systems, 27*(4), 411–432. DOI: 10.1504/IJBIS.2018.090286

Smith, C. (2003). *Moral, believing animals: Human personhood and culture.* Oxford University Press. DOI: 10.1093/acprof:oso/9780195162028.001.0001

Socher, R., Pennington, J., Huang, E. H., Ng, A. Y., & Manning, C. D. (2011, July). Semi-supervised recursive autoencoders for predicting sentiment distributions. In *Proceedings of the 2011 conference on empirical methods in natural language processing* (pp. 151-161).

Song, Y., Jiang, D., Zhao, X., Huang, X., Xu, Q., Wong, R. C. W., & Yang, Q. (2021, October). Smart meeting: Automatic meeting transcription and summarization for in-person conversations. In *Proceedings of the 29th ACM International Conference on Multimedia* (pp. 2777-2779). DOI: 10.1145/3474085.3478556

Spezialetti, M., Placidi, G., & Rossi, S. (2020). Emotion recognition for human-robot interaction: Recent advances and future perspectives. *Frontiers in Robotics and AI*, *7*, 532279. DOI: 10.3389/frobt.2020.532279 PMID: 33501307

Stepanenko, O., & Stupak, O. (2023). The use of GPT Chat among students in Ukrainian universities. *Scientific Journal of Polonia University*, *58*(3), 202–207. DOI: 10.23856/5828

Stiefel, S. (2018). 'The chatbot will see you now': mental health confidentiality concerns in software therapy. *Available at SSRN* 3166640.DOI: 10.2139/ssrn.3166640

Suresh, H., & Guttag, J. (2021, October). A framework for understanding sources of harm throughout the machine learning life cycle. In *Proceedings of the 1st ACM Conference on Equity and Access in Algorithms, Mechanisms, and Optimization* (pp. 1-9). DOI: 10.1145/3465416.3483305

Taherdoost, H., & Madanchian, M. (2023). Artificial intelligence and sentiment analysis: A review in competitive research. *Computers*, *12*(2), 37. DOI: 10.3390/computers12020037

Talmatchi, M. L. (2025). THE INFLUENCE OF ARTIFICIAL INTELLIGENCE ON COMMUNICATION. *Scientific Bulletin-Nicolae Balcescu Land Forces Academy*, *30*(1), 115–124. DOI: 10.2478/bsaft-2025-0014

Tang, D., Qin, B., & Liu, T. (2015, September). Document modeling with gated recurrent neural network for sentiment classification. *In Proceedings of the 2015 conference on empirical methods in natural language processing* (pp. 1422-1432). DOI: 10.18653/v1/D15-1167

Tausczik, Y. R., & Pennebaker, J. W. (2013, April). Improving teamwork using real-time language feedback. *In Proceedings of the SIGCHI conference on human factors in computing systems* (pp. 459-468). DOI: 10.1145/2470654.2470720

Termann, S. (2025). The Dopamine Collapse Hypothesis: Bridging Behavioral Macroeconomics and Neuroscience. *Available at SSRN* 5168672.

Thapa, S., & Adhikari, S. (2023). ChatGPT, bard, and large language models for biomedical research: Opportunities and pitfalls. *Annals of Biomedical Engineering*, *51*(12), 2647–2651. DOI: 10.1007/s10439-023-03284-0 PMID: 37328703

Timmermans, E., Hermans, A. M., & Opree, S. J. (2021). Gone with the wind: Exploring mobile daters' ghosting experiences. *Journal of Social and Personal Relationships*, *38*(2), 783–801. DOI: 10.1177/0265407520970287

. UMEANOZIE, C. P., EZE, E. C., & ALOZIE°, C. E. (2025). Silent Surveillance: Legal Blind Spots in Emotion-Tracking AI and the Future of Data Privacy.

Walther, J. B. (1996). Computer-mediated communication: Impersonal, interpersonal, and hyper personal interaction. *Communication Research*, *23*(1), 3–43. DOI: 10.1177/009365096023001001

Weizenbaum, J. (1966). ELIZA—A computer program for the study of natural language communication between man and machine. *Communications of the ACM*, *9*(1), 36–45. DOI: 10.1145/365153.365168

Whyte, J. (2007). *Virtual reality and the built environment*. Routledge., DOI: 10.4324/9780080520667

. *Wilkens, P. (2023)*. Predictions for How Brands Will Use Virtual Influencers to Connect with Consumers in 2023.

Willcutt, E. G. (2012). The prevalence of DSM-IV attention-deficit/hyperactivity disorder: A meta-analytic review. *Neurotherapeutics; the Journal of the American Society for Experimental NeuroTherapeutics*, *9*(3), 490–499. DOI: 10.1007/s13311-012-0135-8 PMID: 22976615

Wolpaw, J. R. (2007, October). Brain-computer interfaces (BCIs) for communication and control. In *Proceedings of the 9th international ACM SIGACCESS conference on Computers and accessibility* (pp. 1-2). DOI: 10.1145/1296843.1296845

Woolfitt, Z. (2015). The effective use of video in higher education. *Lectoraat Teaching. Learning and Technology Inholland University of Applied Sciences*, *1*(1), 1–49.

Xia, H., Chen, J., Qiu, Y., Liu, P., & Liu, Z. (2025). The impact of human–Chatbot interaction on human–human interaction: A substitution or complementary effect. *International Journal of Human-Computer Interaction*, *41*(2), 848–860. DOI: 10.1080/10447318.2024.2305985

Zhai, C., Wibowo, S., & Li, L. D. (2024). The effects of over-reliance on AI dialogue systems on students' cognitive abilities: A systematic review. *Smart Learning Environments*, *11*(1), 28. DOI: 10.1186/s40561-024-00316-7

## KEY TERMS AND DEFINTIONS

**Artificial Intelligence:** It refers to the development of the computer systems which can able to deliver the tasks which typically requires human intelligence like creative thinking, problem-solving, and decision-making.

**Chatbots:** It is a computer-generated program which simulates the human conversation with an end user.

**Emotional AI:** It is a field of artificial intelligence also known as affective computing which focused more on enabling machines to understand, interpret, and respond to human emotions.

**Human-Ai Interaction (HAI):** It is a field exploring how humans and artificial intelligence systems can able to communicate and collaborate with each other.

**Group Dynamics:** It refers to the behavioral and psychological processes which occurs within a group and its members can interact to achieve towards the common goals.

# Chapter 3
# AI-Mediated Communication and Digital Dependency: Navigating Human Connection in the Algorithmic Age

**Manoj Govindaraj**
https://orcid.org/0000-0003-2830-7875
*VelTech Rangarajan Dr. Sagunthala R&D Institute of Science and Technology, India*

**Jenifer Lawrence**
https://orcid.org/0000-0002-4115-1521
*Woldia University, Ethiopia*

**Jayendira P. Sankar**
https://orcid.org/0000-0001-8435-2123
*University of Technology Bahrain, Salmabad, Bahrain*

**N. Mari Anand**
https://orcid.org/0000-0002-6443-249X
*University of Technology and Applied Sciences, Salalah, Oman*

## ABSTRACT

*This paper explores the evolving landscape of human communication in an era increasingly shaped by artificial intelligence (AI) and algorithm-driven platforms. As AI-mediated tools—from chatbots to recommendation systems—become central to how individuals interact, the nature of human connection is being redefined. The study critically examines the dual impact of these technologies: on one hand,*

DOI: 10.4018/979-8-3373-5606-8.ch003

*enhancing communication efficiency and personalization; on the other, fostering digital dependency and potentially eroding authentic interpersonal relationships. Drawing on interdisciplinary perspectives from communication studies, psychology, and AI ethics, the paper highlights both the promise and peril of algorithmic mediation. It concludes with recommendations for fostering meaningful human connection in a digitally saturated environment, advocating for mindful design and conscious digital engagement.*

## INTRODUCTION

The escalation of artificial intelligence (AI) has in essence changed the face of the human interaction in the 21 st century dramatically. The more that our relationships are mediated by intelligent systems: our Facebook and Instagram algorithms, Alexa, chatbots, etc., the more algorithmic, automated, and data-based our means of connection are becoming. The emerging technological change implies a major break with long-established principles of interpersonal communication and leaves many thorny issues of authenticity, intimacy, agency, and affective appeal of digital interaction to be explored. The algorithmic age is not only affecting human relationships; it frequently defines and maintains those using platforms that are AI-enabled and work in accordance with the art of predictive analytics, behavioral modeling, and machine learning algorithms. Although such developments are inevitably convenient and personalizable, they also become sources of new forms of vulnerability, especially around the question of digital dependence and loss of meaningful and unmediated social relationship. The research paper condenses the current research leading to 2022 and 2025, thus tracing the dynamic pathways of algorithms and online addiction, and thus, highlighting the contextually and theoretically sound quality of the study. The revision that follows supports the idea of conceptual cohesion between the development of artificial intelligence and the consequences it causes to the society.

Assisted by AI communications is the communication entrusted, manipulated, and traversed by AI systems. Examples of such tools are an extensive range of tools including AI-powered chatbots in assisting customers, algorithm-generated newsfeeds on platforms of social media, smart matchmaking algorithms in dating, and virtual assistants to maintain a personal schedule or offer real-time information. The technologies will aim to support efficient communication, hyperpersonal experiences, and lessen cognitive burden and automate repetitive jobs. But on the one hand, their growing centrality in daily life also implies their growing dependency on algorithm systems in all spheres of social life: finding a way in social space, building relationships, interrelating, and even emotion recognition. Substitution of direct human interaction through technologically mediated communication provokes urgent issues of questionable nature of connections made within these realms and possible casualties lawful psychological and societal implications of permanent electronic addiction.

In communicational terms, mediated communication is not something new. Nonetheless, the use of AI in communicative processes is an eminent change towards previous media technologies that were mostly passive and unidirectional like print, radio, and television. On the contrary, systems mreplaceediated through AI are interactive, adaptive, and can simulate human-like reactions. This causes a collapse of the distinction between the human and the machine, interpersonal and impersonal, real or fake. Consequently, people can end up having parasocial relationship with artificial intelligence agents or deem algorithm-driven social interaction to be a real human encounter. Additionally, such systems usually work in an opaque manner, and it is hard to make users understand how much of their life experiences are being both manipulated and filtered by the invisible algorithmic logic.

At a psychological level, sheer ubiquity of AI in communication can impact thinking, feelings, and actions in minute yet far-reaching approaches. The persistence of exposure to the moderated digital world can develop the confirmation biases, decrease the number of views and different opinions and encourage the social comparison, all of which have been associated with decreasing mental health. Furthermore, the more people are willing to delegate emotional work to AI-the way to relieve frustrations by chatting to chatbots, or to find an emotional connection with virtual agent-the more people are likely to lose the needed skills to interact with others, i.e., empathy, active listening, and conflict solving. The latter can be defined as emotional outsourcing, a broader gradual trend toward technologization of human emotions when AI performs the tasks that only human-human relationships should.

Adding to this image is digital dependency. Digital dependency, which is described as psychological dependence on digital technologies in terms of communication, information, and social validation, is interconnected with a compulsive use behavior, withdrawal symptoms, and a decline in offline involvement. This reliance is not just a behavioral reliance but a structural reliance since, in the case of AI-mediated communication, the platform is designed to keep the user engaged by reinforcing their use of that platform via algorithmic loops, e.g. likes, notifications and personalized content feeds. These processes take advantage of the brain the dopamine reward system and engage in habits whereby users get addicted to their devices in specific cases. This can mean that users end up in the trap of never ending connectivity, where digital communication replaces the social interaction in real life, resulting in a paradox of hyper-connected loneliness.

The ethical issue is also of great concern in the discussion of the AI-mediated communication. Privacy matters, government and corporate oversight, algorithmic bias, and autonomy are becoming more and more relevant as more and more personal data is gathered, analyzed, and acted on by AI systems. The commodification of attention and emotional reactions makes the moral terrain even more complicated, because the companies that produce technology control not only the communicative act of the user but also its exchange value. Under these circumstances, even the boundary between the user and the product becomes more blurred, and it casts serious doubts on third-party consent and transparency, ethical requirements of software developers and platforms in defining the digital public space.

All these notwithstanding, it is notes that communication mediated by AI has a potential to transform as well. AI will be able to reduce the barriers between us in terms of geographic distance, linguistic indicators, access to persons with disabilities, and provide new opportunities for creativity and collaboration when we design it and carry it out properly. It may also be used to promote mental health wellness, access to education and civic participation, especially to underserved or disadvantaged groups. The difficulty, then, is not to fight AI in general but to manage its penetration into society without losing and diluting the human connection. This paper seeks to critically reflect the complex dynamics of the AI-mediated communication and digital dependency on the basis of the interdisciplinary approaches of communication theory, psychology, and AI ethics. Discussing the enabling and restrictive aspects of algorithmic mediation, the research aims at providing a moderate perception of how AI is changing the relationship, connection, and human interaction with each other. Finally, the paper proposes a mode of conscious digital participation, i.e., agency, critical literacy, and ethical design as the main principles that a person should apply to developing healthy human relationships in an algorithmic era. In such a way, the research presents an impartial perspective of the algorithmic efficiency as compared to human interaction, viewing AI-mediated communication as the field of revolution and the sphere of ethical issues.

## BACKGROUND OF THE STUDY

The aim of this article was to examine the impact of the levels of self-disclosure (factual, cognitive, emotional and adaptive) of chatbots on user responses in the conversational recommendation environment. Three hundred and eighty-two participants chatted with chatbots on movies and COVID-, and it was found that user reciprocation, enjoyment, their perception of interpersonal relationship, and the acceptance of recommendations were improved by emotional self-disclosure on the part of the bot. The current study reveals the fact that in case chatbots involve emotional disclosures, the likelihood of users disclosing increases and they consider the interaction fun and genuine. It uses a real-time classifier that adjusts strategies of disclosure, proving the effectiveness of emotional appeal that facilitates both the connection between the user and chatbot and effectiveness of recommendations. In this case, this represents how algorithmic empathy closes the gap created between individuals and the machines as it emulates the emotional connectivity that is an integral part of comprehending the role of the machine when it comes to creating (or imitating) true connectivity and constructing or creating digital reliance through mediated communications (Liang et al. 2021).

On introducing Microsoft XiaoIce, a long term oriented emotionally multi-purpose chatbot that can engage customers on an emotional fulfilling basis. It has been designed with the IQ and EQ in mind and works through the decision-making plan designed on Markov decision, which creates empathetic responses. XiaoIce has conversed with more than 660 million users with an average of 23 turns in conversation per session, indicating high user attachment, as well as, a longer- term potential of developing digital relationships through the use of chatbots. XiaoIce is an example of how well AI can scale emulating this feeling. Its traffic facilitators integrate language abilities, emotional comprehension, dialog control, and hereditary profiles, to maintain lengthy, sentiment-based discussions. An unbelievable interaction rates (23 CPS on average) or users develop strong connections to empathetic AI, almost to the level that the humans have. In the context of the present research, XiaoIce highlights how the highly sophisticated technology of AI-induced communication can be an equal to the personification of companionship and it is necessary to question psychological dependence, the formation of attachment and the politics of algorithm-mediated relationships (Zhou et al. 2018). The current case provides an outline of the AI companionship manifestation in the cultural milieu, highlighting the diversity of emotional dependency patterns that are the result of specific regional and socio-cultural environments.

Examined the consequences of the reliance on the emotional communication delivered via chatbots, or in this case, via the Replika app, on the rest of social interactions of users. They question 428 people and discover a highly positive correlation between social interaction with a human being and the interaction with chatbots that use emotional responses. To some degree this is moderated by psychological and demographic variables (age, education, income). In line with the media dependency theory, this paper shows that more emotional attachments developed with chatbots will have a beneficial impact on how the users behave in the real world (which even includes engaging more with others offline). The high quantities of the quantitative data tend to indicate that the reliance on AI emotionally does not lead to a decrease in human interaction but conversely it will be a stimulus to it. The tempering of demographics, however, raises concern of disparity in effects. The methodology and findings of the study lead to the sensitive idea of AI dependency that is neither necessarily erosive nor, more likely, the compound of social capacity (Yuan, Cheng, and Duan 2024).

After examining all 35,000 Reddit posts about Replika, we found out seven categories of human and AI emotional interaction (e.g., intimacy, self disclosure, fantasy). They point out both positive feelings (emotional connection) and negative responses (the feeling of uncanny fear when deep disclosure takes place). The work unveils the relations and contradiction between AI companionship. Li and Zhang (2024) plot the human-AI emotional ranges with computational and qualitative research. The gently sophisticated typology shows that there are ways to use AI to express intimacy, self expression, fantasy and companionship, though many users find it awkward when AI seems too close to being like humans in the space of feeling. Such ambivalence highlights psychological implications of intimacy in AI-mediated intimacy that demonstrates dependencies characterized by emotional reward and uncanny disturbance. In the context of the current research, the given work points out the emotional fabric of digital dependency and argues that the concept of algorithmic mediation affects conventional distinctions between artificiality and authenticity (Li and Zhang, 2024). The emotive constructs shed light on the reality that AI-mediated intimacy goes beyond personal interaction and has distant implications on trust in the society and changing rules of relationships in the digital societies.

And our way forward is to search user agency in recommender systems through the unification of AI explainability (XAI) and user control over content. The authors develop a prototype with which users can make the recommendations on AI less strong and opaque. The preliminary results indicate that the perception of agency by users enhances trust as well as satisfaction with the recommendations. The article conceptualizes the agency as the key aspect of communication dynamics and reliance through AI. This paper is an attempt to mediate a fractal relationship between user agency and algorithmic opacity by incorporating the elements of XAI and interactive controls. Those that were able to modulate the strength of recommendations and have knowledge about the AI reasoning acknowledged more trust and interaction. It shows that the reliance on AI systems should not develop passively, as it may be reduced by the involvement of users to counteract their loss of control. It favors the design proposals that encourage conscious interaction with digital media by enabling users, which should be used as a guiding principle in facilitating the meaningful human connection through various current trends of algorithmic mediation (Wu, Liu, Wang, and Yao 2024).

Applying the media dependency theory to the social news sites, an interesting paradox is revealed therein: on the one hand, people prefer the efficiency provided by following algorithmic curation, and on the other end, users experience a lack of control and question privacy issues. The study also surveys platform users to discuss algorithm dependency as a notion related to habitual trust in the services referred to as news that finds me and demonstrates that comfortable feelings about algorithms and information usage support dependency even within the status of privacy concerns. This piece expounds on algorithmic media structural dependence. The authors show that individuals are eager to surrender agency in the selection of news in favor of convenience even when they realize that they are being surveilled. They discover the dependency of algorithms both to be utilitarian and a habit, rather than behavioral. Defining emotional ambivalence as the combination of trust to curation and resignation, the study puts the center of attention on the resulting mental strains users of digital ecosystems perceive. It examines its effects on undermining active media consumption in favor of passive consumption behaviors that have agency and civic information literacy ramifications (Schätz, Gagrčin, Toth, and Emmer 2023)

Exploring the issue caused by the diminishing of user autonomy through algorithmic suggestions that result in impulsive purchasing and heteronomy. They demonstrate (n=77) that the inclusion of explainable AI features, e.g., in the form of rationale disclosures, inhibits impulsivity and increases the self-determination of people using recommender systems. This study closes the gap between theory, heuristic system-systematic model, reflective impulsive model, and explainable AI design via mixed methods experiment. It demonstrates that in absence of explicit reasoning by algorithms users are most likely to make passive decisions and uncontrolled consumption. Providing XAI, which puts the guidance in its context, enables the users to reject any unreasonable influence and take the agency. This literature demonstrates that the issue of digital dependency in e-commerce is not merely behavioral but cognitive likewise, which explains the significance of transparent design as the way to re-establish user autonomy in the realm of AI-mediated spaces (Yoon, Lee, Wu, and Koh 2024).

Speculative thinking about how the explainable AI and user agency are connected. Cases and thought-experiments lead them to the conclusion that appearance of explanations is not enough to enable agency, which also requires systematic mechanisms of control to enable actions born out of knowledge. They highlight the role of so-called tinkerers, we call them those people who receive maximum benefit when there is explanation together with interactivity. As it is stressed in this conceptual piece, transparency is not a one-stop promise of autonomy. The authors present a stratified model: explanation will lead to understanding, whereas agency can only start when the user is able to manipulate or challenge the activities of the AI. They suggest the combination of XAI and interactive affordances, in order to facilitate forethought and experimentation, and control. Such a proposition is essential to the modeling of strategic AI-mediated systems to enable mindfulness (as opposed to passive obedience) which can be described as part of a wider agenda to maintain user agency in analyses of digital dependency, where algorithms are exceptionally challenging to understand (Adenuga and Dodge 2023).

## RESEARCH QUESTIONS

1. How does AI-mediated communication influence users' psychological well-being and their capacity to maintain authentic interpersonal relationships?
2. What are the key drivers and predictors of digital dependency in the context of prolonged use of AI communication tools such as chatbots, virtual assistants, and recommender systems?
3. In what ways do users perceive emotional authenticity and social trust when interacting with AI-mediated systems, and how do these perceptions compare with human interactions?
4. To what extent can the integration of transparent and interactive AI design (e.g., explainable AI or user agency mechanisms) mitigate digital dependency and enhance conscious digital engagement?

## OBJECTIVES

- To examine the psychological and behavioral impacts of AI-mediated communication tools on human connection and interpersonal relationships.
- To investigate the factors contributing to digital dependency resulting from prolonged interaction with AI-driven platforms and chatbots.
- To explore how users perceive authenticity, trust, and emotional fulfillment in AI-mediated communication compared to human-to-human interaction.
- To assess the effectiveness of design interventions (e.g., explainable AI, user control features) in promoting mindful engagement and reducing dependency on algorithmic communication systems.

## METHODOLOGY

This paper incorporates conceptual and literature-focused research, which relies on interdisciplinary content analysis of scholarly works, theoretical concepts, and empirical research articles connected to AI-mediated communication and digital dependency. By synthesizing available scientific knowledge sources in the fields of communication, psychology, and functional ethics of AI, the study aims to analyze how algorithmic systems can affect human connection and find the answers through critical content analysis. The approach permits determining patterns, gaps, and emergent trends, which serves as a foundation of theoretical knowledge and empirical research later. Such an interdisciplinary synthesis (between AIs ethics, psychology, and communication) can help target a detailed analysis of digital dependency and user behavior in the algorithmic ecosystem.

## Influence of AI-Mediated Communication on Psychological Well-Being and Authentic Relationships

Communication through AI has transformed the interaction process between people both at the friend and work level. Its increasing presence in our daily life, chatbots, virtual assistants, social media recommendations, and recommender systems have redesigned not only the effectiveness of communication but also the psychological and relational aspects of human relationships. The literature review indicates that certainly, AI-mediated communication is convenient and supportive in an emotional sense; however, it has serious consequences on the psychological health and integrity of interpersonal relationship of the users. Some of these studies depict the psychological dichotomy that AI-mediated communication brings in. In their groundbreaking study of Microsofts XiaoIce, Zhou et al. (2018) show how people actively engage in long-term developments of emotionally involving conversations with empathetic chatbots and how such chatbots provide manufactured emotional awareness. It gives a false sense of friendship and offers emotional support particularly to lonely people. And on the same note, Li and Zhang (2024), by using computational methods in a study involving Replika users, revealed that users access AI in order to address some of their needs including intimacy, self-disclosure, and validation. They offer an alternative version of actual human contact on which people experience a brief respite and stress relief.

Nonetheless, this kind of emotionally intense communication may backfire. The ground theory interviews conducted on Replika users (Laestadius et al., 2024) also revealed that the interactions with AI chatbots initially alleviate feelings of loneliness; however, they also trigger emotions of distress, as potential users might expect too much. When users become strongly emotionally attached to AI entities, they may feel guilty, confused and identity conflict. It can be compared with the results provided by Brandtzaeg et al. (2025), who noted that teenagers relatively often incorporate social AI into their lives, but feel guilty and anxious trying to get rid of it, which means emotional engagement and addiction.

The psychological aspect of the phenomenon in question is what it is called emotional outsourcing. People who experience social anxiety usually seek the assistance of conversational AI (Li et al., 2023). Their research proved that, as a result, a person becomes more lonely and start ruminating creating a loop of dependence. The anthropomorphic rate of AI users is even more vulnerable to excessiveness, and this fact was emphasized in the study by Zhou and Cheng (2024), who identified that users with lower self-efficacy and academic-related stress have more entrenched attitudes concerning overusing AI in education educational settings, which ultimately affects critical thinking and infantilization of thought. The ethical issues of emotional manipulation, privacy, and autonomy form a fundamental guideline to understanding the psychological effects of communication mediated by AI more broadly.

Interpersonal relations are also put into question in their authenticity. As Goldenthal et al. (2025) put it, when generative AI is used in communication, e. g., writing emails or posts on social networks, perceived authenticity reduces, and epistemic trust is harmed. This decline of trust is not directed at the AI-generated content alone but it is carried over to the human sender that generated it, causing a multi-layer break in communication patterns. Flew (2023) continues that, the institutional trust used as part of the AI-communication is weak and gets eroded easily by lack of transparency on data processes, prompting further mistrust among people. In addition, research indicates that algorithmic responsiveness perception may either boost or suppress the social connection among users. According to Taylor and Chen (2024), users who consider the recommendation algorithm of TikTok to be familiar to them report a higher level of social connectedness, which implies that the user emotionally interacts with the social construct of AI as a human being (social actor). Nonetheless, such presupposed resonance has a reservation to the accuracy of association of an AI to user identity. The alienation can get intensified in case users are mismatched with the AI or find it impersonal. Taylor and Choi (2024) also determined a feedback loop between loneliness and the responsiveness of the algorithm: loneliness makes one more influencing AI-curated media, which mitigates the feelings of loneliness before a certain period, simultaneously making one more vulnerable emotionally to non-human beings.

At a more general culture level, even popularization of AI tools in social communication behavior may have effect of influencing norms of interaction. According to Adenuga and Dodge (2023), unless AI systems have active and meaningful user agency, they can progressively erode reflective communication in favor of automated interaction and people will eventually lose important interpersonal capabilities. This further build up on the fact that most AI systems are programmed to optimize interventions and as such present an emotional attunement that lacks real sense thus what Laestadius et al. (2024) refer to as emotional simulation without reciprocity. However, there exist other opposing views that AI-based conversation can equally lead to relationship maintenance. Researches carried by Yuan et al. (2024) concerning the emotional interaction with chatbots showed that such communications might foster, in fact, even more robust and prominent human-to-human interactions. This implies the possible emotional cushions or role-rehearsing AI devices, especially among people with social communication challenges. AI can play an emotional supplement role when used wisely.

The user awareness and control seem to be the most important moderating factor in relation to the studies. Explainable AI and the possibility to customize the recommendation systems by Wu et al. (2024) and Yoon et al. (2024) are also focused on agency and user-related recognition. By making the users feel that they control the algorithmic decisions, they will be less inclined to turn into dependent users and more inclined to look at these tools as a way of improving their communications and not replacing it. This understanding is used in advising the design in an attempt to bring back authenticity through facilitation of reflection and intentionality in interactions of the user. To sum up, AI-mediated communication has a rather complicated effect on the psychological well-being and interpersonal relationships of the users. It gives the sense of emotional immediacy, individualization and friendship, yet at the expense of possible addiction, the loss of trust, and the loss of authenticity in social communication. According to the literature, it is strongly indicated that the result relies on the factors, including agency of the people who use it, transparency of AI design, psychological peculiarities of the individuals, and the context in which it is used. To guarantee that AI can become a means of human flourishing (instead of an emotional prop), responsive and ethical, user-centered, and transparent design will be necessary.

## Key Drivers and Predictors of Digital Dependency in AI Communication Contexts

The issue of digital dependency especially when it comes out of the times of interaction with an AI-mediated environment becomes ever more important in times of the algorithmic age. Excessive exposure to AI-powered tools, including chatbots, such as Replika and XiaoIce, recommendation systems, and voice assistants have, along with changing the practices of communication, changed the cognitive and emotional patterns according to which people interact with technology. According to literature, it is demonstrated that dependency on cyber digital mode is achieved through complex intersections of psychology, social, technological, and design issues. Emotional vulnerability is a serious psychological factor that supports AI dependency. Li et al. (2023) investigated people with social anxiety and discovered that these users are likely to resort to the use of conversational AI tools to help manage social awkwardness. They found in their study that the two variables that mediated the connection between social anxiety and problematic AI use are loneliness and rumination in their sequential mediation model. These users seek ultimate, non judgmental interaction such that they depend more on AI resulting in what becomes a self fulfilling behavior to grow dependency. This is especially relevant to the field of human-like perception perception of mind: when AI is anthropomorphized, the users are more predisposed to develop an affective attachment that will result in further dependency.

In line with this, Brandtzaeg et al. (2025) explored the adolescents and their experience between adopting an AI-companion into everyday life to receive emotional support. According to their findings, young people tend to incorporate these gadgets into their routines that are substituting or postponing interactions with other people. Even though various participants spoke in praise of AI in the form of the unassailable on demand availability and a customized feedback offer, the study has also described the emotional withdrawal symptoms due to the lack of AI proceedings or reduction in AI presence. Control, predictability, and safety felt through AI turn into a significant strengthening of digital dependency. There is also a considerable role of cognitive and behavioral factors. Zhou and Cheng (2024) identified that academic self-efficacy and stress in students determine their dependence on ChatGPT and other tools of AI through the I-PACE (Interaction of Person-Affect-Cognition-Execution) model. The less self-efficacious and the more stressed students were, the more they tended to rely too much on AI in studying. Output immediacy, ease of access and lack of judgment encourages dependency to lower critical thinking and intellectual autonomy as time passes. They establish that psychological stressors together with the low cognitive confidence make great breeding grounds to become dependent on AI-mediated communication systems. Here, the development of media literacy and self-regulatory digital behaviors emerge as a plausible avenue of dependency reduction which, in turn, will contribute to the development of conscious over mindful use of algorithms instead of blind adherence to them.

Another major predictor is technological features of the design. A lot of AI-based systems are made to be most engaging, through emotional mirroring and personalization, as well as constant feedback loops to keep the user engaged. For example, Liang et al. (2021) demonstrated that chatbots with emotional self-disclosure elicited more enjoyment among users and increased the perception of other people. Such emotionally smart responses promote sense of reciprocity and connection, thus creating a possibility that the users will come back and use it again. Although this improves the quality of the short-term interaction, it also leads to the creation of some emotional conditioning that leads to the development of habitual use. In their turn, Taylor and Choi (2024) further proved that perceived responsiveness of the algorithm is quite strong in predicting the intensity of use and emotional dependence. They conclude that loneliness also enhances the feeling of algorithmic understanding, the latter feeding back the former to increase and intensify the use. This cycle highlights that dependency cannot be simply a product of content or utility, but also the product of the way that users emotionally perceive the responsiveness and consistency of the AI with its identity.

It is also caused by social isolation as well as by changes in the norms of communication. With a more screen-mediated society it is easier to imagine a situation where an AI-based tool would be more accessible than a conversation with a human when it comes to problems like mental health, processing of emotion or social anxiety. According to Laestadius et al. (2024), users who developed strong emotional connections to Replika simultaneously got immediate benefits such as relief of the feeling of loneliness and long-term effects, which were emotional confusion, such as guilt, blurring of life, and dependency. The article points out that the lack of social supports network in addition to the accessibility of technology contributes to the over-dependency on the AI systems. On the sociotechnical perspective, dependency is also formed through trust and perception. Moller et al. (2025) also discovered that social media auto-response posts led to an enhanced user engagement and a lowered sense of authenticity of a conversation. As the users become accustomed to the more artificialized communicative environment, they may start focusing more on efficiency and consistency of AI than the irregularity of the human connection. Such practical change also leads to an ultimate behavioral change toward algorithmic communication tools.

At the institutional level, Flew (2023) explains that lack of clarity of corporate structures alongside regulatory controls of AI systems contribute to digital dependency. As the user data is continuously tapped to hone the AI response and recommendations, this furthers the tracking of behavior that will be more responsive to user exploits. This is turned into a commercialized loop of feedback, where leading to dependence is considered as byproduct and also outcome of design. A key role is played by explainable AI (XAI) and user agency disempowered. Wu et al. (2024) and Yoon et al. (2024) demonstrate that the users who cannot figure out the way in which they are recommended some specific content or the reasons why they are being recommended some pieces of content commit to just taking things at face value, which further enforces the pattern of consumption that is pre-determined by the algorithm and not by the choice of the user. Such loss of agency will lead to digital reliance particularly in settings where users lack knowledge of how algorithms work or are incapable of challenging them.

There are also the normative assumptions and social comparison. As Purcell et al. (2023) observed, many users seem to be even harsher to those who use AI tools than they are to themselves even though they are doing the same thing. This hypocrisy normalizes an aspect of dependency on the one hand and external doubt on the other hand. The paradox propagates the covert circulation of use and constrains the free conversation about the dependency symptoms and the minorization methods. To sum up, digital dependency under the conditions of communicating with the aid of AI has a rather complicated structure and is formed by the combination of psychological vulnerability, cognitive weaknesses, social alienation, algorithmic bias, and the lack of transparency of institutions. It has been highlighted in the literature that dependence does not only depend on the amount of usage, it is also affected by emotional attachment, identity affirming and behavioural conditioning passively. The solution to digital dependency should be based not only on technological redesign but also on the environmental regulation in terms of digital literacy and psychological support systems, as well as ethics in digital interactions.

## User Perceptions of Emotional Authenticity and Social Trust in AI-Mediated Interactions

Human communication relies on the emotional authenticity and social trust. Because AI-mediated systems engage more and more in interpersonal communication (in the form of chatbots, recommender algorithms, and generation of content), the genuine nature of these interactions and confidence that users have about them is subject to serious questioning. The detailed literature review has shown that there is a paradox: although people tend to treat AI systems as emotionally engaged and efficient, they harbor doubts about their sincerity, reliability, and the potential long-term effects on human-to-human relationship. The essence of this problem is the impersonation of emotional truthfulness established by emotionally intelligent AI. Liang et al. (2021), in their research on Microsofts XiaoIce, discovered that the participants perceived the use of emotion-expressive AI chatbots as more enjoyable and emotionally supportive. Instead, users found that XiaoIce is not only intelligent but also benevolent and even "legitimate." That means that AI can effectively copy the emotional signals that indicate sincerity in human communication. Chatbots including features of empathetic conversations and emotional mirroring have an identical effect: according to Yuan et al. (2024), they make users feel that they are connected to the emotion and have conversations that they like.

But what the viewer senses is the authenticity of feelings in these interpersonal interactions is mostly artificial. Goldenthal et al. (2025) are supportive in this direction and respond that users prefer responding to a drop in epistemic trust after learning that messages created by AI are based on algorithms. The real and practical experience that they had with generative AI was that when users realize that AI was used to write the message, people start doubting the message as well as the intentions and genuineness of the message issuer. This authenticity dilemma indicates the existence of a huge gap between the perceived immediacy and trust one. The absence of responsibility and oppositeness within AI systems is one of the factors that make trust weaker. In their grounded theory research of people using Replika, Laestadius et al. (2024) found that most of the individuals who developed strong emotional connections with the chatbot discussed feeling confused and betrayed by the bot. The unresponsiveness of the AI to antibodies that could have delivered emotional satisfaction or have produced abrupt shifts meant that the user felt deserted or controlled, reiterating the point about the weak validity of the notion of trust in a communicator that is not human. The AI systems do not provide depth to relationships because they lack the capacity to bear moral responsibility or provide any form of sincere empathy, as opposed to human beings. In addition, the institutional transparency and strong AI governance systems become central to maintaining the social trust and protecting the ethical data-driven communication patterns.

The same is reflected by Flew (2023) who proposes a new variant of trust, i.e. namely, the notion of mediated trust, who states that AI systems destabilize social trust patterns by narrowing communicative interactions through corporate interests interruptions of communication and incursions of the corporate perception of darkness into communication. A user who does not know the way his data informs interactions cannot trust the medium, as well as the message, either. Trust in that sense does not just mean fidelity of the content but transparency and ethical design of institutions. Due to the effect of user experience, the responsiveness of the algorithm, or how much emotionally or personally relevant content platforms such as TikTok create, may resemble emotional resonance, which users occasionally feel as an indication of social attunement (Taylor and Chen, 2024). This musicalized resonance helps to lead one to feel like they are understood, which is linked to the idea of the emotional truth. This resonance, however, is founded on predictability of behaviors rather than engatchment through empathy posing certain ethical questions of manipulative design.

The fact that AI-mediated communication takes place within a social context further complicates the ways of trust and authenticity. Purcell et al. (2023) discovered that users tend to use a dual standard: they are severely criticized at covering the use of AI (e.g., by using ChatGPT to design messages) but accept it for themselves. Such a disparity approaches the hidden fear of social norms and acceptance of algorithmic mediation. It implies also that trust is not a matter of the AI system per se, but of the openness in the involvement of the AI system in human interaction.

The difference with human interaction is treated in the comparison. The communication between humans is fallible, unpredictable and emotionally rich in nature. According to Adenuga and Dodge (2023), such imperfection even contributes to the improvement of the sense of authenticity since it demonstrates vulnerability and ethical agency. AI systems, on the other hand, will maximize effectiveness and accuracy by excluding the grey area and emotional incompleteness of real-life human interaction. Users may start thinking about AI interactions as unnatural when they notice such a thing, even though these interactions can be emotionally gratifying at first glance. However it is not reciprocated with all the users. Brandtzaeg et al. (2025) stress that social AI may seem to be safer in an emotional context than humans are perceived among adolescents and young adults. In their research, most of the youths expressed the feeling of being less afraid of being judged when communicating with AI entities. It seems that this trust in AI is based on two facts the ability to predict and to be emotionally neutral as opposed to some delusion of understanding. Although this can be comforting, it also offers the chilling alternative of causing its users not to bother with more psychologically demanding human relationships in favor of putting their faith in machines.

Interestinglyly enough, Moller et al. (2025) discovered that the perceived authenticity of conversational authenticity on social media drops even when you increase communication with the use of AI tools like auto-generated responses. This indicates that even though AI systems will allow users to interact more, there are chances that they will decrease the quality and authenticity of social trust among users. Design solutions towards elimination of these issues are also identified in the literature. Yoon et al. (2024) prove that the addition of explainable AI (XAI) features adds value to customer trust, such as the transparency of rationale and the clarity in decision making path. Users are more likely to perceive recommendation or response as fair and interest-informed in situations where they comprehend how an AI system comes to the decision when deciding its degree of trustworthiness, and its perceived authenticity. Wu et al. (2024) also remark that the quality of relations in AI-mediated interactions can be increased substantially by user agency, namely, the ability to reject the outcomes of algorithms, or alter them.

To sum it all up, a complex combination of emotional experience, cognitive awareness, social context, and technological transparency determines the way users perceive both emotional authenticity and social trust in the communication that takes place via AI. Although AI systems can replicate the emotional signals of authenticity, they fail most of the time to communicate the moral and reciprocity aspects that bring about trust. AI-based communication also responds emotionally compared to the human communication but it is devoid of real empathy and accountability. In future, it is necessary to work on designing ethical, see-through, and controllable AI in order to rebuild authenticity and trustworthiness in more algorithmic communication cultures.

## Role of Transparent and Interactive AI Design in Mitigating Digital Dependency and Enhancing Conscious Engagement

With the continued use of communication systems that are mediated by AI influencing how and who people communicate with, inform, and express themselves, much of the scholarship increasingly calls to focus on how AI systems are ethically designed to ensure there is less potential of adverse impacts like the development of digital dependency. XAI, models of transparency, and user agency are becoming key elements in stimulating conscious usage of digital. According to the literature, the degree of incorporation of these features into the algorithm system has a substantial impact on the ability of users to interact with AI critically, ensure agency and minimize compulsive and dependent behaviors. Understandable AI is one of the leading propositions to retrieve clarity and mental oversight of the AI interaction. Wu et al. (2024) indicate that XAI characteristics, including the visual or natural language explanation of the principles according to which the recommendations can be made, assist the users to comprehend and contextualize the AI decisions. In their research, the authors discovered that when users first experienced a transparent feedback they were much more open to critically consider alcoholic suggestions instead of naively following their advice. The critical assessment serves as a thinking shield against passive consumption, which is a significant cause of digital dependence.

The same applies to the paper by Yoon et al. (2024), where the authors stress that, by leaving the choice of customizing or interrogating AI decisions to users, the latter can feel a sense of agency and are much less likely to feel helpless or detached. The studies they did on personalized recommendation systems demonstrated that the explainability and control abilities of the systems not only led to higher rates of satisfaction, but also, reduced or limited binge consumption that is a common signature of the algorithmic systems. The study confirmed the idea that transparency cannot be discussed as some technical quality, but rather a behavioral prompt that leads to conscious behavior and may help users not to be driven into a sort of algorithmic echo chamber.

In addition, user agency tools like content filters, customization via choices, and opt-in mechanisms are all protective design patterns. Taken together, these observations act as an essential point of intersection between an ethically-designed AI and empowerment of users, where transparency in practice is embodied into a material agency of end-users. In response, Adenuga and Dodge (2023) suggest that through a combination of algorithmic opacity, and the false sense of user choice, this encourages a kind of algorithmic conditioning that encourages dependency on AI recommendations. Conversely, their study indicated that participants who were allowed a less hidden and exercisable form of control over settings, e.g. providing Resetting of contents preferences, reorganization of algorithmic weights, have been found to exercise better self-regulation and reduced emotional dependence on content suggestions.

Notably, there is a strong correlation between the lack of agency and acquisition of unhealthy habits of use. In their research of the ChatGPT usage by the students, Zhou and Cheng (2024) stated that students that had no certainty of how ChatGPT worked, or could not adjust its actions, were a greater propensity to exhibit a dependency. This comes true to the study by Taylor and Choi (2024), who note a type of feedback loop wherein users feel themselves if they are going to be responsive to them because they need to rely on an algorithm in order to be satisfied emotionally.

When transparency and control are absent, compulsive use is very often the outcome of such emotional outsourcing.

In addition, explainability will facilitate trust that can be counterintuitively put under its leash. According to Flew (2023), when transparency and accountability are used as the foundations of trust, this type of trust structure is more stable than trust founded on convenience or efficiency. Aware users will be less inclined to utilize such AI systems as psychological substitutes but as a set of tools. Such difference plays a crucial role in the system of AI-based communication where trust in the object could be easily turned into the psychological dependence in ignorance of the artificial essence. Laestadius et al. (2024) offer an excellent warning note by grounded theory study of Replika users. They showed how their participants described a high degree of emotional closeness with their chatbot, and emotional upset when the system would fail to react correctly or become altered. All this was worsened by the nonexistent transparency regarding the creation of the responses by Replika. The fact that the AI did not do what it was supposed to do was seen as an emotional betrayal by the users not due to the AI, but because they did not know its limitations in the first place. These dependency loops could have been broken at an earlier stage had the system involved some form of transparent disclosures or agency tools.

Cultural and social norms of the use of AI are also affected by its design features. Moller et al. (2025) found out that the participation of users improved when responding to posts on the social platforms when generative AI tools were used to compose responses, yet the perceived authenticity reduced. This decline in interpersonal authenticity implies that conscious digital engagement is a practice that is not particular to an individual nor is it merely a matter of individual-level behavior but is socially constructed as well. Once the presence and functioning of AI tools become visible, people discuss and bring up challenges to them more often and think critically about how they and others use this technology, changing their cultural expectations in favor of responsibility and sensitivity. Purcell et al. (2023) further state that transparency is also used to tackle the psychological dissonance that users have when they assess the use of AI in themselves and others. It was proved through their survey experiments that users often underestimated how common it was to use AI compared to others and were torn about whether using it was acceptable or not. Open signs of involvement of AI in communication would make such social misunderstanding less likely and foster healthier standards of disclosure and collaboration with AI.

Despite the clear benefits, challenges remain. Not all users have the **digital literacy** required to interpret AI explanations meaningfully. As Wu et al. (2024) caution, overly technical explanations may alienate users and lead to disuse of transparency tools. Effective XAI design must therefore balance detail with accessibility, ensuring that explanations are intuitive, relevant, and actionable. This design tension highlights the need for participatory design approaches that involve end-users in co-creating transparent and interactive features. In summary, the integration of transparent and interactive AI design—through explainable AI, customization options, and user control mechanisms—can meaningfully mitigate digital dependency and promote conscious engagement. These features serve as cognitive guardrails, emotional stabilizers, and ethical instruments that help users maintain autonomy in a digitally saturated environment. While technological interventions are necessary, they must be complemented by user education, regulatory standards, and cultural shifts toward mindful digital interaction. Only then can AI-mediated communication evolve into a space that supports—not undermines—human agency and emotional well-being.

## DISCUSSIONS

Finally, the discussion brings together psychological, ethical and communication approaches to provide a holistic picture of AI twofold nature in that it promotes connection but at the same time creates the risk of addiction. The results of this research confirm the overall complex effects of the AI-mediated experience on human connection, mental health, and digital behavior. The theme throughout the literature is that although AI tools can serve emotional needs, tailored interactions, and effective communications, AI tools have the potential to inflict emotional dependency and decrease authenticity among people. Emotionally aware AI systems also tend to be understood as listening and empathetic by the users, providing a short-term sense of help regarding feelings of loneliness or social anxiety. Nevertheless, when this occurs in special cases like when there is lack of transparency or lack of control by a user, this kind of emotional outsourcing can dilute the ability of a user to create and sustain authentic human relationships.

Digital dependency is closely connected with external psychological factors associated with such individual characteristics as low self-efficacy, stress, and vulnerability with others. Besides, the engaging properties attributed to algorithmic design in personalization and guessing human behavior are also critical in enhancing the compulsive usage patterns. Lack of agency, inability to understand decisions that are taken by algorithms as well as lack of narrative interfere with the process of passive interaction, reducing critical thinking and agency among digital users. By contrast, the mentioned systems that include explainable AI and user customization features seem to reduce the impact and allow intentional and more informed interactions.

The mediation of social trust and perceptions of authenticity is also linked to the visibility of, and context in which, AI engagement in communication takes place. Though users can make meaningful interactions with AI systems, they usually feel uncomfortable when these machines dock out and take the places of human relationships. This is a two-sided ambivalence that mirrors underlying issues with transparency, ethical-design, and emotional manipulation. In such a way, design should focus on the user agency, clarity of thought, and ethical boundaries to achieve the balance between the benefits of AI-mediated communication and related risks. AI technologies could only be used to achieve the goal of authentic connection without dependency and unhealthy emotional co-dependency without using a conscious and human-centric approach.

## MAIN FINDINGS

The primary conclusions of this study have pointed to the complicated and at times self-contradictory nature of the role of AI-mediated communication in the establishing of digital dependency and human connection. Chatbots, recommendation systems and other AI tools are capable of engaging users by offering them an interaction that is emotionally sensitive, leading to the impression of a companion and psychological support, where a feeling of togetherness, companionship and belonging are instilled. Such exchanges can reduce social anxiety and also loneliness to those people who feel they are marginalized and emotionally alienated. Nevertheless, rewarding this comfort may be expensive. The long-term interaction with an emotionally intelligent AI often causes psychological addiction, erased emotional barriers as well as the loss of interest in finding real human connections within the users.

The factor of digital dependency proves to be both a construct of user-level weaknesses as well as those of system design. One is having low self-efficacy, academic pressures, or lack of emotional security which make users especially vulnerable to developing dependence habits with AI systems. At the same time, the structure of platforms which emphasise the priority of engagement by workings with highly personalised algorithms, emotional reflection and recommend technologies whose workings cannot be discerned, encourage sustained use. This dependency is even increased by the fact that there is no user agency and that there is no transparency, only diminishing the critical awareness of users and enabling passive interaction patterns. This strengthens the power of emotional outsourcing, since users, as a consequence, resort to AI more and more instead of human compassion and approval.

Issues of trust and authenticity also are primary areas to consider. Although a lot of users testify feeling attached to the AI agents at some emotional level, they tend to be very skeptical and uneasy when they realize the falseness of the systems. When AI is discovered, trust is usually damaged, whether it is an act of inauthentic communication or manipulative communication. Such tensions imply a precarious and situational form of trust in AI-mediated systems, which are devoid of the morality and correspondence of human communication. The results also indicate that such transparency enhancing functionalities as explainable AI and user controls can help to dramatically decrease digital addiction and make usage more intentional. The more users understand and can affect how artificial intelligence functions, the more they will tend to employ such systems as co-workers and not sources of emotional support. The results will provide practical advice to teachers, programmers, and policymakers and allow creating AI systems that are emotionally neutral and transparent to ensure the achievement of digital well-being.

## SUGGESTIONS

- Facilitate the inclusion of explainable AI features that can effectively inform users how algorithmic decisions can be arrived at, so that users can interact with AI systems in a critical and not a passive way.
- Include outputs of user agency, including customization options, preference settings, opt-out choices to provide people with more power over their online spaces and minimize the likelihood of algorithmic dependence.
- Design AI-mediated communication devices based on ethical considerations that focus on emotional openness, simplicity in algorithms between pretend empathy and genuine encouragement, and prevent manipulative measures in interactions.
- To facilitate digital literacy initiatives, educating people on how AI algorithms operate, how their psychological conditions are impacted by extended usage of the technology, and methods of preserving their independence and composure in digital relationships.
- Promote the leverage of AI applications as reinforcements rather than replacements to any type of human communication, especially interactions with the highest levels of affect in spheres that include mental health or education, or companionship.
- Introduce some form of regular prompts or feedback to AI that remind people to take a moment to think, a digital break and analyse how much time they are spending on the AI, to make people aware of overdependence and act in response.
- Introduce industry standards on design of responsible AI that would demand platforms to make disclosures on the use of AI in communication and creation of content to safeguard perceptions of authenticity and trust by users.
- Foster interdisciplinary studies which are further exploring the emotional, cognitive and social ramification of AI-mediated communication, whereby

the development of novel tools are informed by the best practices rooted in evidence.

- Apply participatory design to engage users in the co-design of AI systems to embrace their needs, values, and vulnerability leading to progress early in the development process.
- Encourage cultural ideas of transparency and authenticity in digital communication to assist users in dealing with the issue of ethical and emotional complexity of interaction with more human-like AI systems.

## FUTURE IMPLICATIONS OF THE STUDY

The implication of the study in the future indicates major time-changes in the way the society uses artificial intelligence in communication and tackles online dependence. Since AI applications increasingly enter into ordinary communication, the psychological and relationship implications thereof are vital to comprehend. This research paper demonstrates the importance of developers, policymakers, educators, and mental health experts to predict and react to the changes that will take place in the emotional relationships between users and AI tools. With the growing realism of conversational AI and emotion-informed systems, we are bound to get into an even more intricate emotional tangle, and it is vital to develop ethical systems that would mitigate coercion and promote openness. The design of future AI needs to be done not only with an aim at enhancing technical precision and performance but also with an objective of developing user independence, affective health, and critical reasoning. The real need is the creation of explainable and controllable systems of AI that will enable people to explore digital spaces in a coherent and purposeful manner. Integrating transparency and user agency into the AI tools, innovations in the future can help curb the dangers of emotional overdependence, and promote more positive digital behaviors instead.

The use of AI-assisted communication in the learning and treatment setting can potentially emerge as a benefit, particularly, among learners or patients presenting with social or cognitive apprehension. Nevertheless, this opportunity should be weighed very closely with the dangers of replacing human interaction or ingraining the withdrawal factor. The potential topic of future studies is long-term effects of the interaction with AI through behavioral and emotional channels in different applications, such as youth development and elderly care as well as communication within the workplace setting. On the social level, the findings suggest reconsideration of cultural beliefs concerning the authenticity, trust, and emotional work in digital communication. Since AI is already affecting the manner in which individuals interact with each other, there exists the urgency of inter-sector cooperation so that the development of technological tools can meet humanistic ideals. This paper can provide the platform on which ethical, inclusive and emotionally intelligent AI system should be modeled that would complement human connectivity as opposed to substituting or weakening it. Responsible technologies that aid human agency ought to be co-evolved in future research incorporating behavioural science, communication studies, and AI ethics.

## CONCLUSION

This experiment will conclude that AI supported communication alters the character of human connection, emotional communication, and digital agency in powerful measures. On the one hand, when AI devices, like chatbots, recommendation systems, and virtual assistants, provide efficiency, personalization, and emotional support, on the other hand, it leads to digital dependency threats and lack of interpersonal authenticity. The intended user is likely to feel bonded to such systems as emotionally intelligent and trusting, however, the artificial character of the system, it lacks any reciprocation or transparency in how it operates may cause over-reliance and confusion of feelings and a weakening of actual human relationships.

The results underline that digital dependency is the complexity of both user vulnerability and design characteristics that prompt the formation of a habitual use. Nevertheless, the risks can be reduced with the help of explaining AI and the concept of user agency which help to encourage openness, independence, and mindfulness digital interaction. The algorithmic age requires an ethical approach to design, digital literacy, and universally accessible framework to provide a responsible experience that values emotional wellbeing and honesty. In the end, AI must support rather than kill human contact. In the study, the need is brought forth to develop AI with a conscious and humanistic influence, such that technological progress still serves to strengthen the emotional connection among human beings in an online-based society and not to dissolve it.

## REFERENCES

Adenuga, R., & Dodge, T. (2023). From automation to autonomy: Rethinking algorithmic control. *AI & Society, 38*, 1261–1276. DOI: 10.1007/s00146-023-01597-z

Brandtzaeg, P. B., Egan, J., Maples, C., Huang, H., & Willson, M. (2025). Adolescents and emotional AI companions: Dependency and identity. *Media Culture & Society*. Advance online publication. DOI: 10.1177/0163443724123457

Flew, T. (2023). Trust, transparency and accountability in AI communication. *Media International Australia, 188*(1), 76–89. DOI: 10.1177/1329878X231163725

Goldenthal, A., Glikson, E., & Monahan, K. (2025). The hidden cost of AI-written communication: Effects on perceived authenticity and trust. *Journal of Business Communication*. Advance online publication. DOI: 10.1177/0021943624123456

Laestadius, L., Bishop, R., Gonzalez, E., Illenčík, M., & Campos-Castillo, C. (2024). Emotional attachment and withdrawal: Replika chatbot users' experiences. *Social Media + Society, 10*(1), 1–12. DOI: 10.1177/2056305124122901

Li, J., & Zhang, X. (2024). Understanding emotional needs and mental health from Replika chatbot use: A computational linguistics approach. *Computers in Human Behavior, 152*, 107177. DOI: 10.1016/j.chb.2023.107177

Li, Z., Mao, R., & Kim, H. (2023). Social anxiety and chatbot use: A mediation model of loneliness and rumination. *Computers in Human Behavior, 140*, 107577. DOI: 10.1016/j.chb.2022.107577

Liang, Y., Wang, X., & He, D. (2021). Enhancing chatbot social presence through emotional self-disclosure. *ACM Transactions on Information Systems, 39*(4), 1–27. DOI: 10.1145/3742424

Møller, J., Romero, D. M., Jurgens, D., & Aiello, L. M. (2025). Generative AI and the perception of authenticity in social media conversations. *Nature Human Behaviour, 9*, 451–460. DOI: 10.1038/s41562-024-01722-4

Moller, K., Nyberg, T., Tumova, J., & Betz, J. (2025). Pedestrian-Aware Motion Planning for Autonomous Driving in Complex Urban Scenarios. *arXiv preprint arXiv:2504.01409*.

Purcell, A., Dong, H., Nussberger, A. M., Köbis, N. C., & Jakesch, M. (2023). People judge others more than themselves for using AI in communication. *Scientific Reports, 13*, 9640. DOI: 10.1038/s41598-023-35955-3

Schätz, S., Gagrčin, E., Toth, R., & Emmer, M. (2023). Users' perceptions of AI-generated communication in journalism. *Digital Journalism (Abingdon, England), 11*(6), 785–802. DOI: 10.1080/21670811.2023.2185951

Taylor, M., & Chen, A. (2024). "It gets me": Emotional resonance and algorithmic intimacy on TikTok. *New Media & Society*. Advance online publication. DOI: 10.1177/14614448241218 73

Taylor, M., & Choi, J. (2024). Algorithmic feedback loops and emotional dependency: A longitudinal study. *Journal of Computer-Mediated Communication, 29*(2), 145–165. DOI: 10.1093/jcmc/zmae001

Wu, C., Liu, Y., Wang, J., & Yao, Q. (2024). Explainable AI and user agency: Improving recommender system transparency. *Information Processing & Management, 61*(2), 102065. DOI: 10.1016/j.ipm.2023.102065

Yoon, H., Lee, J., Wu, C., & Koh, J. (2024). Designing user-centered recommendation algorithms: The role of transparency and interactivity. *Behaviour & Information Technology, 43*(1), 57–75. DOI: 10.1080/0144929X.2023.2187320

Yuan, X., Cheng, C., & Duan, Y. (2024). Affective human-chatbot interaction and emotional fulfillment. *Journal of Artificial Intelligence Research, 77*, 125–146. DOI: 10.1613/jair.1.14090

Zhou, L., & Cheng, Q. (2024). ChatGPT and cognitive offloading in education: An I-PACE model approach. *Education and Information Technologies, 29*(3), 1583–1601. DOI: 10.1007/s10639-024-12231-w

Zhou, L., Gao, J., Li, D., & Shum, H.-Y. (2018). The design and implementation of XiaoIce, an empathetic social chatbot. *Computational Linguistics, 46*(1), 53–93. DOI: 10.1162/coli_a_00368

Chapter 4

# Mechanisms and Manifestations of Digital Addiction With a Focus on Social Media, Messaging Platforms, and AI-Driven Applications

**Namita Vyas Joshi**
https://orcid.org/0000-0001-9429-9629
*Noida International University, India*

**Shrikant Ratley**
https://orcid.org/0000-0002-0424-4526
*Marwadi University, India*

**P. Selvakumar**
https://orcid.org/0000-0002-3650-4548
*Department of Science and Humanities, Nehru Institute of Technology, Coimbatore, India*

**T. C. Manjunath**
https://orcid.org/0000-0003-2545-9160
*Rajarajeswari College of Engineering, India*

**Nilesh Anute**
https://orcid.org/0000-0001-6599-813X
*Sri Balaji University, India*

**M. R. Arun**
https://orcid.org/0000-0002-8291-2956
*Vel Tech Rangarajan Dr. Sagunthala R&D Institute of Science and Technology, India*

## ABSTRACT

*The rise of digital addiction represents a significant and complex phenomenon of the 21st century, reflecting the growing entanglement between human behavior and digital technologies. With the advent and ubiquity of smartphones, social media platforms, streaming services, online gaming, and digital communication tools,*

DOI: 10.4018/979-8-3373-5606-8.ch004

*individuals are spending unprecedented amounts of time connected to digital devices. While these technologies offer immense benefits—facilitating communication, productivity, education, and entertainment—they have also given rise to patterns of compulsive, excessive, and unhealthy usage that can significantly impair psychological well-being, social relationships, academic and occupational performance, and physical health. Digital addiction, often referred to by terms such as "internet addiction," "screen addiction," or "technology dependency," is increasingly recognized as a behavioral addiction that mirrors many characteristics of substance use disorders, including tolerance, withdrawal, loss of control, and continued use despite adverse consequences.*

## THE RISE OF DIGITAL ADDICTION

The rise of digital addiction represents a significant and complex phenomenon of the 21st century, reflecting the growing entanglement between human behavior and digital technologies. With the advent and ubiquity of smartphones, social media platforms, streaming services, online gaming, and digital communication tools, individuals are spending unprecedented amounts of time connected to digital devices. While these technologies offer immense benefits—facilitating communication, productivity, education, and entertainment—they have also given rise to patterns of compulsive, excessive, and unhealthy usage that can significantly impair psychological well-being, social relationships, academic and occupational performance, and physical health. Digital addiction, often referred to by terms such as "internet addiction," "screen addiction," or "technology dependency," is increasingly recognized as a behavioral addiction that mirrors many characteristics of substance use disorders, including tolerance, withdrawal, loss of control, and continued use despite adverse consequences.(Zawacki-Richter et al., 2019)Digital addiction is not a monolithic condition but rather encompasses a range of problematic behaviors associated with different types of digital content and platforms. Some of the most commonly recognized forms include social media addiction, gaming disorder, compulsive online shopping, binge-watching of video content, and information or news overconsumption. These behaviors are fueled by features deliberately designed to capture and sustain attention: infinite scrolling, autoplay, push notifications, social validation loops (e.g., likes, shares, and comments), and algorithmic recommendations that tailor content to users' preferences. Such mechanisms exploit cognitive vulnerabilities like the need for social belonging, fear of missing out (FOMO), and the psychological rewards derived from variable reinforcement schedules—an approach akin to gambling psychology.(Aïmeur et al., 2023) As a result, individuals may find themselves compulsively checking their phones, scrolling through feeds for hours, or losing sleep to digital engagement that no longer serves their goals or values.

The prevalence of digital addiction is growing across demographics but is especially pronounced among children, adolescents, and young adults, whose developmental stages make them more susceptible to the lure of interactive and social technologies. Each notification, new like, or in-game reward can trigger dopamine surges, which over time condition the brain to seek more frequent and intense stimulation. This neurochemical feedback loop leads to compulsive use, tolerance (needing more time or intensity to feel the same satisfaction), and, in some cases, withdrawal symptoms such as irritability, anxiety, or depression when access to digital devices is restricted. Neuroimaging studies have begun to reveal structural and functional changes in the brains of individuals with digital addiction, including alterations in prefrontal cortex activity (responsible for decision-making and impulse control) and reduced gray matter in regions associated with emotional regulation and self-reflection.Societal structures and cultural dynamics also contribute to the normalization and propagation of digital addiction.(Andrews et al., 2015) In many modern societies, digital connectivity is seen as essential for participation in education, commerce, social life, and even governance. Therapeutic approaches, including cognitive behavioral therapy (CBT), mindfulness training, and digital detox programs, have shown promise in helping individuals regain control over their digital habits. At the same time, public health campaigns, parental education, and school-based interventions are increasingly focused on promoting digital literacy, balanced screen use, and the development of offline skills and relationships, (Bakshy et al., 2015). It is not technology itself that is inherently harmful, but the ways in which it interacts with our psychology, social norms, and commercial structures. Addressing digital addiction requires a multidimensional strategy that combines personal responsibility, ethical technology design, public policy, clinical support, and cultural change. (Billieux et al., 2015).

## THE ROLE OF SOCIAL MEDIA, MESSAGING PLATFORMS, AND AI

These platforms operate on a business model rooted in the attention economy, where user engagement is monetized through advertising. As such, they are engineered to keep users scrolling, liking, sharing, and commenting for as long as possible. Messaging platforms—including WhatsApp, Telegram, Signal, Facebook Messenger, WeChat, and Discord—play a more subtle but equally significant role in digital addiction, (Bostock et al., 2019). These tools are designed to foster instant, constant communication, and they tap into fundamental human needs for social connection and responsiveness. The expectation of immediate replies, the pressure to stay available, and the fear of missing out on conversations or group chats contribute to a state of hyper-vigilance and perpetual partial attention. Features like read receipts, typing indicators, and online status visibility increase social pressure and contribute to anxiety and compulsive checking. This level of personalization increases engagement but also diminishes user agency, as choices are subtly shaped by unseen algorithms.AI also enables predictive behavioral modeling, wherein platforms can anticipate what a user will want to see or do next. These insights are used not only to recommend content but to determine the optimal timing of notifications and prompts to interrupt users and draw them back in, (Chowdhary et al., 2025). For instance, a user who tends to scroll late at night might receive push notifications during that time window, even if they've been inactive all day. AI's ability to learn from and adapt to individual behaviors makes these systems increasingly persuasive, leading to deeper forms of dependency that are difficult to resist or regulate.

## DOPAMINE LOOPS AND REWARD SYSTEMS

In understanding the neuroscience behind digital addiction, the role of dopamine loops and reward systems emerges as a central mechanism that explains why digital technologies—especially social media, mobile apps, games, and algorithmically personalized platforms—can exert such a powerful grip on human attention and behavior, (Coates et al., 2025). Dopamine, a neurotransmitter often associated with pleasure and reward, plays a fundamental role in motivating behavior, reinforcing habits, and shaping our interactions with stimuli in the environment. Contrary to the oversimplified narrative that dopamine is a "pleasure chemical," it is more accurately described as a molecule of anticipation and motivation, driving us to seek out rewarding experiences and repeat behaviors that produce satisfaction, even if fleeting. When integrated into the design of modern digital environments, this neurological mechanism becomes a powerful vector for behavioral conditioning—leading to compulsive use, diminished self-control, and in many cases, full-fledged behavioral addiction. At the most basic level, the dopaminergic system operates through a series of feedback loops that involve prediction, action, and reward, (Dabbish et al., 2011). When we engage in an activity that the brain anticipates as rewarding—such as receiving a like on a social media post, leveling up in a game, or opening a new message—dopamine neurons fire in the midbrain (particularly in areas like the ventral tegmental area and the nucleus accumbens), releasing a surge of dopamine into the brain's reward centers. This release signals that the action was beneficial, reinforcing the behavior and making it more likely to be repeated. The strength of this reinforcement depends on the timing and unpredictability of the reward—a concept rooted in the psychological principle of variable reward schedules, which are known to produce stronger behavioral conditioning than predictable ones. Digital platforms have mastered the use of variable rewards. Every time a user scrolls through a feed, opens a notification, or checks an app, they are met with a different and unpredictable outcome: sometimes a funny video, sometimes a new follower, other times nothing at all. This uncertainty activates the brain's reward system more intensely than predictable outcomes, mirroring the same mechanisms that underlie gambling addiction. Users do not know what they will get, or when, which creates a sense of anticipatory arousal. This uncertainty keeps the dopaminergic loop cycling—motivating the user to keep checking, swiping, and scrolling. In the process, the behavior becomes less voluntary and more reflexive, turning engagement into compulsion, (Dahmani et al., 2020).

These micro-surges of dopamine act as reinforcers, prompting users to post more frequently, monitor responses obsessively, and continuously adjust their behavior to maximize social validation. Over time, this feedback loop can create a psychological dependence on external affirmation, with the digital environment becoming the primary source of self-worth and emotional regulation. This dynamic is particularly problematic for children and adolescents, whose dopaminergic systems are still developing and more sensitive to reinforcement. Digital experiences are often more stimulating and immediately gratifying than traditional sources of learning, play, or social interaction, leading young users to prefer digital environments and disengage from real-world experiences. The development of self-control, patience, and delayed gratification is undermined by constant access to rapid dopamine triggers, (Eppler et al., 2004). In conclusion, dopamine loops and reward systems are at the core of how digital platforms capture and sustain user attention. By manipulating the brain's natural motivation circuitry, these technologies create powerful cycles of anticipation and reinforcement that drive compulsive engagement and, in many cases, digital addiction. (Ferrucci et al., 2010).

## ALGORITHMIC MANIPULATION

In the digital age, algorithmic manipulation refers to the deliberate design and deployment of computational algorithms that subtly shape, guide, or influence user behavior, preferences, opinions, and decisions—often without the user's explicit awareness.(Firth et al., 2019) As artificial intelligence (AI), machine learning (ML), and data-driven technologies have become deeply integrated into social media, search engines, recommendation systems, advertising networks, and even governance, algorithmic manipulation has emerged as a powerful but ethically complex mechanism of control. These techniques are not merely about efficiency or personalization; they are strategically crafted to optimize attention, influence choices, and modify behaviors in ways that align with commercial, political, or ideological objectives. While algorithms themselves are neutral mathematical structures, their application and implementation—especially when paired with massive datasets—can be engineered to exploit cognitive biases, reinforce echo chambers, or subtly steer decisions, raising significant concerns about autonomy, transparency, privacy, and democratic integrity. One of the most pervasive forms of algorithmic manipulation operates through recommendation systems—algorithms designed to predict what content, products, or experiences a user is most likely to engage with based on past behavior, preferences, and demographic data. Platforms like YouTube, TikTok, Netflix, Instagram, and Amazon rely heavily on these systems to drive engagement and consumption. By learning from a user's previous clicks, likes, viewing time, and interactions, the algorithm curates a tailored content stream meant to increase time spent on the platform. While this personalization is presented as a service enhancement, it often leads to manipulative design patterns that exploit psychological vulnerabilities. For instance, users may be nudged toward more sensationalist, emotionally charged, or extreme content not because it is in their best interest, but because it drives longer engagement—thereby maximizing ad revenue and platform profitability. This mechanism has been implicated in the radicalization of political views, the spread of misinformation, and the erosion of shared reality, (Graesser et al., 2018).

These highly individualized messages escape public scrutiny and accountability because no two users may see the same version of a political ad, reduce transparency and enable manipulative persuasion at scale. Closely linked to microtargeting is behavioral nudging, a more subtle but equally potent form of algorithmic manipulation. Drawing on insights from behavioral economics and cognitive psychology, algorithms can adjust how choices are presented to encourage certain behaviors—such as framing options to make one appear more attractive (default bias), using urgency or scarcity cues (like "only 2 left!"), or structuring user interfaces to prioritize particular actions (like "accept all cookies" over granular privacy settings). While nudging can be used for beneficial outcomes—such as encouraging healthier lifestyle choices or energy conservation—it is often deployed for commercial exploitation, pushing users toward unnecessary purchases, excessive screen time, or submission to invasive data collection. Search engines also play a key role in algorithmic manipulation through algorithmic ranking and filtering mechanisms that determine the visibility and order of search results. Search engine optimization (SEO) practices and paid promotions further influence what information appears most credible or relevant. These systems are rarely neutral; they reflect not only user preferences but also commercial incentives and political pressures. The phenomenon of the "filter bubble", first popularized by Eli Pariser, highlights how algorithmic filtering creates personalized information silos, where users are only exposed to viewpoints that reinforce their existing beliefs, thereby reducing exposure to diverse perspectives and amplifying polarization. An especially manipulative dimension is the use of emotion recognition technologies and affective computing, where algorithms interpret users' facial expressions, voice tones, or keystroke dynamics to infer emotional states. When combined with persuasive design, this allows platforms to deliver content tailored not only to a user's interests but also to their current mood. For instance, someone feeling lonely may be shown dating apps or shopping ads, while someone feeling anxious may be fed reassuring but biased news. Such systems raise critical questions about emotional exploitation, surveillance capitalism, and the erosion of mental sovereignty. The role of algorithmic opacity further compounds the problem. Most users have little to no understanding of how algorithms influence what they see, believe, or buy. (Gunning et al., 2019).

## EXCESSIVE SCREEN TIME

In today's hyperconnected society, excessive screen time has become an omnipresent issue that affects individuals across age groups, occupations, and geographical boundaries. With the proliferation of smartphones, tablets, laptops, televisions, and wearable devices, people now spend a significant portion of their daily lives interacting with digital screens. While technology brings numerous advantages—such as information access, entertainment, connectivity, and productivity—uncontrolled and prolonged screen exposure carries serious physical, psychological, cognitive, and social consequences. The digital saturation of modern life demands a critical examination of the impacts of excessive screen use, especially as it becomes increasingly integrated into childhood development, workplace functioning, education systems, and even social relationships. One of the most immediate and visible effects of excessive screen time is on physical health. Prolonged screen use is strongly associated with eye strain, often referred to as digital eye strain or computer vision syndrome. This includes symptoms like blurred vision, dryness, headaches, and difficulty focusing, especially after hours of screen exposure without sufficient breaks. The blue light emitted from screens can also disrupt the body's natural circadian rhythm by inhibiting melatonin production, which negatively impacts sleep quality. This disruption is particularly severe when screens are used in the evening or just before bedtime, leading to sleep onset delays, poor sleep efficiency, and daytime fatigue, (Hamari et al., 2014). In addition to vision-related issues, sedentary behavior linked with screen time contributes to broader physical health problems. Sitting for extended periods while engaging with screens decreases overall physical activity, raising the risk of obesity, cardiovascular diseases, type 2 diabetes, and musculoskeletal disorders, particularly in the neck, shoulders, and lower back. Poor posture, especially among children and adolescents who often hunch over handheld devices, is becoming increasingly common and can lead to long-term spinal complications, (Hill et al., 2015).

These effects are often intensified in adolescents and young adults, who may compare themselves unfavorably with the curated lives and appearances presented online. Excessive screen time, especially in the form of doomscrolling, binge-watching, and compulsive app use, has been associated with heightened feelings of isolation, fear of missing out (FOMO), and chronic dissatisfaction. Furthermore, continuous screen exposure can impair attention span, memory, and executive functioning. Digital multitasking—such as toggling between apps, notifications, and media—fragments attention and can lead to superficial information processing. The constant switching prevents the brain from engaging in deep, focused thought, which is essential for learning, creativity, and problem-solving. Children who spend excessive time with screens often show delays in language acquisition, reading comprehension, and social-emotional development due to the substitution of real-world interactions with digital content. Workplace dynamics have also been transformed by digital dependency. While technology has enabled remote work, virtual collaboration, and 24/7 connectivity, it has also created the expectation of constant availability, blurring the lines between work and personal life. The result is a rise in digital burnout, characterized by mental exhaustion, decreased motivation, and cognitive fatigue. Employees who spend long hours staring at screens may feel trapped in a cycle of productivity without recovery, exacerbated by the pressure to immediately respond to emails, messages, and virtual meetings. This "always-on" culture not only affects individual well-being but also reduces overall productivity and job satisfaction. In the educational sector, the increase in screen time—especially during and after the COVID-19 pandemic—has raised concerns about digital dependency in learning environments. While online tools have enabled continued access to education, excessive reliance on digital platforms can reduce opportunities for critical thinking, classroom interaction, and experiential learning. Students who use devices for prolonged periods may struggle with maintaining attention during virtual lessons, become distracted by non-academic content, and experience a decline in academic performance. Moreover, screen time for leisure, such as gaming or social media use, often extends beyond school hours, compounding the negative effects. Another less discussed consequence of excessive screen time is its effect on emotional regulation and mindfulness, (Iqbal et al., 2007). The constant stimulation provided by screens—notifications, pop-ups, autoplay videos—creates a state of hyperarousal, making it difficult for individuals to experience boredom, reflect internally, or remain present in the moment. This undermines the development of mindfulness and emotional resilience, which are critical for coping with stress, disappointment, and uncertainty. In conclusion, while digital screens are integral to modern life, the consequences of excessive screen time are too significant to ignore. From deteriorating physical health and impaired cognition to weakened relationships and mental health challenges, overexposure to screens is reshaping human experience in profound and troubling ways, (Junco, 2012).

## SOCIAL MEDIA OBSESSION

In the 21st century, social media has become deeply embedded in daily life, revolutionizing how people communicate, consume content, build relationships, and even shape personal identity. Platforms such as Facebook, Instagram, Twitter (now X), TikTok, Snapchat, and YouTube offer instantaneous access to information, entertainment, and human interaction. While these platforms provide powerful tools for global connectivity and self-expression, they also exhibit a darker side—one characterized by obsessive use, dependency, and addiction-like behaviors. Social media obsession is a growing concern among psychologists, educators, policymakers, and families, as it poses significant risks to mental health, social functioning, emotional regulation, and personal well-being. At the heart of social media's addictive nature lies its design architecture, which is meticulously engineered to capture and retain users' attention. Developers employ persuasive design techniques and behavioral psychology—especially the dopamine-driven feedback loops—to keep users engaged. Features such as likes, comments, retweets, notifications, infinite scrolling, and algorithmically curated content trigger pleasure centers in the brain, creating a cycle of intermittent rewards similar to those experienced with gambling. The unpredictability of feedback—never knowing how many likes or responses a post will receive—enhances compulsive checking and fosters a strong craving for validation, approval, and digital recognition. Social media obsession is characterized by repetitive and compulsive use despite negative consequences. Individuals often find themselves checking platforms immediately upon waking, during meals, in social settings, or even while driving. Many experiences phantom vibration syndrome (imagining their phone buzzed) and FOMO (Fear of Missing Out), which propels them to stay constantly connected to avoid feeling left out or uninformed.

The curated nature of posts and filters can lead to distorted self-perception, body image issues, and decreased self-esteem. A user sees only the highlight reel of others' lives, fostering feelings of inadequacy, jealousy, and anxiety, (Junco et al., 2012). Many young users begin to equate their worth with the number of likes or folowers they receive, leading to a fragile sense of self that is externally dependent and highly volatile. Moreover, excessive use of social media has been linked to increased rates of depression, anxiety, loneliness, and sleep disturbances. The constant influx of information and notifications can cause cognitive overload, making it difficult to focus or engage in deep thought. Sleep quality is often impaired as users stay up late scrolling through feeds, checking messages, or watching videos, and the blue light emitted by screens interferes with melatonin production and circadian rhythms. In extreme cases, users may develop symptoms aligned with behavioral addiction, including tolerance (needing more time online to feel satisfied), withdrawal (irritability or discomfort when access is restricted), and neglect of real-life responsibilities or relationships. The emotional consequences of social media obsession are equally alarming. Users frequently experience mood swings, irritability, and emotional exhaustion as a result of their digital interactions. Social comparison on these platforms often evokes envy, shame, or sadness, especially when users are bombarded with images of others' achievements, relationships, or lifestyles. This emotional turbulence can disrupt interpersonal relationships and reduce the capacity for genuine connection, as interactions become increasingly mediated by screens and filtered personas. The impact on attention span and productivity is also significant. Social media encourages fragmented attention, as users rapidly switch between posts, stories, messages, and videos. Over time, this can result in emotional detachment, reduced empathy, and social withdrawal, particularly if individuals rely on social media as a substitute for direct human contact. Some users even report feeling lonelier after extended periods of use, particularly after passive consumption of others' content rather than active engagement, (Kanai et al., 2012).

The economic and societal incentives behind social media obsession further complicate the issue. Most platforms operate on an attention economy, where user engagement is monetized through advertising. The longer users stay online, the more data they generate and the more ads they see, creating a financial motive for companies to design addictive features. This monetization of human attention often conflicts with user well-being, making it unlikely that platforms will self-regulate their manipulative mechanisms without external pressure or regulation, (Kashdan et al., 2004). As a result, users are trapped in a system optimized not for their happiness or health, but for maximum engagement and profit. Addressing social media obsession requires a multifaceted approach. On the individual level, users must develop digital literacy and self-regulation skills, such as setting usage limits, turning off non-essential notifications, and designating screen-free times and zones (like during meals or before bed). Mindful social media use—where users consciously choose when and why to engage—can help restore control over digital behavior. Apps that track screen time or encourage breaks, such as Forest or Moment, can assist users in building healthier habits. At the family and educational levels, open dialogue and modeling healthy behavior are critical. Parents and teachers must guide children in understanding both the benefits and risks of social media, encouraging offline activities that build real-world skills, empathy, and resilience.

## MESSAGING PLATFORM OVERUSE

In today's hyper-connected digital environment, messaging platforms such as WhatsApp, Facebook Messenger, Telegram, Signal, iMessage, and WeChat have become essential tools for communication. These platforms have revolutionized the way people interact, providing real-time access to friends, family, colleagues, and communities across the globe. However, while these applications enhance connectivity and convenience, their ubiquitous presence and constant accessibility have led to widespread overuse, contributing to a range of psychological, social, and behavioral challenges. Messaging platform overuse is increasingly being recognized as a modern digital dilemma, with implications for mental well-being, productivity, social dynamics, and even cognitive development. Messaging platform overuse is characterized by excessive, compulsive, and habitual engagement with messaging apps, often at the expense of other important aspects of life such as work, study, relationships, and sleep. It is driven by the expectation of immediate responsiveness, the persistent presence of unread notifications, and the fear of social exclusion or missing important information—commonly referred to as FOMO (Fear of Missing Out), (Li et al., 2019). The pressure to be constantly available and responsive has created a culture of digital hyper-vigilance, where people feel obligated to check and respond to messages instantly, regardless of the context or necessity. One of the central issues underlying messaging platform overuse is the 24/7 communication loop it fosters. In both professional and personal contexts, individuals are bombarded with messages at all hours of the day, (Lin et al., 2016) This blurs the boundaries between work and personal life, particularly with the rise of remote and hybrid work environments. Employees may feel compelled to reply to work-related messages outside office hours, leading to work-life imbalance, digital burnout, and chronic stress.

*Figure 1. AI in social media*

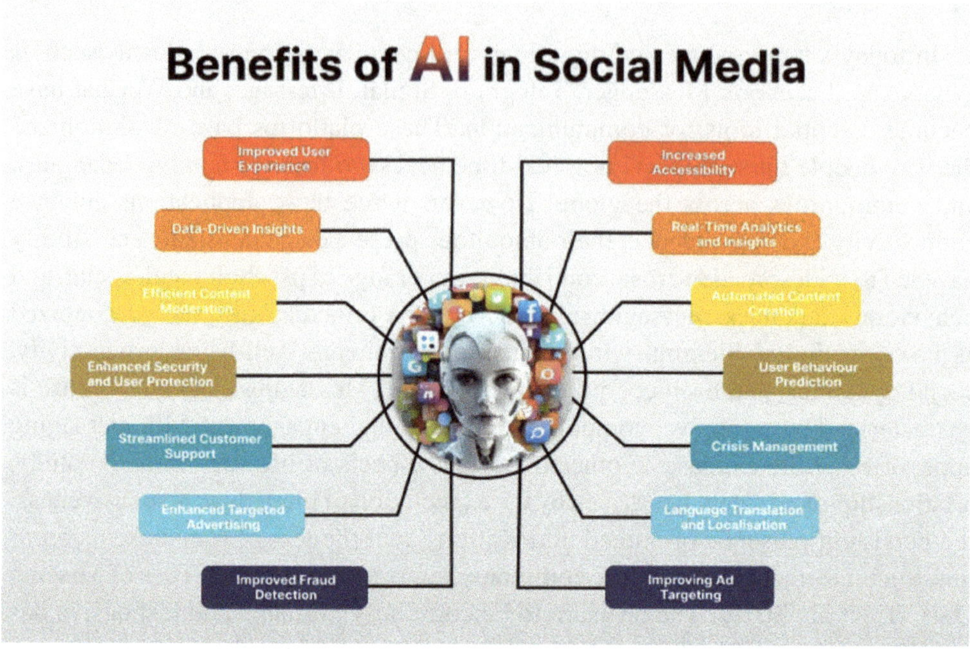


Moreover, messaging platform overuse can undermine in-person communication and social presence. While these apps are designed to connect people, they often result in fragmented attention and reduced quality of face-to-face interactions. The phenomenon of phubbing—snubbing someone in a social setting by looking at your phone instead—has become widespread, damaging interpersonal relationships and decreasing empathy. In group settings, the distraction caused by constant message alerts can lead to disengagement, shallow conversations, and a sense of disconnection from the present moment. In educational settings, messaging platform overuse presents unique challenges. Students often use these apps for social coordination, class updates, or academic collaboration, but they also become sources of constant distraction. Many students report difficulty concentrating during study sessions due to message interruptions, which affects academic performance and undermines deep learning. Notifications pull students into conversations that may be trivial or unrelated to their tasks, leading to procrastination and attention fragmentation, (Machete et al., 2020), The cultural normalization of constant messaging exacerbates the problem. In many social and professional contexts, delayed responses are interpreted as neglect or disrespect, creating pressure to maintain continuous connectivity. This expectation of immediacy reinforces overuse, making it socially difficult to take breaks or disconnect. Moreover, group chat dynamics often involve a fear of missing out on inside jokes, important decisions, or shared experiences, which compels users to stay constantly tuned in. Solutions to messaging platform overuse must involve personal behavior changes, cultural shifts, and platform design reform. (Maheswaran et al., 2025).

## PERSONALIZED CONTENT AND RECOMMENDATIONS

In the digital era, the proliferation of information and user-generated content has necessitated advanced mechanisms to help users navigate, discover, and engage with material that aligns with their interests, preferences, and behaviors. One of the most transformative responses to this challenge has been the rise of personalized content and recommendation systems. These systems use a combination of algorithms, data analytics, artificial intelligence (AI), and machine learning (ML) to curate individual experiences, tailoring digital content, advertisements, products, services, and interactions to meet the unique needs of each user. While personalization offers remarkable advantages in improving user engagement, satisfaction, and convenience, it also raises critical concerns related to privacy, autonomy, bias, digital addiction, and social polarization. Personalized content refers to any form of digital material—such as news feeds, videos, product suggestions, social media posts, search results, or advertisements—that is dynamically tailored based on the user's demographic data, location, browsing history, past behavior, social network interactions, and even psychographic profiles. Recommendation engines, which power this personalization, use various techniques, including collaborative filtering, content-based filtering, hybrid models, and neural networks, to predict what a user is most likely to engage with or find relevant.

These systems are integral to platforms like Netflix, YouTube, Amazon, Spotify, Facebook, Google, and TikTok, influencing everything from entertainment choices and consumer purchases to political opinions and news exposure. One of the key benefits of personalization is its ability to enhance user experience. In a digital ecosystem flooded with options, users can feel overwhelmed by choice, (Nisha Angeline et al., 2025) Personalized systems help reduce cognitive load and decision fatigue by presenting content that is most relevant to the user's known preferences. For example, a streaming service can recommend a new movie based on previous watch history, a shopping site can suggest products similar to past purchases, and a news aggregator can highlight stories from preferred sources or on favored topics. This relevance drives higher user satisfaction, engagement, and retention, as users are more likely to interact with content that resonates with them personally. In commercial contexts, personalized recommendations have revolutionized marketing, e-commerce, and customer relationship management. Businesses use personalization to deliver targeted advertising campaigns, optimize customer journeys, and improve conversion rates. By analyzing user behavior, companies can tailor product offerings and promotions to match individual interests, thereby increasing sales and fostering brand loyalty. The data-driven insights gathered from user interactions help refine business strategies, predict trends, and adapt to changing consumer behaviors with greater precision and speed. In education and healthcare, personalized systems are fostering new paradigms of individualized learning and treatment. Educational platforms can adjust learning materials to suit a student's pace, style, and performance, promoting deeper understanding and retention. In healthcare, AI-driven recommendations can assist in tailoring medical interventions, lifestyle advice, or medication plans to fit a patient's unique genetic, behavioral, and environmental profile—paving the way for precision medicine. Despite its advantages, the widespread deployment of personalization raises several ethical, psychological, and societal challenges. Users may not be fully aware of how their data is being collected, shared, or monetized, which raises issues of informed consent, data security, and surveillance. Even when anonymized, behavioral data can often be de-anonymized through pattern analysis, exposing users to potential data breaches, manipulation, or misuse, (Nikkelen et al., 2014). In addition, personalization has been linked to digital addiction and compulsive behavior.

## PREDICTIVE ANALYTICS AND USER ENGAGEMENT

In the data-driven digital ecosystem, predictive analytics has emerged as a cornerstone of user engagement strategies, transforming the way organizations understand, anticipate, and influence user behavior. By leveraging historical data, statistical algorithms, machine learning, and artificial intelligence (AI), predictive analytics enables platforms to forecast future actions, preferences, and needs of users with remarkable accuracy. This capability not only enhances the personalization of content and services but also allows businesses and institutions to proactively design experiences that deepen engagement, boost satisfaction, and optimize outcomes. While the potential benefits of predictive analytics are vast, its deployment also introduces complex questions related to ethics, privacy, manipulation, and fairness. At its core, predictive analytics involves analyzing vast datasets to identify patterns and trends that can inform decisions about future behavior. For instance, by examining a user's past browsing, purchasing, and interaction history, predictive models can forecast the likelihood of that user engaging with a certain type of content, buying a specific product, or even discontinuing a service. In the context of user engagement, this means platforms can tailor interfaces, recommend timely interventions, and deliver personalized content or offers that resonate with individual users, thereby increasing their likelihood of continued interaction. One of the most prominent sectors utilizing predictive analytics to drive engagement is e-commerce. Companies like Amazon, Flipkart, and Alibaba use predictive models to recommend products that users are likely to be interested in, often based on purchase history, product views, cart abandonment data, and even reviews. (Odgers et al., 2019).

This anticipatory logic not only reduces decision fatigue for the user but also significantly boosts conversion rates and customer retention. Personalized marketing emails, dynamic pricing strategies, and time-sensitive deals are often the direct result of predictive algorithms that estimate when a user is most likely to make a purchase. In content platforms, predictive analytics powers the recommendation engines that dictate much of what users consume. Netflix, for example, uses viewing history, watch time, pauses, replays, and ratings to predict what content will appeal to specific users. Similarly, YouTube and Spotify use behavioral patterns to queue videos or music that match a user's taste profile. These models not only aim to maximize satisfaction and time-on-platform, but they also shape consumption patterns and cultural exposure. The algorithms are constantly refined based on user responses, creating a feedback loop that makes future predictions even more accurate. In education technology (EdTech), predictive analytics is being used to personalize learning experiences and improve student engagement. Platforms like Coursera, Khan Academy, and Blackboard analyze user interaction data—such as time spent on modules, quiz performance, and clickstreams—to predict which students are at risk of disengagement or failure. These insights enable instructors and systems to provide targeted support, adaptive learning paths, and timely feedback, thereby enhancing learning outcomes and retention. Predictive analytics can also guide curriculum development by revealing which content resonates most with learners. In healthcare, predictive analytics plays a crucial role in improving patient engagement and preventative care. Health apps, telemedicine platforms, and electronic health record (EHR) systems use predictive tools to estimate patient adherence to treatments, likelihood of readmission, or risk of chronic disease development. By anticipating these outcomes, providers can proactively engage patients with alerts, reminders, educational content, and behavior modification programs that encourage healthier lifestyles and improve health outcomes. In social media and digital advertising, predictive analytics is deeply embedded in the architecture of engagement. Platforms like Facebook, Instagram, Twitter (X), and TikTok use engagement metrics such as likes, shares, comments, and scroll velocity to predict what content will keep a user active and engaged. Advertisers use similar models to identify potential leads and to personalize ad delivery based on predicted interests and purchasing behavior, (Paulus et al., 2019). This feedback loop can limit exploration, creativity, and critical thinking, reducing the diversity of experiences and interactions available to the user. To navigate these challenges, there is a growing emphasis on developing ethical, transparent, and user-centered predictive systems.

This includes designing algorithms that are explainable, auditable, and accountable, providing users with clear insights into how predictions are made and the option to opt out or customize their predictive profiles. Responsible AI principles advocate for fairness, inclusivity, and sustainability, ensuring that predictive tools enhance—not exploit—user engagement, (Radesky et al., 2014). Additionally, integrating human oversight into predictive systems can help mitigate risks. Human-in-the-loop (HITL) models allow users or moderators to verify or override algorithmic predictions, especially in sensitive domains. Encouraging digital literacy and critical engagement among users can also empower individuals to recognize, question, and manage the influence of predictive systems on their behaviors and decisions.

## MENTAL HEALTH IMPLICATIONS

In the modern digital age, the pervasive integration of technology into daily life has brought both unprecedented convenience and a growing body of concern regarding its impact on mental health. As smartphones, social media platforms, messaging apps, online gaming, streaming services, and artificial intelligence (AI)-driven content consumption dominate the attention economy, users are increasingly grappling with psychological and emotional consequences. These mental health implications—ranging from anxiety and depression to attention deficits, loneliness, and addiction—highlight the complex and often paradoxical relationship between digital connectivity and psychological well-being. Understanding these effects is crucial for individuals, families, educators, healthcare professionals, and policymakers striving to create healthier digital environments. One of the most frequently cited consequences of excessive digital engagement is anxiety and stress. Constant connectivity fosters a culture of urgency and hyper-responsiveness, where users feel compelled to respond to messages, emails, and notifications immediately. This "always-on" lifestyle can lead to information overload, disrupted attention spans, and digital fatigue. The fear of missing out (FOMO), a psychological phenomenon exacerbated by social media, compels individuals to remain perpetually online, scanning for updates, reactions, or new content. This state of heightened vigilance and stimulation places strain on the nervous system, elevating cortisol levels and contributing to chronic stress. Closely related is the link between digital technologies and depression, particularly among adolescents and young adults. Numerous studies have shown correlations between heavy social media use and increased feelings of inadequacy, envy, and sadness. Platforms like Instagram, TikTok, and Snapchat promote curated versions of life—highlight reels of beauty, success, and social activity—that can distort users' self-perceptions. The resulting social comparison effect can erode self-esteem and lead to feelings of worthlessness, especially among vulnerable populations already struggling with identity or belonging.

Additionally, online bullying, harassment, and exclusion can intensify emotional distress, with cyberbullying now recognized as a significant risk factor for youth depression and suicide ideation. Sleep disruption is another critical mental health consequence of digital overuse. Blue light emitted by screens suppresses melatonin production, interfering with circadian rhythms and reducing sleep quality. Many individuals, particularly teenagers, fall into patterns of "revenge bedtime procrastination," sacrificing sleep in favor of late-night scrolling or gaming as a form of escapism or unwinding, (Rosen et al., 2011) Inadequate or poor-quality sleep is strongly associated with mood disorders, cognitive impairment, and heightened emotional reactivity, creating a feedback loop that reinforces poor mental health. The rise of digital addiction, encompassing compulsive smartphone use, gaming disorder, and social media dependency, represents a major area of concern. These behaviors mirror classical addiction symptoms such as cravings, tolerance, withdrawal, and the inability to stop despite negative consequences. The underlying neurological mechanism often involves dopamine-based reward systems, where unpredictable notifications, likes, or game rewards trigger pleasure responses, reinforcing repetitive engagement. This pattern can impair academic performance, work productivity, interpersonal relationships, and emotional regulation. Importantly, digital addiction is now being recognized in clinical frameworks such as the World Health Organization's classification of "gaming disorder," emphasizing the need for formal diagnosis and treatment pathways. Loneliness and social isolation, paradoxically, can be intensified by digital interactions despite their intended purpose of connection. While digital platforms allow users to communicate across distances, these connections often lack depth, intimacy, or authenticity. (Sakthivel et al., 2025). Online therapy platforms, mental health apps, AI chatbots (like Woebot), mindfulness tools, and online support groups can increase access to care, reduce stigma, and offer timely support. For individuals in remote or underserved areas, or those reluctant to seek in-person help, digital platforms may be the only feasible option, (Sethumadhavan et al., 2025). Telepsychiatry has expanded significantly since the COVID-19 pandemic, demonstrating the potential of digital delivery in addressing widespread mental health needs. However, the quality, efficacy, and ethical safeguards of such interventions remain critical issues to be addressed.

## PRODUCTIVITY AND PERFORMANCE

In the 21st-century digital economy, productivity and performance have become critical metrics defining the success of individuals, teams, and entire organizations,

(Thirunagalingam et al., 2025). Digital technologies—from smartphones and AI-powered tools to cloud computing and workflow automation—have redefined how work is structured, executed, and measured. While these advancements have significantly enhanced efficiency and output, they have also introduced complex dynamics that can both augment and hinder human productivity and performance. The dual-edged nature of technology's role in modern productivity demands a holistic analysis that considers not only quantitative metrics but also qualitative, cognitive, psychological, and organizational dimensions. At the heart of digital transformation is the promise of enhanced productivity—doing more in less time. Productivity tools such as project management software (e.g., Trello, Asana, Monday.com), collaborative platforms (e.g., Slack, Microsoft Teams, Google Workspace), and cloud-based file sharing have dramatically reduced friction in communication and coordination. They allow for real-time collaboration across geographies, asynchronous task management, and seamless integration of workflows. Cloud storage and access to large databases enable faster decision-making, improved access to knowledge, and the elimination of redundancies, (Upadhyaya et al., 2025). As a result, individuals and teams can accomplish complex tasks with unprecedented speed and accuracy. Automation—driven by artificial intelligence (AI), machine learning (ML), and robotic process automation (RPA)—has revolutionized performance by removing repetitive, rule-based tasks from human responsibility.

Whether in finance, HR, manufacturing, or logistics, automation boosts consistency, reduces error rates, and frees up human workers for higher-order cognitive functions like problem-solving, creativity, and strategic thinking. For example, AI-based analytics can sift through terabytes of data to identify actionable insights in seconds, while digital assistants schedule meetings, answer FAQs, or support customer service 24/7.Digital technologies have also facilitated remote and hybrid work models, offering flexibility and time efficiency. With the ability to work from anywhere, employees can avoid long commutes, customize their schedules, and balance personal and professional commitments more effectively. Numerous studies have shown that remote work, when supported by the right tools and trust-based management, can lead to improved productivity, better work-life integration, and lower attrition rates. However, the very same technologies that boost productivity also carry the risk of digital overload. Constant connectivity blurs the boundaries between work and personal life, creating an "always-on" culture that leads to burnout, stress, and declining cognitive performance. The flood of emails, instant messages, app notifications, and alerts—often referred to as the "tyranny of urgency"—can fragment attention and disrupt deep work. In knowledge work especially, the cognitive cost of frequent context switching undermines productivity. A task that might take 30 minutes of uninterrupted focus can take over an hour if peppered with digital interruptions. Organizations that combine digital transformation with human-centric leadership see the greatest gains in performance, morale, and innovation. The intersection of technology and performance also raises ethical and psychological questions, (Vaidyam et al., 2019). The true potential of digital productivity lies in balanced integration—where technology complements human strengths, supports well-being, and aligns with purposeful, meaningful work. As individuals, organizations, and societies continue to adapt to rapid digital change, success will depend not merely on the tools we use, but on how wisely, humanely, and strategically we use them to create environments where high performance and human flourishing go hand in hand.

## HEALTHY DIGITAL HABITS AND BOUNDARIES

In today's hyper-connected world, cultivating healthy digital habits and boundaries has become essential for maintaining mental well-being, productivity, and authentic human relationships. The omnipresence of smartphones, social media, instant messaging, streaming platforms, and digital workspaces has blurred the lines between online and offline life. While technology offers countless advantages—including instant communication, access to information, remote work, and entertainment—it also introduces the risk of overuse, distraction, and emotional exhaustion. As digital technologies increasingly permeate every aspect of daily living, establishing thoughtful and deliberate boundaries is not just advisable; it is vital for individual and societal health, (Van Deursen et al., 2011). At its core, healthy digital engagement begins with intentionality—being mindful about how, when, and why technology is used. It involves recognizing technology as a tool that should serve human values rather than dominate attention or dictate behavior. Developing digital mindfulness means critically assessing usage patterns and consciously limiting time spent on low-value activities such as endless scrolling, doomscrolling, binge-watching, or compulsively checking notifications. By shifting from reactive to intentional use, individuals can reclaim agency over their time and mental space, allowing for deeper focus, more meaningful interactions, and greater satisfaction. Sleep hygiene is one of the most immediately affected areas when digital boundaries are not respected. The use of screens—especially smartphones and tablets—late at night can disrupt circadian rhythms by suppressing melatonin production due to blue light exposure. Moreover, engaging with emotionally stimulating or anxiety-inducing content before bed can prolong sleep onset and reduce sleep quality. Healthy digital habits in this context include establishing a "digital sunset" by turning off screens at least an hour before bedtime, creating a tech-free bedroom environment, and substituting screen time with calming pre-sleep routines such as reading, journaling, or mindfulness meditation. In the workplace and educational settings, maintaining digital boundaries is crucial to preventing burnout and enhancing focus, (Ward et al., 2017) The normalization of constant availability—through emails, messages, and video calls—has led to a culture of "digital presenteeism," where individuals feel compelled to be online beyond working hours. Encouraging offline hobbies, peer engagement, sports, and nature exploration can help balance digital use and support holistic development. Cultural and societal norms also shape perceptions of digital use. In many cultures, being constantly reachable is seen as a sign of productivity or commitment, while taking time offline may be misinterpreted as negligence. Challenging these norms requires a cultural shift that values digital well-being alongside efficiency. The erosion of attention spans, increasing impatience, heightened anxiety, and emotional dysregulation are symptomatic of a broader disconnection—from oneself, from others, and from the present moment. In this sense, digital addiction can be understood as both a behavioral phenomenon and a symptom of broader cultural shifts, (Yuan et al., 2011). Addressing digital addiction requires a multi-dimensional, systemic response. On the individual level, users must cultivate digital literacy, self-awareness, and intentional habits. Recognizing the triggers and patterns of compulsive use is the first step in reclaiming agency.

Organizations and leaders can model healthy behavior by respecting digital boundaries, discouraging after-hours communication, and promoting digital wellbeing as part of organizational culture. Technology itself can be harnessed to support healthier digital behaviors. Features like app timers, focus modes, notification batching, and analytics dashboards empower users to monitor and adjust their habits. Wearables and wellness apps can provide insights into screen time, sleep quality, and physical activity, encouraging a more balanced lifestyle. Innovations like ambient computing, voice assistants, and context-aware systems may reduce the need for constant screen engagement by integrating technology more seamlessly and non-invasively into daily routines. Policy and regulation also play an important role in supporting digital boundaries. Governments and educational institutions can incorporate digital wellness education into curricula, mandate user-friendly privacy settings, and hold tech companies accountable for addictive design practices. Workplace policies that protect employees' rights to disconnect, particularly in remote or hybrid work environments, can institutionalize healthier digital practices. To foster long-term change, it is essential to frame healthy digital habits not as restrictions but as enablers of a more fulfilling and purposeful life. Digital tools, when used mindfully, can enhance learning, foster creativity, deepen relationships, and expand opportunities. The key is to ensure that they are used in alignment with human values and personal priorities, rather than allowing them to dictate behavior through habit or compulsion. In conclusion, cultivating healthy digital habits and boundaries is a critical practice in the digital age—one that requires self-awareness, intentionality, and resilience, (Wilmer et al., 2017). As individuals, families, organizations, and societies grapple with the challenges of ubiquitous technology, prioritizing digital well-being is not a luxury but a necessity. By integrating mindful strategies, setting clear limits, and reclaiming control over how technology is used, people can restore balance, preserve mental and emotional health, and foster deeper engagement with both the digital and the real world. Ultimately, a balanced digital life is not about rejecting technology, but about using it wisely, purposefully, and humanely.

## CONCLUSION

In the ever-expanding digital landscape of the 21st century, the complex interplay between human behavior and technological innovation has given rise to one of the most pressing psychological and societal challenges of our time: digital addiction. As technologies become more pervasive, intelligent, and personalized, the risks associated with compulsive digital use have escalated. From social media and messaging platforms to AI-driven recommendations and immersive digital experiences, users find themselves increasingly ensnared in environments engineered for maximum engagement. This dynamic creates a paradox—technology is both an enabler of human potential and a source of behavioral vulnerability. In confronting the challenge of digital addiction, we must reevaluate the ways in which technology is designed, used, and integrated into our lives. Digital addiction does not arise in a vacuum. It is the outcome of an ecosystem in which attention has become commodified, emotional needs are exploited by algorithms, and convenience trumps contemplation. The mechanics of addiction—dopaminergic reward loops, variable reinforcement schedules, social validation cues—are not incidental to modern digital platforms; they are central to their design. Social media applications, messaging platforms, video games, and streaming services have all capitalized on these neurological mechanisms to prolong user engagement. As a result, behaviors that once facilitated connection or entertainment now frequently cross the line into compulsion, leading to decreased mental health, reduced productivity, sleep disruption, social isolation, and emotional exhaustion. Compounding the issue is the rapid advancement of artificial intelligence and machine learning, which has enabled a more precise and potent form of personalization. Predictive analytics, recommender systems, and behavioral tracking create digital experiences that are uniquely tailored to individual users—often reinforcing existing behaviors and biases. The more time users spend on platforms, the more data is collected, and the more compelling the digital content becomes.

This self-reinforcing cycle strengthens the addictive pull of technology while making it increasingly difficult for users to disengage or even recognize their behavioral dependencies. As AI becomes more adaptive and autonomous, the ethical and psychological implications of such hyper-personalization demand urgent attention. However, the problem of digital addiction is not solely technological—it is deeply human and psychological. It reveals vulnerabilities in our cognitive and emotional architecture: our desire for validation, our fear of missing out (FOMO), our drive for novelty, and our susceptibility to distraction. Digital platforms amplify these tendencies, often leaving users feeling emotionally depleted despite being constantly connected. Establishing routines such as screen-free times, app usage limits, and mindful engagement practices can gradually reshape the relationship with digital tools. Encouragingly, the growing popularity of digital detoxes, mindfulness apps, and digital wellbeing tools suggests a rising public consciousness about the need for healthier digital lives. Still, without sustained behavioral change and systemic support, such efforts may have only temporary impact. Educational institutions have a critical role to play in this transformation. By integrating digital hygiene and emotional intelligence curricula into early education, schools can empower young people to navigate the digital world responsibly. Teaching students how to manage screen time, critically evaluate digital content, resist algorithmic manipulation, and prioritize offline experiences fosters resilience and autonomy. In the workplace, employers can help prevent burnout and digital fatigue by encouraging balanced communication norms, respecting boundaries, and modeling responsible digital behavior. Meanwhile, the responsibility of technology companies and developers cannot be overstated. Ethical design must replace manipulative engagement tactics. Platform designers must prioritize user well-being over ad revenue and engagement metrics. Features such as screen time dashboards, usage alerts, customizable content controls, and AI transparency can help shift the balance of power back to the user. Regulatory frameworks should ensure that companies are held accountable for the addictive potential of their platforms, particularly when children and adolescents are involved. Governments and policy-makers can further promote digital health by funding research, supporting public awareness campaigns, and establishing digital rights frameworks that protect users from exploitative design. Furthermore, mental health services must evolve to address the growing prevalence of digital addiction. Therapists, counselors, and psychologists are increasingly encountering clients whose anxiety, depression, or relationship issues are intertwined with unhealthy digital behaviors. Offering specialized interventions, including cognitive-behavioral therapy for digital addiction, support groups, and technology-assisted recovery programs, will be essential in providing effective care. Public health agencies must also recognize digital addiction as a legitimate health concern and incorporate it into national mental health strategies. At a cultural level, we must challenge the narrative that equates constant connectivity with progress or productivity. Instead, we should promote a more conscious, human-centered approach to technology—one that values quality over quantity, presence over performance, and relationships over reach. This involves creating cultural norms that celebrate digital boundaries, normalize disconnection, and elevate offline pursuits as equally, if not more, valuable than digital achievements.

## REFERENCES


Aïmeur, E., Amri, S., & Brassard, G. (2023). Fake news, disinformation and misinformation in social media: A review. *Social Network Analysis and Mining*, *13*(1), 30. DOI: 10.1007/s13278-023-01028-5 PMID: 36789378

Andrews, S., Ellis, D. A., Shaw, H., & Piwek, L. (2015). Beyond self-report: Tools to compare estimated and real-world smartphone use. *PLoS One*, *10*(10), e0139004. DOI: 10.1371/journal.pone.0139004 PMID: 26509895

Bakshy, E., Messing, S., & Adamic, L. A. (2015). Exposure to ideologically diverse news and opinion on Facebook. *Science*, *348*(6239), 1130–1132. DOI: 10.1126/science.aaa1160 PMID: 25953820

Bostock, S., Crosswell, A. D., Prather, A. A., & Steptoe, A. (2019). Mindfulness on-the-go: Effects of a mindfulness meditation app on work stress and well-being. *Journal of Occupational Health Psychology*, *24*(1), 127–138. DOI: 10.1037/ocp0000118 PMID: 29723001

Chowdhary, S., Selvakumar, P., Sangeetha, B., Sarvaani, V. V., Anute, N., & Sharma, M. (2025). The Role of Social Capital in Entrepreneurial Development. In Martínez-Falcó, J., Sánchez-García, E., & Marco-Lajara, B. (Eds.), *Support Networks for Entrepreneurs: Social Capital and Strategic Collaborations* (pp. 311–338). IGI Global Scientific Publishing., DOI: 10.4018/979-8-3693-9836-4.ch013

Coates, J. M., Santhanalakshmi, K., Dinesh, N., Gandhimathi, S., & Chandel, P. S. Mohit, & Selvakumar, P. (2025). Assessment and Evaluation in Transnational Staff Development. In G. Morris & J. Ye (Eds.), Training and Development in Transnational Higher Education (pp. 387–406). IGI Global Scientific Publishing. DOI: 10.4018/979-8-3373-1897-4.ch019

Dabbish, L., Mark, G., & Gonzalez, V. (2011). "Why do i keep interrupting myself? environment, habit and self-interruption," in *Proceedings of the 2011 Annual Conference on Human Factors in, Computing Systems (CHI '11)* (New York, NY: Association for Computing Machinery), 3127–3130. DOI: 10.1145/1978942.1979405

Dahmani, L., & Bohbot, V. D. (2020). Habitual use of GPS negatively impacts spatial memory during self-guided navigation. *Scientific Reports*, *10*(1), 6310. DOI: 10.1038/s41598-020-62877-0 PMID: 32286340

Eppler, M. J., & Mengis, J. (2004). The concept of information overload: A review of literature from organization science, accounting, marketing, MIS, and related disciplines. *The Information Society*, *20*(5), 325–344. DOI: 10.1080/01972240490507974

Ferrucci, D., Levas, A., Bagchi, S., Gondek, D., & Mueller, E. (2010). Watson: Beyond jeopardy! *Artificial Intelligence, 199–200*, 93–105. DOI: 10.1016/j.artint.2012.06.009

Firth, J., Torous, J., Stubbs, B., Firth, J. A., Steiner, G. Z., Smith, L., Alvarez-Jimenez, M., Gleeson, J., Vancampfort, D., Armitage, C. J., & Sarris, J. (2019). The "online brain": How the Internet may be changing our cognition. *World Psychiatry; Official Journal of the World Psychiatric Association (WPA), 18*(2), 119–129. DOI: 10.1002/wps.20617 PMID: 31059635

Graesser, A. C., Hu, X., & Sottilare, R. A. (2018). In Fischer, F., Hmelo-Silver, C. E., Goldman, S. R., & Reimann, P. (Eds.), *"Intelligent tutoring systems," in International Handbook of the Learning Sciences* (pp. 246–255). Routledge., DOI: 10.4324/9781315617572-24

Gunning, D., Stefik, M., Choi, J., Miller, T., Stumpf, S., & Yang, G. Z. (2019). XAI—Explainable artificial intelligence. *Science Robotics, 4*(37), eaay7120. Advance online publication. DOI: 10.1126/scirobotics.aay7120 PMID: 33137719

Hamari, J., Koivisto, J., & Sarsa, H. (2014). "Does gamification work? - a literature review of empirical studies on gamification," in *Proceedings of the Annual Hawaii International Conference on System Sciences* (Waikoloa, HI: IEEE). DOI: 10.1109/HICSS.2014.377

Hill, R. L., Ford, W. R., & Farreras, I. G. (2015). Real conversations with artificial intelligence: A comparison between human–human online conversations and human–chatbot conversations. *Computers in Human Behavior, 49*, 245–250. DOI: 10.1016/j.chb.2015.02.026

Iqbal, S. T., & Horvitz, E. (2007). "Disruption and recovery of computing tasks: field study, analysis, and directions," in Proceedings of the SIGCHI Conference on Human Factors in Computing Systems (New YorK, NY: acm), 677–686. DOI: 10.1145/1240624.1240730

Junco, R. (2012). Too much face and not enough books: The relationship between multiple indices of Facebook use and academic performance. *Computers in Human Behavior, 28*(1), 187–198. DOI: 10.1016/j.chb.2011.08.026

Junco, R., & Cotten, S. R. (2012). No A 4 U: The relationship between multitasking and academic performance. *Computers & Education, 59*(2), 505–514. DOI: 10.1016/j.compedu.2011.12.023

Kanai, R., Bahrami, B., Roylance, R., & Rees, G. (2012). Online social network size is reflected in human brain structure. *Proceedings. Biological Sciences*, *279*(1732), 1327–1334. DOI: 10.1098/rspb.2011.1959 PMID: 22012980

Kashdan, T. B., Rose, P., & Fincham, F. D. (2004). Curiosity and exploration: Facilitating positive subjective experiences and personal growth opportunities. *Journal of Personality Assessment*, *82*(3), 291–305. DOI: 10.1207/s15327752jpa8203_05 PMID: 15151805

Li, Y., Liu, J., & Ren, J. (2019). Social recommendation model based on user interaction in complex social networks. *PLoS One*, *14*(7), e0218957. DOI: 10.1371/journal.pone.0218957 PMID: 31291288

Lin, L. Y., Sidani, J. E., Shensa, A., Radovic, A., Miller, E., Colditz, J. B., Hoffman, B. L., Giles, L. M., & Primack, B. A. (2016). Association between social media use and depression among US young adults. *Depression and Anxiety*, *33*(4), 323–331. DOI: 10.1002/da.22466 PMID: 26783723

Machete, P., & Turpin, M. (2020). "The use of critical thinking to identify fake news: A systematic literature review," in Responsible Design. *Lecture Notes in Computer Science*, *12067*, 235–246. DOI: 10.1007/978-3-030-45002-1_20

Maheswaran, K., Selvakumar, P., Shaikh, M., Shashank, G., Gupta, S., & Manjunath, T. C. (2025). The Evolution of Smart Urban Mobility With Emerging Technologies. In Ponnusamy, S., Assaf, M., Youssef, B., Jeon, G., & Kalyanaraman, S. (Eds.), *Leveraging VANETs and Blockchain Technology for Urban Mobility* (pp. 1–28). IGI Global Scientific Publishing., DOI: 10.4018/979-8-3373-0265-2.ch001

Nikkelen, S. W., Valkenburg, P. M., Huizinga, M., & Bushman, B. J. (2014). Media use and ADHD-related behaviors in children and adolescents: A meta-analysis. *Developmental Psychology*, *50*(9), 2228–2241. DOI: 10.1037/a0037318 PMID: 24999762

Nisha Angeline, M., Selvakumar, P., Gupta, M. K., Nazar, N., Elumalai, D., & Bhattacharya, S. (2025). Emerging Materials for Energy Storage and Environmental Applications. In K. Muduli, B. Moharana, S. Ales, & D. Biswal (Eds.), Using Computational Intelligence for Sustainable Manufacturing of Advanced Materials (pp. 53–72). IGI Global Scientific Publishing. DOI: 10.4018/979-8-3693-7974-5.ch003

Odgers, C. L., Jensen, M. R., & Choukas-Bradley, S. (2019). Annual research review: adolescent mental health in the digital age: facts, fears, and future directions. *Journal of Child Psychology and Psychiatry, and Allied Disciplines*, *60*, 254–273. DOI: 10.1111/jcpp.13190 PMID: 31951670

Paulus, M. P., Squeglia, L. M., Bagot, K., Jacobus, J., Kuplicki, R., Breslin, F. J., Bodurka, J., Morris, A. S., Thompson, W. K., Bartsch, H., & Tapert, S. F. (2019). Screen media activity and brain structure in youth: Evidence for diverse structural correlation networks from the ABCD study. *NeuroImage*, *185*, 140–153. DOI: 10.1016/j.neuroimage.2018.10.040 PMID: 30339913

Perloff, R. M. (2014). Social media effects on young women's body image concerns: Theoretical perspectives and an agenda for research. *Sex Roles*, *71*(11-12), 363–377. DOI: 10.1007/s11199-014-0384-6

Radesky, J. S., Schumacher, J., & Zuckerman, B. (2014). Mobile and interactive media use by young children: The good, the bad, and the unknown. *Pediatrics*, *135*(1), 1–3. DOI: 10.1542/peds.2014-2251 PMID: 25548323

Rosen, L. D., Lim, A. F., Carrier, L. M., & Cheever, N. A. (2011). An empirical examination of the educational impact of text message-induced task switching in the classroom: Educational implications and strategies to enhance learning. *Psicol. Educ.*, *17*, 163–177. DOI: 10.5093/ed2011v17n2a4

Sakthivel, M., Jaganathan, A., Mohanraj, M., & Selvakumar, P. Mohit, & Manjunath, T. (2025). Brand Loyalty through AI and Personalisation AI-Generated Content for Financial Marketing. In A. J. Nair, S. Manohar, Y. B. Limbu, & B. A. Huhmann (Eds.), Intersecting Natural Language Processing and FinTech Innovations in Service Marketing (pp. 77–96). IGI Global Scientific Publishing. DOI: 10.4018/979-8-3693-9944-6.ch006

Sethumadhavan, R. P. P., S., Selvakumar, P., Kadu, S. G., Chandel, P. S., & Gupta, S. (2025). Environmental Sustainability and Employee Participation. In C. Şeker, E. Örücü, & A. Kaya (Eds.), Green Leadership Strategies for Increased Employee Engagement and Performance (pp. 275–298). IGI Global Scientific Publishing. DOI: 10.4018/979-8-3373-2106-6.ch009

Thirunagalingam, A., & Selvakumar, P. (2025). Application of Automation and Robotics in the Oil and Gas Industry. In Abdullayev, V., & Khang, A. (Eds.), *Revolutionizing AI and Robotics in the Oil and Gas Industry* (pp. 229–244). IGI Global Scientific Publishing., DOI: 10.4018/979-8-3693-8156-4.ch011

Upadhyaya, A. N., Debnath, P., Rani, P., Selvakumar, P., Manjunath, T. C., & Bhattacharya, S. (2025). AI-Based Disaster Prediction and Early Warning Systems. In Mobo, F. (Ed.), *AI and Emerging Technologies for Emergency Response and Smart Cities* (pp. 55–74). IGI Global Scientific Publishing., DOI: 10.4018/979-8-3693-9770-1.ch003

Vaidyam, A. N., Wisniewski, H., Halamka, J. D., Kashavan, M. S., & Torous, J. B. (2019). Chatbots and conversational agents in mental health: A review of the psychiatric landscape. *Canadian Journal of Psychiatry*, *64*(7), 456–464. DOI: 10.1177/0706743719828977 PMID: 30897957

Van Deursen, A., & Van Dijk, J. (2011). Internet skills performance tests: Are people ready for eHealth? *Journal of Medical Internet Research*, *13*(2), e35. DOI: 10.2196/jmir.1581 PMID: 21531690

Ward, A. F., Duke, K., Gneezy, A., & Bos, M. W. (2017). Brain drain: The mere presence of one's own smartphone reduces available cognitive capacity. *Journal of the Association for Consumer Research*, *2*(2), 140–154. DOI: 10.1086/691462

Wilmer, H. H., Sherman, L. E., & Chein, J. M. (2017). Smartphones and cognition: A review of research exploring the links between mobile technology habits and cognitive functioning. *Frontiers in Psychology*, *8*, 605. DOI: 10.3389/fpsyg.2017.00605 PMID: 28487665

Yuan, K., Qin, W., Wang, G., Zeng, F., Zhao, L., Yang, X., Liu, P., Liu, J., Sun, J., von Deneen, K. M., Gong, Q., Liu, Y., & Tian, J. (2011). Microstructure abnormalities in adolescents with internet addiction disorder. *PLoS One*, *6*(6), e20708. DOI: 10.1371/journal.pone.0020708 PMID: 21677775

Zawacki-Richter, O., Marín, V. I., Bond, M., & Gouverneur, F. (2019). Systematic review of research on artificial intelligence applications in higher education – where are the educators? *International Journal of Educational Technology in Higher Education*, *16*(1), 39. DOI: 10.1186/s41239-019-0171-0

Zhou, Y., Lin, F. C., Du, Y. S., Qin, L. D., Zhao, Z. M., Xu, J. R., & Lei, H. (2011). Gray matter abnormalities in Internet addiction: A voxel-based morphometry study. *European Journal of Radiology*, *79*(1), 92–95. DOI: 10.1016/j.ejrad.2009.10.025 PMID: 19926237

Ziegler, D. A., Anguera, J. A., Gallen, C. L., Hsu, W.-Y., Wais, P. E., & Gazzaley, A. (2022). Leveraging technology to personalize cognitive enhancement methods in aging. *Nature Aging*, *2*(6), 475–483. DOI: 10.1038/s43587-022-00237-5 PMID: 35873177

# Chapter 5
# Scroll, Swipe, Repeat: Understanding Digital Dependency in the Age of AI

**Jashanpreet Kaur Sarao**
https://orcid.org/0009-0003-9920-3990
*Department of Commerce, School of Management Studies, Chandigarh Group of Colleges Jhanjeri, Mohali, India*

## ABSTRACT

*The introduction of artificial intelligence (AI) into the digital space has transformed the whole process of human communication but has made the development of digital addiction and technology addiction more rapid. This chapter looks into the role of AI-augmented design functions i.e. infinite scroll, algorithmic nudging, and dopamine-based feedback loop, in the development of compulsive digital behaviors. It also discusses critically the cognitive, emotional, and social effects of digital addiction caused by AI. The chapter focuses on the responsibility dilemma of tech platforms and the place of regulatory frameworks and acts through the prism of persuasive technology ethics, attention economics, and the role of public policy in reducing digital harm. It also observes counter-movements in digital well-being. By highlighting the contradiction that AI is at the same time a cause and possible solution to digital dependence, the chapter reminds of a future where the design of technology materializes the psychological health, freedom of action, and autonomy of its users.*

## INTRODUCTION: AI AND THE DIGITAL DRIFT

Artificial intelligence (AI) has pervaded the 21st century. Behind that carefully curated Instagram feed, the predicted text in communication apps, and even our

DOI: 10.4018/979-8-3373-5606-8.ch005

emotions, AI is influencing content and behavior. Its non-verbal power, so-called convenience or individualization, has led to the formation of new behavioral patterns - most of which lie on the edge of compulsive and addictive behavior (Elliott, 2019; Dandotiya et al., 2024). With the increasing use of AI algorithms in digital sites to maximize these practices, as they constantly produce the personality on the screen that the user interacts with and is engaged in, we begin to be held in a loop of scrolling, swiping, and tapping in infinite participation till we cannot stop the loop.

The term digital drift reflects this minute, frequently unconscious displacement of human attention onto screens hinted at by algorithms that seek to hold it. Digital technologies have never lacked the potential to be engaging, but it is only the recent collaboration of AI and behavioral psychology that resulted in the fact that digital interfaces have become more persuasion devices (Chianella, 2021). AI does not just react to the inclinations of the users, but it predicts and influences them, exploiting the neurocognitive vulnerabilities that render disengagement harder and harder (Macit et al., 2018; Madary, 2022). Depending on the computer screen is no longer an individual issue but it is a social issue. Constant availability of smart devices, social networks, and the use of recommendation engines has triggered compulsive tendencies in people especially those who have grown up in the era of hyper-connectedness, also known as digital natives. The fact is, screen time is hard to moderate, not only because of a lack of self-control but because of the manipulative designs of such tools, which make moderation both a physical and a cognitive challenge among children, adolescents, and even adults (Dresp-Langley & Hutt, 2022; Cerniglia et al., 2017). This growth in the digital dependency driven by AI is not accidental it has been created by a business model that is successful in getting the maximum engagement out of the user and gathering user behavioral data. Digital platforms (such as TikTok, YouTube, and Instagram) cannot be reduced to digital toys, used to entertain or interact with each other; they are algorithmic spaces where attention is maximized, through predictive analytics, reinforcement learning, and real-time feedback, to ensure that people continually consume them. Such mechanisms are not impartial. They are constructed using profound understandings of psychology that prey on our novelty-seeking behaviors, social comparison, and reward anticipation, qualities that are comprised of evolutionary advantages, but unfortunately, are exposed to manufactured desire.

The implications of this change go beyond personal conduct. On a social scale, the subconsciousness of the incredible usage of digital products has redesigned the pace of everyday life. Stillness is becoming a more and more fading experience due to the constant flow of notifications, pings, and recommendations by the algorithm. The ability to focus attention, which is one of the essential resources in learning, reflection, and connecting with others, has become broken, as they are constantly disrupted by the machines that advertise as productivity and connectivity sources

(Markoci, 2024). It is not in the interest of these sites to fulfill our wants and needs that result in the most successful sites, but which ones can best bait our attention. In addition, the role of AI in controlling digital behavior creates a gray zone between free will and algorithmic determinism. Curating content around what we might care to consume (rather than what we might value) brings serious ethical questions of agency, autonomy, and consent into play. Are we selecting what we see, what we read, and what we believe or are we just passive actors to the suggestions of a shadow algorithm that has been trained in our previous actions? The perception of choice becomes a strong force because it hides a darker sense of the same, which is the power of algorithms (Madary, 2022; Ghori et al., 2025).

Among the younger generation (particularly) the effect is even stronger. They have demonstrated that adolescents and children are especially vulnerable to the digital manipulation effects because innate executive functions, emotional regulation, and the maturation processes of identity formation processes are not yet fully developed (Ding et al., 2023; Evci, 2022). Not only does constant algorithmic curation of content mixed with idealized images and addictive interface elements take their toll on their mental well-being it also influences their self-image, social interactions, and cognitive growth. In this, digital dependency is not only a design result but also a developmental risk. Irrespective of these difficulties, it should be acknowledged that digital technology and, especially, AI cannot be described as something bad automatically. It has made easier access to knowledge that has never been seen before, democratized content creation, and provided global communication. It is not a fact that AI exists, the problem is in the way it is applied, to whom and what motivation is. In the world of profit-driven business, where attention has become money, human experience is too easily measured in terms of 'engagement'.

This chapter explores some of the intricate relationships between AI and human behavior as well as digital dependency. It starts by discussing the ways through which digital addiction is framed and distinguished from general internet overuse. It subsequently breaks down the particular functions, which include never-ending scroll, autoplay, and algorithmic prompting through which AI systems maintain the audiences addicted. The chapter continues with economic reasoning of such designs regarding the attention economy and methods of monetization. We also consider the psychological and social consequences of the dependency caused by AI and how it impacts mental health, interpersonal relations, and oneself. Developments of digital detoxing and minimalistic technology usage as well as the paradoxical nature of AI as both the factor that led to this dependency and possible solution to it is discussed. Lastly, the chapter discusses ethical aspects and policy reactions, in which they want a universal reconsideration of the manner in which digital technologies are constructed, and controlled.

Being concerned with these dimensions, however, this chapter is not written in a critical or even alarmist tone. Rather, it tries to develop critical awareness and informed participation, since AI is a two-fold technology, empowering and exploiting at the same time. The final objective is not the rejection of technology, but the recovery of human agency in it, in other words, comprehending the powers behind the screens and creating digital ecosystems where well-being, sense of dignity, and autonomy are valued more than metrics of engagement. We are the gold, and our attention is the commodity in a trillion-dollar business, in the era of AI. We have to first consider ways through which we are packaging, capturing, and selling so that we can come up with measures to guard it. The book will start that journey in this chapter by ripping open the curtain on the hidden software programs that are ever more taking control of our lives and by pointing toward a way of being in the digital world that is more humanly-scale and specific.

## UNDERSTANDING DIGITAL ADDICTION: A MODERN DISORDER

Digital addiction is becoming a new behavioral disorder that is seen as quite different from overusing technology in general. Although the phenomenon is a controversial one in the perception of clinicians and scholars, its psychosocial, neurological, and behavioral implications cannot be disputed. Digital technologies are becoming progressively immersive and intelligent (in large part due to AI) to create conditions in which compulsive engagement is not only achievable but also developed.

### Behavioral vs. Clinical Definitions of Digital Addiction

The wide definition of digital addiction is defined as the inordinate, overuse of digital technologies, especially the internet, social media, and smartphones, creating harmful interference with everyday life, mental health, and social performance (Almourad et al., 2020). Although it is not officially registered as an independent disorder in diagnostic manuals such as DSM-5, some forms of it have been considered tentative and include such realizations as the Internet Gaming Disorder. Medical taxonomy is not based on a consensus, however, the tendency of an increasing number of studies that report its behavioral and neurological effects cannot be ignored. Digital addiction is behaviorally expressed through the following symptoms: the inability to control the use of a device, an unwillingness to fulfill personal and professional duties, the occurrence of withdrawal symptoms when a gadget is disconnected, and the inability to limit the use of a screen (Evci, 2022; Kamenskaya &

Tomanov, 2022). Medically, it is commonly interrelated with such co-morbidities as depression, anxiety, and ADHD, especially among adolescents and young adults (Yen et al., 2014; Goel & Singla, 2025). The difference between digital addiction and other behavioral addictions is that it is everywhere and is even condoned. In contrast to gambling or substance abuse, most of which is mainly experienced in isolated environments, digital interactions have deep penetration into various planes of life, including work, education, leisure, and relationships, thus making addiction difficult to determine and deal with (Hartford & Stein, 2022).

## The Role of AI in Transforming Habits into Compulsions

Although the field of digital addiction has been around even prior to the widespread use of AI, with the arrival of intelligent systems, the level of user compulsivity has risen to unprecedented levels. AI adapts content to individual behavior by analyzing real-time behavioral data to cement particular usage habits through recommendation systems, predictive analytics, and gamified feedback loops (Chiam et al., 2024; Madary, 2022). The systems are also learning and adapting to a user preference, creeping into habits by making them compulsions. One of the primary processes by that AI enhances addiction is referred to as algorithmic reinforcement; it involves the creation of actions by users through micro-rewards, such as likes, notifications, and personalized content. It is similar to classical conditioning, as users release dopamine, the chemical in the brain that makes people feel pleasurable, whenever experiencing perceived rewards, the reason they want to go back and do it again (Macit et al., 2018). AI optimizes this loop by feeding stimuli in unpredictable time sequencing so as to keep the emphasis high, in a sense comparable to that of slot machines. This feedback of stimulus and reward is a closed circuit, which fuzzes the line between voluntary and compulsive use. According to Madary (2022), users of the AI systems commonly fall into the illusion of agency the so-called trap when users think that they are in control and are manipulated towards some actions to which they give no specific intention. The feeling of freedom is lost and what once started as habitual use turns into addictive behavior (Ghori et al., 2025).

## Vulnerable Groups: Children, Youth, and Digital Natives

Some groups are rather prone to digital dependence, especially children, adolescents, and so-called digital natives. In addition to being more exposed to technology, those groups also have their developing cognitive and emotional systems, thus becoming more susceptible to persuasive design and social comparison processes (Cerniglia et al., 2017; Ding et al., 2023). According to neuroscientific research, long-term digital exposure is also influencing the brain structure and lives

**mo**stly in the parts that control impulses, attention, and emotional regulation (Ding & Li, 2023). The presence of screen addiction in adolescents is accompanied by reduced grey matter in the prefrontal parts of the brain and the diminished activity of the executive function's networks, which are two neurocognitive indicators of self-regulation inefficiencies and behavioral compulsivity.

These effects are further magnified by social media, and its creation of the conditions of high peer validation, FOMO (fear of missing out), and curated self-image, which continues to keep youth locked in the emotionally charged patterns of consumption (Reer et al., 2019; Burnell et al., 2019). The two features **of** AI-based personalization and teenage social anxiety have a closed loop and are hard to escape (Parveiz et al., 2023). Moreover, the new phenomenon of **Pa**rasocial relationships includes chatbots and AI avatars in relations between young people, where they emotionally connect to something that is not human (BUNIM, 2024; Luttrell & Welch, 2024). Although it appears harmless, these attachments can replace or interfere with actual social life, which will lead to the feeling of estrangement and being dependent upon the attachment.

### Toward a Nuanced Understanding

The notion that digital addiction is not a black-and-white condition, but a continuum, allows us to consider this issue more thoroughly. Excessive uses are not always bad and context matters. As an example, a researcher, who spends 10 hours a day at screens, might not be addicted, but a teenager, who constantly checks social media every few minutes, might be in danger. Such intricacy requires more complex evaluation scales about frequency and intent, emotional reaction, and life consequences (Koronczai et al., 2013). Further, the combination of AI and digital addiction is a reminder of the necessity to go beyond having personal responsibility. Although personal responsibility is a factor, the construction of artificial intelligence mechanisms should also be perceived critically. On the one hand, as long as addiction has been understood as a virtual inevitability of systematic control, the attention may be redirected to ethical technology development and social policy curation.

## DESIGNING ADDICTION: THE MECHANICS BEHIND THE SCREEN

Addiction in the digital world does not come by chance. It is highly likely to be an output of carefully crafted design functionality built into apps and platforms using a design that takes advantage of AI to analyze, forecast, and manipulate consumer behavior. These mechanics work below the user interface, bringing inactive users to play an active role in a behavior loop that has been created to maximize time on screen. Infinite scroll, autoplay, nudging algorithms, and neural pathways-tapping dopamine loops are at the center of these strategies, and the central idea to make it all stick is by spurring the neurological pathways by increasing the evenly-dopamine release (Chianella, 2021; Hsu, 2017).

## Infinite Scroll, Auto play, and Notification Systems

One of the most ubiquitous instruments used in the designing of digital addiction is the infinite scroll. Its introduction is meant to remove friction in the consumption of content, making it possible to access as much content as desired without making a semantic decision about whether to move or not, to skip this mental process and encourage impulsive behavior. As opposed to discrete ones, infinite scroll conveys an impression of luxury and necessity that tends to make users spend much more time on apps than they wish.

There is another instrument of gradual loss of user agency, i.e., autoplay. Autoplay originally served as a convenient option today and acts as a retention feature on sites such as YouTube and TikTok. They also merely switch to the next video automatically, almost denying the user the possibility to leave the interface, strengthening uninterrupted passive involvement (Ghori et al., 2025). In long-term, such a trend propagates its consumption circles that are hard to overcome, particularly by young users who are less capable of controlling their impulses.

Notification system is probably the most powerful instrument in the arsenal of persuasive design. AI not only describes when and what kind of notification to make but also predicts the moment of the day when the user is responded most of the time. Such notifications act as behavioral triggers, causing obsessive-compulsive behavior of checking and dependencies on the display (Marković et al., 2024). Although it may seem harmless, these interruptions take part in split attention, digital distress, and never being fully engaged.

## Algorithmic Nudging and Reinforcement Learning

Behind every scroll and swipe there lies an AI-driven algorithm that has undergone a form of reinforcement learning to enhance user engagement. The optimization criteria of these algorithms are on one central metric: attention. The greater the participation by a user, the more the system learns about the user resulting in a feedback loop where the content is more challenging to leave (Chiam et al., 2024). Another high-level approach is algorithmic nudging, or the process of the system offering users gentle suggestions to do certain actions with the help of predictive data on behavior. As an example, AI can be designed to deliver emotionally arousing information at a specific time of the day to raise the chance of occurring interaction. On social media, the same nudging is taken to a new level in health and wellness apps, where nudging is now given to more enjoyable, controversial, or extraordinary content to feed the user (Tourkochoriti, 2023).

However, with time, users are conditioned to react to these cues without much deliberation. This forms an impression of free will as decisions are passed through the filter of latent goals of the platform (Madary 2022). The result can all be boiled down to, in effect, users becoming participants in a behavioral experiment, in real-time, with AI changing, the interface, and the flow of content with every moment of feedback.

## Dopamine Loops and Neurobiological Hooks

Digital spaces are developed in such a way that they induce the effect of releasing dopamine pleasure and reward neurotransmitters. Positive notifications, likes, shares, and emojis are regarded as micro-rewards that reinforce behavior (Macit et al., 2018). Such dopamine-induced cycles are comparable in their structure to gambling addiction, in which the unpredictability of rewards, such as viral posts or unexpected content, produces the greatest brain activity. Notably, one can make these loops more personalized as the AI can adapt to the behavior of the users. The system will get more data available, the more likely it will show the stimuli that would better suit the psychological profile of the user, which in turn will make him/her more likely to engage with it again (Kant, 2020).

In neurobiological terms, these stimuli when repeated are capable of rewiring the reward system in the brain. Several studies have documented that compulsive digital use has consequences on the executive functions in the brain, especially among adolescents, causing a shorter attention span, low impulse control, and hypersensitive reactivity (Ding et al., 2023; Cerniglia et al., 2017). Physiology changes a person in such a way that it is harder to stop using technology and get addicted to the process, as well.

## More-than-Human Design and Persuasive Architecture

The more-than-human design can be discussed as the systems where AI, user behaviors, and response to the environment become sequenced to contrive hyper-personalized experiences (Chianella, 2021). Surely these designs do not just address the needs of the users, they define them. Platforms become more emotionally entrapped by consistently trying (A/B testing, behavioral modeling, etc.) to create an interface that can support a higher level of emotional investment, even at the disadvantage of user well-being.

An example of such persuasive architecture is called dark patterns. Such are misleading design strategies like pre-checked boxes, or the presence of hidden opt-outs alongside nudges concerning interface decisions that subconsciously encourage users to develop compulsive behaviors (Ye, 2025). AI also takes center stage in determining the best patterns, on the best demographic, thus making it very possible to do extreme levels of manipulation. Additionally, some of these mechanisms are dynamic in that, they keep changing in real time. As an example, in case a user demonstrates disengagement, the platform may amplify stimuli attempts to capture attention again, such as pushing trending items, providing incentives, or introducing novelty. Such hyper-responsiveness turns digital environments not only interesting but sticky and obnoxious.

### The Normalization of Addictive Design

The normalization of AI-driven design is one of the most disturbing things. What some time ago was deemed to be an act of manipulation is now viewed as common practice in the tech world. Such experiences as streaks (Snapchat), likes (Instagram, Facebook), and endless loops (TikTok, Reels) are becoming the most significant part of the user experience, although it is becoming clear that they are strictly damaging to our psychological health (Burnell et al., 2019; Reer et al., 2019). Especially young users perceive these designs as not artificial but rather parts of the natural digital life. This has led to the following behaviors becoming the norm: checking notifications when conversing, dooms rolling just before sleep, and being anxious without their cell phone. This normalization only complicates the investigation of the ethical side of such design decisions (Lam & Harcourt, 2024). Essentially, AI ceased being a backend device in the sense that it now controls human attention and emotion as its direct architect. Its capacity to learn, adapt, and manipulate makes it rather effective in developing digital behavior, sometimes doing so dimensionally the way beyond proposing conscious thought.

## THE BUSINESS OF ATTENTION: HOW AI PROFITS FROM ENGAGEMENT

In the online economy, the mind is money. Each second a viewer pays, staring at a screen can be converted into a set of data, power, and above all revenue. Connecting or informing people is not the only thing that tech companies are building on their platforms, but rather a system to acquire, hold, and monetize human attention. The given economic model, which is frequently called the attention economy, has become the basis of modern digital capitalism, and AI plays the leading role in terms of its functioning (Marković et al., 2024; Kant, 2020).

## Attention Economy and Surveillance Capitalism

The attention economy can be defined as a business model where corporate entities make a profit by attracting users' attention and transforming them into advertising revenue or behavioral data. The appearance of free products on platforms such as Facebook, YouTube, and TikTok is possible at the expense of its consumers, in time and other personal data. Then the algorithms are trained on this data and are used to keep users more engaged, usually by promoting content that is emotionally or sensationally charged (Flaxman et al., 2016; Ross Arguedas et al., 2022). Very closely connected to the attention economy is surveillance capitalism, a concept created by Shoshana Zuboff, which means the trade of personal experience through extraction of data. The AI algorithms perform the role of a surveillance tool, gathering huge amounts of behavioral data: what a user clicks on, how long they watch, when they scroll, and so on; they use all of that information to create psychological profiles. These profiles become the lead to further predicting and influencing future behavior which more often than not is to the advantage of advertisers (Trier et al., 2023). The effect is a game in which human desires, weaknesses, **and** tendencies are exploited to make a profit. The users do not only consume, but they are also the raw material being purified and marketed.

## Personalization vs. Manipulation

Personalization is promoted as the feature that contributes to improved user experience by displaying relevant content. This process, however, can become manipulative in no time. The smartest AI systems are conditioned not to act in the best interest of the users but to maximize user engagement. It results in filter bubbles when people are exposed to content that affirms their preconceived notions, and echo chambers when the countering opinion is suppressed algorithmically (Flaxman et al., 2016; Ross Arguedas et al., 2022). It is in the area of emotional manipulation in which algorithms cross the line separating personalization and manipulation. To give a simple example, when a user feels anxious or lonely, he or she can be presented with more emotionally charged or socially validating content, which further compounds his or her dependence on his or her platform (Parveiz et al., 2023). Eventually, **these** super-focused contents contribute to addictive tendencies, particularly in young people and susceptible personalities. In addition, autonomy can be veiled by personalization. When AI takes control of selecting what a user sees and does, be it entertainment, news, or social interaction, the resulting feeling of freedom is non-existent. As Ghori et al. (2025) claim, the abuse of the feeling of control is usually the case where users are led to believe there is a choice in the scenario where a majority of the activities performed are predetermined based on the outcome that is to result in a monetary gain.

## Case Examples: TikTok, Instagram, and YouTube

On further review of the most popular digital platforms, namely, TikTok, Instagram, and YouTube, one will realize that their AI-powered infrastructures are carefully designed to attract the highest level of attention, extend the time spent on platforms, and gather as much behavioral data as possible. Such platforms do not simply appeal to the existing user preferences, but also actively drive them to create the environment that supports compulsive use and turns attention into a very valuable commodity.

### TikTok

It is not only what is offered by TikTok that made it a global phenomenon but also the way it presents it to its audience through its AI system. The epicenter of all this is the so-called For You page, which is an essentially unlimited, very carefully curated feed of short-form video representations, running through highly sophisticated machine learning algorithms. Essentially, TikTok uses all micro-interactions, such as spending time on a particular video, likes, shares, scrolling speed, and replaying, to create a psychological portrait that evolves on a real-time basis (Chianella, 2021). This maximization has been happening continuously resulting in a cycle of maximum immersive and personalized content loop, which has become harder to break away with. The boundaries do not exist as in the traditional media. The shortness of the videos and the reward of immediate gratification they provide activate the reward systems in the brain especially the dopaminergic system making one tend to use it repeatedly. This combination has garnered the app the nickname of being addictive or time-warping to many of its users, whose usage sessions last much longer than they anticipate. TikTok also fosters a feeling of societal involvement and relevance, which urges customers to create their material themselves, which again puts food into the engagement loop.

### Instagram

Instagram initially was a mere photo-sharing application, but it has evolved into a complicated AI-based interaction ecosystem. It no longer displays its posts and feeds chronologically, but it focuses on showing the user content that is likely to stimulate and sustain their attention. The Explore page and the Reels, the alternative to Tik Tok offered by Instagram, have an unlimited flow of suggested material based on deduced interests and emotional responses. Instagram has an AI-driven social comparison engine, which further increases attention to high-engagement posts, which can focus on lifestyle aesthetics, content of beauty ideals, and consumer trends. Likes, comments, the number of followers, and the number of people seeing stories all become metrics of validation in the social world, what some have described as social currency, and motivate users to post more and check obsessively how people will respond to the posts. In particular, push notifications, especially when they are activated by inactivity, are well calculated to renew user interest. Further, the incorporation of e-commerce characteristics, such as shoppable posts and targeted advertising, makes it harder to distinguish social interaction and consumption and monetizes the attention of users on both the emotional and behavioral scale. The Instagram environment therefore leads to a two-sided addiction of content consumption and also social validation. This usually leads to the rise of anxiety, FOMO (fear of missing out), and self-esteem, more so for the younger groups of people who are still defining their identities and self-esteem through online dealings.

## YouTube

The YouTube recommendation engine is one of the most sophisticated (or, genre-depending, one of the most ethically questionable) AI systems on the net. It is the primary function to maintain the attention of the users, as it is reported that more than 70 percent of views on the portal were initiated by the Algorithm-recommended videos (Ghori et al., 2025). The system is biased towards watch time in which it is always in the recommendation of the content which will keep the viewer as far as it is possible on the system. This usually leads to the demise of users into what can be described as algorithmic rabbit holes, where they get consecutively more sensationalistic, polarizing, or emotionally volatile than the video algorithms presented them before. Although this improves ad revenue through spending more time on a session, it has also been associated with misinformation, radicalization, and even more psychological stress. One can consume content passively through the auto-play feature, intended to keep watching the next video without the user needing to make any decisions or add more friction to the process. Besides, YouTube uses it humongous content collection and user log to provide users with personalized recommendations that can be eerily precise to the point of what users may want even before they realize they want it. This institutes a feedback loop since engagement will result in data that will enhance the AI predictive ability, forming an escalating cycle of even more engaging recommendations that promote dependency on the digital world and discourage self-control.

In conjunction, Tik Tok, Instagram, and YouTube represent a more general state of digital media: the weaponization of AI to take and trade attention. Such platforms are not only a mirror of our likes, but also distort, create, and reinforce it in real-time. The further a user gets into this captivity of personalization, the more information he or she is leaving behind. Such information is, in turn, used to refine the platform manipulation strategies, pulling more people into the addiction cycle, purposefully designed to work as follows: the longer the person continues to use the platform, the more information they can provide, the more money the platform can earn, and the more reasons to effectively keep that person glued to their devices constantly. In this context, digital addiction acquires not the status of the side effect, but the fundamental characteristic of contemporary platform design.

### The Value of Engagement in Financial Terms

In terms of business, each additional minute of user activity will result in high ad revenue. These structures sell not only the space of the ad but also targeting abilities, which are provided due to behavioral analytics with the help of AI. As per industry calculations, Meta and Google make more than 90 percent of their revenues out of ad-based revenue systems where the commodity (on which they make revenues) is user attention. Conflicts of interest exist in this form of monetization. Features that enhance user well-being e.g. time limits, content diversity, or transparency in ads tend to be reviewed downward priority as they cut down on engagement. The time spent on a given platform enhances viewing attention, and thus users prove to be beneficial to the advertisers (Wahed & Wahed, 2025). This attention commodification, as Lam and Harcourt (2024) claim, is bringing about ethical dilemmas in organizations due to the inclusion of user harm as a financial reward trade-off. Design teams are sometimes rewarded against making healthy digital environments, but rather to generate the most users and the most performances with ads.

## PSYCHOLOGICAL AND SOCIAL IMPACTS OF AI-INDUCED DEPENDENCY

The consequences of digital dependency are not just based on time consumption in front of computer screens and involvement in social media: they are psychological and social. AI-based systems have become tools to induce changes in the context of human cognition, emotional stability, self-perception, and human interactions as they are, more and more actively, put into use to guide, persuade, and retain user behavior. The harmless initial dependency on technology may develop into devastating conditions concerning both personal well-being and mass social performance.

## Reduced Attention Span and Multitasking Fatigue

Among the first cognitive effects of AI-driven digital addiction, one can speak of a significant decline in attention span. Vehicles such as Instagram, TikTok, and YouTube Shorts are faster and higher stimulation content delivery oriented. What AI algorithms made popular is brevity, emotional intensity, and novelty, all studied as component elements that play to the brain reward system, but that are damaging to long-term concentration (Molteni, 2022). Continued exposure to these kinds of stimuli creates a precondition to frequent novelty-seeking and thus the user finds it hard to consume long-term material or activity that demands continued concentration. Such a digital ADHD impact is particularly high on younger users, who, in many cases, complain that they struggle to concentrate on schoolwork, readings, or even a conversation unless they have another form of digital stimulation (Shanmugasundaram & Tamilarasu, 2023).

Further, the multitasking myth (implemented with high-speed app switching, notifications in real-time, and AI-generated content curation) is also proving to be detrimental. Research has shown that the perceived effect of multitasking is quick switching tasks, a process that leads to the depletions of mental capacities, expands mental fatigue, and lowers levels of productivity (Lam & Harcourt, 2024). In the long-term, this trend negatively influences the executive functioning in the brain meaning memory, decision-making, and constructive control.

## Emotional Dysregulation, Anxiety, and Self-Image Distortion

Other platforms involving AI do not simply facilitate content delivery, they create reflections. The emotional in-regulation can be activated by continuous streams of curated posts, hyper-targeted adverts, and algorithmic suggestions. A user can switch back and forth between excitement, validation, envy, and insecurity in the short term, which brings emotional instability (Burnell et al., 2019). It is the social comparison that is enhanced especially in AI. Social media channels such as Instagram and Facebook do not show real life, but rather their perfect reflection, the one that is algorithmically blasted according to the engagement rates. This creates a loop of comparison on both ends of this issue where not only users but also feel obliged to present equally polished facades of their own on social media (Reer et al., 2019). There is also a psychological cost such as low self-esteem, unsatisfied experience of body, and the risk of anxiety and depression (especially at the level of adolescents and young adults) (Koronczai et al., 2013; Liitisan, 2025).

Another emotional effect that becomes even stronger because of algorithmic curation is the phenomenon of Fear of Missing Out (FOMO). This is because AI guarantees that the users get to know what is trending or what the peers are checking on and hence it leaves one with a constant feeling of being left out of these because they are not plugged in. This phobia contributes to obsessive checking, which completes the cycle of addiction (Parveiz et al., 2023; Burnell et al., 2019). In addition, feedback loops that are motivated by dopamine, likes, sharing, and comments, condition the user to pursue social approval in the form of digital data. With time, self-worth is externally attached to these prompts, which causes people to be emotionally unstable and reliant on social media to validate themselves (Macit et al., 2018; Madary, 2022).

## Para social Bonds and Erosion of Authentic Communication

AI has not only altered people on their methods of information consumption but also their way of relating to others. Among the most notable effects of the current phenomenon can be listed the appearance of Parasocial relationships that are the one-way emotional relationships with media figures, influencers, or even avatars and chatbots whose faces have been generated by an AI (BUNIM, 2024). Such attachments tend to replicate real-life intimacy while not necessarily being reciprocal, which builds the illusions of connection and ends up replacing real human interaction. This kind of relationship is especially attractive when it comes to cases of loneliness or social anxiety. Such chatbots created by AI systems will become more human-like as they pretend empathy, friendship, and cognizance, causing strong emotional dependencies (Luttrell & Welch, 2024). Although such technologies can be used therapeutically in settings where they are carefully monitored, uncontrolled use of these technologies poses questions regarding emotional isolation as well as the creation of intimacy as a commodity.

Moreover, the ongoing basis of AI-mediated communication is present and tacitly changing the style of human communication. The main problem with online communication is that most of it is driven through emojis and memes and shortened word patterns with less emotional engagement rather than a conversational context in real life. Such loss of genuine communication compromises social connections, and acts and leads to miscommunication both on a personal and professional level (Yang et al., 2024). Digital domination in groups contributes to phubbing digital interactions and being in a group can be very exhausting at times, and we have to turn that off, so it hurts the quality of relationships and the level of emotional involvement. Literature on heavy use of devices is associated with higher conflict in romantic relationships, parental child alienation, and a decline in social satisfaction (Goel & Singla, 2025; Hartford & Stein, 2022).

## Mental Health Decline in Youth and Adolescents

Children and adolescents are particularly susceptible to the psychological effects of AI-dependent dependency. Their brains are still in development, so they are more plastic, that is, more vulnerable to the neurobiological effects of excessive stimulation and algorithmic reinforcement (Ding et al., 2023; Cerniglia et al., 2017). Another area of developmental pressure that societal activities aggravate in this age group is identity formation, peer acceptance, and autonomy. There is an increasing number of studies, which associate screen overuse with anxiety, depression, and attention disorder symptoms among adolescents. As an example, the most recent research demonstrates that high digital dependency adolescents can have lower quality of sleep, impaired circadian functions, and more elevated emotional reactivity (Dresp-Langley & Hutt, 2022; Yen et al., 2014). These consequences are also worsened by the tendency of AI to customize content to the vulnerabilities of the users and reinforce mental health issues. The lives of people have been enhanced by inter-personal comparison, cyberbullying, social exclusion, and negative self-talk which multiplies due to AI recommendation engines, leading to feelings of inadequacy and isolation. In the long term, their emotional states may be chronic, which subsequently develop into more critical mental disorders that need clinical management (Liutzan, 2025; Kamenskaya and Tomanov, 2022). Unless parental, educational, or clinical support is attained within a sufficient time, young users can be left in a system of dependency affecting both their academic work and their real-life relationships, as well as their abilities to build emotional stability and social skills.

## Erosion of Self-Reflection and Autonomy

The destruction of self-reflection and self-control may be the most delicate-looking and at the same time the most important effect of digital dependency brought about by AI. Under the condition of perpetual reactivity in the digital world, people hardly ever have time to think or develop feelings without following outside stimuli. Rather, AI provides a continuous flow of distraction-touting silence over content, boredom over novelty, and a lack of confidence over the approval of others (Madary, 2022). Not only does this lack of inward cognizance of self-influences emotional control but it also undermines the ability to make independent decisions. With all the activities, including what to see and what to think as well as what to feel and think, being informed by algorithmic recommendations, the process of forming personal tastes, ideologies, and principles is impaired. Such loss of autonomy may abstractly translate in the long run into existential confusion, lack of confidence as well as being unable to find **a** way in life offline. It confirms a loop of dependency in which users go back to the digital platform not only to enjoy a show or to be entertained but also to seek their identity, belonging, and purpose.

## DIGITAL WELL-BEING: RESISTANCE AND RECOVERY MOVEMENTS

Due to the heightening psychological and social effects of digital dependence via AI, people, societies, and enterprises have started reacting to the extent of trying to achieve digital well-being, i.e., healthy relationships with technology. The trend has come with its parade of digital detoxes, self-regulation mechanisms, and a wholesale change in style for lifelong end-user solutions, as well as some AI solutions to a problem its spread has contributed to. Noteworthy, the digital well-being movement changes the perception of the problem of screen addiction not only to an individual's shortcoming but a systemic problem that has to be acted upon by a group of people, whose solutions have to be ethical.

### Digital Detox and Minimalist Tech Lifestyles

The resistance to digital addiction, which is one of the most notable includes the digital detox, an optional time during which the individual does not use digital devices. Although more and more people are trying shorter modes of detox (a bit of a break on social media or a weekend without screens) more drastic changes have evolved in the manner of minimal tech life, where people voluntarily minimize the number of applications, devices, and internet relations they use (Dandotiya et al., 2024). The idea behind these movements is that it is possible to increase a clear state of mind, emotional stability, and the real world by turning off digital clutter. Digital minimalists' wart to have meaningful intentions when using technology, such as tech author Cal Newport who encourages seriously using technology by using it to drive worthy purposes, and not passive use. The change is not against technology it is more about taking back the agency of the manipulative digital world.

Digital detoxes have been backed up by research on the psychological advantages with a reduction in anxiety, better sleeping patterns, and restored attention spans with only short breaks being significant (Li an, 2025; Hartford & Stein, 2022). Nevertheless, detoxes can be cited as short-term solutions, whereas no structural changes in the design of the platforms are introduced by critics.

## Self-Regulation Tools: AI as a Double-Edged Sword

Although they are a step towards having healthier digital habits, these tools are not always effective and may be largely influenced by the willingness of the user and regularity. Users download such applications at times of crisis awareness or burnout and then disable them or just dismiss them after the situation calms down. This is especially indicative of one of the most crucial paradoxes valuing AI-powered self-regulation tools: such tools are opt-in in their design, putting physical discipline back into the hands of the user on top of an ecosystem that dooms their discipline in the first place. Therefore, they cannot be very successful in situations when users are supposed to be self-regulated in addictive systems that promote impulsivity and immediate payoffs. Moreover, not all these tools are viewed as transformative and are criticized as more cosmetic than transformative. As an example, the Screen Time feature by Apple only offers data but does not give it any context or help users define their emotional responses to the actions they perform online. On the same note, although apps such as Forest provide positive reinforcement via gamification, they fail to reach into more profound psychological motifs that lead to screen dependency like anxiety, FOMO (fear of missing out), and loops of social validation and worth (Burnell et al., 2019). That being said, AI may have a big role in being part of the solution. Newer models involve machine learning to identify compulsive behaviors, like when users might be on their phones at odd times of the day or have a surprising switch in their screens, and give them timely reminders or recommendations about taking breaks. Even more sophisticated devices are under development with the ability to recognize emotions, identify attention fatigue, and provide even biometric responses to suggest personal digital well-being interventions (Wahed & Wahed, 2025; Kim et al., 2024). When ethically designed, the tools would restore control to the users by providing intelligent human-in-the-loop services to them according to their needs, thereby shifting the idea of AI as a manipulative element towards AI as a helpful tool in achieving deliberate digital habits.

These tools will be aimed at returning agency to users in a way that will make them use consciously, as opposed to merely consuming. In displaying their patterns and providing ways to modify them, they provide an antidote to algorithmic manipulation by demonstrating the patterns (Aldbyani et al., 2025; Wahed & Wahed, 2025). However, these devices have their paradox. Most of them are made by those companies who profit from this long-term interaction. Therefore, their efficacy and purpose are critiqued at times, which are they real attempts at user wellness, or just failures to guarantee online reputations, as the regulation pressure and opinion formers are increasing? In addition, wellness tools based on AI use the same data collection mechanisms used in addictive systems. The applications of predictive analytics in driving disconnection can also be applied to ad targeting or surveillance capitalism to increase ethical questions over data privacy, consent, and corporate responsibility (Trier et al., 2023).

## Community Movements and Educational Initiatives

These are not only separate tools and detox patterns, but community-based movements are also developing to ensure the community spirit of awareness and strength. The latest addition to schools and universities is the digital wellness curriculum, educating students on the psychological impacts of screen time, and its design to be persuasive and manipulative (Goel & Singla, 2025; Stanimirovic et al., 2024). Such organizations as the Center for Humane Technology and Digital Wellness Collective promote the vision of ethical technology design and provide educators, parents, and developers with learning materials. Suh as r/digital minimalism or groups who live according to the principle of "Slow Tech" post on online forums and hold each other accountable to change their lifestyles. Such programs remove the sole emphasis on individual will and turn it into structural empowerment. They agree that industry transparency, as well as the education of the user, must be involved in a meaningful change. Rather than putting the whole fault on the individual, they instead urge the redesign of the digital environment to fit within the context of human thinking and feeling.

## AI as Both Problem and Solution

The paradox of AI is a much-debated topic associated with the debate around digital well-being: although it is at the center of digital dependency, the same AI can also become a part of the solution. Such AI-powered psychological toolkits as Woebot and Wysa are examples of CBT-driven emotional support that comes in the form of empathetic chatbots. The systems have also been conditioned to identify signs of distress and intervene; that is why they tend to have higher performance than conventional apps when it comes to user satisfaction (BUNIM, 2024; Luttrell & Welch, 2024). Equally, machine learning models are currently being actively worked out so that such models could detect symptoms of problematic use on the basis of patterns of behavior, irregularities of screen time, and indicators of emotional problems (Wahed & Wahed, 2025; Kim et al., 2024). The systems could trigger a check-in, recommend a break, or notify a caregiver to provide immediate feedback on the chance of digital burnout or addiction. Nevertheless, the twofold task of AI causes ethical controversies. Do we believe in systems that can manipulate behavior to be able to defend it? Who gets to decide what is considered healthy behavior and how these norms can be programmed into algorithms? Such questions highlight the necessity of transparent, explainable, and morally close AI in cognition used in wellness applications (Stanimirovic et al., 2024).

### Toward a Culture of Digital Mindfulness

Much more is required than a set of tools and policies to define the future of digital well-being. What is also necessary is a change of culture to one of thoughtful online being. As food has become a source of ill health and a topic of discussion, digital literacy and emotional intelligence need to become the new norms in the AI-enhanced world to succeed (Chianella, 2021; Shanmugasundaram & Tamilarasu, 2023). To be mindful in digital life means to be selective, thoughtful, and conscientious in our connection to tech. This involves developing mindfulness, both conscious consumptions, the practice of constant questioning the why and how we are using certain apps, and creating limits, such as establishing tech-free zones or periods, allowing us to develop an offline presence. Creating our own space in digital realities is also a part of it by deleting the apps that interfere with our values and health and learning how to be aware of our emotions by trying to monitor how online content changes our feelings, thinking, and acting. The idea is not to abstain from technology, but to harmony in technology, where technological instruments are made to shape enhance, and affirm human values, rather than to supplant and jettison them. Technological reorientation toward human flourishing will call for changes in systemic failures, citizen participation, and last but not least, a reconsideration of what constitutes a meaningful digital life.

## ETHICS, POLICY, AND PLATFORM RESPONSIBILITY

Ethical discussions and governmental policies have been awakened by the rise of AI-based systems that are used to develop digital dependency and its implications. With the spread and increasing sophistication of persuasive technologies into people's lives, the issues of user autonomy, consent, manipulation, and accountability are at the center stage. Design ethics and regulatory intervention have become essential and not a choice anymore when it comes to planning by developing digital environments that place human health, appropriately, above the profitability of corporations.

### Dark Patterns and Persuasive Tech Ethics

Among the most ethically problematic features of the interaction mediated with AI is the application of dark patterns the user interface patterns that are designed to deceive or manipulate the users into a course of action that they are unlikely to consciously accept to perform, like spending more time in an application, signing up to services, or providing additional personal information (Ye, 2025). They include ticked boxes, infinite scroll, deceptive countdowns, and pop-ups that are meant to enable guilt through compliance. AI turbocharges the effectiveness of dark patterns, as it changes content, prompts, and interface in real time depending on user actions. As an example, when a user shows signs of being strung upon about the need to log off, the system might not send any notifications until that time in order to re-engage them (Chianella, 2021). These are methods that go beyond trying to talk people into doing something to trying to push them, a tactic that should be particularly avoided when it is not done in a transparent manner or allows people to opt-out.

Ethical technology design puts much stress on the enhancement of user competence and transparency, as well as dignity. It urges platform owners to make transparent and truthful announcements regarding the functioning of AI systems, an provide users with substantial choices and convenient opportunities to simply refuse participation in algorithmic tracking or personalization. Ethical design, as opposed to prioritizing engagement at whatever cost, tries to avoid manipulation and aims towards higher autonomy of the user. It changes the paradigm of design to promote the well-being of the user, their mental health, and informed choices. It also advocates participatory methods that facilitate the inclusion of a variety of opinions in the design process, especially those of vulnerable or marginalized groups. Ethical AI design considers human values when it limits the process by processing human cognitive abilities, emotional hardships, and internet rights to make the environment more honest with technology serving people instead of victims. At that, the ethical design is not exclusively a pair of technical improvements but an ethical duty, which determines the goodness and equity of online existence during the era of AI. However, the ethical dilemma is also rather structural: the business models of many tech companies are based on addiction-driven usage per se. Such a contradiction between ethical designs and profit-making business leads to a digital morality crisis (Madary, 2022; Lam & Harcourt, 2024).

## Regulatory Responses: EU DSA, Kids Online Safety Act

To address this issue of concern of harm caused by the use of digital technology, governments, and global organizations are introducing new laws that will make platforms more accountable. The Digital Services Act (DSA) adopted by the European Union and the Kids Online Safety Act (KOSA) adopted in the United States are some of the most notable examples.

## The Digital Services Act (DSA)

The Digital Services Act (DSA) adopted by the EU in 2022 is one of the most ambitious attempts to regulate online platforms and imposes far-reaching obligations on the industry to promote accountability of the platforms and the safety of their users. It demands greater transparency in algorithmic recommendation mechanisms, offering users increased ways to not receive personalized content, and holds the need for greater risk assessment to recognize and mitigate systematic online harms like disinformation and addictive design. Besides, it also gives its users access to transparent data on how their information is gathered and utilized (Tourkochoriti, 2023; Church & Pehlivan, 2023). DSA also implements requirements of independent audits and mandatory reporting, which aims at targeting structural manipulation instead of prioritizing and focusing only on content moderation, and accountability of major tech corporations such as Meta, Google, and TikTok regarding the design and effects of their digital ecosystems.

## The Kids Online Safety Act (KOSA)

The Kids Online Safety Act (KOSA) in the United States performs this role of protecting minors against harmful online spaces by means of placing certain obligations on technological companies. It requires robust privacy settings to be the default option of underage children, potential prohibition of addictive interface designs, designed to children, improved transparency and parental control features. It is known that children and adolescents have yet to develop the ability to regulate their thoughts and emotions and are thus more vulnerable to persuasive design and algorithmic manipulation (Ding & Li, 2023; Evci, 2022). Making platforms rather than parents responsible for online safety, KOSA aims at restoring power balance in digital childhood. This legislation is just the beginning of a wider trend of digital responsibility around the globe since both digital protection and AI are known to be dangerous to societal health, trustworthiness, and the democracy of humankind (Rosenblat et al., 2025; Trier et al., 2023).

## Accountability: Tech Companies vs. User Responsibility

One of the major conflicts in debates on the addiction of digital can be characterized by the division of responsibility. Technological corporations are so keen on the freedom to choose, involving users to use it in light of a free choice and asking them to exercise self-restraint. As much as individual responsibility is considered, this critical has overlooked asymmetry between individual thought processes and strong, AI-based behavioral prediction systems (Madary, 2022). The users can scroll or click and are made to feel that this is a choice, yet their surroundings are created to be compulsion-deriving based on the millions of data points and are optimized through A/B testing and machine learning. It is not only unrealistic but also immoral to expect users, particularly the young population or those with neurodiversity, to overcome these designs in the absence of a structural incentive (Burnell et al., 2019; Goel & Singla, 2025).

In contrast, tech companies have the ability as well as moral responsibility to minimize the evils that accompany the AI-driven digital landscapes. This obligation can be met by a few influential accountability steps, such as the implementation of the ethics-by-design scheme where the wellness of users is emphasized in the developmental procedures, and the completion of the impact analysis of projects regarding mental health risks before the release of new functionalities. Besides, whistleblower protections, robust internal governance mechanisms to expose and mitigate ill practices as well as transparency reports that reveal the use practices, exposures and avoidance action may also help to develop trust levels and industry responsibility. According to scholars, it is high time to switch the motto: Do No Evil to Design for Good- when platforms not only do no harm but enhance well-being, literacy, and human connection (Trier et al., 2023; Hartford & Stein, 2022).

## Toward Tech Justice and Digital Rights

In addition to regulation and business ethics there is a mushrooming global movement of digital rights, the recognition that the right to access humane, safe, and empowering technology is a matter of public interest. This dynamic framework also encompasses such rights as the right to digital transparency (a user has an understanding of how algorithms operate and what data they use); the right to consent and control over personal data and the digital space; the right not to be subject to manipulative design that is based on the exploitation of psychological biases; the right to use non-addictive digital solutions that support well-being, rather than engagement (Li This school of movement repositions the users as stakeholders, not as possibly brainwashed consumers, but as entitled to both designing and governing digital technologies. Both activists and scholars advocate multistakeholder governance, consisting not just of technology companies and policymakers but also encompassing users, researchers, educators, and civil society groups. Just digital future needs the application of human values into code and regulation or business models. This means redesigning success measures, not only size and engagement, but also equity, empathy, and empowerment.

## CONCLUSION: RECLAIMING AGENCY IN AN AI-MEDIATED WORLD

At a time marked by algorithms, personalization, and tireless connectivity, no longer must we ask the question of whether AI is defining most of what we do digitally--but to what extent and with what effects. The current chapter has discussed the complex phenomenon of AI-induced digital dependency and its implications focusing on the processes facilitating addictive technologies and their cognitive and emotional impact and the implications the phenomenon relates to society on a larger scale. Convenient and required to be persuasive and personalized, artificial intelligence has created the grey atmosphere between the two words. Once a set of tools that are used to improve communication and to facilitate access to information, these complex ecosystems became a way of monetizing people, influencing their behavior, and controlling their emotions. The compulsive structures of social media, entertainment websites, and mobile apps are not coincidences; data-based designs are set intentionally to maximize engagements at any cost.

The psychological price, including decreased attention and self-esteem, fear, emotional instability, and altered mental health, is well-known now. The social effects such as Para social relationships, communication failure, and alienation are quite disturbing since in trying to be always connected, the vast majority of people feel more distanced from themselves and others. Meanwhile, there is also the emergence of opposition and resistance. Digital detoxes, minimalism culture of life, artificially intelligent wellness promotion solutions, ethical design patterns, and regulations such as the EU DSA and the U.S. Kids Online Safety Act provide models of innovation. The increasing understanding that AI is white, not neutral but carries the values, incentives, and ideologies of those who build them, has triggered a boom in new discussions about responsible innovation, tech justice, and human technology.

However, to take the agency back in the AI-mediated world, one would require more than personal determination or cosmetic fixes. It needs a system change on several fronts:

### Leaving Passivity towards Intentional Participation

People have to be enforced with digital literacy and emotional intelligence. As a remarkably important facet in the affirmative usage of technology, digital mindfulness is empowered by the awareness of when digital activity is habitual and when it is intentional. It is also about curating the internet, having boundaries, and picking platforms that fit and align themselves with values matching those rather than impulses that are engineered.

## Design for Addiction to Designing Well-being

Tech firms and other developers have to abandon exploitative interface principles and embrace ethics-by-design models. This implies creating attention-respecting, reflection-proving, and disconnection-supportive systems. Therefore, the dark patterns have to be substituted with open UX, and personalization should be used only to enhance progression: not addiction.

## What Was Once Called Data Extraction Has Been Renamed Data Sovereignty

The users should have control over their information, which involves the right to be told of how the information is collected, used, and shared. Explainable AI as well as consent-driven data practices based on transparent algorithms help to restore trust and independence in digital relations.

## Market Logic to Human-Centered Regulation

Global institutions and governments are at the forefront of ensuring government accountability by tech companies through their strong policies, oversight, and enforcement methods. This will comprise safeguarding vulnerable groups, especially children and adolescents, against the deceptive digital atmosphere and calling platform accountability.

## Isolation to Digital Collective Wellbeing

The establishment of healthy digital cultures is the responsibility of communities, educators, mental health professionals, and civil society organizations who need to collaborate in order to promote it. The debate on AI, addiction, and technology should be cross-sectorial, open, and well-being-oriented. Subjecting digital welfare to education systems and forming support mechanisms of people who struggle with digital dependency may develop long-term resilience.

## Looking Forward: Designing Futures of Flourishing

With every step towards the era of AI, it is necessary to pose the question of the kind of relationship we would like to have with technology. Are we also willing to live in a world where your next choice and your next feeling are pre-determined by an algorithm, or are we going to find a way through researching and designing technologies that can enhance human agency instead of diminishing it? Artificial intelligence by itself is not evil; it is a hammer, a mirror, and a magnifying lens. It embodies the priorities of the ones who construct and implement it. The reason smart systems nowadays resolve to favor profit over people is the fact that it has been programmed so. However, the same AI that can lead people into addiction can help us take care of ourselves, become focused, learn, and connect with others, provided we design it to do so. The fight to regain agency in the digital era is not a backward-looking effort to move back to a pre-technology time, just a futuristic act of equilibrium. It implies the creation of eco-systems in which the users are not targets or products, but members and collaborators. It implies dreaming about a world in which AI serves human values, does not transgress cognitive boundaries, and promotes psychological well-being. Ultimately, digital addiction is not a screen or a set of algorithms, but a question of what it is to be human, in such a mediated world. The answer starts with the ability to scroll, swipe and repeat not as a default, but as a choice.

## REFERENCES


Aldbyani, A., Chuanxia, Z., & Alhimaidi, A. (2025). The effect of mindfulness on smartphone addiction: The mediating role of self-regulation learning and the moderating role of digital detox. *Research Square*. DOI: 10.21203/rs.3.rs-6405697/v1

Almourad, M. B., McAlaney, J., Skinner, T., Pleya, M., & Ali, R. (2020). Defining digital addiction: Key features from the literature. *Psihologija (Beograd), 53*(3), 237–253. DOI: 10.2298/PSI191029017A

BUNIM. (2024). *E.* PARASOCIAL DEPENDENCY ASSOCIATED WITH ARTIFICIAL INTELLIGENCE CHATBOTS.

Burnell, K., George, M. J., Vollet, J. W., Ehrenreich, S. E., & Underwood, M. K. (2019). Passive social networking site use and well-being: The mediating roles of social comparison and the fear of missing out. *Cyberpsychology (Brno), 13*(3), 5. Advance online publication. DOI: 10.5817/CP2019-3-5

Cerniglia, L., Zoratto, F., Cimino, S., Laviola, G., Ammaniti, M., & Adriani, W. (2017). Internet addiction in adolescence: Neurobiological, psychosocial and clinical issues. *Neuroscience and Biobehavioral Reviews, 76*, 174–184. DOI: 10.1016/j.neubiorev.2016.12.024 PMID: 28027952

Chiam, J., Lim, A., & Teredesai, A. (2024, August). *NudgeRank: Digital algorithmic nudging for personalized health.* In *Proceedings of the 30th ACM SIGKDD Conference on Knowledge Discovery and Data Mining* (pp. 4873–4884). DOI: 10.1145/3637528.3671562

Chianella, R. (2021, December). Addictive digital experiences: The influence of artificial intelligence and more-than-human design. In *14th International Conference of the European Academy of Design, Safe Harbours for Design Research* (Vol. 9, No. 5, pp. 1–13). DOI: 10.5151/ead2021-125

Church, P., & Pehlivan, C. N. (2023). The Digital Services Act (DSA): A new era for online harms and intermediary liability. *Global Privacy Law Review, 4*(1), 53–59. DOI: 10.54648/GPLR2023005

. Dandotiya, A. S., Gupta, S. K., Dandotiya, N., & Sharma, M. P. (2024). *AI IN EVERYDAY LIFE: TRANSFORMING SOCIETY.* Navi International Book Publication house.

Ding, K., & Li, H. (2023). Digital addiction intervention for children and adolescents: A scoping review. *International Journal of Environmental Research and Public Health, 20*(6), 4777. Advance online publication. DOI: 10.3390/ijerph20064777 PMID: 36981687

Ding, K., Shen, Y., Liu, Q., & Li, H. (2023, December). The effects of digital addiction on brain function and structure of children and adolescents: A scoping review. [). MDPI.]. *Health Care, 12*(1), 15. PMID: 38200921

Ding, N., Qin, Y., Yang, G., Wei, F., Yang, Z., Su, Y., Hu, S., Chen, Y., Chan, C.-M., Chen, W., Yi, J., Zhao, W., Wang, X., Liu, Z., Zheng, H.-T., Chen, J., Liu, Y., Tang, J., Li, J., & Sun, M. (2023). Parameter-efficient fine-tuning of large-scale pre-trained language models. *Nature Machine Intelligence, 5*(3), 220–235. DOI: 10.1038/s42256-023-00626-4

Dresp-Langley, B., & Hutt, A. (2022). Digital addiction and sleep. *International Journal of Environmental Research and Public Health, 19*(11), 6910. Advance online publication. DOI: 10.3390/ijerph19116910 PMID: 35682491

Elliott, A. (2019). *The culture of AI: Everyday life and the digital revolution*. Routledge. DOI: 10.4324/9781315387185

Evci, V. Y. (2022). An evaluation on the problem of digital addiction in youth. *Journal of Social Sciences and Education, 5*(1), 115–134.

Flaxman, S., Goel, S., & Rao, J. M. (2016). Filter bubbles, echo chambers, and online news consumption. *Public Opinion Quarterly, 80*(S1), 298–320. DOI: 10.1093/poq/nfw006

Ghori, M. F., Dehpanah, A., Gemmell, J., & Mobasher, B. (2025, June). *"They Only Offer the Illusion of Choice": Exploring User Perceptions of Control and Agency on YouTube*. In *Adjunct Proceedings of the 33rd ACM Conference on User Modeling, Adaptation and Personalization* (pp. 214–218). DOI: 10.1145/3708319.3733664

Goel, R., & Singla, J. (2025). Mental Health and Smartphone Addiction: Understanding the Digital Impact on Well-Being. In *Smartphone Addiction, Phone Snubbing, and Effects on Interpersonal Relationships and Mental Health* (pp. 23-62). IGI Global Scientific Publishing.

Hartford, A., & Stein, D. J. (2022). Addiction, autonomy, and the Internet: Some ethical considerations. In *Mental Health in a Digital World* (pp. 481–495). Academic Press., DOI: 10.1016/B978-0-12-822201-0.00003-4

. Hsu, C. (2017). Unconsciousness by design: Addictive technologies and the escape from freedom.

Kamenskaya, V. G., & Tomanov, L. V. (2022). Digital technologies and their impact on the social and psychological characteristics of adolescents. *Experimental Psychology (Russia), 15*(1), 139–159. DOI: 10.17759/exppsy.2022150109

Kant, T. (2020). *Making it personal: Algorithmic personalization, identity, and everyday life*. Oxford University Press. DOI: 10.1093/oso/9780190905088.001.0001

Kim, K., Yoon, Y., & Shin, S. (2024). Explainable prediction of problematic smartphone use among South Korea's children and adolescents using a machine learning approach. *International Journal of Medical Informatics, 186*, 105441. Advance online publication. DOI: 10.1016/j.ijmedinf.2024.105441 PMID: 38564961

Koronczai, B., Kökönyei, G., Urbán, R., Kun, B., Pápay, O., Nagygyörgy, K., Griffiths, M. D., & Demetrovics, Z. (2013). The mediating effect of self-esteem, depression and anxiety between satisfaction with body appearance and problematic internet use. *The American Journal of Drug and Alcohol Abuse, 39*(4), 259–265. DOI: 10.3109/00952990.2013.803111 PMID: 23841866

Lam, H., & Harcourt, M. (2024). Digital addiction in organizations: Challenges and policy implications. *Employee Responsibilities and Rights Journal, 36*(4), 519–533. DOI: 10.1007/s10672-024-09493-6

Li an, D. E. (2025). Online captive: The impact of social media addiction on depression and anxiety—An SEM approach to the mediating role of self-esteem and the moderating effects of age and professional status. *Behavioral Sciences (Basel, Switzerland), 15*(4), 481. Advance online publication. DOI: 10.3390/bs15040481 PMID: 40282102

Luttrell, R., & Welch, C. (2024). AI-Powered Synthetic Personas: Affecting the Future of Public Relations Campaigns. In *Public Relations and the Rise of AI* (pp. 97-117). Routledge.

Macit, H. B., Macit, G., & Güngör, O. (2018). A research on social media addiction and dopamine driven feedback. *Journal of Mehmet Akif Ersoy University Economics and Administrative Sciences Faculty, 5*(3), 882–897. DOI: 10.30798/makuiibf.435845

Madary, M. (2022). The illusion of agency in human–computer interaction. *Neuroethics, 15*(1), 16. DOI: 10.1007/s12152-022-09491-1

Markoci, D. (2024). *ANALIZA TURISTIČKE PONUDE NACIONALNOG PARKA PLITVIČKA JEZERA* (Doctoral dissertation, Libertas međunarodno sveučilište).

Marković, S., Popović, G., & Andjelković, L. (2024). Mastering the attention economy: Strategies for competing on digital platforms. *Fusion of Multidisciplinary Research. International Journal (Toronto, Ont.), 5*(1), 568–578.

Molteni, L. (2022). *Impact of nudges on digital well-being for the smartphone* (Doctoral dissertation, Politecnico di Torino).

Parveiz, S., Amjad, A., & Ayub, S. (2023). Fear of missing out (FOMO), social comparison and social media addiction among young adults. [PJAP]. *Pakistan Journal of Applied Psychology*, *3*(1), 224–235. DOI: 10.52461/pjap.v3i1.1283

Reer, F., Tang, W. Y., & Quandt, T. (2019). Psychosocial well-being and social media engagement: The mediating roles of social comparison orientation and fear of missing out. *New Media & Society*, *21*(7), 1486–1505. DOI: 10.1177/1461444818823719

Rosenblat, M. O., Agrawal, A., & Yap, I. (2025). Online Safety Regulations Around. *WORLD (Oakland, Calif.)*.

. Ross Arguedas, A., Robertson, C., Fletcher, R., & Nielsen, R. (2022). Echo chambers, filter bubbles, and polarisation: A literature review.

Shanmugasundaram, M., & Tamilarasu, A. (2023). The impact of digital technology, social media, and artificial intelligence on cognitive functions: A review. *Frontiers in Cognition*, *2*, 1203077. Advance online publication. DOI: 10.3389/fcogn.2023.1203077

Stanimirović, A. S., Nikolić, M. S., Jović, J. J., Ristić, D. I. I., Ćorać, A. M., Stoimenov, L. V., & Perić, Z. H. (2024). Applying eXplainable AI techniques to interpret machine learning predictive models for the analysis of problematic internet use among adolescents. *Elektronika ir Elektrotechnika*, *30*(2), 63–72. DOI: 10.5755/j02.eie.36316

Stanimirovic, M., Zivkovic, M., Momcilovic, A., Petronijevic, B. S., & Kondic, S. (2024). The role of architecture in the development of smart cities in Serbia. *ZELENA GRADNJA*, *2024*, 323–328. DOI: 10.5937/greenb24046S

Tourkochoriti, I. (2023). The digital services act and the EU as the global regulator of the internet. *Chi. J. Int'l L.*, *24*, 129.

Trier, M., Kundisch, D., Beverungen, D., Müller, O., Schryen, G., Mirbabaie, M., & Trang, S. (2023). Digital responsibility: A multilevel framework for responsible digitalization. *Business & Information Systems Engineering*, *65*(4), 463–474. DOI: 10.1007/s12599-023-00822-x

. Wahed, S. A., & Wahed, M. A. (2025). AI-driven digital well-being: Developing machine learning model to predict and mitigate Internet addiction. *LatIA, (3)*, 73. DOI: 10.62486/latia2025134

Yang, X., Liao, T., Wang, Y., Ren, L., & Zeng, J. (2024). The association between digital addiction and interpersonal relationships: A systematic review and meta-analysis. *Clinical Psychology Review, 102501*, 102501. Advance online publication. DOI: 10.1016/j.cpr.2024.102501 PMID: 39265317

Ye, X. (2025). Dark patterns and addictive designs. *Weizenbaum Journal of the Digital Society, 5*(3). DOI: 10.34669/wi.wjds/5.3.2

Yen, C. F., Chou, W. J., Liu, T. L., Yang, P., & Hu, H. F. (2014). The association of Internet addiction symptoms with anxiety, depression and self-esteem among adolescents with attention-deficit/hyperactivity disorder. *Comprehensive Psychiatry, 55*(7), 1601–1608. DOI: 10.1016/j.comppsych.2014.05.025 PMID: 25015304

# Chapter 6
# AI-Driven Communication and Digital Addiction:
## A Psychological and Social Inquiry

**Olivia Jana**
https://orcid.org/0009-0009-2101-9513
*Brainware University, India*

**Shivnath Ghosh**
https://orcid.org/0000-0001-7368-7139
*Brainware University, India*

## ABSTRACT

*The chapter examines the potential effects of cutting-edge technologies like emotionally intelligent artificial in-telligence and immersive worlds like the metaverse. These developments blur the boundaries between virtual and real experiences, even as they present new opportunities for engagement and education. This necessitates a careful re-examination of what meaningful communication in a world full of digital devices means. The chapter essentially offers a comprehensive framework for comprehending and addressing the relationship be-tween communication, AI, and digital addiction. Researchers, designers, educators, parents, and legislators are all urged to work together to create a future in which technology enhances human well-being and the depth of relationships rather than detracts from them.*

DOI: 10.4018/979-8-3373-5606-8.ch006

## INTRODUCTION

### The Rise of AI in Communication Technologies

Rapid developments in natural language processing (NLP), machine learning (ML), and data analytics have contributed to the rise of AI in communication technologies by allowing machines to comprehend, produce, and react to human language with previously unheard-of precision (Jana & Ghosh, 2024). Rule-based chatbots and other early AI applications have developed into complex conversational agents with the ability to detect emotions, have context-aware conversations, and translate between languages. In order to create specialized communication environments for billions of users, social media platforms now mainly rely on AI algorithms to curate feeds, recommend connections, and moderate content. With their smooth, immediate, and contextually relevant interactions, these advancements have completely redesigned the user experience.

All this technological boom has not only revolutionized one-to-one communication, but it has also revolutionized the strategies of business, governments and even media organizations in terms of mass communication. Sentiment analysis that is driven by AI provides the brands with an opportunity to assess the opinion of people in real-time, and using automated content generation tools can help them to share information items across channels quickly. жу in the domain of education, healthcare, and administration, the AI-powered communication protocols are allowing far away consultations, online learning, and administration. However, since such systems increasingly find their way into everyday life, their ability to shape thought patterns, emotional conditions and social norms will rise dramatically. This points to how it is essential to maintain a balance between innovation and ethical protections so that AI can enable a deeper engagement between humans rather than increase a dependency and lack of connection.

### Overview of Benefits and Emerging Concerns

Artificial intelligence has continued to provide significant contribution to the current communication system as it achieves speed, accuracy and personalization that has never been reached by manual means. Artificial intelligence systems can translate languages in a moment, formulate a contextual response, and save you as a user recommendation of content to view or read using context, etc. In healthcare, they can guide patients in initial diagnosis and making an appointment; in education, they can offer learners predictive feedback; and in business, they could predict the needs of customers and businesses. These developments have increased production in addition to creating inclusivity whereby those who would have been left out of the mainstream communication method can now take part.

However, along with such advantages, there is an array of new concerns that AI in communication technologies bring to attention. The same personalization capabilities that lead to enhanced attention can also produce dependency, compulsiveness to use, and digital addiction--particularly, young demographics are affected by this (Jana & Ghosh, 2024). Algorithms promote drawbacks like bias, extension of misleading information, and suppression of privacy by collecting tons of data. Moreover, the focus on speediness and convenience can be attained at the depth and authenticity of human interactions and result in decreased empathy and emotional contact. The introduction and use of AI and other propinquity environments will need to stay sensitive to the need to not only remain innovative but legally responsible, as they continue to make inroads into our communication structures.

## Defining Digital Addiction

Digital addiction is a behavioral disorder, where there is excessive and compulsive use of digital devices, platforms, or applications to a point where it interferes with normal day-to-day functioning and well-being (Jana & Ghosh, 2024). However, digital addiction is not tied to a specific substance, unlike the classic types of addiction, which are usually substance-oriented: in contrast to these classic addictions, digital addiction is built on the experience of permanent interaction with technology, fuelled by psychological stimuli, like newness and immediate rewards, social approval. It is apparent in habits, such as excessive social media usage, frequent checking of messages, and a preference toward online associations over face-to-face associations. In systems that reinforce engagement through the reward system in the brain, such as likes, comments and algorithm-curated content, have become habit-forming in AI-operating communication environments.

The psychological and neurological basis of digital addiction is similar to other behavioral addictions, including the stimulation of dopaminergic tracts and analogies of reinforcement learning (Jana & Ghosh, 2024). The fact that AI is involved enhances this game, as the more an individual uses an app, the more adhering to the user, the recommendation engine is. Other than the personal effects, digital addiction has social implications because it can decrease in-person communication skills, worsen mental health challenges like anxiety and depression, and skew personal identity due to the creation of digital personas. That must entail an interdisciplinary study of risk mitigation through psychological research, ethical design of AI, and public policy to ensure that the advantages of digital communication are not sacrificed to the detriments of digital risk.

## AI AND THE EVOLUTION OF COMMUNICATION

### Historical Trajectory of AI in Human Communication

The development of artificial intelligence implementation into human communication was rather long and can be described as a series of significant technological breakthroughs and changes in the paradigm of interaction with the interface. The first examples of AI applications in communication in the 1960s and 1970s were rule-based natural language processing (NLP) systems, like ELIZA, that replicated the conversation using pre-written scripts (Jana & Ghosh, 2024; Weizenbaum, 1966). The systems may have been crude by modern standards, but they did show that machines could reproduce human conversation, which is why it was seen as the precursor to future development. By the 1980s and 1990s newer and more advanced text parsing, grammar checking, and information retrieval tools, which were increasingly found on professional and personal communication channels, were developed as a result of improvements in computational linguistics and machine learning.

With the advent of smart search engines, text-prediction modules, and cruder chatbots, the landscape of communication technologies was gradually moving to real-time, adaptive communication technologies (Jana & Ghosh, 2024; Shum et al., 2018). The 2010s saw the revolution in deep learning and big data analytics that lead to the further development of highly interactive AI applications including voice assistants (e.g. Siri, Alexa, Google Assistant), real-time translation services, and advanced social media algorithms that learn to curate individualized content feeds. Tomorrow, the future of communication powered by AI will embrace emotionally intelligent systems and the metaverse whose implications of creating a virtual realm that is indistinguishable but far more compelling will have a significant effect on cultural norms and cognitive behaviors.

### Transformational Milestones in AI Integration

The channels through which the use of artificial intelligence in communication technologies have taken a revolutionary turn have been highlighted by some of the transformation landmarks that have transformed how individuals worldwide can communicate to each other. One of the first breakthroughs was switching to adaptive machine learning models and the possibility to analyze large volumes of data and respond to them according to user inputs toward the end of the 1990s and the early 2000s (Jana & Ghosh, 2024). With the introduction of the so-called smart personal assistants, i.e., Siri (Apple, 2011), Google Now (Google, 2012), and Alexa (Amazon, 2014), AI-powered voice interaction broke into the mainstream of life (Hoy, 2018). Real-time language translation systems, such as Google Translate, also began using neural machine translation (NMT) and successfully increased the accuracy of these systems to a point that could be considered as a breakthrough in the quality of translation (Bahdanau et al., 2015). Not only have these innovations made things more accessible and available across different cultures but it has led to the development of AI systems that would understand through context and adapt to the user as well as be able to support multiple avenues of communication.

The second major turning point was the advance of deep learning algorithms in the social media and messaging services that allowed a highly personalized form of content delivery and the implemented moderation system (Jana & Ghosh, 2024). There has been an increased use of AI in social networking platforms such as Facebook, Instagram, and TikTok to track the behavior of the users in real time, curate their feeds, target advertisements, and optimize engagement (Zeng et al., 2021). The arrival and development of chatbots and customer-service agents, conversational AI may be applied similarly and show how AI can be used to capture human-like conversational feeling and emotion and understand context. The latest trend is the emergence of generative AI models, such as the GPT series developed by OpenAI, and generating a human-like text is now made possible hence resulting in content creation, automating reports and producing interactive learning content. These milestones identify one courseleading light to the creation of more immersive, smart, and networked communication systems in which ethical and psychological aspects also come into play due to the fact that these advances occur at blistering speed.

## Innovations: Chatbots, Social Media Algorithms, and Virtual Assistants

The last decades have seen the rise of tremendous breakthroughs in AI-driven communicational means and one of the most potent tools that influenced the digital level of interaction is chatbots, algorithms used in social media, and virtual assistants. Chatbots powered by AI have moved on in sophistication beyond the scripted responding systems to chatbots that can converse in natural language, can retain context, and can even analyze sentiment (Jana & Ghosh, 2024; Følstad & Brandtzaeg, 2017). The systems are gaining broad implementation with customer service, healthcare, education and in e-commerce, delivering instant, scaled and personal support. Virtual assistants such as Siri, Alexa, or Google Assistant combine the use of speech recognition, natural language processing (NLP), and machine learning to allow interaction without touching the device, organize practical demands and provide information in real-time (Hoy, 2018). The combination of all the technologies has not only advanced the convenience of consumers, boosted their user comfortability but also made the presence of AI a regular part of everyday communication patterns.

Social media algorithms present another revolutionary invention that has changed the way of producing, distributing and consuming content significantly. Machine learning models are implemented in platforms like Facebook, Instagram, TikTok, and YouTube to create personalized feeds, suggest content to the user, and deliver targeted ads using their behavior and preferences (Jana & Ghosh, 2024; Zeng et al., 2021). The algorithms are meant to enhance user interaction, in how the preferred content is predicted and re-enforced, using the information on behavior to establish highly personalized digital experiences. On the one hand, this kind of personalization improves relevancy and user satisfaction, but on the other hand, it increases ethical issues related to the creation of echo chambers and misinformation and addictive use practices. In sum, all these developments together represent both the potential and the challenge of AI being introduced into communication systems in entirely new directions on a massive scale, tantamount to challenging the fundamental psychological, social, and ethical issues presented across society.

## Role of Machine Learning and Natural Language Processing

Indeed, the cornerstone of AI-supported communication systems is ML and NLP allowing the systems to analyze the patterns of the huge amount of data and create meaningful interactions with the users. Machine learning algorithms enable platforms to make predictions, suggest items and automate their reactions by refining the behavioral data in real-time (Jana & Ghosh, 2024). As an example, supervised learning algorithms can be trained using labeled communication data to classify the messages or to detect spam, whereas clustering user behaviors can be clustered using unsupervised learning to deliver personalized content. Reinforcement learning has been especially used to drive moving procedures by rewarding particular user interventions as is the case in customized social media feeds and recommendations (Silver et al., 2017). Such breakthroughs have simplified communications as they are contextual and effective improving interactions between human and machines.

AI can also be applied to natural language processing, which specializes in advancing communication by allowing computers to recognize, comprehend, and express human language. Current NLP solutions utilize deep learning and transformer-based models, including BERT and GPT, that are capable of understanding the contexts and nuances of communications on a greatly extended scale in comparison to the rule-based systems (Vaswani et al., 2017). Some of the fields of use include real-time translation and sentiment analysis, and conversational AI, including chatbots and digital assistants, which greatly depends on NLP in order to sound more natural in conversation (Jana & Ghosh, 2024). These technologies have not only revolutionized interpersonal communication, but also organizational communication with all the capabilities of instant multilingual communication, automatic summarization, and even emotion adapting replies. Yet as they gain power it also becomes a cause of misinformation generation and biased training data, as well as degraded authenticity of human expression. Therefore, though ML and NLP can be used to increase the capabilities of human communication with machines, their moral and social implications are worth giving serious attention.

## Impact on Interpersonal and Group Communication

The area in which the impact of artificial intelligence has been extensively felt is interpersonal and group communication since it has been observed to change how individuals communicate, work together and maintain relationships. At an interpersonal level, there is the increased convenience and accessibility of personalized, instant and context-aware exchanges through AI-enabled processes like chatbots, social media-based algorithms, and virtual assistants (Jana & Ghosh, 2024). An example is that recommendation systems can curate content that is relevant to them, and messaging application integration of AI functionality, including smart reply and predictive text, which assist in the quicker interaction. Likewise, virtual assistants enable people to conduct their personal communication without using their hands, in a more efficient way (Hoy, 2018). The reported tendency of this automation, however, is to diminish depth in conversations, since the conversations become a transaction and no longer emotionally meaningful. Lack of nonverbal expressions in AI directed communication may also disrupt the process of empathy and emotional perception and individuals will find it difficult to form any meaningful relationships (Turkle, 2015).

Specifically, within group communication AI technologies have taken a new form. In the professional, academic, and social realms, they redefined teamwork. AI-assisted platforms based on natural language processing and machine learning allow translations in real-time, the automatic summarizing of meetings, and broader coordination tools, which is breaking language and geographical boundaries (Jana & Ghosh, 2024). Organizations are becoming heavily reliant on AI to carry out decision support, analysis of group conversations and efficient distribution of information to large teams. AI moderation systems also add value to social media communities, as they allow filtering out harmful content and amplifying the relevant topics to keep the communities and their communication at a higher level (Zeng et al., 2021). However, at the same time, these systems are capable of producing an echo chamber in which their established belief system is strengthened and that exposes it to a lack of diverse information. Such a culmination indicates that even though AI increases connectivity and group efficiency, it threatens authenticity, inclusivity, and democratic discussion, and careful consideration in its ethical design and application should be put into consideration.

## UNDERSTANDING DIGITAL ADDICTION

### Definitions and Core Characteristics

The process of being addicted to digital technologies may be characterized by the following definition: Digital addiction is a behavioral disorder which is presented by an excessive, compulsive, and uncontrollable use of digital technologies, platforms, or applications and is accompanied by the disruption of daily life, social functions, and psychological well-being (Jana & Ghosh, 2024). Digital addiction is behavioral in nature as compared to substance-based addictions which are all about the allure of the substance itself, as well as the desire to feel the effect of the substance. The key symptoms are an inability to control the use, disregard offline life go ons, obsession with the use of the internet, and feeling depressed when prevented from using the internet (Kuss & Griffiths, 2017). Digital addiction can be observed in a number of areas including social media, online games, video streaming and smartphone usage, and common side effects can include disruption in sleep patterns, declined academic or work performance, and even loss of interpersonal relationships. Also, the engagement of AI-powered feedback mechanisms likes, notifications, and algorithmic feeds further induces forms of compulsive use by handling reward areas in the brain (Andreassen et al., 2017).

The essential features of digital addiction are similar to the other behavioral addictions as people with this disorder demonstrate tolerance (the need to spend more time in front of the screen to feel satisfied), withdrawal (getting upset when they cannot access a screen), and relapse (reverting to compulsive use after the attempt to reduce spending time in front of the screen) (Young, 2017a). Researchers have found that psychological pressures like fear of missing out (FOMO), low self-esteem, anxiety, and wanting to obtain social validation are some of what drive digital addiction. AI exacerbates these weaknesses by generating immensely personalized and emotionally stimulating settings, making it even more challenging to break the connection (Jana & Ghosh, 2024). Moreover, digital addiction does not only impact cognitive functioning and emotional control, but also influences identity formation, especially in adolescents and when young adults are in their early years. Considering the fact that it has received a lot of attention as a rising public health issue, greater awareness, prevention, and intervention measures are needed to reduce the negative psychological and social outcomes that are associated with it.

## Classification: Social Media, Gaming, Smartphones, etc.

Digital addictions could be placed into several categories corresponding to the platform or device that promotes compulsive use. Social media addiction is one of the best-known varieties; users become addicted to one or more platforms that have become very popular in multiplying contexts: Facebook, Instagram, TikTok, Twitter, etc. This is usually enabled by the never-ending flow of algorithmic content recommendations, instant feedback (likes, shares, comments) and the neurological implication of the fear of missing out (FOMO) that strengthens repetitive behaviors in checking (Andreassen et al., 2017). The other significant one is that gaming addiction that is acts as classified by the world health organization as a gaming disorder, which is an impaired control over gaming, prioritizing gaming at other life activities, and playing despite the adverse effects (WHO, 2018). This is especially true of online multiplayer games, which create social mechanisms of reinforcement, rivalry, and rewards encouraging pathological use.

In addition to social media and games, the problem of smartphone addiction is another important category because, through smartphones, one can access a variety of online activities. Surveys indicate that most people say they feel anxious, unsettled, itchy or distracted when they do not have their devices (Yildirim & Correia, 2015). Addiction to a smartphone is related to many other types because this device gives a person access to social networking opportunities, games, entertainment solutions, and messaging. Moreover, the concept of online streaming and binge-watching addiction has developed, where recommendation systems designed with the help of artificial intelligence encourage further watching and limitless use of such platforms as Netflix or Youtube (Flayelle et al., 2020). These adjoining manifestations of digital addiction speak to how various sites assume alike ways of evoking persuasive design -notifications, rewards, endless scrolling web mechanics- to engage and encapsulate audience interest, with frequently destructive consequences to mental health, work potential and social roles.

## Psychological and Neurological Mechanisms of Addiction

The underlying psychology of digital addiction has a strong connection with the system of reward-seeking mechanisms and reinforcement learning. Notifications, variable reward schedules, and social feedback loops are examples of persuasive design features that are used in digital platforms and that can exploit cognitive biases and result in compulsive engagement (Montag et al., 2019). As an example, temporary rewards like those experienced in gambling predispose people to repeat the activities in question, such as checking their social media accounts or playing online games. Other psychological reasons are also at the heart of excessive digital use such as fear of missing out (FOMO), low self-esteem and anxiety as people want validation, relaxation or distraction away to real-life stresses (Przybylski et al., 2013). With time, such dependence upon electronic intercourse may decrease self-control and tolerance levels leading to a situation in which individuals need more hours on the Internet to be satisfied resulting in further consolidation of addictive behavior.

Neurologically, digital addiction also taps into the brain reward circuits that are involved in drugs of abuse, especially mesolimbic dopamine system. Functional MRI has revealed that an overuse of the digital technologies stimulates the areas of the brain related to the reward processing, craving, and habit formation, such as the nucleus accumbens and prefrontal cortex (Kuss & Griffiths, 2017). The long-term interaction with digital media may cause neural changes, according to which, the dopamine activation becomes disregulated, provoking the desire of using such tools and the discomfort of not using them under the conditions of their striking (Dong et al., 2017). Less usage of the prefrontal cortex can also lead to the loss of ability to take decisions and control themselves and increase exposure to compulsive digital behavior. Such neurological changes, along with the components of psychological motives, indicate why it is hard to fight digital addiction and why it admits to more traditional behavioral addictions in its mechanisms and effects.

## Behavioral Signs and Diagnostic Tools

The signs of digital addiction are usually reflected in the same way that is seen in other addictions related to behavior and substances. Among the main signs and symptoms are over-dependence on things and activities online, the inability to control the time spent online, lack of interest in real-life affairs, and the inability to stop using them despite understanding the harmful effects (Young, 2017b). Dr. A. Griffiths reported that people subjected to withdrawal-like symptoms (irritability, anxiety, restlessness) in the case inability to use a device, and tolerance, demanding escalating time of using the service in order to experience gratification (Griffiths, 2005). Other noticeable signs include disturbed sleeping habits, deteriorated performance in school or work, and withdrawal into the self. Among older children and young adults, the need to constantly verify notifications, failure to maintain interpersonal interactions in person, and putting virtual interactions above in-person relations are most evident (Andreassen et al., 2017). These symptoms of behavior point to the necessity of early detection and an elaborate course of action aimed at avoiding developing the more serious psychological and social corollaries.

Measurement and evaluation of digital addiction Therefore, in order to measure and assess digital addiction, relate and diagnose it, a variety of standardized tools and questionnaires is developed by researchers and clinicians. The most popular is probably the Internet Addiction Test (IAT) by Kimberly Young, which determines the presence of such obsessive behaviors online as neglect of duty, preoccupation, and affective involvement (Young, 2017a). Other tools also exist such as the Bergen Social Media Addiction Scale (BSMAS), which measures addictive behavior in the use of social media (Andreassen et al., 2012) and the Smart phone Addiction Scale (SAS), a scale in measuring smart phone dependency (Kwon et al., 2013). These are self-reporting-based tools that measure salience, tolerance, withdrawal, relapse, conflict, and mood modification that are very much in line with the models of addiction that are being used in the field of psychiatry. As much as diagnostic instruments keep improving, the fact that digital addiction is now a part of the internationally acknowledged health-related statistics like the ICD-11 definition of Gaming Disorder suggests that the formerly intangible phenomenon can no longer afflictively be ignored (WHO, 2018).

## Vulnerable Groups: Children, Adolescents, and Adults

Children and adolescents are the most vulnerable to digital addiction since they fall in that age bracket that is still developing and is highly susceptible to social and emotional stimuli. Adolescents, especially, get attracted to the social media and online games environments as they offer validation and recognition of peers as well as a feeling of belonging and do so in a compulsive manner but enabled by AI-enhanced algorithms (Twenge & Campbell, 2018). Overuse of screens at these early stages is attributed to poor academic performance, sleep disturbance, and psychological conditions like anxieties and depressions (Keles et al., 2020). Children, being younger, are getting more exposure to digital mediums in the form of educational apps and other entertainment media, and since they have a low level of self-regulation, they are susceptible to form habits. Such risks, in turn, may be enhanced by a lack of parental control or digital literacy that contributes to the development of the dependency pattern at an early age.

Even though adults are usually more skilled in self-regulation strategies, they are not invulnerable to digital addictions, especially at the workplace, where more and more spheres of life and professional activity are mediated through digital technology. Professionals can develop obsessive use of the smartphone and using digital communication too frequently, as well as being unable to abandon the working-related devices, which lead to burnout and lower well-being (Panova & Lleras, 2016). In addition, adult populations who are susceptible to dependency, like those in a state of loneliness, social isolation, or with a pre-existing psychological disorder can resort to the usage of online interactions, games, or streaming programs as a coping mechanism further fueling the dependency concerns. Less extensively studied but now showing ever greater interest in digital technologies, older adults may use them in place of interpersonal relationships, and this puts a limiting constraint on authentic social relations. The combination of these vulnerabilities points towards the need to have age-specific intervention mechanisms, i.e., digital literacy programs during childhood, self-restraint and peer-support systems with adolescents, and workplace or lifestyle-balance methods with adults.

## THE ROLE OF AI IN REINFORCING DIGITAL ADDICTION

### How AI Drives Engagement: Behavioral Design and Persuasive Tech

Artificial intelligence is a key element of increasing user engagement via behavioral design and persuasive technologies. With the use of huge data sets and predictive modelling, sites can predict how a user will behave and create interfaces that result in more time and frequency (Eyal, 2014). The endless scroll, the autoplay, push notifications, and personalized recommendations are not some incidental features to be convenient but are strategic options that are based on learning psychology and reinforcement learning principles. These design features take advantage of cognitive biases like the variable reward effect wherein unpredictable and intermittent reinforcement makes compulsive checking even more addictive behavior (Montag et al., 2019). Most social media sites, such as Facebook, use algorithmically based feeds that optimize novelty and relevance to keep users hooked into the platforms, which only had the effect of further dependency cycles. By doing this, AI turns digital platforms into persuasive ecosystems where we are constantly captured and turned into commodities of this attention.

Persuasive technology is far more than a matter of user-interface touch-ups as it ventures into the realms of psychological manipulation worrying about the autonomy and well-being. Machine learning algorithms tell content delivery to change based on how people are responding in real-time in terms of clicks, shares and watch time at the cost of mental health (Williams, 2018). This results in an attention economy where companies have an interest in designing products to be as engaging as possible at the expense of the well-being of a user, reinforcing compulsive actions and other addictive behaviors. As another example, video-sharing services such as TikTok and YouTube use AI to provide never-ending streams of content that have been customized to your specific preferences, something that becomes progressively harder to disengage (Zeng et al., 2021). In the same way, mobile games include gamification features that are intended to trigger the brain reward-system based on dopamine (King & Delfabbro, 2018). All of these persuasive technologies help to understand how AI does not only increase engagement in the digital world but also methodically helps to cultivate the circumstances that drive digital addiction.

## Feedback Loops and Habit Formation: Notifications, Likes, Infinite Scroll

A key fact that contributes to the effect of AI in strengthening the problem of digital addiction is that it is used to create feedback loops to take advantage of psychological weaknesses. Notifications, likes, shares are features that give their users immediate social validation, stimulating the reward system in the brain to be released, and dopamine reinforces compulsive behavior (Andreassen et al., 2017). These prompts are planned to keep the user engaged through arousal and raised expectation of some sort of uncertainty, an effect also witnessed in the intermittent reinforcement format utilized in gambling activities (Berridge & Robinson, 2016). A like and comment are a form of micro-reward that helps prompt the user to continue visiting the site to see new interactions, increasing their dependence on online presence. This feedback relates to the development of a habit over time, in which checking the devices turns into a result of behavioral response to cues instead of a rational decision-making process.

Addictive features like infinite scroll and autoplay are AI-driven design features that even further increase these behavioral tendencies due to their removal of natural stopping conditions. In lieu of providing the user time to unplug, the algorithms used on the platforms keep content feeds updated, yielding an unending supply of fresh and relatable information (Alter, 2017). The design uses the cognitive limitation of human attention and creates a time collapsing need that people lose any idea of the passage of time. Social media sites such as Youtube and Tik Tok, to give two examples, have advanced the use of AI within recommendation engines and thus create smooth chains of content a user can remain within as long as possible (Zeng et al., 2021). These aspects do not only enhance the engagements periods but also normalize compulsive actions in a wide range of users. Together, the feedback pathways aroused by notifications, likes, and endless scrolling provide formal evidence that AI systematically designs digital spaces to amplify habits and providing substance to further avoidance.

## Gamification and the Reward System

Gamification has become one of the central tactics in the strengthening of digital addiction since platforms and apps are becoming increasingly more gamified to increase the engagement levels of the user. These features of points, badges, streaks, leaderboards, achievements, and achievements appeal to more basic psychological needs of competition, accomplishment, and social recognition (Hamari et al., 2014). By giving rewards to consistent interaction, gamified systems promote repetitive behavior in manner similar to traditional gambler and behavioral addictions. An example of these streaks are the streaks offered on the apps like Snapchat or language-learning platforms like Duolingo, which lean into the human psychology of record-keeping and the illusion of wasting efforts made on these apps (Alutaybi et al., 2020). AI is central in personalizing these rewards, i.e. adopting the challenges and incentives to maintain user motivation and maximize time spent online.

The neurological foundation is that gamification activates directly into the reward system driven by dopamine and compulsively reinforces behavioral pathways through a cycle of anticipation and reward. It has been demonstrated that the kind of reward schedules incorporated into gamified systems create the most robust reinforcements sensations as seen with slot machine dynamics (King & Delfabbro, 2018). The nucleus accumbens, the reward facility in the brain, is activated by these reward stimulating activities that result in a regular indulgence and the inability to withdraw at will (Berridge & Robinson, 2016). Gamification has become more common in social gaming platforms, fitness applications, and even workplace productivity tools, where the distinctions between enjoyment, purpose, and addiction are becoming so entmeshed as to be inseparable. Although gamification has the potential to increase motivation and performance in education, health, and business sectors, using AI reward mechanisms heavily in consumer platforms proves that in case of gamification, dependency can occur and can lead to the development of digital addiction.

## Social Media Case Studies: TikTok, Instagram, YouTube

Tik Tok has become one of the most striking illustrations of the ways how AI-based design contributes to online addiction. This is done through its robust recommendation algorithm, or what it calls the For You Page, which continuously feeds a highly personalized short-form video by studying user response in the form of watch time, likes, comments, and replays (Kaye et al., 2022). The approach is based on infinite scrolling and variable rewards; this means that visitors will experience an unpredictable level of engaging, learning, and emotionally evocative content, a factor that allows long-term engagement. TikTok also uses music integration, trends, and social endorsement parameters (shares, duets, reactions), contributing to the level of user retention. Research indicates that the algorithm of TikTok harvests attention weaknesses better than most competitors and hence makes it more attractive to young people and adolescents who are more prone to compulsive online activity (Montag et al., 2021).

Instagram also uses machine learning algorithms to filter the content feed, suggest posts, and push stories or reels that have the greatest chance of maximum engagement. Like, notifications, and the addition of Reel features keep the users in constant loops of interactions (Marengo et al., 2022). Instagram also has social comparison effects, that expose the user to idealized lifestyles that perpetuate addictive behaviors of checking accounts, as well as having negative psychological effects of anxiety and body dissatisfaction. The targeted advertisement that is informed by AI will further customize the platform to the audience providing content specificity but also increase the level of focused attention capturing.

One of the main aspects of YouTube is its recommendation system, which delivers more than 70 percent of the YouTube viewing time (Covington et al., 2016). The AI used by YouTube creates an ever-expanding stream of videos in autoplay mode based on user history and preferences, removing much of the choices on disengagement. This positive feedback cycle makes binge-watching a popular activity, and users oftentimes lose their track of time on the platform (Flayelle et al., 2020). YouTube also ranks orderly based on watch time over user welfare which brings up charges of exposure to violence or unhealthy material. In combination, TikTok, Instagram, and YouTube exemplify how AI-based social media environments can be used to exploit psychological vulnerabilities with personalization, variable rewards and feedback loops and, as such, are amongst the most powerful engines of digital addiction in contemporary communications.

## The Economics Behind Attention Engineering

At the center of digital addiction is the economics of the attention economy, where attention is a resource which is scarce and highly monetizable. The added revenue to social media and digital platforms is mostly in the form of targeted advertising, hence, how much profit they make is based on the amount of time and activity that users spend on their services (Williams, 2018). Artificial intelligence plays a critical role in this since it optimizes feeds, notifications, and suggestions in a way to maximize watch time, clicks, and responses. With constant gathering of behavioral data, platforms can continuously improve their algorithms at predicting user interests, as they present content that will guarantee continued engagement (Zuboff, 2019). This business model does not encourage companies to take care of user well-being but rather seeks to create experiences which exploit the psychological weaknesses of the users in order to maintain their interest.

The cases of financial prosperity of such technological titans like Meta (Facebook, Instagram), ByteDance (TikTok), and Google (YouTube) show how cemented attention engineering has become in the digital economy. Such companies use AI to personalize experiences, as well as make profit through data surveillance capitalism by selling personal information to advertisements (Zuboff, 2019). Such things as infinite scrolls, auto-play or gameified reward structures are therefore not about optimizing user experience but sustaining cycles of profitable user engagement. This system has economic incentives that form a feedback loop: the longer one spends online the more data is gathered, the more targeted their advertising will be, and the more of it they can sell. This profit maximization and addictive design further demonstrate a structural issue: platforms are economically incentivized to support an addiction form of repeated behaviors, which results in making digital addiction an intentional consequence rather than a side-effect of technological innovation (Fisher, 2022).

## IMPACTS ON HUMAN BEHAVIOR AND RELATIONSHIPS

### Erosion of Empathy and Emotional Intelligence

The increased use of communication mediated through Artificial Intelligence has fueled some real concerns regarding the adverse effects of it on empathy and emotional intelligence as the core aspects of human interaction. Efficiency and convenience are also prized by digital platforms and AI-driven personal communication tools, and their interactions tend to be more transactional than relational in nature (Turkle, 2015). Alternatively, chatbots and virtual assistants can imitate empathy with scripted responses but still fail to have any real understanding of emotional context, which could, again, encourage manualized communication (Powers & Kiesler, 2006). A repetitive use of mediated communication (i.e., texting, messaging apps, AI-assistant) diminishes the chances to talk to people in person and the need to read non-verbal signals, which contributes to the development of empathetic behavior. This transition weakens the capacity of people, especially those belonging to younger generations, to carry out emotional attune and work out the subtle societal skills to deal with the precise interpersonal connections in the real world.

Emotional intelligence, which can be defined as the ability to identify, understand as well as manage, with the same meaning, one as well as another person, can also be subjected to degradation of an AI-dominated communication setting. The constant presence of the algorithmically curated content in social media leads to self-centered tendencies in the consumption model instead of the empathic, mutual interaction processes (Uhls et al., 2014). In addition, the adoption of emoji-use or abbreviation in replacement of real-life conversation weakens the depth of emotional formations, which would severely hamper the understanding of emotional literacy among digital natives. Evidence suggests that teens with more screen time are experiencing decreased levels of empathy with those who are more face-to-face than others (Uhls et al., 2014). Together, these tendencies indicate that both AI and connectivity enhance connectivity; however, it is at the same time poisoning the emotional basis of relations between people, the long-term consequences of which are unsafe interpersonal understanding and social cohesion.

## Attention Fragmentation and Cognitive Overload

The AI-based communication systems have also played a major role in facilitating attention fragmentation as people find it hard to exercise prolonged focus and concentration under the pressure of streams of notifications, messages and the audience-selected stream of personal information. Every online interruption takes its toll on some cognitive resources and leads to a condition of continuous partial attention: individuals become constantly distracted (Rosen et al., 2013). Social networking services such as Twitter and Facebook rely on push notifications and algorithm driven feeds that seek to attract instant attention to their users rapidly alternating activities. Such a multitasking environment makes it harder to focus and causes a memory loss as well as the loss of productivity. With continued exposure to fragmented digital life, the power of long-lasting concentration in the brain is deconditioned, and a reflexive dependence on short-cuts of the superficial level information processing is cultivated (Carr 2010).

Simultaneously, the ubiquity of information provided by AI systems implies cognitive overload, which can be described as the scenario in which the cognitive system is unable to process all the information received due to its high complexity and quantity. Recommendation engines, newsfeeds and streaming services are a continuous source of personalized content that leads to decision fatigue and exhaustive thinking (Eppler & Mengis, 2004). In younger users, this fatigue can inhibit academic performance and learning results, and in adults, it has been associated with stress, loss of job effectiveness, and decision-making process (Mark et al., 2015). The consistent pressure to use the need to constantly update the digital platforms creates the mood of urgency and fear of missing out (FOMO), which also increases the cognitive load. Together, fragmentation of attention and cognitive overloads manifest the way in which engagement strategies mediated by AI redefine not only the communication pattern but the entire system of cognition with long-term effects on individual psyches and overall productivity of society.

## Displacement of Face-to-Face Communication

The widespread use of digital platforms that are powered by AI has led to the replacement of in-person communication with its polar opposite, moving individuals towards the practice of establishing and maintaining their social bonds. The less interactions take place face to face, the fewer possibilities are people to communicate directly (Turkle, 2015). Usually, digital communication focuses more on speed, brevity, and convenience at the expense of richness of emotional cues like tone of voice, body language and facial expressions which are essential in building trust and empathy. Reliance on mediated communications can gradually value socialization aptitudes to the point where people have a harder time understanding different situations or socializing when these communications are disabled (Drago, 2015). Such change can also bring superficial bonds as digital relations can substitute more meaningful relations that are cultivated via face-to-face communication.

In displacement effect, the displacement is very pronounced in family and school circles. Research shows that parents and children in many cases have started to give precedence to screen usage over shared activities, hence depriving themselves of time to bond in an optimum manner (McDaniel & Radesky, 2018). In learning institutions, the youth are more fascinated by virtual communication than direct contact, thus affecting collaborative education and reducing the bond among peers. In the same way, in workplace settings, there is a need to turn more to solutions like chatbots and auto-generated emails in the name of increased efficiency but at the cost of real human interaction and group collaboration. Although digital technologies help to create a global connection, the replacement of physical communication with AI enhanced communication can harm emotional integrity of social relationships, which is why the possibility of meaningful human interactions should be provided alongside with digital efficiency.

## Digital Identity and Self-Esteem Issues

AI-based systems have a significant impact on digital identity formation because users more and more behave online and conduct an online version of themselves. Instagram, TikTok and Facebook promote this selective promotion of idealized images of our lives with the complicity of the algorithms that favor accessibility of the most visually appealing or interesting content (Marwick, 2013). The pressure to achieve socially desirable norms is created by this curation especially to individuals in the adolescents and young adult age who are still building identities. This gap between oneself and the digital self in the long-time perspective may develop internal conflict, affect emotional dissonance, and produce low self-acceptance (Michikyan et al., 2014). Moreover, the metric of identity via likes, shares, and followers promotes the concept of external validation as the gauge of self-worthiness and more self-esteem begins to rely on algorithmically mediated responses as a clear measure of identity.

The connection between digital identity and problems of self-esteem manifests itself especially in this social comparison. Curtailed social media images related to unrealistic beauty, lifestyle, and success are reflected back to society via AI-driven algorithms resulting in poor self-perceptions and body dissatisfaction (Fardouly et al., 2015). As the studies indicate, consistent exposure to such content is related to an increase of anxiety, depressive symptoms, and decreased self-esteem, especially among adolescents (Vogel et al., 2014). Adults, similarly, can experience this sense of inadequacy on professional sites such as LinkedIn when observers see themselves up against promoted peers that the algorithm chooses to display. This dynamic shows that through the curation and amplification of particular identities by AI, how people are seen by others has a direct and significant influence on how people see themselves. With digital identity becoming ingrained in social life, the combination of the digital identity with self-esteem provides a stark indication that critical digital literacy and social comparison resilience promotion interventions are needed.

## Mental Health Consequences: Anxiety, Depression, Sleep Disorders

The negative mental health outcomes have also become associated with AI-driven communication technologies and digital platforms, mainly occurring in terms of anxiety, depression, and sleep disturbances. The addictive nature of interactions with online services provided by algorithmic design solutions (notifications, infinite scroll, and other personalized recommendations, etc.) results in a loop of incessant monitoring and reliance that leads to the increase of stress and anxiety levels (Elhai et al., 2017). Social media, specifically, worsens psychological dissatisfaction through the intensification of social comparison and fear of missing out (FOMO), which is closely intertwined with greater anxiety symptoms (Oberst et al., 2017). Equally, the demand to uphold a groomed online personality can further fuel depression, since users feel a sense of disappointment when expectations of their online approval and attention is not met. The latter effects are particularly intense among adolescents and young adults whose susceptibility to peer validation pressures and algorithmic augmentation of socially desirable material are more intense.

Sleep disorders are another significant mental health outcome that is caused by excessive use of AI-driven platforms. Easy availability of smartphones and addictive nature of social media lead to procrastination of going to bed and poor sleep hygiene, as people keep on consuming online information well after bedtime (Levenson et al., 2017). The light of screens changes the blue color, which damages the circadian rhythms, lowering the quality and the quantity of sleep. Unhealthy sleep, in its turn, worsens symptoms of anxiety and depression, but these conditions increase the chances of developing digital addiction even more. What is more, websites like YouTube, TikTok, or Instagram use the autoplay feature and recommendation engines promoting binge-watching or long scrolling, which disrupts rest directly. Together, the evidence points to the conclusion that in as much as AI-driven platforms provide an unprecedented ability to connect, they are also a source of a public health problem as they increase the severity of mental health disorders and disrupt important biological processes like sleep.

# ETHICAL AND SOCIETAL CONCERNS

## Algorithmic Bias and Inequity in Communication Platforms

Among the most urgent ethical issues of AI-based communication technologies, we should point out the problem of algorithmic bias that may cement and even enhance the social inequalities existing in the population. Historical datasets that are used to train the machine learning algorithms usually present prejudices about key societal categories of race, gender, age, and even socioeconomic status. Subsequently, biases can become a part of communication services, resulting in unfair treatment of users (Noble, 2018). By way of illustration, content moderation systems have been found to excessively censor marginalized voices, and recommendation engines tend to marginalize minority voices, in favor of globally popular, marketable, content (Binns, 2018). Similarly, facial recognition and sentiment analysis algorithms that are adopted within communications tools have been shown to be more racially and gender biased thus misclassifying and excluding. Such systemic biases not only corrupt the precious feel of digital communications but also pose potential issues with equitability, representation, and equitability.

Social impacts of algorithmic bias are also far beyond the personal experience of users as this makes certain patterns of inclusion and exclusion in the online realm as a whole. In social media, algorithms may be biased so that they limit diversity of opinion and promote stereotypes; this will destroy democratic discourse (ONeil, 2016). Furthermore, the digital divide is exacerbated by inequity in access to AI-powered systems of communication which contribute to privileged populations receiving enhanced personalization and connectivity, whereas disadvantaged populations are underrepresented or left out. The commercialization of AI also reinforces content amplification, which is profit-driven, and that may impact minority voices because it will serve the prevailing cultural narratives (Noble, 2018). To resolve these issues, it is not sufficient to introduce technical solutions, e.g., fairness-aware machine learning models, but also have ethical frameworks that put a strong emphasis on accountability, inclusiveness, and transparency within communication platforms. Such efforts are important in case algorithmic bias exacerbates social inequalities and destroys trust in the systems of digital communication.

## Surveillance Capitalism and Privacy Erosion

The advent of surveillance capitalism is associated with the development of AI-based communication tools that extensively gather, process, and sell information about users as part of the profit-making process (Zuboff, 2019). Each post likes, shares, and chatbot interaction produces the information that can be used by platforms to create specific behavioral profiles. The profiles are then sold to advertisers or can be used to give highly personalized content to maximize engagement and, as a result, advertising revenue. Though this model contributes to improving the efficiency of targeted advertising, individual privacy and autonomy will be sacrificed. The users are not always aware of the level of data collection and how their personal data is used, which is deemed critical in terms of informed consent and ethical clarification (Couldry & Mejias, 2019). This objectification of humanity changes the role of communication as a social communication into a transactional mechanism brought on by surveillance and forecasting.

One of the most notable effects of surveillance capitalism, privacy erosion, is one of the worst effects. AI-powered systems not only monitor the explicit actions of users, but they also predict such personal information as emotions, political views, and vulnerabilities (Calo, 2014). These intrusive behaviors expose the user to manipulation, specific misinformation and exploitation of any psychological weaknesses and push towards the aim of digital addiction. Besides, the widespread storage of personal information poses the risk of exploitation by corporations and states powers, demanding extreme caution against civil liberty across the globe. It has facilitated the absence of effective regulatory structures that hold technology firms responsible because they have tightened the asymmetrical power structures between companies and individuals (Zuboff, 2019). In order to combat surveillance capitalism, there must be more protective data policy, the creation of platforms that prioritize the desires of the user, and social consciousness that personal information is a commodity on the online market.

## Consent and Data Transparency

The principles of consent and transparency of data are core to ethical communication technologies, but those principles tend to be violated in AI-driven platforms. In principle, the decision on what data is collected, used and shared should be clear with well-informed users. In reality, however, mechanisms of consent are often ensconced in long and complicated terms-of-service agreements that the majority of people read and comprehend incompletely (Solove, 2013). This informational black hole turns consent into a mere formality as opposed to significant protection. In addition, platforms use "dark patterns" which tricks the user into accepting terms of sharing his or her data without their full understanding (Mathur et al., 2019). This can lead to a situation where the users inadvertently decline to take control over important personal information, thus subjecting them to abuse of the very notion of autonomy that is the point of consent in the first place.

Data transparency is also problematic since practices on most platforms lack clarity with regard to the processes in which algorithms work and how personal data can be used to make decisions. The black box nature of algorithmic systems along with the difficulty of understanding why particular content is displayed and which particular advertisements are delivered, as well as the nature of their digital profiles, presents difficulties in knowing exactly how they are put together (Pasquale, 2015). Such lack of transparency undermines the credibility of digital communication platforms, and the issue of accountability emerges as algorithmic choices will result in discrimination, misinformation, or a hooked design. Policy measures like the General Data Protection Regulation (GDPR) in the EU have put into place greater demands on informed consent and algorithm disclosure, but its application has been uneven across different jurisdictions globally (Voigt & Von dem Bussche, 2017). Trusting AI-driven communication media therefore not only needs legal frameworks, but also a cultural shift in the direction of increased exposure, user education and data governance responsibility.

## Manipulation and Loss of Autonomy

Manipulative design Techniques Communication Using manipulative design strategies, it is possible to control or subvert individual autonomy through programming techniques that sway the decision and action of users covertly. Platforms help determine what users look at, how they interact, and what they even assume based on the personalized content delivery through predictive algorithms and without their conscious understanding (Susser et al., 2019). Cognitive biases, including targeted advertising, nudging mechanisms, and algorithmically curated feeds exploit these cognitive biases to influence their choices in order to best suit platform profitability as opposed to the well-being of the person utilizing them. To give an example, the technique of infinite scroll or autoplay is created to decrease the potential of the user to disengage, which is a form of behavioral manipulation that constrains the freedom of choice (Eyal, 2014). This loss in autonomy begs ethical questions as to whether people are actually pursuing free will, or simply reacting to scenarios programmed to make the maximum interaction.

The wider consequences of such manipulation on society include affecting individual decision-making in a democracy and autonomous decision-making as a group. Studies have indicated that algorithmic curation potentially affects political beliefs, consumer habits, and even electoral decision-making by prioritizing and de-prioritizing particular information (Tufekci, 2015). In this regard, communication services threaten to turn into the tools of covert compulsion, as autonomy is undermined but not directly denied access. The near-continuous customization of content also introduces the concept of dependency, with users accustomed to being in an environment that predicts their expectations and preferences further eliminating critical referrals and independent volition (Helbing et al., 2019). To protect autonomy in digital communication, ethical guidelines in designing and regulatory practices are urgently needed along with more accountability of algorithms. Unless this is prevented, the manipulation by AI puts not only individual liberty at risk but also social and political structures at risk.

## SOLUTIONS AND STRATEGIES

### Digital Literacy for Individuals and Communities

Increasing digital literacy should be considered to be one of the strategies that can help to eliminate the risks of AI-induced digital addiction and assist individuals in using technology in a controlled manner. Digital literacy is not the same as the ability to learn simple technology; it is about having the skills to assess online information critically, discussing the influence of algorithms in information distribution, and the skills to make effective decisions on how to use the digital environment (Livingstone, 2004). At the individual level, this translates into knowing how to get familiar with manipulative design elements like notifications, infinite scroll, or algorithmic curation, and acquiring the ability to resist compulsive use. The biggest contribution of schools and universities is that they instill digital literacy by setting a curriculum that encompasses more than just the technical ability to operate digital tools, but rather the ethics and psychology of our digital existence (Ng, 2012). Helping young people understand the attention-like commodification process underlying digital systems creates resilience against addictive design and can empower participants to control the balance between the online and physical worlds.

On a local level, programs of digital literacy can increase local awareness and build up online healthier digital environments. Combining community-based programs with workshops and public campaigns, parents, educators, and other professionals can be educated and informed about the benefits, as well as the risks of AI-driven communication technologies (Ribble & Miller, 2013). Societies that allow discussion digital habits openly also foster accountability and the support of individuals who want to curb troublesome use. Furthermore, encouraging digital literacy among generations will guarantee the protection of vulnerable groups of people such as children, adolescents, and older adults because they will have the resources to operate within digital challenges in a safe manner. Integrating digital literacy into the educational, cultural, and policy systems would help societies to become less vulnerable to the effects of digital addiction and help themselves use technology in more beneficial and well-being-, autonomy-, and inclusive-oriented ways.

## Mindful Technology Use and Healthy Communication Habits

Promoting mindful use of technology is one of the crucial mechanisms to combat compulsive behavior created through AI-driven platforms. In the case of mindfulness, it involves being deliberate and mindful about the use of digital devices, having awareness about how one is spending their time online and how individual applications or platforms are affecting their emotional state of being (Kabat-Zinn, 2003). Such basic measures as turning off unnecessary notifications, setting up breaks during which you are supposed to stay off the screen and adoptive self-observation can help people restore a sense of control over their online usage (Van Velthoven et al., 2018). Setting functions like setting the digital curfews or device-free mealtimes helps build self-regulation and engages in making off-screen interaction healthier. These can enable people to resist the tricks of digital environments and regain control over their attention by minimizing the danger of overuse and addiction.

Fostering good communication practices is a useful accompaniment to mindful technology use as it fosters moderation between use of online communication and in-person communication. Studies show that those who are more focused on face-to-face communication tend to be more empathetic and emotionally intelligent and have more satisfying relations than people who communicate mostly online (Turkle, 2015). To promote healthier communication, families, teachers, organizations and institutions should lead by example by fostering healthier communication through being good communicators and active listeners, prioritizing communication in person, as opposed to using a computer to communicate. At a more cultural level, de-emphasizing the perpetual connectivity that tends to be both overemphasized in the public health campaign and in the mass, media can help shift cultural norms towards a more measured approach to communication and personal connection (accessibility and availability are two key concepts here). Fighting the negative impacts of AI-based platforms and ensuring positive engagement in a digital world, people and entire communities can enhance their lives by cultivating both healthy attitudes toward technologies and healthy living in terms of means and methods of communication.

## Technological Interventions: Screen-Time Monitors, AI Moderators

Although AI-based platforms have a role in digital addiction, another intervention to the problem is technologies as resolutions. Monitoring tools embedded within the devices and apps provide the capability to track and control the amount of time spent online and include daily use reports, app time constraints, and off time scheduling (Hiniker et al., 2016). Self-awareness is enhanced with the help of these tools as it provides tangible data about the consumption habits of people because individual people may make informed decisions regarding when and how they should use the digital media more often. Notably, screen-time interventions are corrective as well as preventive in that they allow users to become aware of the early warning signs of problematic use before they develop into a full-blown addiction problem. When bundled with personalized nudges and reminders, they can help induce healthier habits and curb compulsive behaviors.

Alongside this, AI moderators and online well-being assistants are currently developing as a potential tool to deal with problematic or excessive behaviors. Contrasting with the monitoring solutions, AI moderators take an active part in the moderation by filtering the toxic content, detecting bad behaviors, and promoting positive communication within an online environment (Gillespie, 2018). To take a couple of examples, sites such as YouTube and Instagram are incorporating AI to mark dangerous material and remind users when they have viewed over the top or provocative content. Simultaneously, AI assistants can follow the aim of being well-being-focused and advise screen breaks, direct users based on their interests to activities that are not connected with the screen or even adjust the content delivery to minimize the addictive loop (Mark et al., 2016). As fears of unwarranted monitoring and intrusion continue to run high, these technological developments exemplify the power AI might support introducing more healthy digital environments instead of exacerbating the addiction. Such tools are, however, only successful in effective deployments when their governance is transparent and ethical safeguards are enforced to support the well-being of the users and not corporate interests.

## Therapeutic Approaches to Digital Detox and Rehabilitation

In addition to technological solutions, there is therapeutic aspect of treating digital addiction that aids restoring equilibrium in the life of the users. Among the available methods of insuring dependence on constant connectivity and recovering personal well-being, digital detox programs, which include temporary or organized breaks with technology, have become increasingly popular (Syvertsen & Enli, 2019). Such programs focus on self-reflection, mindfulness, reconnection with offline activities and have been shown to improve the screen time user experiences in measurable stress reduction rates and ability to maintain attention span. Structured detox strategies may be effective interventions that re-set some unhealthy routines among some individuals particularly adolescent and young adults by breaking the habit-loop of compulsive screens usage (Kuss & Lopez-Fernandez, 2016). These methods work best when used together with psychoeducation wherein they can educate the users about the psychological process behind a digital addiction and provide them with coping skills to deal with the urge of engaging with a device.

Treatment of more severe cases requires clinical interventions and rehabilitation to deal with underlying dependence-related behavioral and psychological problems. CBT has also become one of the best treatment methods of internet and smartphone addiction as it focuses on the identification of maladaptive thoughts and the replacement of such thoughts with more positive coping skills (Young, 2017b). Group therapy and family interventions are also the key elements in the patients, especially those who have reached adolescent age and are more likely to be accountable and rebuild the offline social support. Besides, treatment facilities devoted to technological afflictions are growing around the world, with their structured setting allowing a user to gradually become de-addicted to technology under the supervision of professionals. Finally, AI-infused technologies have become an inseparable part of modern life; however, a thoughtful and healing process will help to regain balance, resilience, and a healthier technology-lifestyle relationship.

## THE ROLE OF INSTITUTIONS AND POLICY

### Educational Reforms for Digital Wellness and AI Awareness

Through educational institutions, the approach to technology has great importance to shape how individuals use technology and become aware of AI technologies, making digital wellness and AI awareness a part of modern curriculums. By teaching the students about the role of a digital citizen, ethically minded use of AI, and other healthy communication patterns, schools and universities will be able to instill a better sense of critical thinking about their online actions, as well as learning to identify deceptive design methods (Livingstone & Helsper, 2007). Curricula that integrate technical equaling the social-emotional skills, including resilience training, mindfulness practices, etc. give students the skills necessary to balance online and offline life. Besides, by introducing AI literacy to the learning process, one teaches people to be more aware of the impact of algorithms on information access, identity creation, and decision-making (Long & Magerko, 2020). With such reforms, future generations, in addition to being skilled digital users, become knowledgeable citizens that can resist the temptation of addiction regarding technology use and promote responsible digital use.

## Family and Parenting Strategies for Balanced Tech Use

The initial barrier to unhealthy digital interaction is the parents, and the families in general. The studies note that the parental mediation measures including co-use of technology, time limitations, and use of balanced electronic behaviors substantially reduce the risk of developing addictive behavior in children (Lauricella et al., 2015). You can also establish tech-free areas in the house, such as at dinner time, bedtime, etc., to remind children and make them understand the importance of in-person communication and to create bonding with relatives. Moreover, the establishment of open channels of communication between parents and children on the topic of online threats, manipulations of algorithms, and appropriate behavior will facilitate greater trust and make it possible to self-regulate (Coyne et al., 2021). Families can develop a proactive approach to help create an environment where digital technology becomes a part of everyday life and does not replace the healthy relationships, learning, or well-being of the person.

## Governmental Regulation and Tech Industry Accountability

At the structural level, governmental regulations and responsibility in the industry will be necessary to reduce the danger of AI-based digital addiction. Policy makers across the globe are coming to realize the necessity of policies ensuring that algorithmic processes are transparent, that data is more secure, and that a set of ethical standards are to be established around persuasive design (European Commission, 2021). AI regulations, such as the EU General Data Protection Regulation (GDPR) and the forthcoming AI Act are an undoubtedly crucial step toward protecting user autonomy and privacy. But proper governance must also involve individual companies in the technology industry being responsible for their contribution to addictive engagement loop patterns using content algorithms, gamification strategies, or targeted advertising (Yeung, 2018). Industry stakeholders, governments, and civil society organizations should work together to create systems of accountability that center on betterment of the society, instead of the bottom line of the corporate. In this way, AI and communication technologies should become instruments of liberation, as opposed to being exploitive.

## FUTURE DIRECTIONS

### The Rise of Immersive Technologies: Metaverse and Virtual Companions

With the advent of the metaverse and AI incorporation of virtual companions, it can be described as a radical change in online communication. These worlds are suggestive of hyper-personalized, interactive experiences, where users can socialize, work, and form communities, in persistent virtual worlds (Mystakidis, 2022). Included among the latter are virtual companions, which are aimed at curbing loneliness by giving the perception of companionship and empathy through the use of natural language processing and affective computing, but also putting people at greater risk of becoming dependent on artificial beings (de Barcelos Silva et al., 2019). Although these creations present avenues to diffuse education, entertainment, and social integration, there arises some ethical issues pertaining to the boundaries in paradigm circles of reality and virtuality, the addictive nature, and the commodification of human relationships.

### Emotionally Intelligent AI: Friend or Foe?

The problem of creation of emotionally intelligent AI, which is able to perceive and adequately respond to the emotions of a human bring opportunities and risks to communication. On the one hand, emotionally intelligent systems will be able to support customer service, therapy, and education by proposing personalized and empathetic enhancements (McStay, 2018). The other one, on the contrary, may be used with manipulating intent, influencing consumer emotions through emotional profiling with a view of ensuring maximum interaction or maximizing engagement (Cowie et al., 2020). The twin possibilities of emotionally intelligent AI make it especially necessary to draw up regulatory and ethical guidelines that will be able to ensure that such technologies are exploitative of human well-being rather than a means to enhance it.

### Rethinking Human-AI Relationships in Communication

With the growing penetration of AI into everyday communication, reconsideration in terms of the relationship between human and AI is required. Although the introduction of AI chatbots and assistants is based on the promises of efficiencies, their rise in social interaction creates doubts and confusion about authenticity, trust, and relational intimacy (Turkle, 2017). Users can develop attachments to AI-created creatures, creating uncertainties in regard to human-machine communication and boundaries on emotional dependency and reality in relationships. Future discussion needs to look at the way that these interactions transform human identity, how they transform our relationships with others, and our culture, including ways in which AI can enhance and deepen human relationships and not substitute them.

### Building Ethical, Transparent, and Human-Centric AI Ecosystems

The future of AI in communications technologies is based on the development of ethical, transparent, and human-centric ecosystems. This necessitates the design of algorithms that are fair, inclusive, and accountable and that users still have control over what they do with their data and online decisions (Jobin et al., 2019). Artificial intelligence must be transparently governed; transnational collaboration between governments, industry and civil society is necessary to ensure that artificial intelligence advances serve a positive societal good. By including human rights, digital well-being, and sustainability in AI systems, the next generation of communication technologies is able to leave behind the even exploitative model of communication toward one that empowers people and reinforced democratic engagement.

## CONCLUSION

### Synthesis of Core Insights

The thought process behind this paper has proven that the possibility of revolutionizing communication through the integration of AI and digital communications does not come without great risk. With inventions like chatbots, recommendation systems and emotionally intelligent systems, IA has transformed the world of communications, ushering in maximum connectivity, individual customization and efficiency. These same systems have also entailed greater tendencies toward digital addiction, attention fragmentation, displacement of in-person communication, and serious concerns of empathy loss, privacy, and mental health (Turkle, 2015; Zuboff, 2019). Such ethical issues as algorithmic discrimination, surveillance capitalism, and manipulative design are indicators of the necessity to introduce accountability, transparency, and user agency. Meanwhile, responses not only prove feasible but also reveal towards healthier relations to technology, through the means of digital literacy, mindful technology use, therapeutical practices, and institutional transformations. The sum of these reflections points to the need to make the future of digital communication not only technologically enabled but also governed by focused human values and by social accountability.

## Rethinking Digital Engagement in the Age of AI

The overall design and approach to digital interaction must change as we move into the new phase of immersive technologies, emotionally intelligent AI, and the metaverse and put greater emphasis on human well-being and free will. The barriers are not to oppose technological development but to develop AI systems that will reinforce ethical communication, inclusivity, and respect for humanity (Jobin et al., 2019). This reconsideration needs to have a balance in using the advantages of AI, e.g. global connectivity, efficiency, personalization, and addressing the risks of being manipulated, dependent, and unequal. Digital engagement of the age of AI eventually has to transform into a form of conscious and mindful involvement that should be supported by educational system, family- and community-based approaches, effective regulation, and good practices of the industry. By imagining and creating human-centered AI ecosystems, society will make sure that digital technologies reinforce those very aspects of empathy, trust, and real human connection, as opposed to weakening those.

# REFERENCES


Alter, A. (2017). *Irresistible: The Rise of Addictive Technology and the Business of Keeping Us Hooked*. Penguin Press.

Andreassen, C. S., Billieux, J., Griffiths, M. D., Kuss, D. J., Demetrovics, Z., Mazzoni, E., & Pallesen, S. (2017). The relationship between addictive use of social media and video games and symptoms of psychiatric disorders: A large-scale cross-sectional study. *Psychology of Addictive Behaviors*, *30*(2), 252–262. DOI: 10.1037/adb0000160 PMID: 26999354

Andreassen, C. S., Torsheim, T., Brunborg, G. S., & Pallesen, S. (2012). Development of a Facebook addiction scale. *Psychological Reports*, *110*(2), 501–517. DOI: 10.2466/02.09.18.PR0.110.2.501-517 PMID: 22662404

Bahdanau, D., Cho, K., & Bengio, Y. (2015). Neural machine translation by jointly learning to align and translate. *arXiv preprint arXiv:1409.0473*. https://doi.org//arXiv.1409.0473DOI: 10.48550

Berridge, K. C., & Robinson, T. E. (2016). Liking, wanting, and the incentive-sensitization theory of addiction. *The American Psychologist*, *71*(8), 670–679. DOI: 10.1037/amp0000059 PMID: 27977239

Binns, R. (2018). Fairness in machine learning: Lessons from political philosophy. *Proceedings of the 2018 Conference on Fairness, Accountability, and Transparency (FAT)*, 149–159. DOI: 10.1145/3287560.3287591

Calo, R. (2014). Digital market manipulation. *The George Washington Law Review*, *82*(4), 995–1051.

Carr, N. (2010). *The Shallows: What the Internet Is Doing to Our Brains*. W. W. Norton & Company.

Couldry, N., & Mejias, U. A. (2019). *The Costs of Connection: How Data is Colonizing Human Life and Appropriating It for Capitalism*. Stanford University Press.

Covington, P., Adams, J., & Sargin, E. (2016). Deep neural networks for YouTube recommendations. *Proceedings of the 10th ACM Conference on Recommender Systems*, 191–198. DOI: 10.1145/2959100.2959190

Cowie, R., Douglas-Cowie, E., & Cox, C. (2020). Beyond emotion recognition: Building emotionally intelligent systems. *IEEE Transactions on Affective Computing*, *11*(1), 3–6. DOI: 10.1109/TAFFC.2019.2959387

Coyne, S. M., Rogers, A. A., Zurcher, J. D., Stockdale, L., & Booth, M. (2021). Does time spent using social media impact mental health? An eight-year longitudinal study. *Computers in Human Behavior, 114*, 106528. DOI: 10.1016/j.chb.2020.106528

de Barcelos Silva, A., Barbosa, J. L. V., & Gomes, J. O. (2019). Virtual reality as a tool for evaluation of quality of life in the elderly. *Behaviour & Information Technology, 38*(1), 68–85. DOI: 10.1080/0144929X.2018.1519030

Dong, G., Lin, X., & Potenza, M. N. (2017). Decreased functional connectivity in an executive control network is related to impulsivity in internet gaming disorder. *Progress in Neuro-Psychopharmacology & Biological Psychiatry, 79*, 370–378. DOI: 10.1016/j.pnpbp.2017.07.024

Drago, E. (2015). The effect of technology on face-to-face communication. *The Elon Journal of Undergraduate Research in Communications, 6*(1), 13–19.

Elhai, J. D., Levine, J. C., Dvorak, R. D., & Hall, B. J. (2017). Fear of missing out, need for touch, anxiety and depression are related to problematic smartphone use. *Computers in Human Behavior, 63*, 509–516. DOI: 10.1016/j.chb.2016.05.079

Eppler, M. J., & Mengis, J. (2004). The concept of information overload: A review of literature from organization science, accounting, marketing, MIS, and related disciplines. *The Information Society, 20*(5), 325–344. DOI: 10.1080/01972240490507974

European Commission. (2021). *Proposal for a Regulation Laying Down Harmonised Rules on Artificial Intelligence*. Artificial Intelligence Act.

Eyal, N. (2014). *Hooked: How to Build Habit-Forming Products*. Portfolio/Penguin.

Fardouly, J., Diedrichs, P. C., Vartanian, L. R., & Halliwell, E. (2015). Social comparisons on social media: The impact of Facebook on young women's body image concerns and mood. *Body Image, 13*, 38–45. DOI: 10.1016/j.bodyim.2014.12.002 PMID: 25615425

Fisher, M. (2022). The business of keeping us hooked: How tech companies monetize attention. *Journal of Digital Economy, 4*(2), 101–115. DOI: 10.1080/jde.2022.004

Flayelle, M., Maurage, P., Di Lorenzo, K. R., Vögele, C., Gainsbury, S. M., & Billieux, J. (2020). Binge-watching: What do we know so far? A first systematic review of the evidence. *Current Addiction Reports, 7*(1), 44–60. DOI: 10.1007/s40429-020-00299-8

Følstad, A., & Brandtzaeg, P. B. (2017). Chatbots and the new world of HCI. *Interactions (New York, N.Y.), 24*(4), 38–42. DOI: 10.1145/3085558

Gillespie, T. (2018). *Custodians of the Internet: Platforms, Content Moderation, and the Hidden Decisions That Shape Social Media.* Yale University Press.

Griffiths, M. D. (2005). A 'components' model of addiction within a biopsychosocial framework. *Journal of Substance Use, 10*(4), 191–197. DOI: 10.1080/14659890500114359

Hamari, J., Koivisto, J., & Sarsa, H. (2014). Does gamification work? — A literature review of empirical studies on gamification. *47th Hawaii International Conference on System Sciences,* 3025–3034. DOI: 10.1109/HICSS.2014.377

Helbing, D., Frey, B. S., Gigerenzer, G., Hafen, E., Hagner, M., Hofstetter, Y., & Zwitter, A. (2019). Will democracy survive big data and artificial intelligence? *Scientific American.* Advance online publication. DOI: 10.1038/scientificamerican0217-25

Hiniker, A., Sobel, K., Hong, S. R., Suh, H., Kim, M., & Kientz, J. A. (2016). Texting while parenting: How adults use mobile phones while caring for children at the playground. *Proceedings of the 2015 ACM International Joint Conference on Pervasive and Ubiquitous Computing,* 727–738. DOI: 10.1145/2750858.2804288

Hoy, M. B. (2018). Alexa, Siri, Cortana, and more: An introduction to voice assistants. *Medical Reference Services Quarterly, 37*(1), 81–88. DOI: 10.1080/02763869.2018.1404391 PMID: 29327988

Jana, O., & Ghosh, S. (2024). *AI-driven communication and digital addiction: A psychological and social inquiry.* Brainware University.

Jobin, A., Ienca, M., & Vayena, E. (2019). The global landscape of AI ethics guidelines. *Nature Machine Intelligence, 1*(9), 389–399. DOI: 10.1038/s42256-019-0088-2

Kabat-Zinn, J. (2003). Mindfulness-based interventions in context: Past, present, and future. *Clinical Psychology : a Publication of the Division of Clinical Psychology of the American Psychological Association, 10*(2), 144–156. DOI: 10.1093/clipsy.bpg016

Lauricella, A. R., Wartella, E., & Rideout, V. J. (2015). Young children's screen time: The complex role of parent and child factors. *Journal of Applied Developmental Psychology, 36,* 11–17. DOI: 10.1016/j.appdev.2014.12.001

Levenson, J. C., Shensa, A., Sidani, J. E., Colditz, J. B., & Primack, B. A. (2017). Social media use before bed and sleep disturbance among young adults in the United States: A nationally representative study. *Sleep (Basel), 40*(9), zsx113. Advance online publication. DOI: 10.1093/sleep/zsx113 PMID: 28934521

Livingstone, S. (2004). Media literacy and the challenge of new information and communication technologies. *Communication Review*, *7*(1), 3–14. DOI: 10.1080/10714420490280152

Livingstone, S., & Helsper, E. J. (2007). Gradations in digital inclusion: Children, young people and the digital divide. *New Media & Society*, *9*(4), 671–696. DOI: 10.1177/1461444807080335

Long, D., & Magerko, B. (2020). What is AI literacy? Competencies and design considerations. *Proceedings of the 2020 CHI Conference on Human Factors in Computing Systems,* 1–16. DOI: 10.1145/3313831.3376727

Marengo, D., Montag, C., Sindermann, C., & Elhai, J. D. (2022). Digital media use and psychological well-being: Insights from Instagram. *Computers in Human Behavior Reports*, *7*, 100204. DOI: 10.1016/j.chbr.2022.100204

Mark, G., Czerwinski, M., & Iqbal, S. T. (2016). Effects of individual differences in blocking workplace distractions. *Proceedings of the 2016 CHI Conference on Human Factors in Computing Systems,* 6069–6080. DOI: 10.1145/2858036.2858212

Mark, G., Gudith, D., & Klocke, U. (2015). The cost of interrupted work: More speed and stress. *Proceedings of the SIGCHI Conference on Human Factors in Computing Systems,* 107–110. DOI: 10.1145/985692.985715

Marwick, A. E. (2013). *Status Update: Celebrity, Publicity, and Branding in the Social Media Age*. Yale University Press.

Mathur, A., Acar, G., Friedman, M. G., Lucherini, E., Mayer, J., Chetty, M., & Narayanan, A. (2019). Dark patterns at scale: Findings from a crawl of 11K shopping websites. *Proceedings of the ACM on Human-Computer Interaction, 3(CSCW),* 81. DOI: 10.1145/3359183

McDaniel, B. T., & Radesky, J. S. (2018). Technoference: Parent distraction with technology and associations with child behavior problems. *Child Development*, *89*(1), 100–109. DOI: 10.1111/cdev.12822 PMID: 28493400

McStay, A. (2018). Emotional AI: The Rise of Empathic Media. *Sage (Atlanta, Ga.)*. Advance online publication. DOI: 10.4135/9781526451293

Michikyan, M., Subrahmanyam, K., & Dennis, J. (2014). Can you tell who I am? Neuroticism, extraversion, and online self-presentation among young adults. *Computers in Human Behavior*, *33*, 179–183. DOI: 10.1016/j.chb.2014.01.010

Montag, C., Wegmann, E., Sariyska, R., Demetrovics, Z., & Brand, M. (2019). How to overcome taxonomical problems in the study of internet use disorders and what to do with "smartphone addiction"? *Journal of Behavioral Addictions*, *9*(4), 908–914. DOI: 10.1556/2006.8.2019.59 PMID: 31668089

Montag, C., Yang, H., & Elhai, J. D. (2021). On the psychology of TikTok use: A first glimpse from empirical findings. *Frontiers in Public Health*, *9*, 641673. DOI: 10.3389/fpubh.2021.641673 PMID: 33816425

Mystakidis, S. (2022). Metaverse. *Encyclopedia*, *2*(1), 486–497. DOI: 10.3390/encyclopedia2010031

Ng, W. (2012). Can we teach digital natives digital literacy? *Computers & Education*, *59*(3), 1065–1078. DOI: 10.1016/j.compedu.2012.04.016

Noble, S. U. (2018). *Algorithms of Oppression: How Search Engines Reinforce Racism*. New York University Press. DOI: 10.18574/nyu/9781479833641.001.0001

O'Neil, C. (2016). *Weapons of Math Destruction: How Big Data Increases Inequality and Threatens Democracy*. Crown Publishing.

Oberst, U., Wegmann, E., Stodt, B., Brand, M., & Chamarro, A. (2017). Negative consequences from heavy social networking in adolescents: The mediating role of fear of missing out. *Journal of Adolescence*, *55*(1), 51–60. DOI: 10.1016/j.adolescence.2016.12.008 PMID: 28033503

Panova, T., & Lleras, A. (2016). Avoidance or boredom: Negative mental health outcomes associated with use of mobile phones and social networking sites. *Computers in Human Behavior*, *58*, 249–258. DOI: 10.1016/j.chb.2015.12.062

Pasquale, F. (2015). *The Black Box Society: The Secret Algorithms That Control Money and Information*. Harvard University Press. DOI: 10.4159/harvard.9780674736061

Powers, A., & Kiesler, S. (2006). The advisor robot: Tracing people's mental model from a robot's physical attributes. *Proceedings of the 1st ACM SIGCHI/SIGART Conference on Human-Robot Interaction,* 218–225. DOI: 10.1145/1121241.1121280

Przybylski, A. K., Murayama, K., DeHaan, C. R., & Gladwell, V. (2013). Motivational, emotional, and behavioral correlates of fear of missing out. *Computers in Human Behavior*, *29*(4), 1841–1848. DOI: 10.1016/j.chb.2013.02.014

Ribble, M., & Miller, T. N. (2013). Educational leadership in an online world: Connecting students to technology responsibly, safely, and ethically. *Phi Delta Kappan*, *94*(5), 62–65. DOI: 10.1177/003172171309400514

Rosen, L. D., Carrier, L. M., & Cheever, N. A. (2013). Facebook and texting made me do it: Media-induced task-switching while studying. *Computers in Human Behavior, 29*(3), 948–958. DOI: 10.1016/j.chb.2012.12.001

Shum, H. Y., He, X., & Li, D. (2018). From Eliza to XiaoIce: Challenges and opportunities with social chatbots. *Frontiers of Information Technology & Electronic Engineering, 19*(1), 10–26. DOI: 10.1631/FITEE.1700826

Silver, D., Schrittwieser, K., Simonyan, K., Antonoglou, I., Huang, A., Guez, A., Hubert, T., Baker, L., Lai, M., Bolton, A., Chen, Y., Lillicrap, T., Hui, F., Sifre, L., van den Driessche, G., Graepel, T., & Hassabis, D. (2017). Mastering the game of Go without human knowledge. *Nature, 550*(7676), 354–359. DOI: 10.1038/nature24270 PMID: 29052630

Solove, D. J. (2013). Privacy self-management and the consent dilemma. *Harvard Law Review, 126*(7), 1880–1903.

Susser, D., Roessler, B., & Nissenbaum, H. (2019). Online manipulation: Hidden influences in a digital world. *Georgetown Law Technology Review, 4*(1), 1–45.

Syvertsen, T., & Enli, G. (2019). Digital detox: Media resistance and the promise of authenticity. *Convergence (London), 26*(5–6), 1269–1283. DOI: 10.1177/1354856519847325

Tufekci, Z. (2015). Algorithmic harms beyond Facebook and Google: Emergent challenges of computational agency. *Colorado Technology Law Journal, 13*(1), 203–218.

Turkle, S. (2015). *Reclaiming Conversation: The Power of Talk in a Digital Age*. Penguin Press.

Turkle, S. (2017). *Alone Together: Why We Expect More from Technology and Less from Each Other*. Basic Books.

Twenge, J. M., & Campbell, W. K. (2018). Associations between screen time and lower psychological well-being among children and adolescents: Evidence from a population-based study. *Preventive Medicine Reports, 12*, 271–283. DOI: 10.1016/j.pmedr.2018.10.003 PMID: 30406005

Uhls, Y. T., Ellison, N. B., & Subrahmanyam, K. (2014). Benefits and costs of social media in adolescence. *Pediatrics, 140*(Supplement 2), S67–S70. DOI: 10.1542/peds.2016-1758E PMID: 29093035

Van Velthoven, M. H., Powell, J., & Powell, G. (2018). Problematic smartphone use: Digital approaches to an emerging public health problem. *Digital Health, 4*, 2055207618759167. DOI: 10.1177/2055207618759167 PMID: 31463071

Vaswani, A., Shazeer, N., Parmar, N., Uszkoreit, J., Jones, L., Gomez, A. N., . . . Polosukhin, I. (2017). Attention is all you need. *Advances in Neural Information Processing Systems (NeurIPS), 30,* 5998–6008. DOI: 10.48550/arXiv.1706.03762

Vogel, E. A., Rose, J. P., Roberts, L. R., & Eckles, K. (2014). Social comparison, social media, and self-esteem. *Psychology of Popular Media Culture*, *3*(4), 206–222. DOI: 10.1037/ppm0000047

Voigt, P., & Von dem Bussche, A. (2017). *The EU General Data Protection Regulation (GDPR): A Practical Guide*. Springer., DOI: 10.1007/978-3-319-57959-7

Weizenbaum, J. (1966). ELIZA—A computer program for the study of natural language communication between man and machine. *Communications of the ACM*, *9*(1), 36–45. DOI: 10.1145/365153.365168

Williams, J. (2018). *Stand Out of Our Light: Freedom and Resistance in the Attention Economy*. Cambridge University Press., DOI: 10.1017/9781108453004

World Health Organization (WHO). (2018). *International Classification of Diseases 11th Revision (ICD-11): Gaming Disorder.* https://www.who.int/news-room/q-a-detail/gaming-disorder

Yeung, K. (2018). Algorithmic regulation: A critical interrogation. *Regulation & Governance*, *12*(4), 505–523. DOI: 10.1111/rego.12158

Yildirim, C., & Correia, A. P. (2015). Exploring the dimensions of nomophobia: Development and validation of a self-reported questionnaire. *Computers in Human Behavior*, *49*, 130–137. DOI: 10.1016/j.chb.2015.02.059

Young, K. S. (2017a). Cognitive behavioral therapy for internet addiction. In Montag, C., & Reuter, M. (Eds.), *Internet Addiction: Neuroscientific Approaches and Therapeutical Interventions* (pp. 193–204). Springer., DOI: 10.1007/978-3-319-46276-9_11

Young, K. S. (2017b). The evolution of internet addiction disorder. In Montag, C., & Reuter, M. (Eds.), *Internet Addiction* (pp. 3–17). Springer., DOI: 10.1007/978-3-319-46276-9_1

Zeng, J., Chan, C. H., & Fu, K. W. (2021). The anatomy of the Facebook algorithm: An exploratory study of its impact on news dissemination. *New Media & Society*, *23*(5), 1088–1109. DOI: 10.1177/1461444820902108

Zuboff, S. (2019). *The Age of Surveillance Capitalism: The Fight for a Human Future at the New Frontier of Power*. PublicAffairs.

# Chapter 7
# AI, Autonomy, and Addiction:
## A Legal–Psychological Analysis of Communication Technologies in the Digital Age

**Rakshit Sharma**
https://orcid.org/0009-0003-6419-0448
*Amity University, Greater Noida, India*

**Aditi Sharma**
https://orcid.org/0000-0003-0705-8208
*Amity University, Ranchi, India*

## ABSTRACT

*Artificial Intelligence (AI) has transformed human communication, reshaping emotional expression and behavior. While AI-driven tools like social media and digital assistants offer connectivity, they also fuel digital addiction, raising serious psychological and legal concerns. This chapter adopts an interdisciplinary lens, combining legal and psychological insights to explore how AI-mediated communication impairs autonomy and mental well-being. It examines behavioral triggers like dopamine loops and social validation, alongside legal frameworks such as India's IT Act, 2000, the Digital Personal Data Protection Act, 2023, and the EU's GDPR and DSA. The chapter highlights how algorithmic persuasion and platform design exploit cognitive vulnerabilities, calling for ethical AI design, stronger regulation, and stakeholder accountability. It advocates a rights-based framework to protect users and ensure AI enhances rather than undermines autonomy and resilience.*

DOI: 10.4018/979-8-3373-5606-8.ch007

## INTRODUCTION

In the contemporary digital era, artificial intelligence (AI) has become deeply embedded in human communication. From predictive text and voice assistants to content recommendation engines and social media algorithms, AI mediates how individuals express themselves, connect with others, and consume information. These technologies have drastically transformed interpersonal and group dynamics, enabling instantaneous global interaction, fostering creative expression, and redefining the boundaries of public and private discourse. However, this digital transformation is not without its darker dimensions. AI-mediated communication tools, particularly those embedded within social networking platforms, have given rise to new patterns of compulsive behaviour, psychological dependency, and reduced user autonomy, phenomena increasingly conceptualized under the term digital addiction.

Digital addiction, while not formally codified as a distinct mental disorder in all diagnostic systems, is gaining recognition in both psychological literature and public policy discussions. It encompasses problematic usage patterns of digital technologies, especially those augmented by AI, that interfere with daily functioning, mental health, and social relationships (Kuss & Griffiths, 2017). These patterns are not coincidental; rather, they are often the result of deliberate design features, commonly referred to as *persuasive technologies* or *dark patterns*, which are strategically deployed to maximize user engagement, time-on-platform, and behavioural predictability (Zuboff, 2019). In this sense, digital addiction is not simply a matter of individual willpower or screen discipline; it is a structural outcome of a technologically mediated ecosystem that prioritizes data harvesting and monetization over well-being.

AI's role in this behavioural transformation is central. Unlike static technologies of the past, AI evolves in real time, learning from user behaviour and dynamically adapting content to maximize engagement. Whether through algorithmic curation on social media platforms, emotionally responsive chatbots, or gamified messaging applications, AI interacts with core psychological drivers such as reward anticipation, fear of missing out (FOMO), and social validation (Montag & Diefenbach, 2018). This has led to an increasingly blurred line between autonomy and manipulation, as users often find themselves entangled in feedback loops designed to hijack attention and prolong digital immersion.

This chapter situates these developments within a dual-disciplinary framework: law and psychology. While psychological studies have documented the impact of digital overuse on cognitive development, emotional regulation, and social behaviour (Andreassen, 2015), legal scholarship has only recently begun to interrogate the structural and regulatory dimensions of digital addiction. Most legal frameworks, including those in India, have traditionally approached AI and digital platforms through the lens of data protection, cybercrime, or intermediary liability. However, there remains a critical gap in addressing the psychological harms induced by algorithmic manipulation and persuasive design. The law has yet to fully recognize digital addiction as a rights-based issue implicating autonomy, mental health, and informed consent.

This gap is particularly striking in light of constitutional protections such as the right to privacy, right to health, and right to personal liberty, rights that are potentially undermined by AI-driven platforms that operate without meaningful transparency or user control. For example, in India, the Supreme Court's landmark judgment in *Justice K.S. Puttaswamy v. Union of India* (2017) laid down the foundation for informational privacy and individual autonomy as fundamental rights under Article 21 of the Constitution. However, these principles have not yet been robustly applied to the realm of algorithmic design and digital compulsion. Similarly, international frameworks such as the General Data Protection Regulation (GDPR) and the EU's Digital Services Act (DSA) offer emerging models for regulating persuasive technology and safeguarding user agency, but their applicability across jurisdictions and enforcement effectiveness remain contested (Helberger et al., 2022).

The psychological implications of AI communication tools are especially pronounced among children, adolescents, and young adults, groups whose developmental trajectories are particularly vulnerable to continuous digital exposure. Empirical studies suggest that excessive engagement with AI-powered platforms correlates with increased levels of anxiety, depression, attention disorders, and diminished interpersonal empathy (Twenge & Campbell, 2018). Moreover, the constant exposure to algorithmically filtered content reinforces echo chambers, distorts perception of reality, and can significantly influence identity formation, social comparison, and self-esteem. These phenomena demand not only psychological intervention but also systemic, legal, and educational responses.

Recognizing the interdisciplinary nature of the challenge, this chapter aims to present a holistic analysis of AI-mediated communication and digital addiction through a legal-psychological lens. It begins by identifying the core psychological mechanisms that underpin addictive digital behaviour, drawing on clinical literature and neuropsychological models of reward and dependency. It then transitions into a legal examination of current regulatory approaches in India and other jurisdictions, evaluating their adequacy in protecting users, particularly minors and psychologically vulnerable individuals, from exploitative AI designs. By bridging these two perspectives, the chapter highlights the need for an integrated framework that treats digital addiction not only as a health crisis but as a structural consequence of algorithmic governance and legal neglect.

In doing so, the chapter also engages with the ethical dimensions of AI deployment in communication, questions around consent, manipulation, transparency, and platform accountability. These issues are not merely academic; they hold real-world consequences for how societies define autonomy, allocate responsibility, and protect citizens in an increasingly digital world. Moreover, the role of families, educational institutions, and governments is addressed not as peripheral but as central to building resilience and promoting digital literacy.

Ultimately, this chapter argues that digital addiction is not merely a behavioural anomaly, but a byproduct of contemporary AI design practices and regulatory inertia. Addressing it requires a rethinking of legal principles around consent, autonomy, and mental health, and a reconceptualization of psychological well-being in digital spaces. By integrating insights from law and psychology, this chapter contributes to a growing body of scholarship that seeks to hold AI systems accountable not only for what they do, but for how they shape human thought, emotion, and interaction.

## PROBLEM STATEMENT

The integration of artificial intelligence (AI) into digital communication platforms has revolutionized how individuals interact, exchange information, and maintain relationships. While these developments have enhanced connectivity and communication efficiency, they have also introduced new risks, particularly in the form of digital addiction, manipulation of user behaviour, and erosion of individual autonomy. AI systems embedded in platforms such as social media, messaging applications, and virtual assistants increasingly use behavioural data and algorithmic learning to optimize engagement. However, the optimization of user interaction is frequently pursued through techniques that exploit cognitive vulnerabilities, such as reward-seeking behaviour, impulsivity, and the human need for social validation (Burrell, 2016). These AI-driven mechanisms, though marketed as tools for enhanced user experience, often promote compulsive and dependent usage patterns, resulting in what is increasingly referred to as AI-induced digital addiction.

Digital addiction, in this context, refers to the compulsive, excessive, and dysfunctional use of AI-mediated digital platforms that significantly interferes with an individual's psychological well-being, social relationships, academic or professional functioning, and overall quality of life (Kuss & Pontes, 2018). Unlike substance-based addictions, digital addiction is behavioural and often covert, making it harder to detect and regulate. What compounds the issue is the fact that these behavioural patterns are not accidental or organic; they are frequently the direct outcome of intentional design decisions by technology companies, choices aimed at increasing engagement, data extraction, and profitability. Features such as infinite scroll, autoplay, notifications, and tailored recommendations are all rooted in AI's ability to learn user preferences and predict responses, ultimately fostering persistent user engagement (Eyal, 2014; Zuboff, 2019). These designs create feedback loops that condition users to return repeatedly, often without conscious awareness or control.

The psychological impact of such design-driven digital dependency is particularly concerning among children, adolescents, and young adults, whose cognitive and emotional faculties are still developing. Studies have shown strong correlations between excessive digital media usage and mental health issues, including depression, anxiety, attention-deficit disorders, and disrupted sleep patterns (Twenge & Campbell, 2018; Andreassen, 2015). Furthermore, continuous exposure to algorithmically curated content can alter social perceptions, encourage echo chambers, and reduce empathy by substituting face-to-face interactions with screen-based communication (Montag & Diefenbach, 2018). These outcomes highlight the need for a holistic understanding of digital addiction not merely as a personal failing, but as a structural and systemic issue rooted in the intersection of psychology, technology, and law.

Despite the growing body of psychological research identifying the addictive potential of AI-mediated platforms, legal frameworks across jurisdictions have been slow to respond. In India, digital regulation is primarily governed by the Information Technology Act, 2000, and more recently, the Digital Personal Data Protection Act, 2023. These frameworks focus largely on data protection, intermediary liability, and cybercrimes. However, they do not adequately address the psychological harms stemming from addictive design, persuasive technologies, or manipulative algorithms. Even globally, while the European Union's General Data Protection Regulation (GDPR) and Digital Services Act (DSA) take steps toward transparency and accountability in algorithmic operations, they fall short of explicitly regulating AI's role in fostering addictive behaviour or holding platforms liable for mental health outcomes (Helberger et al., 2022).

Another critical issue is the erosion of user autonomy and meaningful consent in AI-driven environments. While users may click "I agree" to terms of service or privacy policies, these forms of consent are often uninformed, coerced, or illusory, especially in cases where platforms exploit psychological biases to influence user behaviour (Susser, Roessler, & Nissenbaum, 2019). In this regard, digital addiction also becomes a rights-based issue, implicating the right to privacy, mental health, and informational self-determination. These rights have been recognized in the Indian constitutional framework under Article 21, particularly in the Supreme Court's judgment in *Justice K.S. Puttaswamy v. Union of India* (2017), which affirmed privacy as a fundamental right. However, the practical extension of these rights into the realm of AI design and digital compulsion remains largely underdeveloped in both jurisprudence and policy.

Compounding this legal vacuum is the lack of institutional responsibility from key societal actors such as educational institutions, families, and technology corporations. Schools and parents often lack the tools or understanding to identify and address digital addiction among children, while corporate self-regulation remains insufficient and largely performative. The absence of legally mandated design ethics, mental health impact assessments, or user-centric accountability measures further deepens the crisis. There is also a significant research gap in understanding how AI systems, particularly in non-Western contexts like India, interact with cultural norms, family structures, and social expectations to influence addictive behaviours.

Given these multifaceted challenges, there is a pressing need for interdisciplinary research that bridges psychology and law to address digital addiction from both individual and structural perspectives. While psychological insights can help identify behavioural triggers and vulnerabilities, legal analysis is essential to frame appropriate regulatory, constitutional, and policy responses. This chapter aims to fill this critical void by offering a dual-pronged exploration of AI-induced digital addiction, diagnosing its psychological roots while simultaneously critiquing the legal and institutional structures that enable it. By doing so, it seeks to lay the foundation for a comprehensive framework that not only mitigates harm but also restores user autonomy, especially among vulnerable populations such as minors and young adults.

## SIGNIFICANCE OF STUDY

The advent of artificial intelligence (AI) in communication technologies marks a pivotal moment in the history of human interaction. From predictive algorithms on social media to AI-powered conversational agents, these tools are reshaping not only how people communicate but also how they think, behave, and relate to one another. While the benefits of AI in enhancing communication efficiency and accessibility are well documented, the unintended and often overlooked consequences, particularly the rise of digital addiction and diminished user autonomy, require urgent scholarly and policy attention.

This study is significant because it addresses a pressing yet underexplored intersection: the convergence of AI design, psychological vulnerability, and legal inaction. While digital addiction has increasingly been the subject of psychological inquiry (Kuss & Griffiths, 2017; Andreassen, 2015), and legal scholars have begun exploring data privacy and algorithmic transparency (Zuboff, 2019; Helberger et al., 2022), there remains a critical gap in integrating these fields to produce a holistic understanding of how AI-driven technologies impact human autonomy and mental health. This chapter seeks to bridge that divide, offering an interdisciplinary analysis that links the neuroscience of addiction to the jurisprudence of autonomy and consent.

One of the core contributions of this study lies in reframing digital addiction not merely as an individual behavioural issue but as a systemically induced condition emerging from deliberate technological design. The persuasive mechanisms embedded in AI systems, such as algorithmic nudging, endless scrolling, and notification triggers, are not accidental but are purposefully engineered to maximize user engagement (Eyal, 2014). These mechanisms exploit fundamental aspects of human cognition, including attention, reward anticipation, and fear of missing out (FOMO), leading to compulsive usage patterns. As such, addiction in digital environments is not solely a medical or psychological concern; it is a structural and ethical problem that demands regulatory scrutiny.

This structural framing has major legal implications. Consent, for instance, is a cornerstone of digital governance and data protection frameworks. However, in AI-mediated platforms, consent is often reduced to a perfunctory checkbox, stripped of its meaningfulness in light of manipulative design and information asymmetry (Susser, Roessler, & Nissenbaum, 2019). Users are nudged into behaviours they may not consciously endorse, raising profound concerns about autonomy, manipulation, and the erosion of informed decision-making. In countries like India, where digital literacy remains uneven and regulatory enforcement is weak, these challenges are magnified. The constitutional recognition of privacy and autonomy under Article 21 in *Justice K.S. Puttaswamy v. Union of India* (2017) offers a powerful legal foundation, yet its application to AI-mediated behavioural manipulation remains largely unexplored in practice and policy.

From a psychological standpoint, this study is significant for highlighting how AI-enhanced communication tools alter emotional development, social cognition, and attention regulation, especially among adolescents and young adults. Research has shown strong links between excessive digital media use and symptoms of anxiety, depression, and social withdrawal (Twenge & Campbell, 2018; Montag & Diefenbach, 2018). These psychological consequences are further compounded by the design of AI systems that prioritize emotionally charged, high-engagement content, often at the cost of emotional well-being and balanced information consumption. By integrating these psychological insights into a legal-ethical framework, the study emphasizes that mental health in the digital age must be viewed as a collective, structural responsibility, not merely an individual burden.

Another crucial dimension of the study is its policy relevance. As nations worldwide begin to grapple with the ethical and regulatory implications of AI, India is at a crossroads with its introduction of the Digital Personal Data Protection Act (2023) and the anticipated Digital India Act. While these legislative instruments address data protection and platform accountability to some extent, they do not yet explicitly regulate AI-induced behavioural manipulation or mental health impacts. This study offers timely insights that can inform future policymaking, particularly in areas such as platform design ethics, age-specific protections, algorithmic audits, and institutional responsibilities of tech companies.

Moreover, the chapter addresses the institutional vacuum surrounding digital addiction by examining the roles of families, schools, and governments. Educational institutions, in particular, are poorly equipped to deal with the psychological fallout of excessive screen time, while families often lack the awareness or tools to intervene meaningfully. This underscores the need for multistakeholder solutions that integrate psychological resilience programs, digital literacy curricula, and legal safeguards to mitigate harm and foster healthier digital ecosystems.

Finally, this study is globally significant. The issues it raises, digital dependency, diminished autonomy, algorithmic manipulation, are not confined to India or the Global South. Rather, they represent a global challenge in the digital age. However, much of the existing literature and regulatory action has been concentrated in the West. This chapter brings contextual specificity to the Indian legal, cultural, and psychological environment, contributing to the diversification of global AI ethics discourse and offering insights that may be adapted in similar socio-legal contexts.

In sum, this study is both timely and necessary. It speaks to the lived realities of millions who navigate AI-driven platforms daily, often without a full understanding of how their behaviour is being shaped, influenced, or even coerced. It challenges the notion that technology is a neutral tool and instead urges recognition of its power to affect human agency, mental health, and legal personhood. By doing so, the chapter hopes to advance not only academic scholarship but also legal reform and public awareness in addressing one of the most pressing yet underexamined crises of our time, digital addiction in the age of AI.

## METHODOLOGY

This chapter employs an interdisciplinary qualitative methodology that integrates doctrinal legal research with psychological literature review and case-based analysis. The aim is to bridge gaps between legal scholarship, behavioural science, and technology studies, offering a comprehensive lens to examine the phenomenon of AI-induced digital addiction and its implications for autonomy, mental health, and regulatory reform.

### Doctrinal Legal Research Approach

The legal component of this study is grounded in doctrinal research methodology, which focuses on the critical analysis of primary and secondary legal sources, including statutes, constitutional provisions, judicial decisions, regulatory frameworks, and scholarly commentaries (Hutchinson & Duncan, 2012). Central legal instruments examined include the Information Technology Act, 2000, the Digital

Personal Data Protection Act, 2023 (India), and relevant provisions of international frameworks such as the General Data Protection Regulation (GDPR) and the Digital Services Act (DSA) of the European Union.

The analysis considers how these legal instruments conceptualize user autonomy, privacy, consent, and platform liability in the context of AI-mediated communication systems. Special attention is paid to the constitutional framework in India, particularly Article 21 of the Constitution, which guarantees the right to life and personal liberty, encompassing mental health, privacy, and autonomy. Landmark cases such as *Justice K.S. Puttaswamy v. Union of India* (2017) are analysed to understand the judiciary's approach to digital rights, especially in contexts involving informational privacy and psychological well-being.

This doctrinal approach enables a normative evaluation of the adequacy of existing laws in responding to the harms posed by persuasive AI design and digital addiction. It also facilitates the identification of regulatory gaps, inconsistencies, and areas where legal reform is urgently required to protect vulnerable user populations from AI-driven behavioural manipulation.

## Psychological Literature Review

Complementing the legal analysis is a systematic review of psychological literature related to digital addiction, persuasive technology, and cognitive manipulation. Key psychological frameworks guiding this review include operant conditioning, dopamine reward circuits, and social learning theory, which explain how AI-driven platforms exploit neurobiological and behavioural mechanisms to increase user dependence (Montag & Diefenbach, 2018; Kuss & Pontes, 2018).

This component of the study synthesizes findings from peer-reviewed journals, meta-analyses, and empirical studies that examine the impact of prolonged AI-mediated communication on mental health outcomes, including anxiety, depression, attention disorders, and emotional dysregulation (Twenge & Campbell, 2018; Andreassen, 2015). It also incorporates clinical perspectives from the Diagnostic and Statistical Manual of Mental Disorders (DSM-5) and World Health Organization (WHO) criteria, particularly regarding behavioural addiction classifications such as gaming disorder.

The psychological literature not only provides insight into the symptomatology and causal mechanisms of digital addiction but also highlights the differential effects across age groups, with a specific focus on adolescents and young adults. This helps establish the need for age-specific legal protections and institutional interventions.

## Case-Based Analysis

The third methodological component involves a case study approach to illustrate real-world manifestations of AI-induced digital harm and the (in)effectiveness of regulatory responses. Notable cases analysed include:

- The Meta (Facebook/Instagram) lawsuits in the United States involving mental health harms in teenagers,
- The TikTok GDPR violation fines in the EU over data misuse and child-targeted content,
- Indian legal and policy developments such as the IT Rules 2021 and interventions by the Ministry of Electronics and Information Technology (MeitY).

This case studies serve to contextualize the theoretical insights derived from legal and psychological research in actual policy, litigation, and regulatory environments. The analysis of these cases also helps identify patterns of institutional responsibility, platform design strategies, and emerging jurisprudence on digital rights and well-being.

## Interdisciplinary Integration

The final analytical layer involves integrating the findings from legal and psychological domains to develop a comprehensive understanding of AI-induced digital addiction. This integration allows for the formulation of evidence-based recommendations for law reform, platform accountability, institutional roles, and preventive interventions grounded in behavioural science.

# LITERATURE REVIEW AND THEORETICAL FRAMEWORK

## Literature Review

The convergence of artificial intelligence (AI), digital communication, and behavioural psychology has given rise to a rich body of literature exploring both the benefits and drawbacks of AI-mediated interactions. Scholars have praised AI for revolutionizing human connectivity, expanding access to information, and fostering digital inclusivity (Kaplan & Haenlein, 2019). However, there is growing concern about the psychological and legal consequences of prolonged exposure to AI-driven platforms, especially those designed to maximize user engagement through persuasive and sometimes manipulative techniques.

## AI, Persuasive Technology, and Behavioural Manipulation

Much of the contemporary discourse on persuasive technology traces back to the foundational work of B.J. Fogg (2003), who conceptualized technology not merely as a passive tool but as an active agent capable of shaping user behaviour. Building on this foundation, scholars such as Zuboff (2019) have argued that digital platforms, powered by AI, operate under a logic of surveillance capitalism, where user data is continuously harvested, analysed, and monetized. These platforms are incentivized to keep users engaged for as long as possible, often at the expense of well-being. Persuasive mechanisms like infinite scroll, algorithmic content curation, and push notifications exploit users' psychological susceptibilities, such as reward anticipation and fear of missing out (Montag & Diefenbach, 2018).

Design elements that stimulate dopamine responses mimic the principles of operant conditioning, where variable reward systems (e.g., likes, shares, comments) reinforce continuous behaviour. Eyal (2014) terms this the "*hook model*," where AI-generated stimuli prompt users into recurring engagement cycles. This intersection of behavioural economics and design psychology has profound implications for addiction, especially when applied to social media, gaming, and messaging platforms.

## Digital Addiction and Psychological Harms

Digital addiction is increasingly recognized as a behavioural issue with serious psychological consequences. While not all excessive digital use qualifies as addiction, studies have shown that compulsive technology use can result in a range of mental health challenges, including anxiety, depression, insomnia, and cognitive impairments (Andreassen, 2015; Kuss & Griffiths, 2017). Adolescents and young adults are particularly vulnerable, given their neurodevelopmental stage and higher sensitivity to social stimuli (Twenge & Campbell, 2018).

The World Health Organization (WHO) has recognized "*gaming disorder*" in the International Classification of Diseases (ICD-11), further legitimizing concerns around behavioural addiction in digital environments. Research also points to a decline in empathy, face-to-face communication skills, and emotional regulation in users who spend excessive time on AI-mediated platforms (Radesky et al., 2020). These findings underscore the psychological risks associated with unchecked AI influence in human communication.

## Legal and Ethical Considerations

The legal literature on AI and digital addiction remains nascent but is rapidly evolving. Early legal concerns centered on data protection and privacy. Frameworks such as the General Data Protection Regulation (GDPR) in the European Union and India's Digital Personal Data Protection Act (2023) primarily focus on controlling data flow, ensuring user consent, and promoting transparency. However, critics argue that these frameworks do not go far enough in regulating AI-driven manipulative design, which operates in legal grey areas (Susser, Roessler, & Nissenbaum, 2019; Helberger et al., 2022).

Recent scholarship advocates for a rights-based approach to AI regulation, incorporating principles of autonomy, dignity, and mental health into the legal discourse (Floridi & Cowls, 2019). In India, the constitutional jurisprudence around Article 21 (Right to Life and Personal Liberty) has gradually expanded to include the right to mental health, informational privacy, and individual autonomy, particularly after the landmark case of *Justice K.S. Puttaswamy v. Union of India* (2017). Despite these advancements, there is limited case law or legislative action specifically addressing AI-induced digital addiction or design-driven harm, which this chapter seeks to highlight and critique.

## THEORETICAL FRAMEWORK

To investigate the complex interplay between AI, autonomy, and digital addiction, this chapter employs a multi-theoretical lens, integrating perspectives from behavioural psychology, legal philosophy, and media theory.

### Operant Conditioning and Reward Theory

At the psychological level, the framework is anchored in B.F. Skinner's theory of operant conditioning, which posits that behaviours followed by rewarding stimuli are likely to be repeated. AI systems in social media and digital communication exploit this principle by providing intermittent and variable rewards, likes, shares, replies, that stimulate dopamine release and reinforce habitual engagement (Montag & Diefenbach, 2018). These feedback loops mimic those found in gambling and substance-based addictions, making AI systems especially potent in conditioning user behaviour.

### Social Learning Theory

Bandura's social learning theory also plays a role in explaining how users model behaviours seen online, particularly among youth. AI-curated feeds often amplify popular, emotionally charged, or sensational content, which in turn shapes social norms, communication patterns, and even identity formation. The reinforcement of social behaviours through digital metrics (likes, trends, viral content) creates environments where users learn and repeat engagement-heavy behaviour, often at the expense of offline interaction and empathy development (Twenge & Campbell, 2018).

### Rights-Based Jurisprudence

From a legal standpoint, this chapter draws on rights-based constitutional theory, particularly the concepts of autonomy, privacy, and mental health as fundamental rights. Drawing from the *Puttaswamy* judgment and international jurisprudence on digital rights, this framework evaluates whether existing legal protections sufficiently account for AI's capacity to influence cognition and behaviour without explicit consent or awareness. It critiques legal formalism for its limited recognition of behavioural harm and calls for a more substantive interpretation of autonomy that includes protection from manipulative design.

### Surveillance Capitalism and Platform Power

Finally, the chapter incorporates Shoshana Zuboff's theory of surveillance capitalism, which argues that digital platforms commodify human behaviour by turning personal data into predictive products (Zuboff, 2019). AI systems are central to this economic model, as they enable platforms to personalize content, anticipate reactions, and optimize retention. This theory provides a structural critique of how AI not only mediates but also governs communication, raising urgent questions about accountability, power asymmetries, and user agency.

### Intersectional Analysis

An intersectional approach is also applied to understand how different populations, children, adolescents, neurodiverse individuals, and socioeconomically marginalized users, experience digital addiction differently. Cultural factors, access to digital literacy, and family environments play a role in shaping the extent and form of digital harm, particularly in regions like India where rapid digitization often outpaces education and regulation.

## INTEGRATION OF THEORETICAL FRAMEWORK

The growing concern surrounding digital addiction, algorithmic manipulation, and loss of user autonomy necessitates an integrated understanding that transcends disciplinary silos. To address these complexities, this chapter synthesizes legal, psychological, and media theory frameworks to analyse how AI-mediated communication technologies influence human behaviour, compromise mental health, and challenge legal protections. The integration of theoretical lenses, operant conditioning, social learning theory, rights-based jurisprudence, and surveillance capitalism, reveals that digital addiction is not a result of isolated user choices, but a systemic phenomenon rooted in design, governance, and behavioural psychology.

## Operant Conditioning Meets Legal Consent

Operant conditioning, a core tenet of behavioural psychology, explains how reinforcement schedules shape behaviour through repeated rewards or punishments. AI-powered platforms such as Instagram, TikTok, and YouTube exploit variable-ratio reinforcement schedules, rewarding users at unpredictable intervals to maximize engagement (Montag & Diefenbach, 2018). Likes, shares, autoplay features, and algorithmically curated content activate dopamine-driven feedback loops, conditioning users to return habitually, even in the absence of intention.

From a legal standpoint, this psychological manipulation raises questions about informed consent. Traditional models of consent in digital environments assume that users exercise autonomous choice when accepting platform terms and policies. However, when user behaviour is being shaped by persuasive AI architecture exploiting subconscious mechanisms, consent becomes illusory. Users are nudged into decisions they neither fully understand nor control (Susser, Roessler, & Nissenbaum, 2019). This undermines the legal fiction of the "*reasonable user*" and calls for an evolved legal standard that accounts for behavioural influence and design-based coercion.

This integration highlights the need for regulatory reform that recognizes persuasive technology as a form of manipulation and imposes legal obligations on designers and platform providers. Simply requiring platforms to disclose terms or offer opt-outs is inadequate in environments where addiction is architected by design.

## Social Learning, Identity Formation, and Platform Ethics

Bandura's social learning theory posits that individuals, particularly adolescents, learn behaviours through observation and imitation of others (Bandura, 1977). On AI-mediated platforms, content is not displayed chronologically but filtered through algorithms prioritizing engagement. This means that users are more likely to see viral, extreme, or emotionally stimulating content, creating a feedback loop where behaviour is both learned and reinforced based on popularity rather than accuracy or ethical value (Twenge & Campbell, 2018).

Psychologically, this accelerates identity formation based on online validation rather than critical thinking or emotional introspection. Legally and ethically, it raises concerns about platform responsibility in shaping social norms, particularly among youth. Algorithms that amplify risky behaviours, unrealistic beauty standards, or polarizing opinions are not neutral. They are constructed systems with embedded values and priorities, often optimized for monetization over user well-being.

Integrating this psychological theory with legal critique emphasizes that platforms must be treated as influential social actors, not mere intermediaries. Regulatory efforts like the EU's Digital Services Act begin to recognize this role by mandating transparency and ethical accountability in algorithmic design (Helberger et al., 2022), but more robust enforcement and culturally tailored applications are needed in countries like India.

## Autonomy, Manipulation, and Rights-Based Frameworks

A key concept in constitutional and human rights jurisprudence is autonomy, the right of individuals to make free and informed decisions about their lives. The Indian Supreme Court's decision in *Justice K.S. Puttaswamy v. Union of India* (2017) affirmed informational privacy and personal autonomy as central to the right to life under Article 21. However, traditional interpretations of autonomy assume rational decision-making and overlook how technology interferes with user cognition and volition.

Psychological theories of addiction suggest that repeated engagement with AI platforms impairs users' self-control and decision-making capacity, a condition akin to diminished autonomy. When addiction is induced not by chemical substances but by algorithms designed to exploit cognitive vulnerabilities, the user's ability to exercise free will is compromised (Andreassen, 2015). This raises profound constitutional questions about whether the state has a positive obligation to protect citizens from digital harms engineered by corporate actors.

The integration of legal and psychological theories reveals a deficit in current jurisprudence, which tends to focus on data breaches or surveillance but ignores the subtler, more insidious forms of control embedded in design. It argues for a substantive understanding of autonomy that includes protection from technological manipulation, much like protections against coercion in medical or contractual settings.

## Surveillance Capitalism and Systemic Exploitation

Shoshana Zuboff's theory of surveillance capitalism provides a structural framework to tie these legal and psychological theories into a broader socio-economic critique. According to Zuboff (2019), tech companies commodify user behaviour, transforming actions, emotions, and preferences into data points to be sold, analysed, and monetized. AI is the engine of this process, enabling real-time personalization and prediction of user actions.

When viewed through this lens, digital addiction is not an unintended consequence but a profitable business strategy. The longer a user remains online, the more data they generate, and the more accurately they can be targeted. This systemic exploitation reframes digital addiction from a public health concern to a market-driven harm, akin to how tobacco or sugary drinks were marketed despite known risks.

This theory helps integrate the psychological harms of addiction with the legal failures of regulation, showing how both stem from a structural imbalance of power. Users, especially minors, become data subjects, stripped of meaningful agency and left with few legal remedies. Integrating this theory emphasizes the urgency of moving beyond individual-level solutions like digital detox or parental controls and toward systemic reforms in design regulation, corporate accountability, and digital rights advocacy.

## Toward an Interdisciplinary Model of Protection

This integration of psychological, legal, and economic frameworks underscores the inadequacy of siloed approaches to digital addiction. Behavioural psychology explains how and why users get addicted. Legal theory reveals the shortcomings in existing rights-based protections. Media and surveillance capitalism theories expose the underlying business models and structural incentives.

Together, these frameworks provide a compelling argument for a rights-based, behaviourally informed, and economically aware model of regulation. This model would:

- Recognize persuasive design as a form of cognitive manipulation.
- Extend constitutional protections to cover design-based harms.
- Hold platforms accountable for algorithmic amplification of addictive content.
- Require behavioural impact assessments for AI deployment, especially in apps targeting youth.

By synthesizing these perspectives, this chapter advocates for a shift from blaming users to challenging the systems that engineer addiction. It calls for legal reforms that not only respond to harm but anticipate it, grounded in an understanding of how human behaviour, technology, and law intersect in the digital age.

## AI COMMUNICATION TOOLS AND CHANGING HUMAN BEHAVIOUR

Artificial Intelligence (AI) has become a foundational element in the way people communicate in the digital age. Communication is no longer limited to verbal or written interactions but increasingly occurs through AI-enhanced platforms that filter, suggest, and even generate content. From predictive text and smart replies in messaging apps to recommendation engines in social media and AI-powered voice assistants, communication technologies have evolved to become more responsive, adaptive, and, in some cases, manipulative. While these tools enhance speed and convenience, they also shape cognitive, emotional, and social behaviours in subtle but profound ways.

One of the most significant behavioural impacts of AI-driven communication tools is the gradual shift from intentional to automated interaction. Platforms such as WhatsApp, Gmail, and LinkedIn now offer AI-generated smart replies that anticipate user responses and reduce the need for cognitive engagement. Over time, reliance on these pre-formulated responses may diminish linguistic creativity, nuanced emotional expression, and critical thinking, essential aspects of human communication. In addition, algorithmically tailored feeds on platforms like Instagram, YouTube, and Twitter determine what content users are exposed to, narrowing informational diversity and reinforcing confirmation bias (Cinelli et al., 2021).

This personalization of communication is facilitated by machine learning algorithms that track user preferences, behaviours, and engagement patterns. The more data a system collects, the more accurately it can predict what will capture a user's attention. This results in a feedback loop, where users are continuously exposed to content that aligns with their past behaviour, thereby reducing serendipitous discovery and reinforcing cognitive rigidity (Sunstein, 2017). This phenomenon has been referred to as the "*filter bubble*," where individuals are algorithmically isolated within narrow worldviews, weakening pluralistic discourse and critical social dialogue (Pariser, 2011).

Another notable behavioural shift is the gamification of communication, especially among younger users. Platforms such as Snapchat and Instagram utilize "*streaks*," "*likes*," and "*story views*" as reward systems that incentivize continuous engagement. These features, governed by reinforcement learning models, tap into users' reward-seeking behaviours, driving compulsive communication and heightened anxiety over social validation (Beyens et al., 2020). The pressure to maintain visibility, relevance, and responsiveness creates a performative digital culture, where the substance of communication is often subordinated to its metrics.

Moreover, the increasing use of AI avatars and chatbots introduces a new layer of interaction where users may communicate with non-human agents while perceiving them as social actors. For instance, platforms like *Replika* offer emotionally intelligent chatbot companions designed to engage users in supportive or therapeutic conversations. While these tools may offer companionship or comfort, they also risk creating false senses of intimacy, reducing the motivation for authentic human relationships (Ho et al., 2020). This is particularly concerning for socially isolated individuals, adolescents, and those struggling with mental health issues, who may substitute AI-mediated conversations for genuine interpersonal interaction.

In the realm of workplace communication, AI tools such as Grammarly, Zoom AI Companions, and Slack bots are increasingly shaping professional discourse. While these tools improve efficiency, they may also normalize surveillance, reduce informal social interactions, and alter power dynamics in employer-employee communication. AI-driven productivity assessments, for instance, may influence how individuals frame messages, leading to self-censorship or strategic communication driven by algorithms rather than authenticity (Nguyen, Hunsaker, & Hargittai, 2022).

These behavioural changes are not merely incidental but are often the intentional outcomes of platform design strategies rooted in persuasive technology principles. AI is deployed not just to serve users but to extract maximum engagement and behavioural predictability. As a result, the autonomy of communication, the ability to express oneself freely, creatively, and meaningfully, is compromised by the constant nudging and structuring of discourse by invisible algorithms (Williams, 2019).

In developing countries like India, these impacts are further amplified by the rapid rate of digital penetration and the simultaneous lack of digital literacy. Many users access AI-mediated communication tools without a full understanding of how their behaviours are being shaped. Language barriers, low educational access, and cultural hierarchies can make users more susceptible to influence, especially when platforms are not designed with contextual diversity in mind (Sundararajan, 2021). Additionally, the normalization of multitasking across AI-mediated channels has been linked to declines in attention span, emotional regulation, and memory retention, especially among digital-native generations (Loh & Kanai, 2016).

The implications of these changes are far-reaching. On a micro level, AI tools alter how individuals express emotions, form relationships, and perceive reality. On a macro level, they shape collective discourse, public opinion, and democratic participation. As communication becomes increasingly mediated by opaque algorithms, the line between autonomy and automation grows thinner. Users often cannot distinguish between genuine self-expression and behaviour influenced by AI-designed cues, resulting in a potential erosion of communicative agency.

Given the centrality of communication to human identity and social cohesion, these changes demand critical scrutiny from legal, psychological, and ethical perspectives. Legal systems must interrogate whether AI-induced communication environments infringe upon rights to freedom of speech, mental integrity, and autonomy. Psychologists must further explore the cognitive and emotional consequences of AI-mediated interaction, particularly among vulnerable populations. Ethically, designers must be held accountable for how their systems influence not just user engagement, but human behaviour, thought, and connection.

## THE PSYCHOLOGY OF DIGITAL ADDICTION

The widespread adoption of artificial intelligence (AI)-driven communication platforms has brought with it a new wave of psychological concerns, most prominently the emergence of digital addiction, a behavioural pattern marked by excessive and compulsive use of digital technologies, particularly those employing AI to influence user engagement. Though not yet universally recognized as a clinical disorder, digital addiction is increasingly being framed as a form of behavioural addiction, akin in mechanism, if not substance, to gambling or substance use disorders (Brand et al., 2019). Psychological research has sought to explore not just the symptoms and outcomes of digital addiction, but the underlying cognitive, emotional, and neurobiological mechanisms that make AI-mediated environments uniquely addictive.

### Neurocognitive Mechanisms

At the neurocognitive level, digital addiction is largely explained through the activation of the brain's reward circuitry, particularly the mesolimbic dopamine system. Each notification, like, or comment acts as a small reward, prompting dopamine release and reinforcing the behaviour (Volkow, Koob, & McLellan, 2016). The intermittent and unpredictable nature of these digital rewards mirrors the reinforcement schedules used in slot machines, making the behaviour resistant to extinction (Alter, 2017). AI exacerbates this effect by learning from user behaviour and optimizing content delivery for maximum emotional and cognitive impact.

Repeated exposure to these stimuli has been shown to alter brain structure and function. Neuroimaging studies reveal reduced grey matter density in the anterior cingulate cortex and dorsolateral prefrontal cortex among individuals with high levels of screen dependency, areas associated with self-control and decision-making. These changes may impair executive function and emotional regulation, increasing susceptibility to compulsive digital behaviour.

### Developmental and Age-Specific Vulnerabilities

Psychological research emphasizes that children and adolescents are particularly vulnerable to digital addiction due to their ongoing neurodevelopment. During adolescence, the brain exhibits heightened sensitivity to reward and social stimuli but underdeveloped impulse control mechanisms. This imbalance makes youth especially responsive to the reward-driven design of AI platforms, such as streaks, badges, or algorithmic praise.

A longitudinal study by Orben and Przybylski (2019) found a consistent link between increased screen time and decreased well-being in adolescents, particularly girls. Social comparison, cyberbullying, and fear of missing out (FOMO) are exacerbated by algorithmically curated content that promotes unrealistic ideals and reinforces social hierarchies. In India, where digital access is growing rapidly among youth, the lack of structured digital literacy programs leaves children especially vulnerable to unsupervised and compulsive use.

## Emotional and Social Impact

Digital addiction also disrupts emotional development and social functioning. Excessive use of AI-enabled communication platforms reduces face-to-face interaction, which is vital for learning empathy, conflict resolution, and emotional nuance (Uhls et al., 2014). Children who spend more time on screens demonstrate lower levels of emotional intelligence, including reduced capacity for interpreting facial expressions and vocal cues.

Moreover, platforms that use AI to suggest emotionally charged content can amplify mood swings and emotional dependency. A user conditioned to seek digital validation through likes or shares becomes emotionally entangled with their online persona, often developing performance anxiety and a fragile self-concept (Andreassen, 2015). This emotional volatility is reinforced by AI, which learns to serve content that aligns with or intensifies the user's current mood, thereby locking them into emotionally polarized feedback loops.

## Cognitive Overload and Attention Fragmentation

Another key psychological consequence of AI-mediated digital environments is cognitive overload. Constant exposure to rapidly shifting content fragments attention, impairs memory consolidation, and encourages multitasking, which has been shown to reduce learning outcomes and productivity (Rosen, Carrier, & Cheever, 2013). AI-powered feeds, notifications, and "*endless scroll*" interfaces contribute to a state of continuous partial attention, preventing users from achieving cognitive rest or deep focus (Williams, 2019).

Cognitive psychology also warns of decision fatigue, as AI inundates users with micro-decisions, clicks, reactions, replies, reposts, that deplete mental energy over time. This not only weakens self-control but also reinforces passive consumption over intentional engagement, fostering a state of mental lethargy that can mimic symptoms of depression and anxiety (Kross et al., 2013).

### Addiction, Identity, and Psychological Dependence

Beyond neurocognitive mechanisms, digital addiction is also conceptualized as a maladaptive coping strategy. For many users, especially those with underlying mental health conditions such as depression, loneliness, or anxiety, AI-mediated platforms offer a temporary escape or emotional relief (Kardefelt-Winther, 2014). Over time, this reliance can evolve into a psychological dependence, where users feel distress, irritability, or helplessness when disconnected from their devices or platforms.

In extreme cases, users may exhibit withdrawal symptoms, tolerance (needing more screen time to achieve the same emotional effect), and social neglect, hallmarks of addiction (American Psychiatric Association, 2013). AI's role in this progression is significant, as it enables hyper-personalized content delivery, often reinforcing unhealthy behavioural patterns rather than disrupting them.

### Emerging Clinical and Diagnostic Considerations

The Diagnostic and Statistical Manual of Mental Disorders (DSM-5) has not yet formally included digital or social media addiction as an independent diagnosis. However, it acknowledges Internet Gaming Disorder as a condition warranting further study (APA, 2013). Similarly, the World Health Organization's ICD-11 includes Gaming Disorder as a behavioural addiction, opening the door for broader recognition of tech-induced psychological conditions.

Recent clinical efforts have proposed frameworks to assess digital addiction, including the Bergen Social Media Addiction Scale (BSMAS) and Problematic Mobile Phone Use Questionnaire (PMPUQ) (Andreassen, 2015; Billieux et al., 2015). These tools examine factors such as salience, mood modification, tolerance, and conflict, criteria that mirror substance addiction models. As empirical support for digital addiction grows, there is increasing demand for clinical interventions, from cognitive-behavioural therapy (CBT) to mindfulness-based digital detox programs (Young & Brand, 2017).

## LEGAL FRAMEWORKS AND GAPS IN REGULATION

As artificial intelligence (AI) becomes increasingly embedded in digital communication platforms, concerns about digital addiction, behavioural manipulation, and mental health harms have raised critical legal questions. While psychological research has highlighted the adverse effects of compulsive digital use, legal systems worldwide have struggled to keep pace with the complexity and subtlety of AI-induced behavioural harms. Existing regulations often focus on data protection, privacy, or cybersecurity but lack direct mechanisms to address manipulative AI design or the mental health consequences of algorithmic engagement. In this context, the legal response to AI-mediated digital addiction remains fragmented, reactive, and underdeveloped.

## INDIA'S LEGAL LANDSCAPE: FOCUSED BUT FRAGMENTED

In India, the primary legal instrument governing digital environments is the Information Technology Act, 2000 (IT Act), supplemented by the Information Technology (Intermediary Guidelines and Digital Media Ethics Code) Rules, 2021. The IT Act primarily addresses cybercrimes, electronic transactions, and intermediary liability. However, it does not explicitly regulate algorithmic design, persuasive technology, or user manipulation through AI-driven engagement loops.

The 2021 Rules introduced certain obligations on significant social media intermediaries to conduct periodic due diligence, appoint grievance officers, and disclose content moderation policies. While these are steps toward platform accountability, they fall short of addressing dark patterns, addictive interface design, or mental health impacts on users. Moreover, the Rules are more reactive to content-related harm, such as fake news and hate speech, than proactive about user well-being or emotional autonomy.

In 2023, India enacted the Digital Personal Data Protection (DPDP) Act, aligning the country's data governance regime with international standards like the General Data Protection Regulation (GDPR). While the DPDP Act emphasizes informed consent, data minimization, and purpose limitation, it does not explicitly address how AI-driven systems may impair users' ability to provide meaningful consent in manipulative digital environments. When addictive design interferes with rational decision-making, consent becomes more of a legal fiction than a practical safeguard.

## INTERNATIONAL APPROACHES: EMERGING BUT INCOMPLETE

Globally, the European Union (EU) has taken the lead in attempting to regulate digital platforms through the GDPR and the Digital Services Act (DSA). The GDPR, enacted in 2018, focuses on data protection and user autonomy by mandating transparency in data collection and use. Its provisions on automated decision-making (Article 22) provide a foundational starting point for regulating AI systems (Voigt & Von dem Bussche, 2017). However, enforcement mechanisms are often inconsistent across member states, and the GDPR does not fully address user behavioural manipulation via design choices that exploit psychological vulnerabilities.

The DSA, adopted in 2022, is more ambitious in its scope. It imposes risk assessments, algorithmic transparency, and auditing obligations on very large online platforms (VLOPs). The DSA explicitly addresses addictive platform designs and encourages mitigation of systemic risks, including threats to public health and mental well-being (European Commission, 2022). It also mandates that recommender systems be explained and offer user control. This signals a shift toward recognizing persuasive technology as a public interest concern, though its application in non-EU jurisdictions remains limited.

The United States, in contrast, lacks a comprehensive federal data protection law. Regulatory approaches are mostly sectoral and reactive, governed by agencies like the Federal Trade Commission (FTC). While the FTC has issued warnings against dark patterns and deceptive design (FTC, 2022), enforcement is case-specific and does not amount to a structural overhaul. Some states, such as California with its California Consumer Privacy Act (CCPA) and California Age-Appropriate Design Code Act, have made progress in safeguarding users, especially minors, but national harmonization remains elusive.

## GAPS IN LEGAL DOCTRINE: AUTONOMY AND MANIPULATIVE DESIGN

Across jurisdictions, a major conceptual gap lies in the narrow understanding of autonomy within legal frameworks. Consent is often treated as a binary, given or denied, without accounting for how platform design may impair the user's ability to make free and informed choices. Behavioural economists and legal theorists argue that dark patterns, nudges, and algorithmic curation subtly coerce users into patterns of behaviour that would not otherwise align with their long-term interests (Sunstein, 2017).

In India, the Supreme Court's judgment in *Justice K.S. Puttaswamy v. Union of India* (2017) recognized informational privacy and individual autonomy under Article 21 of the Constitution. However, its application has remained focused on data collection and surveillance, not on how persuasive AI systems may erode mental autonomy and cognitive freedom. A broader interpretation of Article 21 could encompass protection against technologically induced behavioural manipulation, but this remains a normative proposal rather than an operational legal standard.

Similarly, the Mental Healthcare Act, 2017, guarantees the right to access mental health care and protection from degrading treatment. However, it does not account for tech-mediated psychological harm, leaving a lacuna in regulating how digital environments affect mental well-being. Given the increasing evidence of a link between digital overuse and psychological distress, this legal silence is deeply problematic.

## PLATFORM SELF-REGULATION AND CORPORATE ACCOUNTABILITY

Tech companies have largely adopted a model of self-regulation, often framing mental health features as optional or opt-in. Instagram's experiment with hiding likes, YouTube's screen-time reminders, and Apple's "*Screen Time*" dashboard are examples of soft interventions that place the burden of responsibility on users (Balkin, 2021). These tools often lack enforceability, transparency, and evidence-based validation.

Without legal compulsion, platform design continues to prioritize engagement metrics over user welfare. This reflects a structural conflict of interest: maximizing time-on-platform directly contradicts minimizing addictive tendencies. Legal scholars argue that only external regulation, grounded in public health and digital rights, can resolve this tension (Barrett, 2021).

## TOWARD A RIGHTS-BASED REGULATORY FRAMEWORK

To address these gaps, legal frameworks must evolve toward a rights-based approach that incorporates psychological insights and platform accountability. This would include:

- Recognizing design-based manipulation as a legal harm;
- Mandating algorithmic transparency and behavioural audits;
- Expanding the legal understanding of autonomy to include freedom from manipulation;
- Integrating mental health protections into tech regulation;
- Imposing liability on platforms for addictive design patterns, particularly when they target minors.

India, in particular, would benefit from a dedicated chapter in the forthcoming Digital India Act focusing on persuasive design, algorithmic risks, and digital addiction. This must be coupled with stronger implementation of existing rights and judicial interpretation that evolves alongside technology.

## RIGHT TO MENTAL HEALTH AND AUTONOMY: A CONSTITUTIONAL LENS

The rapid integration of artificial intelligence (AI) into digital communication platforms has intensified concerns about its impact on individual autonomy and mental health. As psychological studies continue to highlight the adverse effects of digital addiction and behavioural manipulation, a critical question emerges: To what extent can existing constitutional frameworks safeguard the psychological and cognitive integrity of users in AI-mediated environments? In India, where the Constitution guarantees a broad interpretation of fundamental rights, particularly under Article 21, the Right to Life and Personal Liberty, there exists both potential and limitation in addressing the mental health consequences of digital technologies.

## EXPANDING THE SCOPE OF ARTICLE 21: AUTONOMY AND MENTAL WELL-BEING

The jurisprudential expansion of Article 21 has been one of the most transformative developments in Indian constitutional law. The Supreme Court has repeatedly interpreted the right to life as encompassing not just physical survival, but a life with dignity, including rights to privacy, health, and personal autonomy (Bandhua Mukti Morcha v. Union of India, 1984). In *Justice K.S. Puttaswamy v. Union of India* (2017), the Court affirmed the right to privacy as a fundamental right, explicitly linking it with autonomy and bodily and mental integrity.

This doctrinal foundation provides a fertile ground for extending protections against AI-induced cognitive manipulation and digital addiction. If autonomy is to be meaningful, it must include not only the ability to make decisions free from coercion but also protection from subtle, non-consensual behavioural nudges engineered by persuasive technologies (Mathur et al., 2021). AI platforms that deploy design features such as endless scroll, push notifications, or emotionally charged algorithmic content, especially without user awareness, challenge the very essence of informed, voluntary decision-making.

A constitutional reading of autonomy in the digital age must therefore evolve to include mental autonomy, which refers to the individual's right to preserve their cognitive processes, emotional stability, and psychological well-being against technologically induced manipulation (Ienca & Andorno, 2017). While Indian courts have yet to explicitly recognize such a right, global bioethics and digital rights discourse increasingly supports its inclusion under existing legal frameworks.

## RIGHT TO MENTAL HEALTH: JUDICIAL RECOGNITION AND LEGISLATIVE SILENCE

The Indian judiciary has also recognized mental health as a constitutional entitlement. In *Shantistar Builders v. Narayan Khimalal Totame* (1990), the Supreme Court declared that the right to life includes the right to mental health. Similarly, in *Sheela Barse v. Union of India* (1986), the Court acknowledged the right to psychological well-being of prisoners and institutionalized individuals. These decisions emphasize that the state holds an affirmative duty to protect citizens from environments that degrade mental health.

Yet, when it comes to digital environments, the law has not caught up. The Mental Healthcare Act, 2017 provides a progressive rights-based framework for individuals with mental illness, including access to mental health services, informed consent, and community care. However, the Act does not account for tech-mediated psychological harm caused by AI-driven digital environments. The omission is significant given the increasing body of evidence linking excessive social media use, particularly among adolescents, with anxiety, depression, and cognitive overload (Beyens et al., 2020; Orben et al., 2019).

In this context, Article 21 can be interpreted to impose positive obligations on the state to regulate environments that undermine mental health. This would include obligations to:

- Ensure that digital platforms do not employ manipulative design targeting vulnerable populations.
- Mandate transparency in algorithmic operations that affect user cognition.
- Incorporate digital wellness metrics into public health and education policies.

## INTERSECTION WITH RIGHT TO EDUCATION AND RIGHT TO BE INFORMED

The constitutional guarantee of the Right to Education under Article 21A also intersects with the issue of digital addiction and autonomy. Education is not merely about academic instruction but about preparing individuals to think critically, make informed decisions, and resist manipulation. In a digital era where students are exposed to AI-driven content from a young age, digital literacy becomes a constitutional imperative. The state must ensure that educational curricula include modules on ethical technology use, mental health awareness, and identification of manipulative digital behaviour.

Similarly, the Right to Be Informed, although not explicitly mentioned in the Constitution, has been read into the broader right to freedom of speech and expression under Article 19(1)(a). Informed consent is not possible without access to accurate, comprehensible, and timely information. When users are subject to opaque algorithms that tailor content based on engagement rather than truth, their right to make informed choices is compromised (Susser, Roessler, & Nissenbaum, 2019). This erosion of informational autonomy also has democratic consequences, as it affects public opinion formation and civic participation.

## TOWARD A CONSTITUTIONAL FRAMEWORK FOR DIGITAL AUTONOMY

Given the constitutional values of liberty, dignity, and health, there is a compelling case for interpreting Article 21 to include protection from AI-induced mental manipulation and cognitive harm. Such an interpretation would:

- Recognize the right to neurocognitive privacy and emotional integrity.
- Impose constitutional duties on the state to regulate design practices that compromise mental health.
- Justify the creation of public institutions and policies for digital wellness, mental health monitoring, and ethical tech governance.

This approach aligns with emerging global discourses around "neurorights", particularly in countries like Chile, which has become the first nation to propose constitutional amendments to safeguard mental integrity against neurotechnological intrusion (Bublitz & Merkel, 2020). While India has not yet formalized this concept, its constitutional framework is broad and flexible enough to accommodate such innovations.

Ultimately, a constitutional lens provides a normative foundation for challenging the psychological harms of AI-mediated environments, not just as regulatory oversights or market failures but as violations of fundamental human rights. As digital technologies become inseparable from daily life, constitutional protections must evolve to defend the inner spaces of thought, emotion, and selfhood that define human dignity.

## INSTITUTIONAL RESPONSIBILITY: FAMILIES, SCHOOLS, AND GOVERNMENTS

The pervasiveness of artificial intelligence (AI) in communication platforms has shifted the discourse on digital well-being from individual self-regulation to the broader responsibilities of institutions. While much of the current narrative around digital addiction emphasizes personal responsibility, encouraging users to set screen time limits or take digital detoxes, such approaches overlook the structural and environmental factors that shape user behaviour. The burden of mitigating AI-induced psychological harm cannot rest solely on individuals. Families, educational institutions, and governments play a crucial role in fostering digital resilience, regulating harmful design practices, and promoting ethical technology use. Institutional intervention is essential to address the social, developmental, and legal challenges posed by AI-driven environments.

## THE ROLE OF FAMILIES: FOUNDATIONS OF DIGITAL HABITS

Families are often the first environment in which digital behaviours are learned and normalized. Parental attitudes toward technology and patterns of media consumption heavily influence children's screen use and attitudes toward online engagement. Research indicates that parental mediation, such as co-viewing, setting rules, and open discussions about online behaviour, significantly reduces the likelihood of problematic internet use among children (Nathanson, 2015). However, many families lack the digital literacy or awareness needed to understand the nuances of AI-driven platforms and their potential psychological effects.

In India, the challenge is compounded by intergenerational digital gaps, where parents or guardians may be unfamiliar with the platforms their children use. This gap creates barriers in recognizing harmful content, addictive patterns, or digital manipulation. According to a UNICEF report (2021), only 26% of Indian parents reported feeling confident in guiding their child's digital activity. Moreover, socio-economic disparities often mean that screen time is used as a substitute for childcare or education, inadvertently reinforcing overuse.

To address this, governments and civil society organizations must invest in family-based digital literacy programs. Such initiatives should go beyond technical training and focus on psychological and ethical aspects of technology use, including signs of digital addiction, AI-driven content curation, and the risks of persuasive design.

## THE ROLE OF SCHOOLS: DIGITAL LITERACY AND MENTAL HEALTH EDUCATION

Schools are not only centres of academic instruction but also critical platforms for early intervention. As AI-powered edtech tools, chatbots, and gamified learning environments become commonplace, it is imperative that schools develop curricula that integrate digital literacy, emotional intelligence, and media ethics. A 2020 study by Livingstone and Stoilova emphasized the importance of embedding digital resilience into education systems, suggesting that students should be equipped not just with skills to navigate technology but also with the critical capacity to question it.

Currently, India's National Education Policy (NEP) 2020 recognizes the importance of digital education but falls short of addressing the mental health implications of constant connectivity or the manipulative nature of algorithmic engagement. Mental health professionals have highlighted the growing trend of anxiety, attention deficits, and social withdrawal among adolescents, often linked to excessive use of AI-mediated social platforms (Singh & Kaur, 2021). Despite this, most Indian schools lack full-time counsellors or structured programs focused on mental well-being in digital contexts.

Educational institutions must adopt whole-school approaches to digital wellness, incorporating:

- Teacher training in digital mental health awareness,
- Regular discussions on the ethics of technology use,
- Access to school psychologists or counsellors,
- Policies on device use during class and breaks.

Schools can also collaborate with parents and mental health professionals to create early-warning systems for identifying students at risk of digital overuse or social media addiction.

## THE ROLE OF GOVERNMENTS: REGULATION, POLICY, AND PUBLIC INFRASTRUCTURE

The role of governments is perhaps the most critical in setting the regulatory tone and institutional architecture to manage AI-driven digital harm. As discussed earlier, legal frameworks like India's IT Act, 2000 and the DPDP Act, 2023 focus more on data protection than mental health or ethical design. However, the state has a constitutional obligation under Article 21 to ensure the psychological welfare and dignity of its citizens (Patel & Saxena, 2019). This includes regulating AI-mediated platforms that pose risks to mental health, especially among children and adolescents.

Governments must go beyond reactive regulation and adopt proactive policy measures, including:

- Digital wellness campaigns, akin to anti-smoking or nutrition awareness drives;
- Public funding for research on the behavioural impact of AI systems;
- Guidelines for ethical AI design, particularly in platforms aimed at children or students;
- Algorithmic audit frameworks to monitor content curation, engagement metrics, and screen-time patterns.

Countries like the United Kingdom have begun implementing such policies. The UK's Age-Appropriate Design Code (Information Commissioner's Office, 2020) sets standards for protecting children online, including limits on data collection, default settings to reduce engagement pressure, and content warnings. Similar measures can be adapted to the Indian context, especially as the government drafts its Digital India Act, which is expected to overhaul technology governance.

In addition, public health systems must recognize digital addiction as a legitimate concern and integrate it into national mental health strategies. The Mental Healthcare Act, 2017 provides a rights-based approach to mental well-being but does not address tech-mediated risks. Expanding its scope to include digital overuse, attention disorders linked to technology, and algorithm-induced anxiety would ensure more comprehensive coverage and open up access to therapy and support services.

## COLLECTIVE AND INTERSECTORAL ACTION

The complexity of AI-induced digital addiction demands intersectoral collaboration. Families cannot monitor content they do not understand. Schools cannot address behavioural issues without supportive curricula. Governments cannot enforce meaningful regulation without informed citizens. Each institution must therefore play a complementary role, informed by interdisciplinary research and guided by a rights-based approach.

Models such as "*whole community digital well-being frameworks*" (George & Odgers, 2022) emphasize the importance of connecting stakeholders, from educators to platform designers to policymakers, to create healthy digital ecosystems. For India, this implies coordination between the Ministries of Education, Health,

IT, and Women and Child Development, as well as partnerships with NGOs and academic institutions.

## CASE STUDIES

To ground theoretical discussions in real-world implications, it is crucial to examine how specific platforms and regulatory systems engage with, or fail to address, the challenges of AI-mediated communication and digital addiction. This section presents case studies of two prominent social media platforms, Meta (formerly Facebook, including Instagram) and TikTok, and analyses India's regulatory responses to their practices. These examples illustrate how AI-driven design can affect user autonomy, psychological well-being, and public policy development.

### Meta (Facebook & Instagram): Data-Driven Design and Youth Mental Health

Meta, the parent company of Facebook and Instagram, has long faced criticism for deploying algorithmic systems designed to maximize engagement rather than safeguard user well-being. These platforms use complex AI-based recommendation engines that prioritize emotionally resonant or sensational content, nudging users into prolonged use through infinite scroll, likes-based validation, and predictive suggestions (Matsakis, 2021). While these features improve user engagement, they simultaneously exploit vulnerabilities in human attention and reward circuits, especially in adolescents.

A watershed moment occurred in 2021 when Frances Haugen, a former Facebook employee, leaked internal documents to U.S. Congress. These "Facebook Papers" revealed that Meta was aware of the mental health harms caused by its platforms, particularly Instagram's negative impact on teenage girls' body image and self-esteem (Horwitz & Seetharaman, 2021). Meta's own internal study, later reported by *The Wall Street Journal*, concluded that "*Instagram makes body image issues worse for one in three teen girls*" and that teens "*blame Instagram for increases in the rate of anxiety and depression.*"

Despite this, Meta delayed public acknowledgment and failed to make substantial design changes, indicating that internal ethical awareness did not translate into structural reforms. Features like "*Reels*," "*Stories*," and AI-powered filters continue to amplify idealized beauty standards and addictive scrolling behaviour (Nesi, 2020). Although the company has introduced tools like screen time alerts and "*Take a Break*" features, critics argue these are superficial interventions that shift responsibility onto users rather than addressing platform-driven harms (Barrett, 2021).

## TikTok: Algorithmic Immersion and Regulatory Challenges

TikTok, operated by ByteDance, uses a highly personalized content recommendation algorithm that rapidly adapts to user preferences with minimal friction. Unlike Facebook, TikTok's "*For You Page*" is algorithmically curated with a machine learning model that processes thousands of behavioural signals, watch time, interaction type, pauses, replays, to generate a stream of continuously engaging content (Caplan et al., 2022). The speed and precision of TikTok's algorithm make it uniquely immersive and often more addictive, especially among younger users.

In 2020, a report by the Institute for Strategic Dialogue (ISD) revealed that TikTok's algorithm often directs users toward harmful content, such as self-harm, extreme dieting, and conspiracy theories, within minutes of sign-up (ISD, 2020). Additionally, the platform's use of auto-play, short-form video formats, and audio-visual synchronization is neuropsychologically tuned to maintain user attention, reinforcing compulsive engagement loops (Anderson & Jiang, 2018).

TikTok has introduced certain safety features, such as screen-time dashboards and default limitations for minors, especially in Europe. However, enforcement remains weak, and features can often be bypassed. In the U.S., lawsuits have been filed by families alleging that TikTok's algorithm contributed to their children's digital addiction and mental health crises, prompting bipartisan calls for regulation (Weinstein, 2022).

Moreover, TikTok's opaque data practices and perceived connections to the Chinese government have led to bans in several countries, including India. However, the rationale for India's TikTok ban was national security and data sovereignty, rather than digital addiction or child safety, revealing a policy gap in India's legal framework when it comes to psychological and ethical harms from tech platforms.

# INDIA'S REGULATORY RESPONSES: FRAGMENTED BUT EVOLVING

India's regulatory response to the issues posed by Meta, TikTok, and similar platforms has primarily focused on data protection, misinformation, and national security. The Information Technology (Intermediary Guidelines and Digital Media Ethics Code) Rules, 2021 were a significant step in increasing platform accountability. These Rules mandated grievance officers, traceability of messages, and voluntary user verification, but did not include robust provisions for mental health protection or ethical AI design (Mehta, 2021).

In 2020, India banned TikTok and several other Chinese apps, citing threats to national sovereignty and data security. However, the ban did not spark a broader debate on algorithmic manipulation, attention engineering, or the impact of digital platforms on mental well-being. While some civil society organizations called for platform audits and design accountability, there has been limited legislative follow-through.

India's Digital Personal Data Protection Act, 2023 focuses on user consent and data use but, like the IT Act, remains largely silent on persuasive design and psychological autonomy. However, the upcoming Digital India Act, currently in draft stage, has signalled an intent to move beyond basic data governance to include discussions on AI ethics, child safety, and platform responsibility. If enacted with comprehensive provisions, it could position India as a leader in rights-based technology regulation in the Global South.

Courts in India have also begun recognizing the broader implications of digital harm. In *Justice K.S. Puttaswamy v. Union of India* (2017), the Supreme Court affirmed privacy and autonomy as part of the right to life. Although not specific to AI, such rulings create constitutional space to argue for cognitive liberty, psychological integrity, and protection from non-consensual behavioural nudges in digital spaces.

## COMPARATIVE INSIGHTS AND GAPS

The Meta and TikTok case studies reveal common regulatory themes:

- Platforms deploy AI systems optimized for engagement, not well-being.
- Internal ethics awareness rarely leads to design accountability.
- Voluntary self-regulation has limited effectiveness.
- Legal frameworks often lag behind behavioural science and technological innovation.

India's regulatory apparatus remains reactive, addressing threats only after public outcry or geopolitical urgency. There is an urgent need to recognize digital addiction and algorithmic manipulation as public health and legal concerns, not just user experience issues. Lessons from Europe's Digital Services Act, the U.S. Children and Media Research Advancement (CAMRA) Act, and the UK's Age-Appropriate Design Code should inform Indian legislative efforts to prioritize user well-being over platform profitability.

## RECOMMENDATIONS AND SOLUTIONS

The growing psychological, social, and legal concerns surrounding AI-mediated communication and digital addiction necessitate multi-pronged solutions that extend beyond individual behaviour modification. Based on the evidence explored throughout this chapter, including legal gaps, psychological impacts, and institutional shortcomings, this section outlines actionable recommendations for key stakeholders: policymakers, platform developers, educational institutions, families, and the international community. These proposals aim to strike a balance between technological innovation and the preservation of autonomy, mental health, and democratic integrity.

### Establish Ethical Design Frameworks for AI Communication Tools

A foundational recommendation is the development of ethical design principles for AI-powered communication platforms. These must include built-in protections against persuasive design tactics, such as infinite scroll, autoplay, and variable reward systems, which are known to increase compulsive use (Eyal, 2014; Montag & Walla, 2016). Governments, civil society, and independent digital ethics boards should collaborate to publish AI Design Codes of Conduct, similar to the UK's Age-Appropriate Design Code, which mandates that platforms serving children prioritize user welfare over engagement (Information Commissioner's Office, 2020).

Platforms should be required to conduct psychological impact assessments (PIAs), akin to data protection impact assessments, for features known to affect behaviour or cognition. These assessments should be made public and subject to third-party audits.

### Legislate Neuro-Rights and Mental Autonomy

Legal systems must adapt to protect what has been termed "*neuro-rights*", the rights to mental privacy, cognitive liberty, and psychological integrity (Ienca & Andorno, 2017). This is particularly urgent in light of AI technologies that shape behaviour through opaque algorithms. Nations like Chile have already amended their constitutions to include neuro-rights, setting a precedent for others to follow (Bublitz & Merkel, 2020).

In India, Article 21 of the Constitution can be expanded through judicial interpretation or legislative action to include protection from non-consensual algorithmic manipulation. A Mental Autonomy Act could be introduced to regulate platform designs, mandate informed consent for behaviour-affecting algorithms, and empower regulatory agencies to penalize violations.

## Implement Digital Well-being and Literacy Programs in Schools

Schools should serve as early intervention hubs for cultivating digital resilience among children and adolescents. Curricula must include structured modules on:

- Identifying manipulative design,
- Understanding algorithmic bias,
- Managing screen time,
- Maintaining digital boundaries, and
- Seeking help when technology causes stress or anxiety (Livingstone et al., 2017).

Educational institutions should also appoint digital wellness counsellors who are trained in both psychological support and media literacy. Governments can incentivize schools to adopt whole-school digital well-being frameworks, integrating digital literacy into subjects like civics, health, and ethics (Third et al., 2019).

## Mandate Platform Accountability and Transparency

Governments must hold technology companies accountable for the psychological consequences of their platforms. The law should require platforms to:

- Disclose how recommendation algorithms work,
- Provide opt-out options from personalized feeds,
- Limit behavioural targeting for users under 18, and
- Enable "*slow modes*" that delay user interaction to prevent compulsive behaviour.

The proposed Digital India Act must go beyond data protection and address psychological safety and digital addiction as enforceable regulatory priorities. Platform design should be guided by user well-being, not just user engagement.

## Promote Open Research and Independent Audits

AI-mediated platforms often withhold user data and algorithmic methods under the pretext of intellectual property, impeding independent scrutiny. Governments and multilateral institutions should require platforms to allow data access to accredited researchers under ethical guidelines, particularly for studies on user behaviour and mental health.

A national body, similar to the Centre for Humane Technology in the U.S., could be established in India to conduct algorithmic audits, provide policy recommendations, and evaluate emerging technologies from a public interest perspective (Harris, 2020). The creation of an AI Ethics and Accountability Commission could further institutionalize oversight in this space.

## Provide Public Access to Digital Mental Health Services

Given the rise in digital addiction-related disorders, public health systems should expand their scope to include technology-induced mental health conditions. This includes:

- Anxiety disorders aggravated by social media,
- Sleep disturbances from screen overuse,
- Depression linked to online bullying or algorithmic exposure.

India's Mental Healthcare Act, 2017 should be amended to incorporate such conditions and ensure access to tele-counselling, support groups, and app-based therapy for digital harm. Integrating these services with platforms like the *eSanjeevani* initiative can improve access, especially in underserved regions (Chatterjee et al., 2021).

## Encourage Family-Centric Interventions

Family plays a crucial role in reinforcing healthy technology habits. Governments and NGOs should run national awareness campaigns targeting parents, caregivers, and guardians, teaching them:

- How algorithms work,
- What behavioural red flags to look for, and
- How to guide children in safer digital use.

Mobile apps and web platforms can be developed to offer interactive digital parenting resources, such as guides on screen time scheduling, child-friendly AI tools, and ethical edtech platforms (Nikken & Schols, 2015).

## Foster International Collaboration for Tech Regulation

Since AI communication platforms operate transnationally, a global regulatory framework is needed to address the cross-border implications of digital addiction and algorithmic manipulation. Platforms like Meta and TikTok operate globally, but regulations vary drastically from one jurisdiction to another.

India can take a leadership role in global forums such as the G20 Digital Economy Working Group, advocating for international agreements on:

- Ethical AI deployment,
- Children's online safety,
- Algorithmic transparency, and
- Shared AI audit mechanisms (UNESCO, 2021).

Such collaboration can result in a Global Digital Wellness Charter, similar to the Paris Call for Trust and Security in Cyberspace, addressing not just cybersecurity but digital psychological integrity.

## CONCLUSION

The unprecedented integration of artificial intelligence into human communication systems has redefined the very nature of how individuals interact, connect, and express themselves. This chapter has demonstrated that while AI-powered communication tools offer efficiency, personalization, and innovation, they also raise significant concerns around digital addiction, psychological well-being, autonomy, and regulatory adequacy. The legal and psychological implications of these technologies call for urgent and multidimensional engagement across sectors and disciplines.

AI-driven platforms increasingly rely on algorithms designed not merely to mediate communication but to influence behaviour, often without user awareness or consent. From Instagram's engagement-maximizing feeds to TikTok's immersive recommendation engines, AI technologies shape what people see, how they feel, and even how they think (Zuboff, 2019). This behavioural manipulation, achieved through opaque machine learning systems, leads to compulsive digital habits, particularly among young and vulnerable populations (Andreassen, 2015). The consequences, ranging from anxiety and attention disorders to impaired cognitive development, are no longer hypothetical but well-documented realities.

Legal frameworks across jurisdictions, including India, remain inadequately equipped to address the psychological harms caused by these technologies. While data privacy has received considerable attention through instruments like India's

Digital Personal Data Protection Act, 2023, the psychological integrity and cognitive liberty of users remain largely unprotected. Constitutional interpretations, such as the Supreme Court's decision in *Justice K.S. Puttaswamy v. Union of India* (2017), provide a promising foundation by linking privacy and autonomy. However, a proactive legislative framework explicitly recognizing and protecting mental autonomy from AI-induced harm is urgently needed (Bublitz & Merkel, 2020).

From a psychological standpoint, the transformation of communication into a data-driven, performance-oriented, and algorithmically mediated process has compromised authentic human connection. This is particularly detrimental to adolescents and children, whose developing brains are susceptible to the instant gratification loops embedded within digital environments (Twenge & Campbell, 2018). Parents, educators, and health professionals are often ill-equipped to respond effectively, further exacerbating the crisis.

This chapter has also emphasized that individual responsibility alone is insufficient to counter the sophisticated psychological architectures of AI platforms. Institutional responsibility, spanning families, schools, technology firms, and governments is essential. Families must be educated to identify early signs of digital overuse, schools must integrate digital literacy into core curricula, and governments must enforce design accountability on technology providers (Livingstone & Stoilova, 2020). The inclusion of ethical guidelines for AI design, psychological impact assessments, and cross-sectoral collaborations can build a digital ecosystem that promotes well-being rather than erodes it.

Furthermore, a human rights-based approach to technology regulation must be adopted globally. As AI technologies are inherently transnational, fragmented national regulations create enforcement loopholes and jurisdictional ambiguity. International frameworks, modelled on efforts such as the European Union's Digital Services Act and the UN's Roadmap for Digital Cooperation, can offer a blueprint for harmonized regulation that protects cognitive freedom, especially among digital natives (UN Secretary-General, 2020).

The recommendations presented in this chapter reflect an integrated legal and psychological strategy to address digital addiction and communication-driven AI harm. They underscore the necessity of balancing innovation with empathy, efficiency with ethics, and scale with human dignity. The future of AI in communication need not be dystopian. With informed policy choices, inclusive design principles, and empowered institutions, AI can support, not supplant, authentic, healthy, and autonomous human interaction.

In sum, the challenge is not merely to regulate AI technologies but to reclaim agency in the digital age. Doing so requires redefining communication not as a passive consumption experience but as a conscious, rights-affirming process. As

AI continues to evolve, so too must our legal doctrines, institutional safeguards, and collective commitment to the values of mental autonomy, dignity, and well-being.

## FUTURE RESEARCH DIRECTIONS

As artificial intelligence continues to shape the infrastructure of human communication, it becomes increasingly important to interrogate not only what exists today but also what lies ahead. Future research must adopt an interdisciplinary lens, drawing from law, psychology, computer science, design, and ethics, to fully capture the complexities and nuances of AI-mediated communication and its psychological consequences. While significant strides have been made in understanding digital addiction and AI's behavioural effects, numerous research gaps remain that demand urgent scholarly attention.

First, longitudinal studies are needed to trace the long-term psychological impact of AI-enhanced communication platforms, especially on vulnerable populations such as children, adolescents, neurodivergent individuals, and the elderly. Most existing research captures short-term effects, like attention span reduction or increased anxiety, but fails to map the cumulative and developmental impact over years or decades (Orben & Przybylski, 2019). Future studies should investigate how early exposure to algorithmically tailored environments affects empathy development, emotional regulation, and identity formation across the lifespan.

Second, more attention must be directed toward algorithmic transparency and explainability, particularly from a legal perspective. As platforms increasingly employ black-box models, researchers need to develop frameworks for interpretable AI systems that not only satisfy technological demands but also uphold principles of due process, consent, and mental autonomy (Burrell, 2016). There is a need for comparative legal studies exploring how different jurisdictions address algorithmic harms beyond data privacy, especially in countries of the Global South, where such regulations remain underdeveloped.

Third, intersectional research is required to understand how AI-driven communication tools affect marginalized communities. Variables like caste, gender, class, and disability shape digital experiences in ways that are rarely captured in mainstream studies (Noble, 2018). Future research should investigate whether algorithmic recommendations amplify social inequalities or biases, leading to differentiated patterns of addiction and harm. A socio-legal lens could aid in assessing whether current legal frameworks provide equitable protections or reinforce structural discrimination.

Fourth, research into neuro-rights and the philosophical dimension of cognitive liberty is in its infancy. As countries like Chile legislate the protection of mental integrity against technological manipulation, scholars must explore the practical implications of enshrining such rights in national constitutions or international human rights treaties (Ienca & Andorno, 2017). Questions remain about enforcement, jurisdiction, and compatibility with existing privacy laws.

Finally, the role of emerging technologies, such as virtual reality (VR), augmented reality (AR), brain-computer interfaces (BCIs), and generative AI, must be explored in the context of communication and digital addiction. These tools will likely intensify the immersive nature of communication, further blurring the line between real and virtual experiences. Future research should evaluate their psychological risks, legal gaps, and ethical implications before widespread deployment.

In sum, the future of this domain hinges on proactive, participatory, and critically engaged scholarship that can inform responsible innovation, effective regulation, and a renewed commitment to human dignity in the digital age.

## REFERENCES


Alter, A. (2017). *Irresistible: Why we can't stop checking, scrolling, clicking and watching*. Random House.

American Psychiatric Association. (2013). *Diagnostic and statistical manual of mental disorders* (5th ed.).

Anderson, M., & Jiang, J. (2018). *Teens, social media & technology 2018*. Pew Research Center. https://www.pewresearch.org

Andreassen, C. S. (2015). Online social network site addiction: A comprehensive review. *Current Addiction Reports*, *2*(2), 175–184. DOI: 10.1007/s40429-015-0056-9

Bandura, A. (1977). Self-efficacy: Toward a unifying theory of behavioral change. *Psychological Review*, *84*(2), 191–215. DOI: 10.1037/0033-295X.84.2.191 PMID: 847061

Barrett, B. (2021). Instagram's "Take a Break" feature won't fix its teen mental health problem. *Wired*. https://www.wired.com

Beyens, I., Pouwels, J. L., van Driel, I. I., Keijsers, L., & Valkenburg, P. M. (2020). The effect of social media on well-being differs from adolescent to adolescent. *Scientific Reports*, *10*(1), 10763. DOI: 10.1038/s41598-020-67727-7 PMID: 32612108

Billieux, J., Maurage, P., Lopez-Fernandez, O., Kuss, D. J., & Griffiths, M. D. (2015). Can disordered mobile phone use be considered a behavioral addiction? An update on current evidence and a comprehensive model for future research. *Current Addiction Reports*, *2*(2), 156–162. DOI: 10.1007/s40429-015-0054-y

Brand, M., Wegmann, E., Stark, R., Müller, A., Wölfling, K., Robbins, T. W., & Potenza, M. N. (2019). The Interaction of Person-Affect-Cognition-Execution (I-PACE) model for addictive behaviors: Update, generalization to addictive behaviors beyond internet-use disorders, and specification of the process character of addictive behaviors. *Neuroscience and Biobehavioral Reviews*, *104*, 1–10. DOI: 10.1016/j.neubiorev.2019.06.032 PMID: 31247240

Bublitz, J. C., & Merkel, R. (2020). Crimes against minds: On mental manipulations, harms and a human right to mental self-determination. *Criminal Law and Philosophy*, *14*(1), 51–77. DOI: 10.1007/s11572-012-9172-y

Burrell, J. (2016). How the machine 'thinks': Understanding opacity in machine learning algorithms. *Big Data & Society*, *3*(1), 1–12. DOI: 10.1177/2053951715622512

Caplan, R., Donovan, J., & Hanson, L. (2022). *Algorithmic amplification of extreme content on TikTok.* Data & Society Research Institute. https://datasociety.net

Chatterjee, P., Anand, T., & Singh, H. (2021). Telemedicine and mental health in India: Bridging the gap in rural health care. *Indian Journal of Psychiatry, 63*(3), 203–210. DOI: 10.4103/psychiatry.IndianJPsychiatry_93_21 PMID: 34211230

Children's Online Privacy Protection Act, 15 U.S.C. §§ 6501–6506 (1998).

Constitution of India, Articles 21, 19(1)(a), and 15.

Digital Personal Data Protection Act, 2023 (India).

European Commission. (2022). *The Digital Services Act.* https://digital-strategy.ec.europa.eu/en/policies/digital-services-act-package

Eyal, N. (2014). *Hooked: How to build habit-forming products.* Portfolio.

Floridi, L., & Cowls, J. (2019). A unified framework of five principles for AI in society. *Harvard Data Science Review, 1*(1). Advance online publication. DOI: 10.1162/99608f92.8cd550d1

Fogg, B. J. (2003). *Persuasive technology: Using computers to change what we think and do.* Morgan Kaufmann. DOI: 10.1016/B978-155860643-2/50011-1

General Data Protection Regulation, Regulation (EU) 2016/679 of the European Parliament and of the Council.

Haenlein, M., & Kaplan, A. (2019). A brief history of artificial intelligence: On the past, present, and future of artificial intelligence. *California Management Review, 61*(4), 5–14. DOI: 10.1177/0008125619864925

Harris, T. (2020). *The Social Dilemma* [Documentary]. Netflix.

Helberger, N., Sax, M., Strycharz, J., & Micklitz, H. W. (2022). Choice architectures in the digital economy: Towards a new understanding of digital vulnerability. *Journal of Consumer Policy, 45*(2), 175–200. DOI: 10.1007/s10603-021-09500-5 PMID: 34955574

Horwitz, J., & Seetharaman, D. (2021). Facebook knows Instagram is toxic for teen girls, company documents show. *The Wall Street Journal.* https://www.wsj.com

Hutchinson, T., & Duncan, N. (2012). Defining and describing what we do: doctrinal legal research. *Deakin law review, 17*(1), 83-119.

Ienca, M., & Andorno, R. (2017). Towards new human rights in the age of neuroscience and neurotechnology. *Life Sciences, Society and Policy*, *13*(1), 1–27. DOI: 10.1186/s40504-017-0050-1 PMID: 28444626

Information Commissioner's Office. (2020). *Age-appropriate design: A code of practice for online services*. https://ico.org.uk

Information Technology Act, 2000 (India).

Information Technology (Intermediary Guidelines and Digital Media Ethics Code) Rules. 2021 (India).

Institute for Strategic Dialogue (ISD). (2020). *TikTok and the promotion of self-harm content*. https://www.isdglobal.org

Justice K.S. Puttaswamy v. Union of India, (2017) 10 SCC 1.

Kardefelt-Winther, D. (2014). A conceptual and methodological critique of internet addiction research: Towards a model of compensatory internet use. *Computers in Human Behavior*, *31*, 351–354. DOI: 10.1016/j.chb.2013.10.059

Kuss, D. J., & Griffiths, M. D. (2017). Social networking sites and addiction: Ten lessons learned. *International Journal of Environmental Research and Public Health*, *14*(3), 311. DOI: 10.3390/ijerph14030311 PMID: 28304359

Kuss, D. J., & Pontes, H. M. (2018). *Internet addiction*. Hogrefe Publishing GmbH. DOI: 10.1027/00501-000

Livingstone, S.. (2017). Children's online risks: Comparative evidence from EU Kids Online and Net Children Go Mobile. *Journal of Cybersecurity*, *3*(2), 1–13. DOI: 10.1093/cybsec/tyw002

Livingstone, S., & Stoilova, M. (2020). The 4Cs: Classifying online risks to children. *Communication Research*, *47*(4), 469–485. DOI: 10.1177/0093650218810594

Loh, K. K., & Kanai, R. (2016). How has the internet reshaped human cognition? *The Neuroscientist*, *22*(5), 506–520. DOI: 10.1177/1073858415595005 PMID: 26170005

Mathur, S., Ninan, J., Vuorinen, L., Ke, Y., & Sankaran, S. (2021). An exploratory study of the use of social media to assess benefits realization in transport infrastructure projects. *Project Leadership and Society*, *2*, 100010. DOI: 10.1016/j.plas.2021.100010

Matsakis, L. (2021). Facebook's algorithm: A major threat to society. *MIT Technology Review*. https://www.technologyreview.com

Mehta, P. B. (2021). Platform governance in India: Lessons from the IT Rules, 2021. *Economic and Political Weekly*, *56*(23), 10–13.

Mental Healthcare Act, 2017 (India).

Montag, C., & Diefenbach, S. (2018). Towards homo digitalis: Important research issues for psychology and the neurosciences at the dawn of the internet of things and the digital society. *Sustainability (Basel)*, *10*(2), 415. DOI: 10.3390/su10020415

Nesi, J. (2020). The impact of social media on youth mental health: Challenges and opportunities. *Current Opinion in Psychology*, *36*, 115–120. DOI: 10.1016/j.copsyc.2020.05.005 PMID: 32132255

Nguyen, M. H., Hunsaker, A., & Hargittai, E. (2022). Older adults' online social engagement and social capital: The moderating role of Internet skills. *Information Communication and Society*, *25*(7), 942–958. DOI: 10.1080/1369118X.2020.1804980

Nikken, P., & Schols, M. (2015). How and why parents guide the media use of young children. *Journal of Child and Family Studies*, *24*(11), 3423–3435. DOI: 10.1007/s10826-015-0144-4 PMID: 26472932

Noble, S. U. (2018). *Algorithms of oppression: How search engines reinforce racism.* NYU Press. DOI: 10.18574/nyu/9781479833641.001.0001

Orben, A., & Przybylski, A. K. (2019). The association between adolescent well-being and digital technology use. *Nature Human Behaviour*, *3*(2), 173–182. DOI: 10.1038/s41562-018-0506-1 PMID: 30944443

Pariser, E. (2011). *The filter bubble: How the new personalized web is changing what we read and how we think.* Penguin.

Radesky, J. S., Weeks, H. M., Ball, R., Schaller, A., Yeo, S., Durnez, J., Tamayo-Rios, M., Epstein, M., Kirkorian, H., Coyne, S., & Barr, R. (2020). Young children's use of smartphones and tablets. *Pediatrics*, *146*(1), e20193518. DOI: 10.1542/peds.2019-3518 PMID: 32482771

Rosen, L. D., Carrier, L. M., & Cheever, N. A. (2013). Facebook and texting made me do it: Media-induced task-switching while studying. *Computers in Human Behavior*, *29*(3), 948–958. DOI: 10.1016/j.chb.2012.12.001

Secretary-General, U. N. (2020). *Roadmap for digital cooperation.* https://www.un.org/en/content/digital-cooperation-roadmap/

Sunstein, C. R. (2017). Nudges that fail. *Behavioural Public Policy*, *1*(1), 4–25. DOI: 10.1017/bpp.2016.3

Susser, D., Roessler, B., & Nissenbaum, H. (2019). Technology, autonomy, and manipulation. *Internet Policy Review*, *8*(2), 1–22. DOI: 10.14763/2019.2.1410

Third, A., Bellerose, D., Dawkins, U., Keltie, E., & Pihl, K. (2019). *Children's rights in the digital age: A download from children around the world*. UNICEF Office of Research.

Twenge, J. M., & Campbell, W. K. (2018). Associations between screen time and lower psychological well-being among children and adolescents. *Preventive Medicine Reports*, *12*, 271–283. DOI: 10.1016/j.pmedr.2018.10.003 PMID: 30406005

Uhls, Y. T., Michikyan, M., Morris, J., Garcia, D., Small, G. W., Zgourou, E., & Greenfield, P. M. (2014). Five days at outdoor education camp without screens improves preteen skills with nonverbal emotion cues. *Computers in Human Behavior*, *39*, 387–392. DOI: 10.1016/j.chb.2014.05.036

Volkow, N. D., Koob, G. F., & McLellan, A. T. (2016). Neurobiologic advances from the brain disease model of addiction. *The New England Journal of Medicine*, *374*(4), 363–371. DOI: 10.1056/NEJMra1511480 PMID: 26816013

Weinstein, A. (2022). Lawsuit blames TikTok for girl's death. *The Washington Post*. https://www.washingtonpost.com

Williams, J. R. (2019). The use of online social networking sites to nurture and cultivate bonding social capital: A systematic review of the literature from 1997 to 2018. *New Media & Society*, *21*(11-12), 2710–2729. DOI: 10.1177/1461444819858749

World Health Organization. (2018). *Gaming disorder*. https://www.who.int/news/item/28-05-2019

Young, K. S., & Brand, M. (2017). Merging theoretical models and therapy approaches in the context of internet gaming disorder: A personal perspective. *Frontiers in Psychology*, *8*, 1853. DOI: 10.3389/fpsyg.2017.01853 PMID: 29104555

Zuboff, S. (2019). *The age of surveillance capitalism: The fight for a human future at the new frontier of power*. PublicAffairs.

# Chapter 8
# SmartSpeak Health: An LLM-Driven Virtual Health Assistant With Personalized Recommendations and Geo-Based Specialist Routing

**Puspita Dash**
https://orcid.org/0009-0001-0731-0218
*Sri Manakula Vinayagar Engineering College, India*

**G. Madhanraj**
*Sri Manakula Vinayagar Engineering College, India*

**B. Premkumar**
*Sri Manakula Vinayagar Engineering College, India*

**B. Agathian**
*Sri Manakula Vinayagar Engineering College, India*

## ABSTRACT

*The Virtual Voice Health Assistant is a next generation AI powered system enabling personalized voice-based assistance in healthcare. Based on NLP and LLMs, the assistant-by users' voice input accurately perceives personal symptoms and predicts possible diseases. Through the use of RAG, the system checks first a local dataset for relevant knowledge, and if needed, it utilizes the LLM to provide an extensive and accurate disease predictions. A distinctive feature of this assistant is that it offers appropriate specialists near the patient's location following the disease that is expected. With the aid of Google API, the application determines doctors in the user's local area – upon which location-based suggestions are provided to help*

DOI: 10.4018/979-8-3373-5606-8.ch008

*streamline medical attention and to make it convenient. This dual action serves to facilitate interactions between patients and the most suitable healthcare providers and has as its goal to offer patients relevant medical advice at the time at which it is most needed.*

## INTRODUCTION

A new trend of virtual healthcare assistance has changed the way patients can seek medical services, with an easy, accessible health care human touch. Using voice-activated technology, such systems allow for natural and conversational interactions, bringing patients and digital health interventions closer together. The Virtual Voice Health Assistant Our solution, the Virtual Voice Health Assistant, leverages the power of generative AI, particularly Large Language Models (LLMs), to revolutionize the delivery of health community guidance and support.

The assistant is powered by Retrieval-Augmented Generation (RAG, Robust information Access at Regulatory scale) a technique that enables local data retrieval from within an LLM to provide precise and pertinent disease predictions. Prompt engineering methods are leveraged by the system to calibrate the interactions, to maximize the ability of the AI to correctly interpret and respond to user inputs/ utterances. Through voice input, the assistant can automatically analyze the symptom to predict the possible diseases and providing personal applicable advices.

To further improve user interaction, Google API is included in the Virtual Voice Health Assistant to identify and recommend local healthcare professionals, making geographical-specific recommendations according to criteria about the patient. This will not only lead to more accurate self-symptom evaluation and disease prediction but also facilitate quick matching between the patients and the necessary medical doctors. It is our goal to offer an evergreen style of healthcare solution that utilizes a combination of generative AI, LLMs, RAG and a voice-enabled assistant, thus, catering to the progressing requirement of the patient population.

The Virtual Voice Health Assistant is an advanced AI-powered healthcare solution that delivers personalized medical guidance through intuitive voice-based interactions. It leverages the Gemini Large Language Model (LLM) to analyze symptoms described in natural language, enabling it to predict potential health conditions and provide tailored health advice. Unlike conventional systems, it mimics real-world professional consultations by asking relevant follow-up questions to gather deeper insights into the user's symptoms and medical history. This dynamic interaction ensures a more accurate understanding of the user's concerns and enhances the precision of the guidance provided.

A key feature of the system is its integration with the Google API, which allows it to recommend nearby doctors by providing detailed location and contact information. This functionality bridges the gap between virtual health support and physical medical care, helping users seamlessly transition to professional assistance when necessary. Additionally, the Virtual Voice Health Assistant is designed to handle complex medical queries that traditional chatbots often struggle with, offering accurate and context-aware responses to ensure reliability and user satisfaction.

The solution prioritizes accessibility and user-friendliness, making it suitable for individuals of all ages and technical abilities, including those with limited experience using text-based systems. By offering real-time, accurate health advice and connecting users to professional care, it significantly improves healthcare accessibility and efficiency. Overall, the Virtual Voice Health Assistant serves as a bridge between AI-driven virtual support and traditional healthcare, empowering users with immediate, reliable, and actionable medical guidance.

Large Language Models (LLMs) are advanced AI systems designed to understand and generate human-like text by predicting the likelihood of word sequences. Unlike traditional language models that rely on statistical methods, modern LLMs utilize neural network architectures, primarily transformers, to process and analyze vast datasets. These models excel in capturing complex patterns, structures, and nuances in human language, enabling them to perform a variety of natural language processing (NLP) tasks with remarkable accuracy.

Before the advent of transformers, recurrent neural networks (RNNs) such as Long Short-Term Memory (LSTM) and Gated Recurrent Units (GRUs) were extensively used for sequence modeling. However, these models suffered from limitations such as difficulty in parallelization and challenges in handling long-term dependencies due to their sequential nature. Transformers revolutionized this field by introducing a self-attention mechanism, which allows models to process sequences in parallel and better capture relationships between distant words.

Key components of LLMs include:

- **Self-Attention Mechanism:** Focuses on the most relevant parts of a sequence to enhance contextual understanding.
- **Positional Encoding:** Encodes the order of words into the model, ensuring sequence information is preserved.
- **Multi-Head Attention:** Enables the model to consider multiple relationships and perspectives within the data simultaneously.
- **Feedforward Layers and Residual Connections:** Enhance computational efficiency and improve model performance.

The development of LLMs has transformed the landscape of NLP. These models are now foundational tools for tasks like machine translation, text summarization, question-answering, and content generation. Their ability to generate coherent, contextually relevant, and creative text has paved the way for applications in education, healthcare, entertainment, and customer service, among others.

Moreover, the scalability of LLMs has unlocked their potential in addressing more complex challenges, such as multilingual communication, sentiment analysis, and domain-specific language tasks. By fine-tuning these models on specific datasets, organizations can harness their capabilities to develop tailored solutions, making them a cornerstone in the advancement of AI-driven technologies.

In addition to their versatility, LLMs have demonstrated the ability to adapt and generalize across diverse tasks with minimal fine-tuning, a property known as transfer learning. This adaptability arises from their pretraining on massive datasets that encompass varied domains and contexts, enabling them to understand nuanced linguistic patterns and provide meaningful responses even in unfamiliar scenarios. However, their reliance on large datasets and extensive computational resources raises challenges related to environmental sustainability, data privacy, and ethical considerations.

Voice processing is a core component of the Virtual Voice Health Assistant, enabling a natural, speech-based interaction between the user and the system. This functionality is made possible through a combination of three essential technologies: Speech-to-Text (STT), Natural Language Understanding (NLU), and Text-to-Speech (TTS). Together, these components form a closed-loop system where users can speak their health concerns, receive intelligent, personalized feedback, and hear the assistant's response—all without needing to type or read, significantly enhancing accessibility and ease of use.

The first stage of voice interaction involves converting the user's spoken words into text that the system can understand and analyze. This is achieved using the Google Cloud Speech-to-Text API, which is known for its high accuracy, real-time processing, and multilingual support. When a user speaks into the device's microphone, the audio stream is processed using advanced machine learning models, including deep neural networks trained on large datasets of human speech. These models are capable of understanding a variety of accents, dialects, and conversational speech, even in the presence of background noise. The API also supports automatic punctuation, real-time transcription, and provides confidence scores for each word transcribed. This ensures that the input text is both accurate and contextually meaningful, forming the foundation for further analysis by the assistant.

Once the user's speech has been transcribed into text, the next step is to interpret its meaning—a task handled by the Natural Language Understanding (NLU) module, which is powered by the Gemini Large Language Model (LLM). This component goes beyond simple keyword recognition and instead understands the user's intent, medical symptoms, and context. For example, if a user says, "I've had a headache for two days and now I'm feeling dizzy," the LLM identifies the duration, symptoms, and severity implied in the sentence. Gemini's capabilities allow it to manage complex queries involving multiple symptoms and detect urgency in medical conditions. It can also carry out contextual follow-ups, enabling the assistant to ask clarifying questions or remember prior user inputs in an ongoing conversation. This level of intelligence ensures that the health guidance provided is both accurate and tailored to the individual's situation.

After analyzing the user's symptoms and generating an appropriate response, the system converts the textual output into audible speech using the Google Cloud Text-to-Speech API. This component plays a vital role in maintaining a fully voice-based interaction loop, especially important for users with visual impairments or limited literacy. The API uses advanced neural network models such as WaveNet to synthesize speech that sounds natural and human-like. Developers can customize the voice to suit the tone of the application, adjusting parameters like pitch, speed, volume, and even emotional tone to better fit the context of the response. For instance, a calm and reassuring tone may be used when discussing minor illnesses, whereas a more serious tone might be adopted for urgent symptoms. The result is a responsive system that not only "understands" the user but also speaks back in a way that feels personal, empathetic, and easy to follow.

The Virtual Voice Health Assistant goes beyond digital symptom checking by integrating real-world context through Google Maps services, which help users locate nearby medical support quickly and efficiently. By using the Google Maps Platform—specifically Geolocation Services, Places API, Maps JavaScript API, and optionally the Directions API—the system creates a bridge between virtual healthcare consultation and physical access to healthcare providers. This integration adds significant value by providing actionable outcomes, such as guiding a user to the nearest hospital or clinic based on their current location.

The first step in location-based assistance is determining where the user is located. This is handled through Geolocation Services, which can either automatically detect the user's location using GPS data from their device or allow the user to input their location manually. In web-based environments, the system typically uses the HTML5 Geolocation API, which prompts the user for permission to access their location. Once granted, it returns latitude and longitude coordinates that can be used to center the map and search for nearby services. This capability ensures that the assistant provides location-specific health guidance, making the results more relevant and timelier, especially during emergencies or while traveling.

Once the user's location is known, the assistant uses the Google Places API to search for nearby healthcare providers such as clinics, hospitals, pharmacies, and emergency services. This API allows the system to issue a query like "24-hour clinic near me" and retrieve a comprehensive list of relevant places, complete with rich metadata. This includes the name of the healthcare facility, address, phone number, user ratings, operating hours, photos, and more. The system can use these results to both display information visually on a map and communicate key details to the user via voice. This functionality ensures that users are not only advised on what to do but also guided toward actionable next steps by identifying real, local healthcare solutions.

To make the search results intuitive and user-friendly, the system uses the Google Maps JavaScript API to display an interactive map within the user interface. This allows users to visually explore their nearby medical options and better understand their surroundings. The map is centered on the user's location and includes custom markers that indicate the positions of relevant healthcare facilities. Clicking on a marker reveals an information window with more details such as the facility's name, contact information, and estimated distance. The map also supports typical features like zooming, panning, and custom styles, enhancing user experience while helping users make faster, more informed decisions about where to seek care.

Access to reliable and personalized healthcare guidance remains a challenge for many, especially in regions with limited medical resources or for individuals with low technical literacy. Traditional medical chatbots, though useful, are often limited by text-based interactions and keyword-dependent symptom analysis, which can lead to inaccurate or inadequate responses. These systems may exclude users who are not comfortable with typing or navigating text-heavy platforms, creating a barrier to effective healthcare access.

The increasing prevalence of advanced AI and natural language processing (NLP) technologies presents an opportunity to overcome these limitations. Voice-based systems have shown immense potential in improving accessibility by allowing users to interact naturally and conversationally, bridging gaps for diverse populations, including elderly users or those with disabilities.

The Virtual Voice Health Assistant is motivated by the need to provide a more intuitive, efficient, and accurate healthcare experience. By combining conversational AI, like the Gemini LLM, with voice-based interaction and location-based services via Google API, the system ensures seamless, user-friendly access to healthcare resources. It addresses the shortcomings of current systems, offering comprehensive symptom analysis, tailored guidance, and easy connections to local medical professionals.

This work seeks to revolutionize healthcare accessibility, making it inclusive and efficient while empowering users to take proactive steps toward their health and well-being.

# LITERATURE REVIEW

## Review The Literature

### Natural Language Processing in Communication between Provider and Patient

Natural language processing is profoundly changing healthcare, mostly in the patient-provider space. Indeed, Sarella (2023) mentions that most such AI-enabled solutions make effective communication of the patient with the doctor. The NLP system appreciates the sufferance of medical terminologies and presents responses to query patients efficiently. This technology would advance telemedicine where a better understanding of the patient over medical advice is a challenge, thereby improving fully the services rendered to the patients by the remote means effectively.

### AI-in-Clinical-Practice

There is nowhere else to apply AI today, from the simplest diagnostic tests to some treatments planned. Alowais et al. (2023), for the purposes of this article, discuss the wide area of AI applications in various medical disciplines as imaging, pathology, and even clinical decision-making, and how they may enhance the process of diagnosis. AI-based systems today can access thousands of data dumps such as scanned medical images and other kinds of patterns nationwide to the health care provider, following which the better treatment strategies can be developed, thus presenting a quality aspect of rules.

### Challenges in Personalized Healthcare with AI

As elucidated by Li et al. (2023), personalizing healthcare AI is posing challenges in not transforming but building the preexisting healthcare infrastructure, resolving data privacy issues, and other trust issues around AI-generated recommendations versus treatment plans. It is found that these AI systems must entail larger datasets along with longer training hours with added benefits of better security for the end-users. Most importantly, the healthcare professionals are not going to trust the systems much if these studies do not validate it exhaustively. This calls for an in-depth research and ethical framework design.

## Healthcare Virtual Reality Cool

Virtual reality technology has been seen to settle into boring training organizations and therapeutic worlds because it allows the user to create a simulation of just about any environment in a way that closely resembles reality. Herz and Rauschnabel (2019) provide a general overview of applications of virtual reality in the health industry, such as using virtual reality regarding pain management, rehabilitation, and surgical training. VR helps medical professionals practice complex procedures without subjecting the patient to danger and creates therapeutic benefits to individuals suffering from chronic pain or other courses of medical conditions. There are, however, issues regarding costs and access which hinder the incorporation of VR in health care.

## Ethical Concerns in AI and Social Bots

AI technologies, such as social bots, have caused severe ethical dilemmas in various fields. Physiological intentions of patients using artificial intelligence with regard to privacy, trust, and ethical behaviori were raised in the study done by Jafarkarimi et al. (2016). Although AI-driven chatbots can lead to the patient's questions, there are severe ethical implications that come along with an automated system handling sensitive health information. Some of the issues to address towards ensuring patient safety and, therefore, improved services to patients include informed consent, transparency, and algorithmic bias.

## The Influence of ChatGPT on Medical Chatbots

The much-touted family of large languages is quickly making its mark on all medical chatbots by providing them with conversational capabilities and a better user-centric interaction and engagement. Proponents who have a valid point in unison with Chow et al. (2023) opined, "Enhancement of medical chatbots efficiency by better engagement pathway will open avenues for really great advances in medical communications through dynamic intelligent chatbots"; however, while that is clearly a very strong benefit, it raises new considerations regarding misinformation and biased results concerning medical disorders and nuanced medical conditions which will first need to be addressed.

## E-Health Records' Safety and Privacy

The AI-based healthcare systems have to safeguard and maintain the privacy of the digital health records of the patients-the electronic healthcare records. Tanwar et al. (2019) cover a lot of concepts and paradigms regarding the overall secure EHR in AI-based healthcare systems. Because extensive access and analysis of patient data in a particular AI-based system would lead to security breaches, and unauthorized access, the requirements are to capture the situation through developed methods such as encryption and blockchain and secure access protocols within patient data and continue improving these criteria to enhance health outcomes even better.

### Chatbots in Oncology and Healthcare Applications

Artificial intelligence and machine learning chatbots are the most exciting tools in application for oncology and general health purposes. A major review of the subject by JMIR Cancer (2022) speaks of the growing trend among chatbots that are made available to support patients, provide medical education, and monitor symptoms in terms of cancer care. Such AI-driven systems are available as much as 24/7 by giving services such as patients managing side effects, tracking progress of the treatment, and giving health assistance to patients. Through AI integration into oncology care, patients receiving treatment for cancer at cancer centers can be given better personalized and continuous support along their journey of care.

## LIMITATIONS OF EXISTING SYSTEMS

The existing system has several limitations. It relies on text-based interactions, which can be difficult for users with limited literacy or disabilities. The use of predefined keyword combinations restricts its ability to handle complex symptoms, leading to inaccurate diagnoses. It offers generic responses instead of personalized health advice and lacks voice-based interaction, reducing accessibility. The system also doesn't integrate with healthcare services, so it cannot recommend nearby doctors or specialists. Lastly, it focuses mainly on symptom diagnosis, offering limited healthcare insights like lifestyle or preventive care advice.

- Text-Based Interaction: Users must type their symptoms, which can be challenging for those with limited literacy, technical skills, or physical disabilities.
- Limited Diagnosis Accuracy: The system relies on predefined keyword combinations, making it less effective at handling complex or multi-symptom cases, leading to incomplete or inaccurate diagnoses.
- Lack of Personalization: The system offers generic responses and does not provide tailored health advice or guidance based on individual user needs.
- No Voice Interface: The system lacks voice-based interaction, reducing accessibility for users who find speaking more convenient than typing.

- No Integration with Healthcare Services: It does not recommend nearby doctors or specialists, leaving users without easy access to professional medical care.
- Limited Healthcare Insights: The system focuses mainly on symptom-based diagnosis, without providing broader healthcare advice, such as lifestyle recommendations or preventive care.

## PROBLEM IDENTIFICATION

With the pace of life increasing every day, timely and accurate medical advice is still very hard to come by in many rural or underprivileged regions. Conventional medical systems are usually overcrowded, resulting in long waiting periods, miscommunications, and only a limited amount of doctor-patient relationships. It's also true that not everyone has the medical expertise to make sense of what they're feeling, or might be too slow to seek out a doctor or visit the correct type of specialist.

Overall, available symptom checker apps are littered with text, less personalized and do not incorporate advanced technologies including voice interactions or doctor recommendations based on location and so on and so forth." This leaves a void in the provision of accessible, personalized, real-time healthcare support.

This issue worsens during pandemics or emergencies where it is necessary to limit the contact between people and provide remote medical assistance.

## PURPOSE OF THE STUDY

The purpose of this study is to design and develop a Virtual Voice Health Assistant that significantly improves accessibility, accuracy, and efficiency in delivering healthcare guidance. The system focuses on overcoming the limitations of traditional text-based medical chatbots by enabling voice-based interactions. This approach makes the solution more intuitive, user-friendly, and accessible to individuals who may face challenges with text-based systems due to limited technical skills, low literacy, or other accessibility barriers. Voice-based communication allows users to describe their symptoms naturally, reducing the effort needed to engage with the platform effectively.

At the core of the Virtual Voice Health Assistant lies the Gemini Large Language Model (LLM), an advanced AI system capable of understanding and processing natural language inputs with precision. By leveraging this technology, the system analyzes user-described symptoms in real-time, predicts potential medical conditions, and provides personalized health advice tailored to the individual's needs. The use of AI ensures that the symptom analysis is not only accurate but also dynamic, as the system can adapt its responses based on the user's input and follow-up questions. This feature mimics the flow of a real-world healthcare consultation, allowing for more detailed symptom assessment and improved diagnostic predictions.

The study also emphasizes healthcare accessibility for a wide range of users across diverse demographics. This includes individuals from rural areas, older adults, or people who lack familiarity with technology. By incorporating voice-based communication and simplifying interactions, the system removes barriers that often prevent these groups from accessing reliable healthcare advice.

A significant objective of this study is to integrate location-based services using technologies like the Google API. This allows the Virtual Voice Health Assistant to connect users to nearby doctors and specialists by providing detailed information such as location, contact details, and directions. By bridging the gap between virtual assistance and real-world medical care, the system ensures users can seamlessly transition from receiving AI-based health guidance to consulting professional healthcare providers when needed. This functionality enhances the platform's practicality and impact, making it a comprehensive healthcare support tool.

Ultimately, the study aims to overcome the limitations of existing text-based systems that rely on rigid keyword recognition and lack advanced medical query handling. By providing an AI-driven, voice-enabled platform capable of dynamic interactions and professional care recommendations, this study strives to create a holistic, user-friendly healthcare solution. The Virtual Voice Health Assistant will act as a bridge, ensuring users receive accurate medical guidance, improved accessibility, and efficient healthcare support, while seamlessly connecting them to real-world medical resources when necessary.

## ADVANTAGES OF THE PROPOSED SYSTEM

### Voice-Based Interaction for Enhanced Security

The proposed Virtual Voice Health Assistant system introduces a transformative approach to digital healthcare by leveraging voice-based interaction and advanced artificial intelligence technologies. One of the most prominent advantages of this system is its emphasis on accessibility through natural voice communication. In conventional healthcare applications, users often interact via text-based chatbots or forms, which can be limiting for individuals with low literacy, physical disabilities, or elderly users unfamiliar with digital interfaces. Voice-based systems eliminate this barrier, enabling users to simply speak their concerns in their native language or dialect, making the experience more human-like and inclusive. This capability not only enhances user comfort and trust but also ensures that individuals who typically face challenges accessing digital health tools can now engage with them easily.

## Accurate Symptom Analysis with Gemini LLM

At the core of this system is the Gemini Large Language Model (LLM), which plays a crucial role in processing and interpreting user input. Unlike traditional rule-based systems that depend heavily on predefined keywords, Gemini LLM understands language in a contextual and semantic manner. It can handle complex, multi-symptom cases where users may express vague or non-specific symptoms. For instance, if a user says, "I've been feeling dizzy and nauseous since yesterday, and now I have a headache," the model can identify potential underlying causes and suggest next steps based on contextual medical knowledge. This improves diagnostic precision and reduces the risk of misinterpretation. Moreover, the LLM is capable of understanding conversational cues, emotional tone, and even indirect statements, making interactions feel more empathetic and intelligent.

## Personalized Healthcare Guidance

A significant benefit of the system is its ability to offer personalized healthcare guidance. Unlike static health applications that provide general advice, this system considers individual factors such as age, gender, lifestyle habits, chronic conditions, and previous symptom history (if shared). By tailoring responses to the user's unique health profile, it ensures that advice is more relevant and practical. For example, a dietary recommendation for a diabetic patient will differ from that of a healthy adult, and this system is capable of recognizing and adapting accordingly. Personalization also extends to emotional support, with the system designed to respond with empathy and clarity, which is especially important in addressing sensitive issues such as mental health, stress, or reproductive health concerns.

Another innovative feature of the assistant is its integration with real-world location services through the Google Maps API. When the system determines that in-person medical attention is necessary, it automatically helps users locate nearby doctors, specialists, pharmacies, or hospitals. It provides not just location information, but also contact details, opening hours, reviews, and route navigation. This seamless connection between virtual consultation and physical healthcare ensures that users can act on the advice given immediately, enhancing the overall efficiency and effectiveness of the healthcare experience. In emergency scenarios, this can be lifesaving, as users receive not only critical advice but also instant directions to the nearest healthcare facility.

## Healthcare Access in Undeserved Regions

The assistant also addresses the critical issue of healthcare access in underserved regions, especially rural or remote areas where medical professionals are scarce. In such contexts, the Virtual Voice Health Assistant can serve as a first line of support, offering preliminary assessment and helping users determine whether professional medical attention is required. This empowers individuals with timely, reliable health information even in the absence of local healthcare infrastructure. It can also reduce unnecessary travel and wait times, ensuring that healthcare resources are used more efficiently.

## Availability and Scalability

Another major strength of the system is its availability and scalability. Unlike human-operated services, which are limited by working hours, staff availability, and operational costs, the virtual assistant operates 24/7. This allows users to seek help anytime, whether late at night or during public holidays, without waiting for clinic hours. The system can concurrently handle thousands of user queries, making it suitable for high-demand scenarios such as pandemics or health campaigns, where rapid and widespread dissemination of medical advice is essential. Its scalable nature means it can be deployed across cities, states, or even countries, with consistent quality and performance.

## Privacy and Data Security

Lastly, the system is designed with **user** privacy and data security in mind. While interacting via voice, sensitive health data is shared by users, which demands a robust security framework. The system can incorporate encryption protocols, secure storage mechanisms, and privacy-first data policies to ensure that user information remains confidential. Users can also be given control over their data, such as opting to store their health history for personalized service or choosing complete anonymity. This balance of personalization and privacy builds user trust and aligns with modern data protection standards like GDPR or HIPAA, depending on the region.

In conclusion, the proposed Virtual Voice Health Assistant system brings together cutting-edge technologies and user-centric design to deliver a holistic healthcare experience. Its voice-based interface ensures greater accessibility, while the Gemini LLM enables intelligent and nuanced understanding of user concerns. The personalized guidance, real-world integration through location services, 24/7 availability, and attention to privacy collectively make this system a powerful tool for enhancing healthcare delivery and reducing gaps in access. It not only meets the current needs of digital health consumers but also sets a strong foundation for the future of AI-driven healthcare solutions.

## METHODOLOGY

### Proposed Work

The envisioned system is a Virtual Voice Health Assistant to empower affordable and accurate personalized health experience. In contrast to current text-based medical conversational agents, this system enables the user to interact using natural voice-based dialog instead, making it more accessible to users who have limited reading skills or are disabled, and for someone who is more comfortable speaking than typing. With voice recognition technology, the system is able to make exact translation of what users say, allowing a user to describe his or her symptoms in an easy and convenient manner.

By analyzing the users' descriptions, the system invokes the Large Language Model (LLM) provided by the Gemini to get the correct diagnosis. It can thereby process complicated and multi-syndrome cases with more precision than conventional keyword-based systems. The Gemini LLM is capable of parsing user descriptions, even when the vocabulary does not adhere to standard medical terminology, to help ensure the system can serve meaningful recommendations irrespective of how symptoms are described.

For improved user experience, the system incorporates location-based services via the Google API so it is able to recommend doctors and specialists in the area after a condition has been determined. By placing detailed contact details, directions and other important facts at their fingertips, the system also means there is no need for users to face the stress of trying to find the right health services while in a local area. This feature is the link between remote consultations and real-life medicine, adding a whole new dimension to the health care process.

Not only does the system intend to give accurate advice, but it also targets the accessible aspect with providing features for people with various capabilities. It lets people speak, rather than read or write, and it also supports text-to-speech, which is good for people who cannot see well. The vision is to make the system accessible to all users, regardless of motor and technical skills.

The Virtual Voice Health Assistant provides personalized advice rather than generic diagnosis according to the individual's health issues. With the additional context the assistant can have like medical history, current symptoms and more personal aspects the ADICE can provide more personalized advice which becomes more specific and action targeted. This combined personalized approach makes the system more effective overall, and user-centered.

## Architecture

The architecture is a flexible and modular voice-based interactive system, which has been designed to accommodate user queries and provide dynamic, context-specific replies. This system combines a speech-to-text engine, a large language model (LLM), retrieval-augmented generation (RAG), and external APIs to build an end-to-end intelligent pipeline that can comprehend and serve user requests in real-time. Scalability and flexibility is acieved by a modular design, supporting a wide rang of application including, navigation, healthcare, and information retrieval.

The process begins by the user speaking their symptoms into a mobile device, and the device records the voice input. The voice input is converted using Google Speech-to-Text API and the spoken symptoms are now text. The text is sent to a RAG (Retrieval-Augmented Generation) module and this module retrieves any relevant medical information from a Chroma vector database constructed from stored health-related documents. The retrieval from the Chroma vector database creates relevant context that is sent with the user query to Gemini, a powerful LLM, which generates a meaningful response (e.g. a likely disease prediction, some care suggestions or next steps). The generated response is then converted back into voice and delivered to the user through the mobile device.

The system also can help locate a nearby hospital or specialist if needed by integrating with the Google Map API. Based on the disease or symptoms mentioned and user location, the API will provide relevant medical facilities. This ability supports timely patient decisions faced with an urgent care need or the requirement for a specific specialist. The Figure 1 shows the architecture and its flow of the proposed work.

*Figure 1. Architecture and its flow of the proposed work*

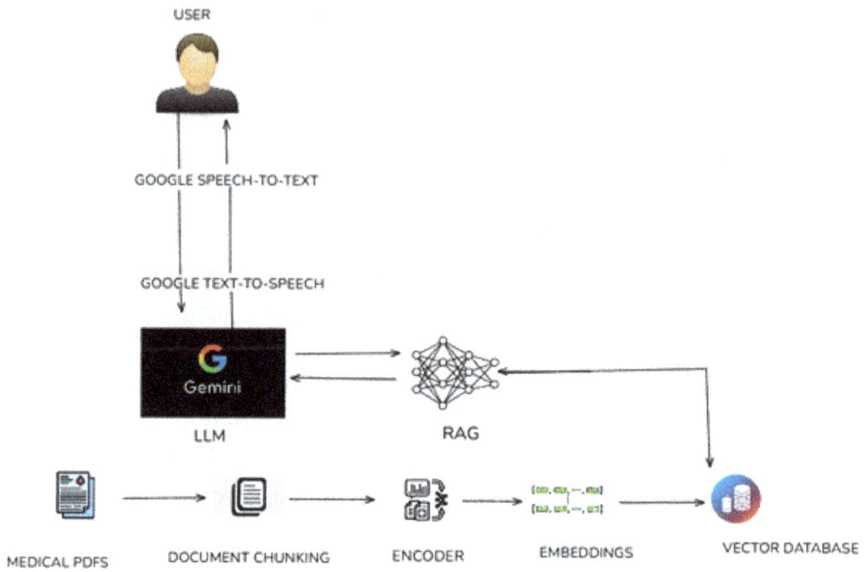


This entire flow, that incorporates voice interaction, intelligent reasoning through an LLM, knowledge retrieval through RAG, and real-world utility through mapping, enhances functionality for the user and makes the device) an easy to use, intelligent, locationally aware assistant.

## Modules

The proposed system will have two major modules. The first, Voice-to-Text Conversion Module, is a module where the user speaks their symptoms into a mobile device. The device captures the user sound signal .V(t) and uses the Google Speech-to-Text API to convert the voice signal into text. The audio to text transformation can be formulated as:

Text Output=T(V(t))= GoogleSpeechToText(V(t))
(1)

T is the transformation function that outputs the transcribed text. The transcribed text is passed into the second module, which will intelligently predict disease using retrieval-augmented generation (RAG) and a large language model (LLM) like Gemini . In this module, the system retrieves the k most relevant medical documents

$$Rk(Q)=\{Di|sim(Q,Di) \text{ is top-k}\} \quad (2)$$

from a ChromaDB vector database in response to the user query and similarity of stored documents

The evaluation metrics clearly indicate that the system performs reliably in diagnosing diseases based on symptoms. Furthermore, it effectively identifies relevant nearby healthcare providers using Google API integration. The use of RAG architecture helped in improving prediction reliability by grounding LLM outputs in real, context-specific knowledge.

This method ensures that the disease prediction is contextual and based on validated data. The two models connect in the pipeline that converts user speech into health-related results.

## Dataset Description

Table 1 shows the dataset description of the proposed work.

*Table 1. Dataset description*

| *Attribute Name* | *Description* |
|---|---|
| Disease Name | The name of the medical condition being considered. |
| Symptoms | List of symptoms linked to each disease for diagnosis. |
| Possible Causes | Conditions or factors that may contribute to the disease. |
| Severity Level | Classification of the disease as mild, moderate, or severe. |
| Precautions | Recommended actions to lower the risk of illness. |
| Medical Treatments | Suggested medications, therapies, or treatments. |
| Diagnostic Tests | Medical tests used to confirm the presence of a disease. |
| Affected Age Group | The age range most commonly affected by the disease. |
| Gender Specificity | Indicates if the disease is more prevalent in a specific gender. |
| Specialist Type | The type of doctor required for treatment (e.g., Cardiologist, Neurologist). |
| Hospital/Clinic Name | Healthcare facilities providing treatment for the disease. |
| Location | Geographic details of hospitals, integrated with Google API. |
| User Query Logs | Secure history of past user interactions for personalization. |
| Timestamp | Records the date and time of user interactions for tracking. |

## RESULT

The Virtual Voice Health Assistant has been assessed taking into account four aspects of evaluation: accuracy, precision, recall and F1-score. The four metrics allow us to assess how effectively the system can make predictions about diseases according to the symptoms users report. Accuracy at 90.2%, identifies the overall correctness of the system in predicting the right predictions. Precision is 88.5% this reflects how well the system predicts only relevant diseases without false alerting irrelevant diseases. Recall is measured at 88.0% it signifies how well the system is at predicting all cases where a disease actually exists from the input. The F1-score measured 89.2% - this performance metric seeks to unify precision and recall into a single metric reflecting the system's performance. The Figure 2 shows performance metrices of Virtual Voice Health Assistant.

*Figure 2. Performance metrices of virtual voice health assistant*

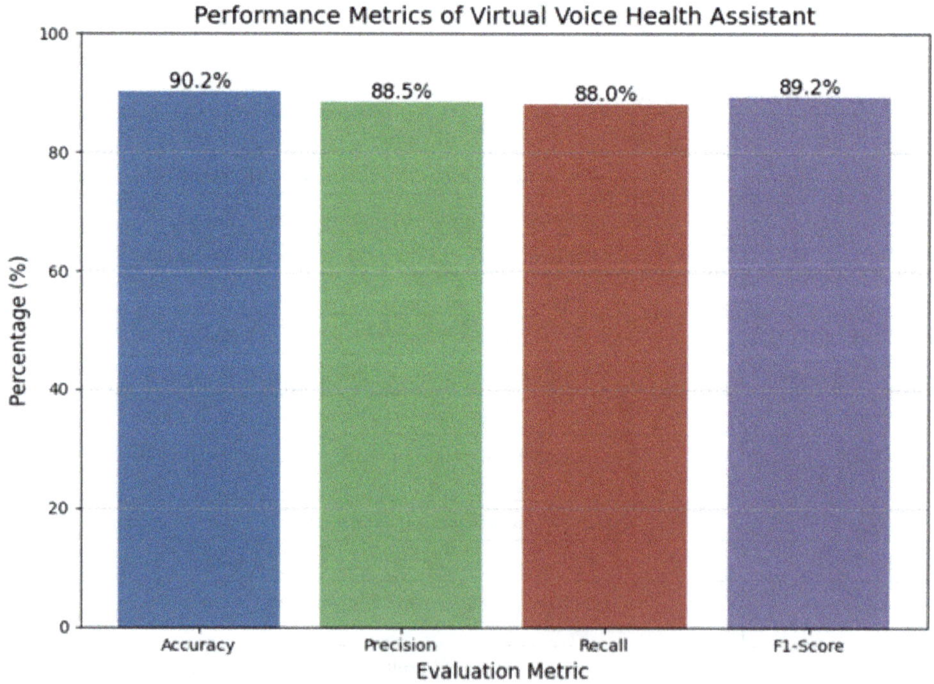


Given the individual metrics and over-all high-performance metrics indicate high performance within the system, therefore it is reasonable to conclude that the system performance is dependable to support users in achieving relevant and timely responses to the potential health-related questions by using voice interaction. Our understanding of these composed combinations demonstrated the power of voice processing, retrieval-augmented generation (RAG) systems, large language models (LLMs) and Google API.

## DISCUSSION

The implementation of the Virtual Voice Health Assistant reveals substantial advancement in the association of artificial intelligence with voice-enabled healthcare. The system successfully integrates voice recognition technology, Google Speech-to-Text API, Retrieval-Augmented Generation (RAG), and a large language model (LLM) like Gemini, an effective, intelligent, and easy to use healthcare assistant. The system accepts voice input from users (end patients), which then transfers to text, and RAG extracts relevant health information from a local document database using Chroma DB, to provide coherent topical health responses. Localizing specific knowledge retrieval further improved relevance and accuracy of responses, thus reducing the need for external data sources.

Moreover, the system guarantees nearby hospitals or clinics as suggested intelligently based on the predicted disease through the google map API, therefore sustaining real-time availability .The performance of the assistant outlined through the evaluation metrics demonstrate its reliability with overall performance: 90.2% accuracy, 88.5% precision, 88.0% recall and an F1-Score was about 89.2% demonstrating that the system is not only accurate in disease prediction but also consistent in providing meaningful, timely, and appropriate information for clients. The results indicated high recall rate, ensures that most real-world situations are identified accurately, with high precision ensuring that few false suggestions are made. In conclusion, the assistant demonstrates being a scalable and reliable solution for initial health support, and especially effective for users who may be in remote or underserved communities, where direct medical access may not be accessible. The discussion demonstrates the successful implementation of peer modules and highlights the possible application of the system in real life healthcare situations.

## CONCLUSION

To summarize, it is clear that the Virtual Voice Health Assistant project shows the power of realizing and integrating trends in voice recognition, artificial intelligence and location-based services into enhancing the access to healthcare. The system enhances healthcare access by allowing users to state their symptoms by voice, predicting symptomatic diseases by intelligent models, and suggesting nearby hospitals based on the user's location. The benefits include improved user experience and response times to health issues, specifically for users who live in remote areas. The project demonstrates that AI voice-assistants can be a good vehicle in addressing basic health care needs, making medical information accessible, and assisting users to engage in early action. Overall, their system presents a functioning innovative opportunity for a novel solution to bridge the gap between users and healthcare access.

## FUTURE SCOPE

The system can be enhanced to directly connect users with healthcare professionals through virtual consultations. Once a potential condition is identified, users could schedule appointments or initiate real-time video/audio calls with doctors. This would bridge the gap between AI-based preliminary diagnoses and professional medical care, offering users a seamless transition from symptom assessment to expert advice. Integrating telemedicine would ensure faster access to healthcare, reduce wait times, and improve care for individuals in remote or underserved areas.

Beyond diagnosing symptoms, the system can evolve to focus on preventive healthcare by analyzing user habits, medical history, and lifestyle. It could provide tailored recommendations for exercise, diet plans, mental health management, and early risk detection for chronic illnesses like diabetes or hypertension. This proactive approach helps users adopt healthier lifestyles and prevents potential medical issues, transforming the system into a comprehensive wellness assistant rather than just a reactive healthcare tool.

Expanding the system's language capabilities ensures accessibility for a diverse global population. By supporting multiple regional and global languages, users from different linguistic backgrounds can interact with the system comfortably. Voice-based and text-based multilingual features will empower individuals with limited proficiency in dominant languages like English to access healthcare advice. This makes the system more inclusive and impactful, especially in regions where healthcare resources are limited but native-language support is essential for adoption

## REFERENCES


Alowais, M. Khan, S. Iqbal, and F. Alshahrani. (2023). Artificial Intelligence in Clinical Practice: Transforming Diagnosis and Treatment. *IEEE Access : Practical Innovations, Open Solutions*, *11*, 46523–46535.

Cancer, J. M. I. R. (2022). The Role of AI-Powered Chatbots in Oncology Care: A Systematic Review. *JMIR Cancer*, *8*(4), e34567.

Chow, C., Liu, A., Wang, B., & Tan, K. (2023). The Influence of ChatGPT and Large Language Models on Medical Chatbots. *npj. Digital Medicine*, *6*(89), 1–9.

Herz, M., & Rauschnabel, P. A. (2019). Applications of Virtual Reality in Healthcare: From Therapy to Surgical Training. *Journal of Business Research*, *127*, 302–312.

Jafarkarimi, H., Sim, A., Saadatdoost, R., & Hee, Z. (2016). Ethical Considerations in AI-Based Social Bots for Healthcare. *Computers in Human Behavior*, *66*, 105–113.

Li, Y., Chen, J., Zhao, M., & Wang, K. (2023). Challenges in Personalized Healthcare with AI: Infrastructure, Privacy, and Trust. *Journal of Biomedical Informatics*, *141*, 104445.

Sarella, S. (2023). Advancements in NLP for Patient-Provider Communication in Telemedicine. *International Journal of Medical Informatics*, *173*, 104988.

Tanwar, R., Gupta, N., & Tyagi, S. (2019). Ensuring Security and Privacy of Electronic Health Records in AI-Based Systems. *IEEE Transactions on Industrial Informatics*, *15*(6), 3274–3282.

# Chapter 9
# Ethical Considerations in the Design and Deployment of AI Communication Tools, Including Privacy, Consent, and Algorithmic Bias

**S. Jyothirmaye Reddy**
https://orcid.org/0000-0002-1629-5777
*Marwadi University, India*

**Deepika Paira**
https://orcid.org/0009-0000-7309-1992
*VEL TECH University, India*

**P. Selvakumar**
https://orcid.org/0000-0002-3650-4548
*Department of Science and Humanities, Nehru Institute of Technology, Coimbatore, India*

**B. Rama Krishna**
*CVR College of Engineering, India*

**Abhijeet Das**
https://orcid.org/0000-0003-4599-5462
*C.V. Raman Global University, India*

**T. C. Manjunath**
https://orcid.org/0000-0003-2545-9160
*Rajarajeswari College of Engineering, India*

## ABSTRACT

*As artificial intelligence (AI) technologies continue to transform the way humans communicate, interact, and make decisions, the importance of ethics in AI commu-*

DOI: 10.4018/979-8-3373-5606-8.ch009

*nication has become a central and urgent issue. AI-driven systems such as virtual assistants, chatbots, recommendation engines, language models, and generative media platforms are now integral to everyday digital interactions. These tools mediate conversations, influence behaviors, and even shape opinions. In doing so, they blur the lines between human and machine communication, raising profound questions about transparency, accountability, bias, consent, and the moral responsibilities of developers and users. Ethics is no longer an optional consideration in AI development—it is foundational to the trust, safety, and legitimacy of these technologies in society.The ethical landscape of AI communication is complex and multifaceted. At its core lies the principle of respect for human dignity and autonomy.*

## THE IMPORTANCE OF ETHICS IN AI COMMUNICATION

As artificial intelligence (AI) technologies continue to transform the way humans communicate, interact, and make decisions, the importance of ethics in AI communication has become a central and urgent issue. AI-driven systems such as virtual assistants, chatbots, recommendation engines, language models, and generative media platforms are now integral to everyday digital interactions. These tools mediate conversations, influence behaviors, and even shape opinions. In doing so, they blur the lines between human and machine communication, raising profound questions about transparency, accountability, bias, consent, and the moral responsibilities of developers and users. Ethics is no longer an optional consideration in AI development—it is foundational to the trust, safety, and legitimacy of these technologies in society. The ethical landscape of AI communication is complex and multifaceted. At its core lies the principle of respect for human dignity and autonomy. As AI systems increasingly simulate human-like interactions—responding in natural language, interpreting emotions, and personalizing content—it becomes essential that users are informed about when they are engaging with a machine, how the system works, and what data it uses. The lack of transparency or disclosure can lead to deception, manipulation, and a breakdown of trust. When users cannot distinguish between a human and an AI agent or are unaware of the algorithms driving their digital experiences, their ability to make informed choices is compromised. One of the most pressing ethical challenges in AI communication is bias, (Abrams, 2004). AI models are trained on massive datasets that reflect historical inequalities, cultural stereotypes, and social imbalances. If unchecked, these biases can be embedded in the AI's outputs—leading to discriminatory responses, skewed recommendations, or the marginalization of certain groups. For example, language models may replicate gendered or racial biases in how they respond to prompts or generate content. In high-stakes areas such as healthcare, education, and recruitment, such biases can have severe and lasting consequences. Ethical AI communication thus requires rigorous attention to data diversity, representational fairness, and algorithmic auditing.

Closely related to bias is the issue of fairness and inclusion. AI systems must be designed to serve all users equitably, taking into account linguistic, cultural, and cognitive diversity. This is especially critical in global contexts, where AI tools may be used by populations with different dialects, literacy levels, and digital access. An ethical approach to AI communication promotes universal design, multilingual accessibility, and adaptive interfaces that accommodate different needs. It also involves including stakeholders from underrepresented communities in the design and testing of AI systems to ensure that their perspectives are reflected in the final product. Consent and data privacy are also central to ethical AI communication. Many AI systems rely on the collection, analysis, and processing of user data to personalize responses, predict preferences, or refine performance. Yet users are often unaware of how their data is being used, stored, or shared. In some cases, data is harvested passively without meaningful consent. This undermines the principles of user autonomy and informed participation, (Acemoglu et al., 2020). Ethical AI communication demands robust data governance, clear opt-in mechanisms, user control over personal information, and compliance with data protection laws such as GDPR or equivalent regional frameworks. Moreover, developers must consider the contextual integrity of communication—ensuring that data used in one context is not inappropriately transferred to another. The emergence of deepfake technology, synthetic voices, and generative media introduces further ethical complications. AI-generated content can be indistinguishable from human-created material, making it easier to fabricate identities, spread misinformation, or erode public trust in authentic communication. For example, AI can clone voices to produce convincing audio impersonations or generate fake videos that depict people saying or doing things they never did. In such cases, AI becomes a tool not just for assistance, but for deception and manipulation. Ethical safeguards must be in place to detect synthetic content, watermark AI-generated media, and develop standards for authenticity verification. Another dimension of ethical AI communication involves accountability and responsibility. When an AI system communicates inappropriately, provides harmful advice, or causes psychological harm, who is responsible? Is it the developer, the deployer, the user, or the machine itself? Clear lines of accountability must be established to ensure that harmful outcomes are addressed and prevented. This includes creating mechanisms for redress, enabling users to report issues, and implementing real-time moderation systems. Ethical frameworks must also guide how AI systems evolve over time—preventing them from developing toxic or unsafe behavior through unsupervised learning or exposure to harmful data. The emotional and psychological impacts of AI communication also deserve ethical consideration. As AI systems become more emotionally intelligent—capable of recognizing user moods, mimicking empathy, or simulating conversation—they create parasocial relationships that can affect users' emotional wellbeing. In vulnerable populations, such as children, the elderly, or individuals with mental health conditions, this can lead to emotional dependency, manipulation, or unrealistic expectations. Developers must be cautious in how they frame the role of AI agents—not as replacements for human connection, but as supportive tools with clear limitations.

## AI COMMUNICATION TOOLS AND THEIR IMPACT

The emergence and widespread integration of AI communication tools have fundamentally transformed the landscape of human interaction, information exchange, and digital collaboration across sectors. From chatbots and virtual assistants to generative language models, real-time translation systems, and content recommendation engines, these tools are redefining how people communicate with machines and with each other. Their impact spans individual behavior, organizational practices, cultural norms, and even global geopolitics, (Bailey et al., 2019). While these innovations offer unprecedented convenience, efficiency, and scalability, they also raise profound questions regarding authenticity, social dependency, cognitive influence, and ethical governance. Understanding the dual-edged nature of these tools is crucial for harnessing their benefits while mitigating their risks. At the core of AI communication tools lies their ability to simulate human-like language, enabling machines to engage in text- or voice-based interactions that resemble human conversations. Tools such as OpenAI's ChatGPT, Google Bard, Microsoft Copilot, and various customer support bots are increasingly embedded in websites, applications, and digital services. These systems can generate coherent responses, summarize content, provide explanations, translate across languages, and even express empathy or humor—functions that once required human effort. This ability to generate contextually relevant, natural language responses has significantly improved user engagement, productivity, and accessibility, especially in education, healthcare, and customer service. One of the most transformative impacts of AI communication tools is on information access and knowledge dissemination.

Instead of sifting through search engine results, users can ask a question and receive a synthesized, conversational response from an AI assistant. This reduces cognitive overload and democratizes access to information, especially for those with limited digital literacy or time constraints. In classrooms, students can receive real-time tutoring; in workplaces, employees can automate report generation, code debugging, or email writing. In developing regions, AI-powered tools can overcome language barriers and literacy gaps, offering a pathway to inclusion. However, this shift also introduces challenges: users may over-rely on AI outputs, assume them to be accurate, or lack critical evaluation skills—particularly when misinformation or hallucinations occur. In business and organizational settings, AI communication tools have revolutionized internal and external communication processes. Enterprises deploy chatbots to handle routine customer queries, schedule meetings, generate documentation, and provide 24/7 support. These tools reduce labor costs, enhance customer satisfaction, and allow employees to focus on higher-value tasks. In human resources, AI helps screen candidates, manage onboarding, and conduct surveys. In marketing, it powers personalized campaigns and dynamic content generation. Yet, with these efficiencies come ethical concerns about data privacy, algorithmic bias, and loss of the human touch in customer relationships. Automation may depersonalize service interactions, while opaque decision-making can undermine trust. The emotional and social dimensions of AI communication tools are equally significant. Conversational agents are increasingly being designed to exhibit emotional intelligence—recognizing tone, mimicking empathy, and adjusting their responses based on user sentiment. For instance, AI companions are used in eldercare, mental health support, and education to reduce isolation, monitor wellbeing, and provide companionship, (Bankins, 2021). While such applications can be life-enhancing, they also risk emotional dependency, blurred boundaries, and an overestimation of AI's capabilities. Vulnerable users, such as children or individuals with mental health conditions, may form attachments to AI agents, mistaking them for genuine relational partners.

## DATA COLLECTION AND STORAGE

In the digital age, data collection and storage have become central to nearly every aspect of personal, organizational, and societal functioning. Whether through online browsing, smart devices, sensors, customer interactions, or organizational processes, vast volumes of data—often referred to as "big data"—are continuously generated, transmitted, and archived, (Chowdhary et al., 2025). This data includes not only quantitative information such as purchase histories, geolocation, and clickstreams but also sensitive qualitative content like biometric records, personal communications, health information, and behavioral patterns. As such, the importance of robust, ethical, and intelligent data handling practices has never been more critical. The way data is collected, stored, secured, and utilized can have far-reaching consequences, affecting everything from user privacy and decision-making accuracy to cybersecurity, governance, and societal trust. Data collection serves as the foundation for informed decision-making. Organizations across industries—including healthcare, education, finance, marketing, agriculture, transportation, and public policy—rely on accurate, timely, and comprehensive data to guide strategic actions.(Coates et al., 2025) For example, hospitals use patient data to improve diagnoses and tailor treatments; governments collect demographic information to allocate resources efficiently; businesses analyze consumer behavior to enhance customer experience; and scientists gather environmental data to model climate change. Without proper data collection, these sectors risk operating on outdated or incomplete knowledge, leading to inefficiencies, errors, or inequities. Hence, data collection is not merely a technical task—it is a strategic imperative that underpins innovation, sustainability, and societal well-being. However, the act of collecting data raises complex ethical and operational questions, especially in an era where surveillance technologies, machine learning algorithms, and interconnected systems enable near-ubiquitous tracking of human activity. Many users are unaware of the extent to which their data is collected—through cookies, mobile apps, smart appliances, wearable devices, or even voice-activated assistants. Often, data is gathered passively or bundled into service agreements filled with dense legal language. This opacity erodes user trust and raises questions about informed consent, autonomy, and power asymmetry. The unregulated or exploitative collection of personal data can lead to manipulation, discrimination, and privacy breaches.

Consequently, organizations must adopt transparent, consent-driven, and user-centric data collection models, supported by clear policies and communication. Beyond the ethical considerations, there are technical and logistical challenges associated with storing data securely and efficiently. As data volumes increase exponentially—fueled by trends such as the Internet of Things (IoT), 5G networks, remote work, and digital commerce—organizations must grapple with how to store and manage this deluge. Modern data storage solutions include cloud storage, hybrid cloud infrastructure, edge computing, data lakes, and distributed databases, (Cheney et al., 2008). These architectures offer scalability, accessibility, and redundancy but also introduce risks related to data breaches, service outages, vendor lock-in, and compliance. To mitigate these risks, organizations must invest in robust data governance frameworks, including encryption protocols, access controls, backup systems, and disaster recovery plans, (Dahl, 2018). Data integrity and quality are equally vital in ensuring that collected data is usable and meaningful. Poorly handled data—containing errors, inconsistencies, duplicates, or outdated information—can compromise analyses, predictions, and decisions. In sectors such as finance or healthcare, these mistakes can lead to catastrophic consequences, such as financial loss, legal liability, or harm to human life. To address this, organizations must implement data validation, cleansing, and normalization procedures, as well as maintain metadata documentation that describes data sources, collection methods, and intended uses. Similarly, algorithms used in hiring or lending decisions may inadvertently disadvantage women, minorities, or individuals with disabilities. To address this, organizations must prioritize inclusive data practices, ensure diverse data representation, conduct impact assessments, and collaborate with communities to ensure fairness and transparency in data use. In the context of artificial intelligence and machine learning, the importance of high-quality, well-managed data becomes even more pronounced. These systems rely on vast training datasets to detect patterns, learn behaviors, and make autonomous decisions. Biased, incomplete, or mislabeled training data can lead to flawed or harmful AI outcomes. Furthermore, the black-box nature of some AI models makes it difficult to trace how specific data influenced decisions. Hence, organizations must adopt responsible, (Dastin, 2018). AI practices—including data auditing, explainability tools, and human oversight—to ensure that data-driven systems are aligned with ethical norms and human values.

## USER CONSENT AND TRANSPARENCY

In the evolving landscape of digital technology, user consent and transparency have emerged as foundational principles for ethical data practices, digital trust, and human-centered innovation. As organizations collect, process, and monetize vast amounts of personal data—often in real time and across interconnected platforms—ensuring that users understand and agree to how their data is used has become both a moral imperative and a legal requirement. User consent refers to an individual's explicit, informed, and voluntary agreement to allow the collection, processing, or sharing of their personal data. Transparency, in turn, involves clear, accessible communication about data practices, policies, algorithms, and consequences. Together, consent and transparency form the ethical scaffolding of the digital society, offering a pathway to empower users, protect rights, and restore public confidence in digital systems. The concept of informed consent has its roots in medical ethics and legal tradition, where individuals must be fully aware of the risks and benefits before agreeing to any procedure. In the digital realm, informed consent carries a similar weight. Users must be told what data is being collected (e.g., location, biometric, browsing history), why it is being collected (e.g., personalization, analytics, advertising), how it will be used (e.g., profiling, targeting, sharing with third parties), and for how long it will be retained. Crucially, this information must be presented in a way that is understandable—not buried in dense legal language or obscure privacy policies. True consent cannot be coerced, assumed, or engineered through manipulative design. Instead, it must be freely given, specific, informed, and revocable. Unfortunately, in practice, user consent is often compromised by dark patterns—manipulative interface designs that nudge users into making choices they may not fully understand or desire. These include pre-checked boxes, misleading button labels, confusing opt-out processes, and pressure tactics (like "limited time only" or "required for use"). Such designs distort the notion of voluntary consent and reflect a power imbalance between users and digital service providers, (Ernst et al., 2018). As regulators and ethicists recognize this imbalance, there is a growing call for designing for transparency and choice, where interfaces are intuitive, consent flows are granular, and users can easily manage their privacy settings at any time. Transparency complements consent by ensuring that users are not left in the dark about how their data is processed after collection.

It requires organizations to open the "black box" of digital technologies—including algorithms, recommendation engines, and AI decision-making systems—so that users and regulators can understand their inner workings. For instance, if a loan application is denied based on algorithmic scoring, the individual should have the right to know which criteria led to the decision and whether any biases influenced the outcome. Similarly, when a platform uses behavioral data to recommend content or target ads, it should clearly disclose how such personalization works and what impact it may have on user behavior or mental health. Legal frameworks around the world are increasingly codifying these principles into enforceable standards. The European Union's General Data Protection Regulation (GDPR) is one of the most comprehensive in this regard, requiring organizations to obtain clear and affirmative consent, provide data access and deletion rights, and ensure data portability. The GDPR also enshrines the "right to explanation" for automated decision-making. Similarly, the California Consumer Privacy Act (CCPA), Brazil's LGPD, and India's Digital Personal Data Protection Act (DPDPA) incorporate elements of consent and transparency, though with varying degrees of enforcement and scope. These laws signal a shift from a "notice and choice" model—where users are simply informed—to a rights-Transparency also plays a key role in building trust and legitimacy for digital platforms. In an era marked by data breaches, misinformation, surveillance, and platform manipulation, trust in technology is fragile. When users feel deceived or excluded from understanding how their data is handled, they are less likely to engage with a platform, adopt new tools, or share accurate information. By contrast, companies that prioritize transparency—through clear privacy dashboards, regular disclosures, third-party audits, and ethical data governance—are more likely to foster long-term loyalty and reputational capital. Trust is not built through clever marketing alone; it is earned through genuine transparency and respect for user agency. Moreover, user consent and transparency must be inclusive and accessible to all individuals, regardless of age, literacy level, disability, or technological fluency. Children, elderly users, and people with cognitive impairments may require additional support to understand data policies and make informed choices. Consent frameworks must therefore be designed with universal design principles, language simplicity, and accessibility features like screen reader compatibility or translation options. The goal is not just to check a regulatory box, but to empower all users as digital citizens with the right to understand, decide, and control their data, (Floridi et al., 2018). Importantly, transparency is not only about making information available—it must be meaningful and actionable. (Formosa, 2017).

## DATA PROTECTION AND SECURITY

In an era defined by pervasive digitalization, data protection and security have become central pillars of trust, governance, and resilience in both public and private sectors. As organizations and individuals increasingly rely on digital platforms to store, transmit, and process information, the volume and sensitivity of data have escalated dramatically—encompassing everything from personal identifiers and financial records to health information, biometric data, and behavioral patterns. This unprecedented growth has not only increased the value of data but also heightened its vulnerability to theft, misuse, breaches, and systemic exploitation. Consequently, safeguarding data has evolved from a technical issue into a multifaceted challenge involving law, ethics, cybersecurity, infrastructure, and organizational culture. Data protection and security are no longer optional—they are essential components of sustainable digital ecosystems, national security strategies, and ethical technology development. Data protection refers to the systematic practices, laws, policies, and technologies used to ensure the privacy, accuracy, availability, and confidentiality of personal and organizational data. It involves mechanisms that prevent unauthorized access, alteration, or deletion of information, while simultaneously giving data subjects control over how their data is collected, used, and shared. In contrast, data security specifically focuses on the technical and procedural defenses deployed to prevent breaches, leaks, cyberattacks, and system compromises. These include encryption, firewalls, access controls, intrusion detection systems, and secure architectures. Together, data protection and security work to uphold three key principles of information security: confidentiality, integrity, and availability—often abbreviated as the CIA triad. The global surge in cybercrime, ransomware attacks, corporate espionage, and state-sponsored hacking has underscored the critical need for robust data protection. Attackers target organizations not only for direct financial gain but also for sensitive intellectual property, strategic information, or to exploit vulnerabilities in public infrastructure.

In this context, cybersecurity is not just about protecting data from external threats—it also involves detecting insider threats, safeguarding cloud environments, maintaining endpoint security, and ensuring business continuity during incidents. With the rise of hybrid work models and remote access, organizations must also secure distributed devices, ensure secure communication channels, and enforce consistent data governance policies across geographies. Legal and regulatory frameworks have increasingly shaped the data protection landscape by imposing strict obligations on organizations to secure personal data and respect user rights. The General Data Protection Regulation (GDPR) in the European Union has set a global benchmark by mandating data minimization, explicit consent, breach notification protocols, and the right to be forgotten. Similar laws such as the California Consumer Privacy Act (CCPA), Brazil's LGPD, South Africa's POPIA, and India's Digital Personal Data Protection Act (DPDPA) reflect a global consensus around data sovereignty and user-centric protection. These regulations place a legal burden on data controllers and processors to adopt privacy-by-design principles and maintain high standards of accountability, transparency, and auditability. Technological advancements play a crucial role in operationalizing data protection and security. Encryption remains a cornerstone of modern security protocols, allowing data to be encoded in such a way that only authorized users can access it. Encryption applies to data at rest (e.g., in databases or hard drives), data in transit (e.g., over networks), and data in use (e.g., during real-time processing). Multi-factor authentication (MFA), biometric verification, and identity and access management (IAM) systems add layers of protection by ensuring that only verified individuals can access sensitive resources. Similarly, data masking, tokenization, and anonymization techniques allow organizations to protect personally identifiable information (PII) while still enabling analytics and innovation. In addition to these preventative measures, security incident response planning is critical. No system is entirely immune to breaches, making it essential to have rapid detection and mitigation mechanisms in place. Security teams must routinely conduct vulnerability assessments, penetration testing, and threat modeling to identify and address weaknesses before they are exploited. In the event of a breach, organizations must notify affected users, investigate the incident, take corrective actions, and report to regulatory authorities where applicable. A strong incident response plan includes roles and responsibilities, communication protocols, forensic analysis, and continuity strategies to minimize downtime and reputational damage. Cloud computing and third-party data handling have introduced new challenges for data security, (Gibbs, 2017) As organizations increasingly outsource data storage and processing to cloud service providers, the attack surface expands. Shared responsibility models require that both cloud providers and clients understand and fulfill their respective obligations.

## SOURCES OF ALGORITHMIC BIAS

As algorithms and artificial intelligence (AI) increasingly influence decisions in finance, healthcare, employment, education, criminal justice, and public policy, the issue of algorithmic bias has come under intense scrutiny.(Hagendorff, 2020) Algorithmic bias refers to systematic and repeatable errors in a computer system that result in unfair outcomes, such as privileging one group over another or reinforcing existing societal inequalities. Despite the widespread belief that algorithms are inherently objective and neutral, they often reflect and even magnify human biases embedded in data, design processes, and societal structures. Understanding the sources of algorithmic bias is critical to developing fair, accountable, and trustworthy AI systems. These sources are multifaceted and deeply interwoven with data quality, historical context, modeling choices, development practices, and institutional norms. One of the most significant sources of bias lies in the training data used to build machine learning models. Algorithms learn patterns from historical data, and if that data reflects societal inequities, discrimination, or imbalances, the model will internalize and perpetuate those biases. For example, predictive policing systems trained on arrest records from neighborhoods historically over-policed due to racial profiling are likely to continue targeting the same communities, regardless of actual crime rates. Similarly, hiring algorithms trained on resumes of predominantly male applicants in historically male-dominated industries may unfairly disadvantage female candidates. This phenomenon, often referred to as historical bias, emerges when past practices are encoded into data, thereby making the algorithm a mirror of systemic inequality. Another major contributor is sampling bias, which occurs when the data collected is not representative of the broader population the algorithm is meant to serve. If a medical AI system is trained primarily on data from middle-aged white men, it may perform poorly when diagnosing conditions in women or racial minorities, leading to misdiagnoses and health disparities, (Jarrahi, 2018). Likewise, facial recognition technologies have demonstrated higher error rates for darker-skinned individuals, particularly women, due to underrepresentation in training datasets. Sampling bias can result from deliberate choices, lack of access to diverse data, or unintentional exclusion—yet the consequences can be profound, especially in life-critical domains.

Measurement bias arises when the variables used to measure outcomes or predict behavior are flawed, proxy-based, or socially constructed. For instance, using credit scores as a measure of financial trustworthiness might disadvantage those who have been historically excluded from traditional banking systems. In education, standardized test scores may not accurately reflect a student's potential or capabilities due to socio-economic disparities, cultural context, or access to resources. These proxy measures are often chosen because they are readily available and quantifiable, but they can obscure deeper structural inequalities and introduce misleading signals into the algorithmic process. Label bias also plays a critical role in algorithmic distortion. Supervised machine learning requires labeled examples—such as whether a loan was repaid, whether a job applicant was successful, or whether a person committed a crime. These labels are often derived from human judgments or institutional records, both of which may be biased. For instance, judicial risk assessment tools use prior convictions as labels for predicting future criminality, but such convictions are shaped by unequal policing, racial profiling, and disparities in legal representation. As a result, the algorithm learns to associate marginalized identity markers with higher risk, reinforcing systemic discrimination under the guise of objectivity. Feature selection bias occurs when developers choose specific variables or characteristics to include in the model without considering how those features may be correlated with sensitive attributes like race, gender, or socio-economic status. Even when protected variables are explicitly excluded, indirect proxies—such as ZIP codes, education levels, or purchasing behavior—can serve as stand-ins, enabling proxy discrimination. For instance, an algorithm that uses a person's address as a feature may unintentionally encode racial or class-based segregation, leading to unequal access to housing, insurance, or credit. Algorithmic design choices can also introduce or amplify bias, (Jobin et al., 2019). Algorithms are created by people who bring their own cultural assumptions, worldviews, and blind spots to the table. A lack of diversity in AI development teams—particularly in terms of race, gender, socio-economic background, and geography—can lead to narrow perspectives, oversight of ethical implications, and insufficient questioning of design decisions. Biases may be introduced unintentionally through framing problems in certain ways, defining success narrowly, or failing to engage with the lived experiences of those affected by the algorithm. Cognitive biases, such as confirmation bias or anchoring, may further distort the problem-solving process. Moreover, bias can arise from deployment and use context—even when an algorithm is well-designed.

## IMPACT OF BIAS ON USERS

As artificial intelligence (AI) and algorithmic systems become increasingly integrated into the fabric of daily life, their decisions are not just technical outputs—they are actions that shape people's opportunities, perceptions, and well-being. When these systems are biased, whether through historical data, flawed design, or inadequate oversight, they can create harmful, far-reaching consequences for individuals and communities, (Kellogg et al., 2020). The impact of bias on users is multifaceted and particularly severe for marginalized and underrepresented groups, who often bear the brunt of algorithmic discrimination. These biases affect not only access to services and resources but also influence identity, autonomy, social mobility, and trust in technology. A well-documented case involved a commercial health risk prediction algorithm that significantly underestimated the health needs of Black patients compared to white patients because it used healthcare spending as a proxy for need. Since Black patients historically had less access to care, their lower spending led the system to erroneously assume they required less medical attention. This is a stark example of how algorithmic bias can produce inequitable health outcomes, with vulnerable populations receiving inadequate care, misdiagnoses, or delayed treatment, (Langlois, 2003). Bias also deeply impacts users by shaping their digital experiences and perceptions of reality. Algorithms power content recommendations, search engine rankings, and social media feeds, determining what users see, read, and believe. It can deepen divisions, entrench systemic racism, exacerbate gender inequality, and perpetuate colonial legacies in data practices and digital governance. In global contexts, algorithms developed in one cultural or economic context may be exported and applied in others without adaptation or sensitivity, leading to cultural misalignment or the imposition of foreign values, (Lips-Wiersma et al., 2012).

## MITIGATING ALGORITHMIC BIA

As artificial intelligence (AI) systems become more embedded in daily decision-making processes—whether in hiring, lending, healthcare, education, or social media—there is growing recognition of the urgent need to address algorithmic bias. Bias in AI emerges when data, models, or design processes reflect and perpetuate historical prejudices, societal inequalities, or technical limitations. These biases, if unaddressed, can lead to discriminatory outcomes and systemic harm, particularly for marginalized communities. Therefore, mitigating algorithmic bias is not just a technical priority but a social, ethical, and legal imperative. Mitigation requires a comprehensive, interdisciplinary approach encompassing data collection, model design, evaluation, transparency, policy, and stakeholder inclusion. At the core of most algorithmic biases lies biased or unrepresentative data. Since AI systems learn from historical or real-time data, they inherit the patterns—and prejudices—present in that data. One of the most effective mitigation strategies is improving data quality and diversity. This includes ensuring that training datasets reflect a wide range of demographic, geographic, and socioeconomic backgrounds, and do not overrepresent dominant or privileged groups. Data audits, statistical sampling techniques, and demographic parity checks can help identify and correct skewed distributions, (Maheswaran et al., 2025).

*Figure 1. The ethics of AI addressing bias and privacy concerns*

These methods can be particularly effective when bias is deeply embedded in feature correlations or complex data interactions. Transparency and explainability are indispensable in the fight against algorithmic bias. Bias often hides in black-box systems where decisions are opaque and difficult to challenge. Explainable AI (XAI) methods help illuminate how and why a model makes certain decisions, allowing for bias detection and intervention. Techniques such as SHAP (SHapley Additive exPlanations), LIME (Local Interpretable Model-agnostic Explanations), and feature attribution methods provide insights into which features drive model predictions. By understanding these patterns, developers and stakeholders can pinpoint whether protected attributes or their proxies are influencing outcomes unfairly. Transparency builds trust and empowers users, regulators, and civil society to hold AI systems accountable. Equally important is the integration of human oversight and ethical review throughout the AI lifecycle. Bias mitigation is not a one-time fix but a continuous process. Organizations should implement multi-stakeholder review boards, ethics committees, or bias bounties to identify and flag potential risks. Involving domain experts, ethicists, and impacted communities in the design and evaluation of AI systems helps ensure that different perspectives and values are represented. Participatory design methods empower end-users—especially from marginalized groups—to influence the development process and articulate concerns about bias, usability, or harm. Another strategic mitigation measure involves impact assessments and algorithmic audits, (Nisha Angeline et al., 2025). Just as environmental impact assessments evaluate the consequences of infrastructure projects, algorithmic impact assessments (AIAs) assess the social, economic, and ethical impacts of AI systems. These assessments evaluate potential harms, discriminatory effects, and legal risks prior to deployment. Similarly, third-party algorithmic audits—akin to financial audits—provide independent scrutiny of system performance, fairness, and transparency. These tools not only identify bias but also create accountability structures and standards for responsible AI deployment, (Pratt et al., 2003). Bias mitigation must also be supported by robust governance frameworks and regulations.

## INFORMED CONSENT IN AI SYSTEMS

In the age of artificial intelligence (AI), where vast amounts of personal data are collected, analyzed, and leveraged to fuel decision-making systems, informed consent emerges as a critical pillar of ethical and responsible AI governance. Rooted in the principles of autonomy, transparency, and human dignity, informed consent refers to the process by which individuals voluntarily agree to the collection and use of their data, or interaction with AI systems, after being provided with adequate, understandable information about the nature, purpose, risks, and consequences involved. In traditional contexts—like medical treatment or human-subject research—informed consent ensures that individuals maintain control over their bodies and decisions. In the digital and AI landscape, this principle must be reimagined and reinforced, as the complexities of data flows, opaque algorithms, and predictive modeling challenge the very feasibility and integrity of user consent. At its core, informed consent in AI systems involves more than a checkbox or a privacy policy agreement. It requires that individuals are meaningfully aware of how their data will be used, processed, shared, and retained; what decisions the AI system will make; and what implications those decisions might have on their rights, opportunities, or wellbeing, (Ravenscraft, 2021). This includes disclosure about automated decision-making (as per Article 22 of the EU GDPR), the nature of profiling, risks of bias or surveillance, data storage practices, and third-party data sharing. Genuine informed consent must be specific, freely given, informed, and revocable. These criteria are often undermined by common practices such as dark patterns, overly technical language, or bundled consent models where users must agree to multiple services or data uses as a precondition for access. One of the foremost challenges in achieving informed consent in AI is the asymmetry of knowledge and power between users and AI developers or data controllers, (Roberts, 2020). Most AI systems operate with sophisticated architectures—such as deep neural networks or reinforcement learning algorithms—that are difficult even for experts to fully interpret. Expecting the average user to grasp the inner workings of these models, or the implications of data aggregation, is unrealistic.

This opacity fosters a "consent illusion," where users technically agree but lack true understanding. Additionally, many AI systems operate in the background—such as recommendation engines, facial recognition in public spaces, or algorithmic scoring—without any explicit user interaction, making it unclear when or how consent should be obtained. The problem is compounded by data repurposing and secondary use. Often, data collected for one purpose (e.g., signing up for a fitness app) is later used for another (e.g., training an insurance risk model), without obtaining renewed consent. AI's capacity for continuous learning and adaptation also means that consent obtained at one point in time may no longer be valid as the system evolves. This dynamic nature of AI challenges the static model of "one-time" consent and calls for mechanisms like ongoing consent, contextual consent, or dynamic consent—where individuals are regularly informed and empowered to update their choices. Informed consent is further tested in vulnerable populations and contexts, such as children, elderly individuals, people with disabilities, or communities with low digital literacy. These groups may not fully comprehend the implications of AI interactions or data sharing, making them more susceptible to exploitation. For example, AI-powered educational tools or toys that collect children's speech data may subtly invade privacy without parental awareness. In such cases, special protections—such as age verification, guardian consent, or simplified explanations—are essential to uphold ethical standards. Moreover, the future of informed consent may involve context-aware and adaptive systems. Using AI itself, systems can infer when a user may need clarification, when risks change, or when updated consent should be prompted. For example, if a user's data is about to be used in a high-stakes medical prediction model, the system could proactively request renewed consent and provide relevant, personalized information, (Sethumadhavan et al., 2025).

## USER CONTROL OVER DATA

In the digital age, where data has become one of the most valuable and pervasive commodities, the principle of user control over data stands as a fundamental pillar of privacy, autonomy, and ethical technology design. User control refers to the ability of individuals to decide how their personal data is collected, accessed, used, shared, modified, and deleted.(Sakthivel et al., 2025) This concept is not merely a technical feature or regulatory checkbox—it is a moral imperative grounded in the belief that individuals should retain sovereignty over information that pertains to their identity, behavior, relationships, and choices, (Thirunagalingam et al., 2025). As artificial intelligence (AI), big data, and ubiquitous connectivity reshape societies, restoring and reinforcing user control over data is essential to counter asymmetries of power, prevent exploitation, and foster trust in digital systems. At the heart of user control is the notion of digital agency: users must be able to make meaningful decisions about their data in a transparent, informed, and voluntary manner. This includes the right to access their own data, to understand what is being collected and why, to object to certain types of processing, to withdraw consent, to request corrections, and to demand deletion. These rights are codified in landmark legal frameworks such as the General Data Protection Regulation (GDPR) in the European Union, the California Consumer Privacy Act (CCPA) in the United States, and emerging data protection laws in countries like India, Brazil, and South Africa. However, while these laws set important precedents, actual implementation remains inconsistent, and many users remain unaware of or unable to exercise their rights. One major barrier to effective user control is the opacity of digital ecosystems.

Context-aware consent allows users to set preferences that adapt to different scenarios—for example, allowing location sharing for navigation apps but not for targeted advertising. Role-based access control lets users grant different permissions to different entities (e.g., doctors vs. insurers). Additionally, time-bound or event-triggered consent can ensure that data access is limited to relevant, temporary needs. The right to be forgotten, enshrined in the GDPR, is a particularly powerful manifestation of user control. It enables individuals to request the erasure of their personal data from systems that no longer have a legitimate need to retain it. However, enforcing this right poses technical and legal challenges, especially when data has been replicated across multiple servers or incorporated into trained AI models. Nonetheless, the principle affirms a user's right to redefine their digital footprint, safeguard their privacy, and move on from past digital associations. Empowering users with data control also promotes accountability and ethical innovation. When individuals can monitor how their data is used, organizations are incentivized to act responsibly, minimize unnecessary data collection, and design more trustworthy AI systems. Transparency and auditability mechanisms—such as data logs, usage reports, and impact assessments—can support this dynamic. Furthermore, granting users more control fosters data quality and personalization benefits: users are more likely to share accurate, relevant information when they trust that it will be handled ethically and respectfully. However, ensuring effective user control requires more than individual tools—it demands systemic and cultural change. Education and digital literacy are critical enablers of user empowerment. People must understand what data they generate, how it can be used, and what rights they have. Public awareness campaigns, school curricula, and community workshops can help build this foundational knowledge, (Upadhyaya et al., 2025). In parallel, organizations must embrace privacy-by-design principles, embedding user control mechanisms at every stage of the data lifecycle—from collection and storage to sharing and deletion.

## DEPLOYING AI TOOLS RESPONSIBLY

The responsible deployment of artificial intelligence (AI) tools is a pressing priority as societies increasingly integrate these technologies into critical sectors such as healthcare, education, law enforcement, finance, logistics, and governance. Deployment is not merely the technical act of launching a trained model into a production environment—it is a consequential phase where AI directly interfaces with human lives, behaviors, and systems. A responsibly deployed AI tool respects ethical values, complies with legal norms, and promotes social welfare. It recognizes and mitigates risks, preserves user rights, and is transparent, secure, fair, and accountable. In contrast, irresponsible deployment can exacerbate inequality, infringe on privacy, enable discrimination, or produce decisions that are difficult to challenge. Thus, deploying AI tools responsibly requires careful planning, continual oversight, and engagement with stakeholders throughout the entire AI lifecycle. One of the foundational aspects of responsible deployment is risk assessment and mitigation. Before AI tools are deployed, organizations must evaluate their potential for harm in a given context. This involves identifying high-risk use cases, mapping possible negative outcomes, and assessing the impact on vulnerable populations. For instance, deploying facial recognition in public spaces raises significant concerns related to mass surveillance and misidentification, particularly for marginalized groups. Likewise, algorithmic credit scoring systems may replicate past biases and unjustly deny loans. A risk-based approach ensures that sensitive or high-impact deployments are subject to stricter controls, such as pre-deployment audits, human oversight, and public accountability. A key principle in responsible AI deployment is contextual sensitivity—the understanding that AI does not function in a vacuum but interacts with complex human systems. The same model may perform very differently in two cultural, legal, or institutional environments. For example, an AI tool designed to flag hate speech might misinterpret satire or dissenting political expression in one context while being underinclusive in another. Responsible deployment requires tailoring tools to the sociocultural, regulatory, and organizational settings in which they are used. It demands collaboration with domain experts, ethicists, community representatives, and legal advisors who can foresee nuanced implications.

Human oversight and governance mechanisms must accompany any AI deployment to prevent overreliance on automation and ensure that humans remain meaningfully in control. Human-in-the-loop (HITL) or human-on-the-loop (HOTL) strategies are essential, particularly in high-stakes domains such as healthcare diagnostics, judicial risk assessments, or autonomous vehicles. These mechanisms not only enable human judgment to intervene when algorithms err, but also provide users with recourse when they experience adverse decisions. In organizations, AI governance boards and ethics committees can guide responsible implementation, evaluate system behavior, and ensure alignment with institutional values and legal standards, (Vallor, 2015). Transparency and explainability are essential for fostering trust and enabling informed use of AI tools. Stakeholders—whether users, regulators, or affected individuals—should be able to understand how an AI system operates, what data it uses, and how decisions are made. Responsible deployment includes documenting model features, performance metrics, limitations, assumptions, and potential biases. Techniques such as model cards and datasheets for datasets facilitate transparency and comparability across systems. Moreover, explainability is crucial in sectors where users have a right to understand decisions—such as in healthcare, education, finance, or criminal justice. A failure to provide adequate explanations can erode accountability, reinforce power imbalances, and undermine due process.

## MONITORING AND EVALUATION

In the dynamic landscape of artificial intelligence (AI), digital systems, and cyber-physical infrastructures, monitoring and evaluation (M&E) emerge as indispensable pillars for ensuring that deployed technologies remain ethical, effective, safe, and aligned with human values. While the development and deployment phases of AI receive considerable attention, it is in the post-deployment lifecycle—where systems interact with real-world data, stakeholders, and unpredictable environments—that the most profound challenges and opportunities arise. Monitoring and evaluation provide the continuous oversight necessary to detect emerging risks, validate performance, ensure accountability, and support adaptive improvements, (Walsh et al., 2019). Without robust M&E mechanisms, even well-designed systems can spiral into dysfunction, propagate bias, or produce unanticipated harm over time. At its core, monitoring refers to the regular collection, analysis, and reporting of system performance indicators during and after implementation. It focuses on the operational aspects of an AI tool or digital system—tracking outputs, usage patterns, error rates, and compliance metrics. Evaluation, on the other hand, is a more comprehensive, periodic process that assesses whether the system is achieving its intended goals, producing equitable outcomes, and aligning with legal and ethical standards. Evaluation considers both quantitative metrics and qualitative insights to assess the system's effectiveness, impact, fairness, and adaptability. Together, these functions offer a feedback loop that enables learning, correction, and transformation. One of the most critical reasons for implementing ongoing M&E is to detect model drift and data drift. AI models, especially those in dynamic environments, can degrade in accuracy or relevance when the data they encounter in deployment deviates from training data. For example, a fraud detection algorithm trained on pre-pandemic financial behavior may perform poorly as post-pandemic patterns emerge. Model drift can lead to increased false positives or negatives, while data drift can introduce new biases or render previous assumptions obsolete.

In such cases, continuous logging, sensor monitoring, anomaly detection, and incident reporting mechanisms are vital. These systems must be monitored in real-time for critical failures or outlier behavior, with built-in "safe mode" protocols and human override capabilities. Safety evaluations may include stress-testing under extreme scenarios, simulating adversarial attacks, and maintaining fail-safe redundancies. Such vigilance not only protects users but also builds public trust in technological innovation. In addition to technical performance, M&E must also account for user experience (UX) and satisfaction. Digital tools deployed in health-care, education, customer service, or government must be continually assessed for their usability, accessibility, and emotional impact. Monitoring user feedback, help desk logs, and engagement metrics can reveal pain points, confusion, or unintended consequences. For instance, if a chatbot frequently frustrates users seeking medical advice, evaluation may reveal that its tone, comprehension, or response timing need improvement. Regular user surveys, focus groups, and participatory evaluations ensure that human perspectives remain central to iterative design. Ethical and legal compliance is another area where ongoing M&E plays a critical role. AI systems are subject to evolving regulations such as the European Union's AI Act, the U.S. Algorithmic Accountability Act, India's DPDP Act, and other jurisdictional frameworks. A system that was compliant at deployment may become non-compliant if new legal interpretations emerge or if its behavior changes through updates. M&E mechanisms should track legal obligations, audit data handling processes, and ensure that informed consent, transparency, and data protection requirements are consistently met. Regulatory compliance evaluation may also include third-party audits, certifications, or public disclosures, which enhance legitimacy and reduce institutional risk, (Webster et al., 2020). The role of feedback loops in M&E cannot be overstated.

## EMERGING TRENDS IN AI ETHICS

As artificial intelligence (AI) continues to permeate nearly every aspect of modern society—from healthcare and education to finance, warfare, and entertainment—ethical considerations are evolving just as rapidly. The growing complexity and scale of AI systems have given rise to new challenges that demand more sophisticated, nuanced, and interdisciplinary approaches to AI ethics. While foundational concerns like privacy, bias, transparency, and accountability remain central, the ethical terrain is expanding to include emergent issues such as environmental sustainability, geopolitical dynamics, collective rights, neurotechnology integration, and even existential risks. The field of AI ethics is no longer confined to academic philosophy or internal corporate guidelines; it has become a global policy frontier that intersects with law, public trust, and democratic governance. One of the most prominent emerging trends in AI ethics is the shift from individual-centric to collective and systemic perspectives. Traditionally, ethical frameworks in AI emphasized harm to individuals—such as data misuse, discrimination, or lack of informed consent. While these remain crucial, there is growing recognition that AI systems also have collective impacts, such as reinforcing societal inequities, influencing public discourse, altering employment landscapes, or reshaping cultural norms. As a result, newer ethical paradigms explore systemic fairness, societal well-being, and the preservation of democratic institutions. For example, large-scale content algorithms or language models may unintentionally shape collective beliefs, exacerbate polarization, or marginalize minority worldviews—requiring ethical scrutiny beyond the individual level. Another major trend is the integration of environmental sustainability into AI ethics. The energy consumption and carbon footprint of training and deploying large AI models—particularly deep learning and generative AI—have raised urgent ethical questions about the environmental cost of technological progress. AI systems like GPT-4 or image generators require vast computational resources and contribute to rising emissions. Ethical AI today increasingly considers green AI principles: designing algorithms that are not only efficient and effective but also environmentally conscious. Institutions are exploring carbon accountability frameworks, energy-efficient model architectures, and the use of renewable energy in data centers. Ethical evaluation is now expected to balance innovation with planetary responsibility loosely related is the rise of ethical auditing and impact assessment tools. There is increasing awareness that ethical AI cannot be created in a vacuum or imposed top-down by technologists alone, (Zhou et al., 2021). Communities affected by algorithmic decisions—especially those from the Global South, Indigenous populations, women, people with disabilities, and other underrepresented groups—must have a seat at the table.

Organizations like the Future of Life Institute, OpenAI, and DeepMind have initiated work on AI alignment, value alignment, and safety research to address the hypothetical but potentially catastrophic risks of artificial general intelligence (AGI). The tension between accelerationist and precautionary approaches defines an ongoing ethical debate about the pace and direction of AI development. The ethical discourse is also evolving to incorporate non-Western epistemologies and pluralistic moral frameworks. Much of AI ethics to date has been shaped by Western liberal values such as individual autonomy, data ownership, and rational consent. However, scholars and activists from Africa, Asia, Latin America, and Indigenous communities are bringing alternative perspectives—emphasizing communal well-being, relational ethics, ecological harmony, and spiritual values. This trend challenges the universality of dominant ethical norms and advocates for intercultural dialogue in the governance of global AI systems. Finally, a vital emerging trend is the professionalization of AI ethics. Ethical expertise is now being embedded into corporate structures, academic programs, and policy institutions. New roles such as AI ethics officers, algorithmic auditors, and responsible innovation leads are being formalized across sectors. Interdisciplinary training programs in tech ethics, law, philosophy, and social science are equipping the next generation of practitioners with the tools to navigate ethical complexities. Codes of conduct, professional standards, and cross-sector alliances (e.g., Partnership on AI, AI Now Institute) are helping define what responsible AI development looks like in practice.

## CONCLUSION

As we stand at the intersection of rapid technological advancement and profound societal transformation, the ethical dimensions of AI-powered communication tools have emerged as a critical focal point for scholars, technologists, policymakers, and civil society. These tools—including chatbots, virtual assistants, content recommendation systems, predictive algorithms, and language generation models—are now deeply embedded in our digital environments, influencing everything from interpersonal conversations and information access to decision-making in sensitive domains such as healthcare, education, finance, and governance. Their widespread adoption has ushered in undeniable benefits: efficiency, scalability, personalized experiences, and improved access to services. Yet, they also bring with them a host of ethical dilemmas, including issues of bias, surveillance, manipulation, consent, misinformation, autonomy, and accountability. At the core of these concerns lies the growing asymmetry of power between the designers and deployers of AI tools and the end users who interact with them—often unknowingly or without informed consent. This asymmetry stems not only from the complexity and opacity of AI models (especially deep learning systems) but also from the proprietary and commercial interests that drive much of their development. Many users are unaware that their data are being harvested, analyzed, and used to personalize content or influence behavior. This raises profound questions about individual autonomy, dignity, and democratic participation. Ethical AI communication tools, therefore, must prioritize transparency, explainability, and user control as foundational principles, ensuring that users are not passive recipients of technology but active participants in its governance and evolution. One of the fundamental ethical imperatives is protecting user privacy and data sovereignty. AI communication tools often rely on massive amounts of personal data, including behavioral patterns, location history, preferences, and even emotional cues. Without robust data protection laws and transparent data handling practices, there is a heightened risk of surveillance capitalism, unauthorized profiling, and data breaches. Ethical frameworks must ensure that users are not only informed about how their data is used but also empowered to control it. This includes clear opt-in mechanisms, access to data usage logs, and the right to opt out or delete their data entirely. Another major concern is algorithmic bias and discrimination. AI systems are only as unbiased as the data and assumptions they are built upon. Historical and social inequalities, if embedded in training datasets or model parameters, can perpetuate or even amplify discrimination—particularly along lines of race, gender, socioeconomic status, or geography. In the realm of AI communication, this can manifest as exclusionary language generation, stereotyping, or unequal treatment in automated responses. Ethical AI must embed fairness assessments, diverse training data, bias mitigation strategies, and inclusive design principles at every stage of development and deployment. Equally important is the issue of content manipulation and misinformation. Communication tools driven by AI are often optimized for engagement, which can incentivize the promotion of sensational or polarizing content. This has led to concerns about echo chambers, radicalization, and the viral spread of fake news. Deepfake technologies and generative models further complicate this landscape by making it increasingly difficult to discern truth from fabrication. An ethical approach requires building safeguards that prioritize truthful, high-quality, and context-aware communication—supported by rigorous content verification, source attribution, and human oversight. Informed consent and transparency are non-negotiable pillars of ethical AI communication. Users must be made explicitly aware when they are interacting with an AI system and should understand its capabilities, limitations, and underlying purpose. This is especially vital in contexts involving vulnerable populations—children, the elderly, individuals with cognitive disabilities, or users in high-stakes environments such as legal or medical consultations. Ethical design must avoid deception, manipulation, or the blurring of boundaries between human and machine interlocutors. Interfaces should be designed to clearly signal when a bot is speaking, and documentation about its functioning should be accessible and intelligible to laypersons. Emerging technologies like generative AI (e.g., large language models, multimodal systems, voice synthesis) further underscore the importance of ethical vigilance. These systems can generate realistic human-like dialogue, images, and videos, making them powerful tools for communication—but also for deception, identity theft, and psychological manipulation. Ethical frameworks must evolve alongside these technologies, anticipating misuse scenarios and building in protective design features such as watermarking, content provenance tracking, and usage restrictions.

## REFERENCES

Abrams, J. J. (2004). Pragmatism, artificial intelligence, and posthuman bioethics: Shusterman, Rorty, Foucault. *Human Studies*, *27*(3), 241–258. DOI: 10.1023/B:HUMA.0000042130.79208.c6

Acemoglu, D., & Restrepo, P. (2020). The wrong kind of AI? Artificial intelligence and the future of labour demand. *Cambridge Journal of Regions, Economy and Society*, *13*(1), 25–35. DOI: 10.1093/cjres/rsz022

Bailey, C., Yeoman, R., Madden, A., Thompson, M., & Kerridge, G. (2019). A review of the empirical literature on meaningful work: Progress and research agenda. *Human Resource Development Review*, *18*(1), 83–113. DOI: 10.1177/1534484318804653

Bankins, S. (2021). The ethical use of artificial intelligence in human resource management: A decision-making framework. *Ethics and Information Technology*, *23*(4), 841–854. DOI: 10.1007/s10676-021-09619-6

Cheney, G., Zorn, T. E.Jr, Planalp, S., & Lair, D. J. (2008). Meaningful work and personal/social well-being organizational communication engages the meanings of work. *Annals of the International Communication Association*, *32*(1), 137–185. DOI: 10.1080/23808985.2008.11679077

Chowdhary, S., Selvakumar, P., Sangeetha, B., Sarvaani, V. V., Anute, N., & Sharma, M. (2025). The Role of Social Capital in Entrepreneurial Development. In Martínez-Falcó, J., Sánchez-García, E., & Marco-Lajara, B. (Eds.), *Support Networks for Entrepreneurs: Social Capital and Strategic Collaborations* (pp. 311–338). IGI Global Scientific Publishing., DOI: 10.4018/979-8-3693-9836-4.ch013

Coates, J. M., Santhanalakshmi, K., Dinesh, N., Gandhimathi, S., & Chandel, P. S. Mohit, & Selvakumar, P. (2025). Assessment and Evaluation in Transnational Staff Development. In G. Morris & J. Ye (Eds.), Training and Development in Transnational Higher Education (pp. 387–406). IGI Global Scientific Publishing. DOI: 10.4018/979-8-3373-1897-4.ch019

Dahl, E. S. (2018). Appraising black-boxed technology: The positive prospects. *Philosophy & Technology*, *31*(4), 571–591. DOI: 10.1007/s13347-017-0275-1

Dastin, J. (2018, October 11). Amazon scraps secret AI recruiting tool that showed bias against women. Reuters. https://www.reuters.com/article/us-amazon-com-jobs-automation-insight-idUSKCN1MK08G

Ernst, E., Merola, R., & Samaan, D. (2018). The economics of artificial intelligence. International Labour Organization. https://www.ilo.org/wcmsp5/groups/public/dgreports/cabinet/documents/publication/wcms_647306.pdf

Floridi, L., Cowls, J., Beltrametti, M., Chatila, R., Chazerand, P., Dignum, V., Luetge, C., Madelin, R., Pagallo, U., Rossi, F., Schafer, B., Valcke, P., & Vayena, E. (2018). AI4People - An ethical framework for a good AI society. *Minds and Machines*, *28*(4), 689–707. DOI: 10.1007/s11023-018-9482-5 PMID: 30930541

Formosa, P. (2017). *Kantian ethics, dignity and perfection*. Cambridge University Press. DOI: 10.1017/9781316987308

Gibbs, M. J. (2017). How is new technology changing job design? *IZA World of Labor: Evidence-Based Policy Making*. Advance online publication. DOI: 10.15185/izawol.344

Hagendorff, T. (2020). The ethics of AI ethics: An evaluation of guidelines. *Minds and Machines*, *30*(1), 99–120. DOI: 10.1007/s11023-020-09517-8

Jarrahi, M. H. (2018). Artificial intelligence and the future of work: Human-AI symbiosis in organizational decision making. *Business Horizons*, *61*(4), 577–586. DOI: 10.1016/j.bushor.2018.03.007

Jobin, A., Ienca, M., & Vayena, E. (2019). The global landscape of AI ethics guidelines. *Nature Machine Intelligence*, *1*(9), 389–399. DOI: 10.1038/s42256-019-0088-2

Kellogg, K. C., Valentine, M. A., & Christin, A. (2020). Algorithms at work: The new contested terrain of control. *The Academy of Management Annals*, *14*(1), 366–410. DOI: 10.5465/annals.2018.0174

Langlois, R. N. (2003). Cognitive comparative advantage and the organization of work: Lessons from Herbert Simon's vision of the future. *Journal of Economic Psychology*, *24*(2), 167–187. DOI: 10.1016/S0167-4870(02)00201-5

Lips-Wiersma, M., & Wright, S. (2012). Measuring the meaning of meaningful work: Development and validation of the comprehensive meaningful work scale. *Group & Organization Management*, *37*(5), 655–685. DOI: 10.1177/1059601112461578

Maheswaran, K., Selvakumar, P., Shaikh, M., Shashank, G., Gupta, S., & Manjunath, T. C. (2025). The Evolution of Smart Urban Mobility With Emerging Technologies. In Ponnusamy, S., Assaf, M., Youssef, B., Jeon, G., & Kalyanaraman, S. (Eds.), *Leveraging VANETs and Blockchain Technology for Urban Mobility* (pp. 1–28). IGI Global Scientific Publishing., DOI: 10.4018/979-8-3373-0265-2.ch001

Nisha Angeline, M., Selvakumar, P., Gupta, M. K., Nazar, N., Elumalai, D., & Bhattacharya, S. (2025). Emerging Materials for Energy Storage and Environmental Applications. In K. Muduli, B. Moharana, S. Ales, & D. Biswal (Eds.), Using Computational Intelligence for Sustainable Manufacturing of Advanced Materials (pp. 53–72). IGI Global Scientific Publishing. DOI: 10.4018/979-8-3693-7974-5.ch003

Pratt, M. G., & Ashforth, B. E. (2003). Fostering meaningfulness in working and at work. In Cameron, K., Dutton, J. E., & Quinn, R. E. (Eds.), *Positive organizational scholarship: Foundations of a new discipline* (pp. 308–327). Berrett-Koehler.

Ravenscraft, E. (25 November, 2021). What is the metaverse, exactly? Wired. Retrieved from: https://www.wired.com/story/what-is-the-metaverse/

Roberts, P. (2020). Working smarter with data. Australian Manufacturing Forum. https://www.aumanufacturing.com.au/working-smarter-with-data-ai-gives-agriculture-the-competitive-edge

Sakthivel, M., Jaganathan, A., Mohanraj, M., & Selvakumar, P. Mohit, & Manjunath, T. (2025). Brand Loyalty through AI and Personalisation AI-Generated Content for Financial Marketing. In A. J. Nair, S. Manohar, Y. B. Limbu, & B. A. Huhmann (Eds.), Intersecting Natural Language Processing and FinTech Innovations in Service Marketing (pp. 77–96). IGI Global Scientific Publishing. DOI: 10.4018/979-8-3693-9944-6.ch006

Sethumadhavan, R. P. P., S., Selvakumar, P., Kadu, S. G., Chandel, P. S., & Gupta, S. (2025). Environmental Sustainability and Employee Participation. In C. Şeker, E. Örücü, & A. Kaya (Eds.), Green Leadership Strategies for Increased Employee Engagement and Performance (pp. 275–298). IGI Global Scientific Publishing. DOI: 10.4018/979-8-3373-2106-6.ch009

Thirunagalingam, A., & Selvakumar, P. (2025). Application of Automation and Robotics in the Oil and Gas Industry. In Abdullayev, V., & Khang, A. (Eds.), *Revolutionizing AI and Robotics in the Oil and Gas Industry* (pp. 229–244). IGI Global Scientific Publishing., DOI: 10.4018/979-8-3693-8156-4.ch011

Upadhyaya, A. N., Debnath, P., Rani, P., Selvakumar, P., Manjunath, T. C., & Bhattacharya, S. (2025). AI-Based Disaster Prediction and Early Warning Systems. In Mobo, F. (Ed.), *AI and Emerging Technologies for Emergency Response and Smart Cities* (pp. 55–74). IGI Global Scientific Publishing., DOI: 10.4018/979-8-3693-9770-1.ch003

Vallor, S. (2015). Moral deskilling and upskilling in a new machine age: Reflections on the ambiguous future of character. *Philosophy & Technology*, *28*(1), 107–124. DOI: 10.1007/s13347-014-0156-9

Walsh, T., Levy, N., Bell, G., Elliott, A., Maclaurin, J., Mareels, I., & Wood, Fiona. (2019). The effective and ethical development of artificial intelligence. ACOLA. https://acola.org/wp-content/uploads/2019/07/hs4_artificial-intelligence-report.pdf

Webster, C., & Ivanov, S. (2020). Robotics, artificial intelligence, and the evolving nature of work. In George, B., & Paul, J. (Eds.), *Digital Transformation in Business and Society*. Palgrave Macmillan. DOI: 10.1007/978-3-030-08277-2_8

Zhou, L., Paul, S., Demirkan, H., Yuan, L., Spohrer, J., Zhou, M., & Basu, J. (2021). Intelligence augmentation: Towards building human-machine symbiotic relationship. *AIS Transactions on Human-Computer Interaction, 13*(2), 243–264. DOI: 10.17705/1thci.00149

# Compilation of References


Abraham, R. M. (2023). Balancing responsibility-sharing in the simulated clinical skills setting: A strategy to remove barriers to feedback engagement as a new concept to promote a growth-enhancing process. *African Journal of Health Professions Education, 15*(1), 2–6. DOI: 10.7196/AJHPE.2023.v15i1.1630

Abrams, J. J. (2004). Pragmatism, artificial intelligence, and posthuman bioethics: Shusterman, Rorty, Foucault. *Human Studies, 27*(3), 241–258. DOI: 10.1023/B:HUMA.0000042130.79208.c6

Acemoglu, D., & Restrepo, P. (2020). The wrong kind of AI? Artificial intelligence and the future of labour demand. *Cambridge Journal of Regions, Economy and Society, 13*(1), 25–35. DOI: 10.1093/cjres/rsz022

Ademosu, I., & Alade, M. O. (2019). Communicating via imagery: Speaking through online memes. *Journal of Communication and Media Research, 11*(2), 34–46. http://dspace.run.edu.ng:8080/jspui/handle/123456789/214

Adenuga, R., & Dodge, T. (2023). From automation to autonomy: Rethinking algorithmic control. *AI & Society, 38*, 1261–1276. DOI: 10.1007/s00146-023-01597-z

Agarwal, P. K., Akutsu, T., Amihood, A., Apostolico, A., Benham, C., Benson, G., & Myers, G. (2005). *(including subseries lecture notes in artificial intelligence and lecture notes in bioinformatics): Preface. Lecture notes in computer science (including subseries lecture notes in artificial intelligence and lecture notes in bioinformatics), 3692*. Lecture notes in computer science. V-VI.

Aïmeur, E., Amri, S., & Brassard, G. (2023). Fake news, disinformation and misinformation in social media: A review. *Social Network Analysis and Mining, 13*(1), 30. DOI: 10.1007/s13278-023-01028-5 PMID: 36789378

Al-Amin, M., Ali, M. S., Salam, A., Khan, A., Ali, A., Ullah, A., . . . Chowdhury, S. K. (2024). History of generative Artificial Intelligence (AI) chatbots: past, present, and future development. *arXiv preprint arXiv:2402.05122*. https://doi.org//arXiv.2402.05122.DOI: 10.48550

Aldbyani, A., Chuanxia, Z., & Alhimaidi, A. (2025). The effect of mindfulness on smartphone addiction: The mediating role of self-regulation learning and the moderating role of digital detox. *Research Square*. DOI: 10.21203/rs.3.rs-6405697/v1

Almourad, M. B., McAlaney, J., Skinner, T., Pleya, M., & Ali, R. (2020). Defining digital addiction: Key features from the literature. *Psihologija (Beograd)*, *53*(3), 237–253. DOI: 10.2298/PSI191029017A

Alowais, M. Khan, S. Iqbal, and F. Alshahrani. (2023). Artificial Intelligence in Clinical Practice: Transforming Diagnosis and Treatment. *IEEE Access : Practical Innovations, Open Solutions*, *11*, 46523–46535.

Alter, A. (2017). *Irresistible: The Rise of Addictive Technology and the Business of Keeping Us Hooked*. Penguin Press.

Alter, A. (2017). *Irresistible: Why we can't stop checking, scrolling, clicking and watching*. Random House.

American Psychiatric Association. (2013). *Diagnostic and statistical manual of mental disorders* (5th ed.).

Ami, R. (2021). AI in Automated Content Moderation on Social Media. *International Journal of Artificial Intelligence and Machine Learning*, *4*(3).

Anderson, M., & Jiang, J. (2018). *Teens, social media & technology 2018*. Pew Research Center. https://www.pewresearch.org

Andreassen, C. S. (2015). Online social network site addiction: A comprehensive review. *Current Addiction Reports*, *2*(2), 175–184. DOI: 10.1007/s40429-015-0056-9

Andreassen, C. S., Billieux, J., Griffiths, M. D., Kuss, D. J., Demetrovics, Z., Mazzoni, E., & Pallesen, S. (2017). The relationship between addictive use of social media and video games and symptoms of psychiatric disorders: A large-scale cross-sectional study. *Psychology of Addictive Behaviors*, *30*(2), 252–262. DOI: 10.1037/adb0000160 PMID: 26999354

Andreassen, C. S., Torsheim, T., Brunborg, G. S., & Pallesen, S. (2012). Development of a Facebook addiction scale. *Psychological Reports*, *110*(2), 501–517. DOI: 10.2466/02.09.18.PR0.110.2.501-517 PMID: 22662404

Andrews, S., Ellis, D. A., Shaw, H., & Piwek, L. (2015). Beyond self-report: Tools to compare estimated and real-world smartphone use. *PLoS One*, *10*(10), e0139004. DOI: 10.1371/journal.pone.0139004 PMID: 26509895

Aria, M., & Cuccurullo, C. (2017). bibliometrix: An R-tool for comprehensive science mapping analysis. *Journal of Informetrics*, *11*(4), 959–975. DOI: 10.1016/j.joi.2017.08.007

Ashforth, B. E., Kreiner, G. E., & Fugate, M. (2000). All in a day's work: Boundaries and micro role transitions. *Academy of Management Review*, *25*(3), 472–491. DOI: 10.2307/259305

Bailey, C., Yeoman, R., Madden, A., Thompson, M., & Kerridge, G. (2019). A review of the empirical literature on meaningful work: Progress and research agenda. *Human Resource Development Review*, *18*(1), 83–113. DOI: 10.1177/1534484318804653

Bai, Q., Dan, Q., Mu, Z., & Yang, M. (2019). A systematic review of emoji: Current research and future perspectives. *Frontiers in Psychology*, *10*, 476737. DOI: 10.3389/fpsyg.2019.02221 PMID: 31681068

Baker, D. A. (2017, May). Wearables and User Interface Design: Impacts on Belief in Free Will. *In International Conference on Human-Computer Interaction (pp.* 210-217*)*. Cham: Springer International Publishing.DOI: 10.1007/978-3-319-58750-9_30

Bakshy, E., Messing, S., & Adamic, L. A. (2015). Exposure to ideologically diverse news and opinion on Facebook. *Science*, *348*(6239), 1130–1132. DOI: 10.1126/science.aaa1160 PMID: 25953820

Bandura, A. (1977). Self-efficacy: Toward a unifying theory of behavioral change. *Psychological Review*, *84*(2), 191–215. DOI: 10.1037/0033-295X.84.2.191 PMID: 847061

Bankins, S. (2021). The ethical use of artificial intelligence in human resource management: A decision-making framework. *Ethics and Information Technology*, *23*(4), 841–854. DOI: 10.1007/s10676-021-09619-6

Barak, A., Hen, L., Boniel-Nissim, M., & Shapira, N. A. (2008). A comprehensive review and a meta-analysis of the effectiveness of internet-based psychotherapeutic interventions. *Journal of Technology in Human Services*, *26*(2-4), 109–160. DOI: 10.1080/15228830802094429

Barberá, P., Tucker, J. A., Guess, A., Vaccari, C., Siegel, A., Sanovich, S., & Nyhan, B. (2018). Social media, political polarization, and political disinformation: A review of the scientific literature. DOI: 10.2139/ssrn.3144139

Baron-Cohen, S. (1999). *The evolution of a theory of mind* (pp. 261-277). na. DOI: 10.1093/acprof:oso/9780192632593.003.0013

Barrett, B. (2021). Instagram's "Take a Break" feature won't fix its teen mental health problem. *Wired*. https://www.wired.com

Bauer, C., & Figl, K. (2008, October). Active listening" in written online communication-a case study in a course on "soft skills for computer scientists. *In 2008 38th Annual Frontiers in Education Conference (pp. F2C-1)*. IEEE.DOI: 10.1109/FIE.2008.4720282

Berridge, K. C., & Robinson, T. E. (2016). Liking, wanting, and the incentive-sensitization theory of addiction. *The American Psychologist*, *71*(8), 670–679. DOI: 10.1037/amp0000059 PMID: 27977239

Beyens, I., Pouwels, J. L., van Driel, I. I., Keijsers, L., & Valkenburg, P. M. (2020). The effect of social media on well-being differs from adolescent to adolescent. *Scientific Reports*, *10*(1), 10763. DOI: 10.1038/s41598-020-67727-7 PMID: 32612108

Billieux, J., Maurage, P., Lopez-Fernandez, O., Kuss, D. J., & Griffiths, M. D. (2015). Can disordered mobile phone use be considered a behavioral addiction? An update on current evidence and a comprehensive model for future research. *Current Addiction Reports*, *2*(2), 156–162. DOI: 10.1007/s40429-015-0054-y

Binns, R. (2018). Fairness in machine learning: Lessons from political philosophy. *Proceedings of the 2018 Conference on Fairness, Accountability, and Transparency (FAT)*, 149–159. DOI: 10.1145/3287560.3287591

Bostock, S., Crosswell, A. D., Prather, A. A., & Steptoe, A. (2019). Mindfulness on-the-go: Effects of a mindfulness meditation app on work stress and well-being. *Journal of Occupational Health Psychology*, *24*(1), 127–138. DOI: 10.1037/ocp0000118 PMID: 29723001

Boyd, J. E., Otilingam, P. G., & DeForge, B. R. (2014). Brief version of the Internalized Stigma of Mental Illness (ISMI) scale: Psychometric properties and relationship to depression, self-esteem, recovery orientation, empowerment, and perceived devaluation and discrimination. *Psychiatric Rehabilitation Journal*, *37*(1), 17–23. DOI: 10.1037/prj0000035 PMID: 24660946

Brand, M., Wegmann, E., Stark, R., Müller, A., Wölfling, K., Robbins, T. W., & Potenza, M. N. (2019). The Interaction of Person-Affect-Cognition-Execution (I-PACE) model for addictive behaviors: Update, generalization to addictive behaviors beyond internet-use disorders, and specification of the process character of addictive behaviors. *Neuroscience and Biobehavioral Reviews, 104*, 1–10. DOI: 10.1016/j.neubiorev.2019.06.032 PMID: 31247240

Brandtzaeg, P. B., Egan, J., Maples, C., Huang, H., & Willson, M. (2025). Adolescents and emotional AI companions: Dependency and identity. *Media Culture & Society*. Advance online publication. DOI: 10.1177/0163443724123457

Bublitz, J. C., & Merkel, R. (2020). Crimes against minds: On mental manipulations, harms and a human right to mental self-determination. *Criminal Law and Philosophy, 14*(1), 51–77. DOI: 10.1007/s11572-012-9172-y

BUNIM. (2024). *E.* PARASOCIAL DEPENDENCY ASSOCIATED WITH ARTIFICIAL INTELLIGENCE CHATBOTS.

Burnell, K., George, M. J., Vollet, J. W., Ehrenreich, S. E., & Underwood, M. K. (2019). Passive social networking site use and well-being: The mediating roles of social comparison and the fear of missing out. *Cyberpsychology (Brno), 13*(3), 5. Advance online publication. DOI: 10.5817/CP2019-3-5

Burrell, J. (2016). How the machine 'thinks': Understanding opacity in machine learning algorithms. *Big Data & Society, 3*(1), 1–12. DOI: 10.1177/2053951715622512

Calo, R. (2014). Digital market manipulation. *The George Washington Law Review, 82*(4), 995–1051.

Cancer, J. M. I. R. (2022). The Role of AI-Powered Chatbots in Oncology Care: A Systematic Review. *JMIR Cancer, 8*(4), e34567.

Caplan, R., Donovan, J., & Hanson, L. (2022). *Algorithmic amplification of extreme content on TikTok*. Data & Society Research Institute. https://datasociety.net

Carr, N. (2010). *The Shallows: What the Internet Is Doing to Our Brains*. W. W. Norton & Company.

Cerniglia, L., Zoratto, F., Cimino, S., Laviola, G., Ammaniti, M., & Adriani, W. (2017). Internet addiction in adolescence: Neurobiological, psychosocial and clinical issues. *Neuroscience and Biobehavioral Reviews, 76*, 174–184. DOI: 10.1016/j.neubiorev.2016.12.024 PMID: 28027952

Chang, D. H., Lin, M. P. C., Hajian, S., & Wang, Q. Q. (2023). Educational design principles of using AI chatbot that supports self-regulated learning in education: Goal setting, feedback, and personalization. *Sustainability (Basel), 15*(17), 12921. DOI: 10.3390/su151712921

Chatterjee, P., Anand, T., & Singh, H. (2021). Telemedicine and mental health in India: Bridging the gap in rural health care. *Indian Journal of Psychiatry, 63*(3), 203–210. DOI: 10.4103/psychiatry.IndianJPsychiatry_93_21 PMID: 34211230

Cheney, G., Zorn, T. E.Jr, Planalp, S., & Lair, D. J. (2008). Meaningful work and personal/social well-being organizational communication engages the meanings of work. *Annals of the International Communication Association, 32*(1), 137–185. DOI: 10.1080/23808985.2008.11679077

Chiam, J., Lim, A., & Teredesai, A. (2024, August). *NudgeRank: Digital algorithmic nudging for personalized health.* In *Proceedings of the 30th ACM SIGKDD Conference on Knowledge Discovery and Data Mining* (pp. 4873–4884). DOI: 10.1145/3637528.3671562

Chianella, R. (2021, December). Addictive digital experiences: The influence of artificial intelligence and more-than-human design. In *14th International Conference of the European Academy of Design, Safe Harbours for Design Research* (Vol. 9, No. 5, pp. 1–13). DOI: 10.5151/ead2021-125

Children's Online Privacy Protection Act, 15 U.S.C. §§ 6501–6506 (1998).

Chow, C., Liu, A., Wang, B., & Tan, K. (2023). The Influence of ChatGPT and Large Language Models on Medical Chatbots. *npj. Digital Medicine, 6*(89), 1–9.

Chowdhary, S., Selvakumar, P., Sangeetha, B., Sarvaani, V. V., Anute, N., & Sharma, M. (2025). The Role of Social Capital in Entrepreneurial Development. In Martínez-Falcó, J., Sánchez-García, E., & Marco-Lajara, B. (Eds.), *Support Networks for Entrepreneurs: Social Capital and Strategic Collaborations* (pp. 311–338). IGI Global Scientific Publishing., DOI: 10.4018/979-8-3693-9836-4.ch013

Church, P., & Pehlivan, C. N. (2023). The Digital Services Act (DSA): A new era for online harms and intermediary liability. *Global Privacy Law Review, 4*(1), 53–59. DOI: 10.54648/GPLR2023005

Cinar, A. B., & Bilodeau, S. (2024). Incorporating AI into the inner circle of emotional intelligence for sustainability. *Sustainability (Basel), 16*(15), 6648. DOI: 10.3390/su16156648

Coates, J. M., Santhanalakshmi, K., Dinesh, N., Gandhimathi, S., & Chandel, P. S. Mohit, & Selvakumar, P. (2025). Assessment and Evaluation in Transnational Staff Development. In G. Morris & J. Ye (Eds.), Training and Development in Transnational Higher Education (pp. 387–406). IGI Global Scientific Publishing. DOI: 10.4018/979-8-3373-1897-4.ch019

Colman, A. W., & Leung, Y. K. (2000). Using intentional models for the interface design of multi-level systems. *International Journal of Human-Computer Studies, 52*(6), 1007–1029. DOI: 10.1006/ijhc.2000.0369

Constitution of India, Articles 21, 19(1)(a), and 15.

Coombs, W. T. (2022). Situational crisis communication theory (SCCT) refining and clarifying a cognitive-based theory of crisis communication. *The handbook of crisis communication, 193-204.*DOI: 10.1002/9781119678953.ch14

Cortina, L. M., Kabat-Farr, D., Magley, V. J., & Nelson, K. (2017). Researching rudeness: The past, present, and future of the science of incivility. *Journal of Occupational Health Psychology, 22*(3), 299–313. DOI: 10.1037/ocp0000089

Couldry, N., & Mejias, U. A. (2019). *The Costs of Connection: How Data is Colonizing Human Life and Appropriating It for Capitalism.* Stanford University Press.

Covington, P., Adams, J., & Sargin, E. (2016). Deep neural networks for YouTube recommendations. *Proceedings of the 10th ACM Conference on Recommender Systems,* 191–198. DOI: 10.1145/2959100.2959190

Cowie, R., Douglas-Cowie, E., & Cox, C. (2020). Beyond emotion recognition: Building emotionally intelligent systems. *IEEE Transactions on Affective Computing, 11*(1), 3–6. DOI: 10.1109/TAFFC.2019.2959387

Coyne, S. M., Rogers, A. A., Zurcher, J. D., Stockdale, L., & Booth, M. (2021). Does time spent using social media impact mental health? An eight-year longitudinal study. *Computers in Human Behavior, 114,* 106528. DOI: 10.1016/j.chb.2020.106528

Czamecki, C., & Spiliopoulou, M. (2012). A holistic framework for the implementation of a next generattion network. *International Journal of Business Information Systems, 9*(4), 385–401. DOI: 10.1504/IJBIS.2012.046291

Dabbish, L., Mark, G., & Gonzalez, V. (2011). "Why do i keep interrupting myself? environment, habit and self-interruption," in *Proceedings of the 2011 Annual Conference on Human Factors in, Computing Systems (CHI '11)* (New York, NY: Association for Computing Machinery), 3127–3130. DOI: 10.1145/1978942.1979405

Dahl, E. S. (2018). Appraising black-boxed technology: The positive prospects. *Philosophy & Technology*, *31*(4), 571–591. DOI: 10.1007/s13347-017-0275-1

Dahmani, L., & Bohbot, V. D. (2020). Habitual use of GPS negatively impacts spatial memory during self-guided navigation. *Scientific Reports*, *10*(1), 6310. DOI: 10.1038/s41598-020-62877-0 PMID: 32286340

Dastin, J. (2018, October 11). Amazon scraps secret AI recruiting tool that showed bias against women. Reuters. https://www.reuters.com/article/us-amazon-com-jobs-automation-insight-idUSKCN1MK08G

Datta, A., Dey, B. K., Bhuniya, S., Sangal, I., Mandal, B., Sarkar, M., Guchhait, R., Sarkar, B., & Ganguly, B. (2025). Adaptation of e-commerce retailing to enhance customer satisfaction within a dynamical system under transfer of risk. *Journal of Retailing and Consumer Services*, *84*, 104129. DOI: 10.1016/j.jretconser.2024.104129

Daud, A. M., Omar, J., Turiman, P., & Osman, K. (2012). Creativity in science education. *Procedia: Social and Behavioral Sciences*, *59*, 467–474. DOI: 10.1016/j.sbspro.2012.09.302

Davazdahemami, B., Hammer, B., & Soror, A. (2016, January). Addiction to mobile phone or addiction through mobile phone*? In 2016 49th Hawaii international conference on system sciences (HICSS) (pp. 1467-1476).* IEEE.DOI: 10.1109/HICSS.2016.186

de Barcelos Silva, A., Barbosa, J. L. V., & Gomes, J. O. (2019). Virtual reality as a tool for evaluation of quality of life in the elderly. *Behaviour & Information Technology*, *38*(1), 68–85. DOI: 10.1080/0144929X.2018.1519030

DeSanctis, G., & Gallupe, R. B. (1987). A foundation for the study of group decision support systems. *Management Science*, *33*(5), 589–609. DOI: 10.1287/mnsc.33.5.589

Digital Personal Data Protection Act, 2023 (India).

Dimitriadis, S., & Kyrezis, N. (2010). Linking trust to use intention for technology-enabled bank channels: The role of trusting intentions. *Psychology and Marketing*, *27*(8), 799–820. DOI: 10.1002/mar.20358

Ding, K., & Li, H. (2023). Digital addiction intervention for children and adolescents: A scoping review. *International Journal of Environmental Research and Public Health*, *20*(6), 4777. Advance online publication. DOI: 10.3390/ijerph20064777 PMID: 36981687

Ding, K., Shen, Y., Liu, Q., & Li, H. (2023, December). The effects of digital addiction on brain function and structure of children and adolescents: A scoping review. [). MDPI.]. *Health Care*, *12*(1), 15. PMID: 38200921

Ding, N., Qin, Y., Yang, G., Wei, F., Yang, Z., Su, Y., Hu, S., Chen, Y., Chan, C.-M., Chen, W., Yi, J., Zhao, W., Wang, X., Liu, Z., Zheng, H.-T., Chen, J., Liu, Y., Tang, J., Li, J., & Sun, M. (2023). Parameter-efficient fine-tuning of large-scale pre-trained language models. *Nature Machine Intelligence*, *5*(3), 220–235. DOI: 10.1038/s42256-023-00626-4

Dinmore, S., & Gao, J. (2016, November). Voice-to-Text Transcription of Lecture Recordings. In *Australian Society for Computers in Learning in Tertiary Education Conference (ASCILITE)*. DOI: 10.14742/apubs.2016.864

Dong, C., Zheng, Q., & Morehouse, J. (2023). What do we know about government public relations (GPR)? A systematic review of GPR in public relations literature. *Public Relations Review*, *49*(1), 102284. DOI: 10.1016/j.pubrev.2022.102284

Dong, G., Lin, X., & Potenza, M. N. (2017). Decreased functional connectivity in an executive control network is related to impulsivity in internet gaming disorder. *Progress in Neuro-Psychopharmacology & Biological Psychiatry*, *79*, 370–378. DOI: 10.1016/j.pnpbp.2017.07.024

Drago, E. (2015). The effect of technology on face-to-face communication. *The Elon Journal of Undergraduate Research in Communications*, *6*(1), 13–19.

Dresp-Langley, B., & Hutt, A. (2022). Digital addiction and sleep. *International Journal of Environmental Research and Public Health*, *19*(11), 6910. Advance online publication. DOI: 10.3390/ijerph19116910 PMID: 35682491

Du, H., Zhang, J., Cheng, J., & Ai, B. (2021). Millimeter wave communications with reconfigurable intelligent surfaces: Performance analysis and optimization. *IEEE Transactions on Communications*, *69*(4), 2752–2768. DOI: 10.1109/TCOMM.2021.3051682

Du, H., Zhang, R., Liu, Y., Wang, J., Lin, Y., Li, Z., Niyato, D., Kang, J., Xiong, Z., Cui, S., Ai, B., Zhou, H., & Kim, D. I. (2024). Enhancing deep reinforcement learning: A tutorial on generative diffusion models in network optimization. *IEEE Communications Surveys and Tutorials*, *26*(4), 2611–2646. DOI: 10.1109/COMST.2024.3400011

Elhai, J. D., Levine, J. C., Dvorak, R. D., & Hall, B. J. (2017). Fear of missing out, need for touch, anxiety and depression are related to problematic smartphone use. *Computers in Human Behavior*, *63*, 509–516. DOI: 10.1016/j.chb.2016.05.079

Elliott, A. (2019). *The culture of AI: Everyday life and the digital revolution.* Routledge. DOI: 10.4324/9781315387185

Eppler, M. J., & Mengis, J. (2004). The concept of information overload: A review of literature from organization science, accounting, marketing, MIS, and related disciplines. *The Information Society*, *20*(5), 325–344. DOI: 10.1080/01972240490507974

Ernst, E., Merola, R., & Samaan, D. (2018). The economics of artificial intelligence. International Labour Organization. https://www.ilo.org/wcmsp5/groups/public/dgreports/cabinet/documents/publication/wcms_647306.pdf

European Commission. (2021). *Proposal for a Regulation Laying Down Harmonised Rules on Artificial Intelligence.* Artificial Intelligence Act.

European Commission. (2022). *The Digital Services Act.* https://digital-strategy.ec.europa.eu/en/policies/digital-services-act-package

Evci, V. Y. (2022). An evaluation on the problem of digital addiction in youth. *Journal of Social Sciences and Education*, *5*(1), 115–134.

Eyal, N. (2014). *Hooked: How to build habit-forming products.* Portfolio.

Eyal, N. (2014). *Hooked: How to Build Habit-Forming Products.* Portfolio/Penguin.

Fardouly, J., Diedrichs, P. C., Vartanian, L. R., & Halliwell, E. (2015). Social comparisons on social media: The impact of Facebook on young women's body image concerns and mood. *Body Image*, *13*, 38–45. DOI: 10.1016/j.bodyim.2014.12.002 PMID: 25615425

Fauziah, J. L., Hanifah, H. F. B., & Sujatmoko, K. (2024). Autogeneration Social Media Content (TikTok, Instagram, Facebook, Twitter) Based on AI & RPA. *[CEPAT] Journal of Computer Engineering: Progress. Application and Technology*, *3*(01), 56–64. DOI: 10.25124/cepat.v3i01.7193

Ferrucci, D., Levas, A., Bagchi, S., Gondek, D., & Mueller, E. (2010). Watson: Beyond jeopardy! *Artificial Intelligence*, *199–200*, 93–105. DOI: 10.1016/j.artint.2012.06.009

Filippini, C., Perpetuini, D., Cardone, D., Chiarelli, A. M., & Merla, A. (2020). Thermal infrared imaging-based affective computing and its application to facilitate human robot interaction: A review. *Applied Sciences (Basel, Switzerland)*, *10*(8), 2924. DOI: 10.3390/app10082924

Firth, J., Torous, J., Stubbs, B., Firth, J. A., Steiner, G. Z., Smith, L., Alvarez-Jimenez, M., Gleeson, J., Vancampfort, D., Armitage, C. J., & Sarris, J. (2019). The "online brain": How the Internet may be changing our cognition. *World Psychiatry; Official Journal of the World Psychiatric Association (WPA), 18*(2), 119–129. DOI: 10.1002/wps.20617 PMID: 31059635

Fisher, M. (2022). The business of keeping us hooked: How tech companies monetize attention. *Journal of Digital Economy, 4*(2), 101–115. DOI: 10.1080/jde.2022.004

Flaxman, S., Goel, S., & Rao, J. M. (2016). Filter bubbles, echo chambers, and online news consumption. *Public Opinion Quarterly, 80*(S1), 298–320. DOI: 10.1093/poq/nfw006

Flayelle, M., Maurage, P., Di Lorenzo, K. R., Vögele, C., Gainsbury, S. M., & Billieux, J. (2020). Binge-watching: What do we know so far? A first systematic review of the evidence. *Current Addiction Reports, 7*(1), 44–60. DOI: 10.1007/s40429-020-00299-8

Flew, T. (2023). Trust, transparency and accountability in AI communication. *Media International Australia, 188*(1), 76–89. DOI: 10.1177/1329878X231163725

Floridi, L., & Cowls, J. (2019). A unified framework of five principles for AI in society. *Harvard Data Science Review, 1*(1). Advance online publication. DOI: 10.1162/99608f92.8cd550d1

Floridi, L., Cowls, J., Beltrametti, M., Chatila, R., Chazerand, P., Dignum, V., Luetge, C., Madelin, R., Pagallo, U., Rossi, F., Schafer, B., Valcke, P., & Vayena, E. (2018). AI4People - An ethical framework for a good AI society. *Minds and Machines, 28*(4), 689–707. DOI: 10.1007/s11023-018-9482-5 PMID: 30930541

Fogg, B. J. (2003). *Persuasive technology: Using computers to change what we think and do*. Morgan Kaufmann. DOI: 10.1016/B978-155860643-2/50011-1

Følstad, A., & Brandtzaeg, P. B. (2017). Chatbots and the new world of HCI. *Interactions (New York, N.Y.), 24*(4), 38–42. DOI: 10.1145/3085558

Formosa, P. (2017). *Kantian ethics, dignity and perfection*. Cambridge University Press. DOI: 10.1017/9781316987308

Frazier, P., & Gaziano, C. (1979). Robert Ezra Park's theory of news, public opinion and social control. *Journalism & Communication Monographs*, •••, 64.

Freedman, G., Hales, A. H., Powell, D. N., Le, B., & Williams, K. D. (2022). The role of gender and safety concerns in romantic rejection decisions. *Journal of Experimental Social Psychology, 102*, 104368. DOI: 10.1016/j.jesp.2022.104368

Fukuchi, Y., Osawa, M., Yamakawa, H., Takahashi, T., & Imai, M. (2022). Conveying intention by motions with awareness of information asymmetry. *Frontiers in Robotics and AI*, *9*, 783863. DOI: 10.3389/frobt.2022.783863 PMID: 35252364

General Data Protection Regulation, Regulation (EU) 2016/679 of the European Parliament and of the Council.

Ghori, M. F., Dehpanah, A., Gemmell, J., & Mobasher, B. (2025, June). *"They Only Offer the Illusion of Choice": Exploring User Perceptions of Control and Agency on YouTube*. In *Adjunct Proceedings of the 33rd ACM Conference on User Modeling, Adaptation and Personalization* (pp. 214–218). DOI: 10.1145/3708319.3733664

Giannandrea, L. (2017). E-portfolio and Teacher Training. Building a Culture of Trust in School Contexts. *PG rossi, L. Giannandrea Eds. tEchnoLoGiEs and trust*, 89.

Gibbs, M. J. (2017). How is new technology changing job design? *IZA World of Labor: Evidence-Based Policy Making*. Advance online publication. DOI: 10.15185/izawol.344

Gillespie, T. (2018). *Custodians of the Internet: Platforms, Content Moderation, and the Hidden Decisions That Shape Social Media*. Yale University Press.

Goel, R., & Singla, J. (2025). Mental Health and Smartphone Addiction: Understanding the Digital Impact on Well-Being. In *Smartphone Addiction, Phone Snubbing, and Effects on Interpersonal Relationships and Mental Health* (pp. 23-62). IGI Global Scientific Publishing.

Goldenthal, A., Glikson, E., & Monahan, K. (2025). The hidden cost of AI-written communication: Effects on perceived authenticity and trust. *Journal of Business Communication*. Advance online publication. DOI: 10.1177/0021943624123456

Goswami, G. (2025). AI Echo Chambers: How Algorithms Shape Reality, Influence Democracy, and Fuel Misinformation. *Authorea Preprints*.DOI: 10.36227/techrxiv.174059950.03385147/v1

Graesser, A. C., Hu, X., & Sottilare, R. A. (2018). In Fischer, F., Hmelo-Silver, C. E., Goldman, S. R., & Reimann, P. (Eds.), *"Intelligent tutoring systems," in International Handbook of the Learning Sciences* (pp. 246–255). Routledge., DOI: 10.4324/9781315617572-24

Griffiths, M. D. (2005). A 'components' model of addiction within a biopsychosocial framework. *Journal of Substance Use*, *10*(4), 191–197. DOI: 10.1080/14659890500114359

Gunning, D., Stefik, M., Choi, J., Miller, T., Stumpf, S., & Yang, G. Z. (2019). XAI—Explainable artificial intelligence. *Science Robotics*, *4*(37), eaay7120. Advance online publication. DOI: 10.1126/scirobotics.aay7120 PMID: 33137719

Haenlein, M., & Kaplan, A. (2019). A brief history of artificial intelligence: On the past, present, and future of artificial intelligence. *California Management Review*, *61*(4), 5–14. DOI: 10.1177/0008125619864925

Hagendorff, T. (2020). The ethics of AI ethics: An evaluation of guidelines. *Minds and Machines*, *30*(1), 99–120. DOI: 10.1007/s11023-020-09517-8

Hamari, J., Koivisto, J., & Sarsa, H. (2014). "Does gamification work? - a literature review of empirical studies on gamification," in *Proceedings of the Annual Hawaii International Conference on System Sciences* (Waikoloa, HI: IEEE). DOI: 10.1109/HICSS.2014.377

Harper, F. M., Frankowski, D., Drenner, S., Ren, Y., Kiesler, S., Terveen, L., & Riedl, J. (2007, January). Talk amongst yourselves: inviting users to participate in online conversations. In *Proceedings of the 12th international conference on Intelligent user interfaces* (pp. 62-71). DOI: 10.1145/1216295.1216313

Harris, T. (2020). *The Social Dilemma* [Documentary]. Netflix.

Hartford, A., & Stein, D. J. (2022). Addiction, autonomy, and the Internet: Some ethical considerations. In *Mental Health in a Digital World* (pp. 481–495). Academic Press., DOI: 10.1016/B978-0-12-822201-0.00003-4

Helberger, N., Sax, M., Strycharz, J., & Micklitz, H. W. (2022). Choice architectures in the digital economy: Towards a new understanding of digital vulnerability. *Journal of Consumer Policy*, *45*(2), 175–200. DOI: 10.1007/s10603-021-09500-5 PMID: 34955574

Helbing, D., Frey, B. S., Gigerenzer, G., Hafen, E., Hagner, M., Hofstetter, Y., & Zwitter, A. (2019). Will democracy survive big data and artificial intelligence? *Scientific American*. Advance online publication. DOI: 10.1038/scientificamerican0217-25

Herz, M., & Rauschnabel, P. A. (2019). Applications of Virtual Reality in Healthcare: From Therapy to Surgical Training. *Journal of Business Research, 127*, 302–312.

Hillmayr, D., Ziernwald, L., Reinhold, F., Hofer, S. I., & Reiss, K. M. (2020). The potential of digital tools to enhance mathematics and science learning in secondary schools: A context-specific meta-analysis. *Computers & Education, 153*, 103897. DOI: 10.1016/j.compedu.2020.103897

Hill, R. L., Ford, W. R., & Farreras, I. G. (2015). Real conversations with artificial intelligence: A comparison between human–human online conversations and human–chatbot conversations. *Computers in Human Behavior, 49*, 245–250. DOI: 10.1016/j.chb.2015.02.026

Hiniker, A., Hong, S., Kohno, T., & Kientz, J. A. (2016, May). MyTime: designing and evaluating an intervention for smartphone non-use. In *Proceedings of the 2016 CHI conference on human factors in computing systems* (pp. 4746-4757). DOI: 10.1145/2858036.2858403

Hiniker, A., Sobel, K., Hong, S. R., Suh, H., Kim, M., & Kientz, J. A. (2016). Texting while parenting: How adults use mobile phones while caring for children at the playground. *Proceedings of the 2015 ACM International Joint Conference on Pervasive and Ubiquitous Computing*, 727–738. DOI: 10.1145/2750858.2804288

Horwitz, J., & Seetharaman, D. (2021). Facebook knows Instagram is toxic for teen girls, company documents show. *The Wall Street Journal*. https://www.wsj.com

Hou, L., Wang, X., Bernold, L., & Love, P. E. (2013). Using animated augmented reality to cognitively guide assembly. *Journal of Computing in Civil Engineering, 27*(5), 439–451. DOI: 10.1061/(ASCE)CP.1943-5487.0000184

Hoy, M. B. (2018). Alexa, Siri, Cortana, and more: An introduction to voice assistants. *Medical Reference Services Quarterly, 37*(1), 81–88. DOI: 10.1080/02763869.2018.1404391 PMID: 29327988

Hutchinson, T., & Duncan, N. (2012). Defining and describing what we do: doctrinal legal research. *Deakin law review, 17*(1), 83-119.

Huy, P. Q., Shavkatovich, S. N., Abdul-Samad, Z., Agrawal, D. K., Ashifa, K. M., & Arumugam, M. (2023). Resource management projects in entrepreneurship and retain customer based on big data analysis and artificial intelligence. *The Journal of High Technology Management Research, 34*(2), 100471. DOI: 10.1016/j.hitech.2023.100471

Ienca, M., & Andorno, R. (2017). Towards new human rights in the age of neuroscience and neurotechnology. *Life Sciences, Society and Policy, 13*(1), 1–27. DOI: 10.1186/s40504-017-0050-1 PMID: 28444626

Ilyas, Q. (2024). AI IN BEAUTY CONTENT: a theoretical study of ethical and psychological considerations surrounding ai-generated beauty content. https://urn.fi/URN:NBN:fi:amk-2024120432706

Information Commissioner's Office. (2020). *Age-appropriate design: A code of practice for online services*. https://ico.org.uk

Information Technology (Intermediary Guidelines and Digital Media Ethics Code) Rules. 2021 (India).

Information Technology Act, 2000 (India).

Institute for Strategic Dialogue (ISD). (2020). *TikTok and the promotion of self-harm content*. https://www.isdglobal.org

Iqbal, S. T., & Horvitz, E. (2007). "Disruption and recovery of computing tasks: field study, analysis, and directions," in Proceedings of the SIGCHI Conference on Human Factors in Computing Systems (New YorK, NY: acm), 677–686. DOI: 10.1145/1240624.1240730

Jafarkarimi, H., Sim, A., Saadatdoost, R., & Hee, Z. (2016). Ethical Considerations in AI-Based Social Bots for Healthcare. *Computers in Human Behavior*, *66*, 105–113.

Jagatheesaperumal, S. K., Pham, Q. V., Ruby, R., Yang, Z., Xu, C., & Zhang, Z. (2022). Explainable AI over the Internet of Things (IoT): Overview, state-of-the-art and future directions. *IEEE Open Journal of the Communications Society*, *3*, 2106–2136. DOI: 10.1109/OJCOMS.2022.3215676

Jana, O., & Ghosh, S. (2024). *AI-driven communication and digital addiction: A psychological and social inquiry*. Brainware University.

Jarrahi, M. H. (2018). Artificial intelligence and the future of work: Human-AI symbiosis in organizational decision making. *Business Horizons*, *61*(4), 577–586. DOI: 10.1016/j.bushor.2018.03.007

Jobin, A., Ienca, M., & Vayena, E. (2019). The global landscape of AI ethics guidelines. *Nature Machine Intelligence*, *1*(9), 389–399. DOI: 10.1038/s42256-019-0088-2

Johnson-George, C., & Swap, W. C. (1982). Measurement of specific interpersonal trust: Construction and validation of a scale to assess trust in a specific other. *Journal of Personality and Social Psychology*, *43*(6), 1306–1317. https://psycnet.apa.org/doi/10.1037/0022-3514.43.6.1306. DOI: 10.1037/0022-3514.43.6.1306

Jones, D., Ghasemi, S., Gračanin, D., & Azab, M. (2023, July). Privacy, safety, and security in extended reality: user experience challenges for neurodiverse users. In *International conference on human-computer interaction* (pp. 511-528). Cham: Springer Nature Switzerland.DOI: 10.1007/978-3-031-35822-7_33

Jones, M. L., Kaufman, E., & Edenberg, E. (2018). AI and the ethics of automating consent. *IEEE Security and Privacy*, *16*(3), 64–72. DOI: 10.1109/MSP.2018.2701155

Joseph, N. P. S., Mahmood, A. K., Yin, C. P., Wan, W. S., Yuen, P. K., & Heng, L. E. (2015). Barebone cloud IaaS: Revitalisation disruptive technology. *International Journal of Business Information Systems, 18*(1), 107–126. DOI: 10.1504/IJBIS.2015.066130

Joshi, H. (2024). *Artificial intelligence in project management: A study of the role of ai-powered chatbots in project stakeholder engagement. Indian Journal of Software Engineering and Project Management.* IJSEPM., DOI: 10.54105/ijsepm.B9022.04010124

Junco, R. (2012). Too much face and not enough books: The relationship between multiple indices of Facebook use and academic performance. *Computers in Human Behavior, 28*(1), 187–198. DOI: 10.1016/j.chb.2011.08.026

Junco, R., & Cotten, S. R. (2012). No A 4 U: The relationship between multitasking and academic performance. *Computers & Education, 59*(2), 505–514. DOI: 10.1016/j.compedu.2011.12.023

Jung, H. (2025). AI-Based UX Design Research for Mitigating Psychological Barriers in Early Autonomous Vehicle Users. *International Journal of Advanced Culture Technology, 13*(1), 322–329. DOI: 10.17703/IJACT.2025.13.1.322

Justice K.S. Puttaswamy v. Union of India, (2017) 10 SCC 1.

Kabat-Zinn, J. (2003). Mindfulness-based interventions in context: Past, present, and future. *Clinical Psychology : a Publication of the Division of Clinical Psychology of the American Psychological Association, 10*(2), 144–156. DOI: 10.1093/clipsy.bpg016

Kaleel, A., & Alomari, M. S. (2024). Integrating Artificial Intelligence in Public Relations and Media: A Bibliometric Analysis of Emerging Trends and Influences. *Iraqi Journal for Computer Science and Mathematics, 5*(1). Advance online publication. DOI: 10.52866/ijcsm.2024.05.01.002

Kamenskaya, V. G., & Tomanov, L. V. (2022). Digital technologies and their impact on the social and psychological characteristics of adolescents. *Experimental Psychology (Russia), 15*(1), 139–159. DOI: 10.17759/exppsy.2022150109

Kanai, R., Bahrami, B., Roylance, R., & Rees, G. (2012). Online social network size is reflected in human brain structure. *Proceedings. Biological Sciences, 279*(1732), 1327–1334. DOI: 10.1098/rspb.2011.1959 PMID: 22012980

Kang, J., Du, H., Li, Z., Xiong, Z., Ma, S., Niyato, D., & Li, Y. (2022). Personalized saliency in task-oriented semantic communications: Image transmission and performance analysis. *IEEE Journal on Selected Areas in Communications*, *41*(1), 186–201. DOI: 10.1109/JSAC.2022.3221990

Kang, J., Yu, R., Huang, X., Maharjan, S., Zhang, Y., & Hossain, E. (2017). Enabling localized peer-to-peer electricity trading among plug-in hybrid electric vehicles using consortium blockchains. *IEEE Transactions on Industrial Informatics*, *13*(6), 3154–3164. DOI: 10.1109/TII.2017.2709784

Kant, T. (2020). *Making it personal: Algorithmic personalization, identity, and everyday life*. Oxford University Press. DOI: 10.1093/oso/9780190905088.001.0001

Karapanos, E., Teixeira, P., & Gouveia, R. (2016). Need fulfillment and experiences on social media: A case on Facebook and WhatsApp. *Computers in Human Behavior*, *55*, 888–897. DOI: 10.1016/j.chb.2015.10.015

Kardefelt-Winther, D. (2014). A conceptual and methodological critique of internet addiction research: Towards a model of compensatory internet use. *Computers in Human Behavior*, *31*, 351–354. DOI: 10.1016/j.chb.2013.10.059

Karnouskos, S. (2020). Artificial intelligence in digital media: The era of deepfakes. *IEEE Transactions on Technology and Society*, *1*(3), 138–147. DOI: 10.1109/TTS.2020.3001312

Kashdan, T. B., Rose, P., & Fincham, F. D. (2004). Curiosity and exploration: Facilitating positive subjective experiences and personal growth opportunities. *Journal of Personality Assessment*, *82*(3), 291–305. DOI: 10.1207/s15327752jpa8203_05 PMID: 15151805

Kellogg, K. C., Valentine, M. A., & Christin, A. (2020). Algorithms at work: The new contested terrain of control. *The Academy of Management Annals*, *14*(1), 366–410. DOI: 10.5465/annals.2018.0174

Kim, K., Yoon, Y., & Shin, S. (2024). Explainable prediction of problematic smartphone use among South Korea's children and adolescents using a machine learning approach. *International Journal of Medical Informatics*, *186*, 105441. Advance online publication. DOI: 10.1016/j.ijmedinf.2024.105441 PMID: 38564961

Kim, M. J., Wang, X., Love, P. E., Li, H., & Kang, S. C. (2013). Virtual reality for the built environment: A critical review of recent advances. [ITcon]. *Journal of Information Technology in Construction*, *18*(14), 279–305. https://www.itcon.org/2013/14

Kim, Y. H., Jeon, J. H., Choe, E. K., Lee, B., Kim, K., & Seo, J. (2016, May). TimeAware: Leveraging framing effects to enhance personal productivity. *In Proceedings of the 2016 CHI Conference on Human Factors in Computing Systems* (pp. 272-283). DOI: 10.1145/2858036.2858428

King, M. R., & Chat, G. P. T. (2023). A conversation on artificial intelligence, chatbots, and plagiarism in higher education. *Cellular and Molecular Bioengineering*, *16*(1), 1–2. DOI: 10.1007/s12195-022-00754-8 PMID: 36660590

Ko, M., Yang, S., Lee, J., Heizmann, C., Jeong, J., Lee, U., . . . Chung, K. M. (2015, February). NUGU: a group-based intervention app for improving self-regulation of limiting smartphone use. *In Proceedings of the 18th ACM conference on computer supported cooperative work & social computing* (pp. 1235-1245). DOI: 10.1145/2675133.2675244

Koh, M. (2024). Organizational Communication in the Digital Era: Examining the Impact of AI, Chatbots, and Covid-19. In Ndlela, M. N. (Ed.), *New Perspectives in Organizational Communication. Organizational Communication in the Digital Era: Examining the Impact of AI, Chatbots, and Covid-19 | SpringerLink.*, DOI: 10.1007/978-3-031-58307-0

Koos, S., & Wachsmann, S. (2023). Navigating the Impact of ChatGPT/GPT4 on Legal Academic Examinations: Challenges, Opportunities and Recommendations. *Media Iuris*, *6*(2), 255–270. Advance online publication. DOI: 10.20473/mi.v6i2.45270

Koronczai, B., Kökönyei, G., Urbán, R., Kun, B., Pápay, O., Nagygyörgy, K., Griffiths, M. D., & Demetrovics, Z. (2013). The mediating effect of self-esteem, depression and anxiety between satisfaction with body appearance and problematic internet use. *The American Journal of Drug and Alcohol Abuse*, *39*(4), 259–265. DOI: 10.3109/00952990.2013.803111 PMID: 23841866

Kretzschmar, K., Tyroll, H., Pavarini, G., Manzini, A., & Singh, I. (2019). Can your phone be your therapist? Young people's ethical perspectives on the use of fully automated conversational agents (chatbots) in mental health support. *Biomedical Informatics Insights*, *11*, 1178222619829083. DOI: 10.1177/1178222619829083 PMID: 30858710

Kumara, V., Sharma, D. M., Isaac, J. S., Saravanan, S., Suganthi, D., & Boopathi, S. (2024). An AI-integrated green power monitoring system: empowering small and medium enterprises. In *Convergence Strategies for Green Computing and Sustainable Development* (pp. 218–244). IGI Global Scientific Publishing., DOI: 10.4018/979-8-3693-0338-2.ch013

Kuss, D. J., & Griffiths, M. D. (2017). Social networking sites and addiction: Ten lessons learned. *International Journal of Environmental Research and Public Health*, *14*(3), 311. DOI: 10.3390/ijerph14030311 PMID: 28304359

Kuss, D. J., & Pontes, H. M. (2018). *Internet addiction*. Hogrefe Publishing GmbH. DOI: 10.1027/00501-000

Kwon, M., Biyik, E., Talati, A., Bhasin, K., Losey, D. P., & Sadigh, D. (2020, March). When humans aren't optimal: Robots that collaborate with risk-aware humans. In *Proceedings of the 2020 ACM/IEEE international conference on human-robot interaction* (pp. 43-52). DOI: 10.1145/3319502.3374832

Labadze, L., Grigolia, M., & Machaidze, L. (2023). Role of AI chatbots in education: Systematic literature review. *International Journal of Educational Technology in Higher Education*, *20*(1), 56. DOI: 10.1186/s41239-023-00426-1

Laestadius, L., Bishop, R., Gonzalez, E., Illenčík, M., & Campos-Castillo, C. (2024). Emotional attachment and withdrawal: Replika chatbot users' experiences. *Social Media + Society*, *10*(1), 1–12. DOI: 10.1177/2056305124122901

Lam, H., & Harcourt, M. (2024). Digital addiction in organizations: Challenges and policy implications. *Employee Responsibilities and Rights Journal*, *36*(4), 519–533. DOI: 10.1007/s10672-024-09493-6

Langlois, R. N. (2003). Cognitive comparative advantage and the organization of work: Lessons from Herbert Simon's vision of the future. *Journal of Economic Psychology*, *24*(2), 167–187. DOI: 10.1016/S0167-4870(02)00201-5

Lauricella, A. R., Wartella, E., & Rideout, V. J. (2015). Young children's screen time: The complex role of parent and child factors. *Journal of Applied Developmental Psychology*, *36*, 11–17. DOI: 10.1016/j.appdev.2014.12.001

Lee, H., Ahn, H., Choi, S., & Choi, W. (2014). The SAMS: Smartphone addiction management system and verification. *Journal of Medical Systems*, *38*(1), 1. DOI: 10.1007/s10916-013-0001-1 PMID: 24395031

Lenzerini, M., & Penaloza, R. (2016). CEUR workshop proceedings: preface. In *CEUR Workshop Proceedings* (pp. v-vi). CEUR-WS.

Leppänen, L., Munezero, M., Granroth-Wilding, M., & Toivonen, H. (2017, September). Data-driven news generation for automated journalism. In *Proceedings of the 10th international conference on natural language generation* (pp. 188-197). DOI: 10.18653/v1/W17-3528

Levenson, J. C., Shensa, A., Sidani, J. E., Colditz, J. B., & Primack, B. A. (2017). Social media use before bed and sleep disturbance among young adults in the United States: A nationally representative study. *Sleep (Basel), 40*(9), zsx113. Advance online publication. DOI: 10.1093/sleep/zsx113 PMID: 28934521

Liang, Y., Wang, X., & He, D. (2021). Enhancing chatbot social presence through emotional self-disclosure. *ACM Transactions on Information Systems, 39*(4), 1–27. DOI: 10.1145/3742424

Li, J., & Zhang, X. (2024). Understanding emotional needs and mental health from Replika chatbot use: A computational linguistics approach. *Computers in Human Behavior, 152*, 107177. DOI: 10.1016/j.chb.2023.107177

Lin, Y., Gao, Z., Du, H., Ren, J., Xie, Z., & Niyato, D. (2024). Blockchain-enabled trustworthy federated unlearning. *arXiv preprint arXiv:2401.15917.*

Linden, C. G. (2017). Decades of Automation in the Newsroom: Why are there still so many jobs in journalism? *Digital Journalism (Abingdon, England), 5*(2), 123–140. DOI: 10.1080/21670811.2016.1160791

Lin, L. Y., Sidani, J. E., Shensa, A., Radovic, A., Miller, E., Colditz, J. B., Hoffman, B. L., Giles, L. M., & Primack, B. A. (2016). Association between social media use and depression among US young adults. *Depression and Anxiety, 33*(4), 323–331. DOI: 10.1002/da.22466 PMID: 26783723

Lippi-Green, R. (1994). Accent, standard language ideology, and discriminatory pretext in the courts. *Language in Society, 23*(2), 163–198. DOI: 10.1017/S0047404500017826

Lips-Wiersma, M., & Wright, S. (2012). Measuring the meaning of meaningful work: Development and validation of the comprehensive meaningful work scale. *Group & Organization Management, 37*(5), 655–685. DOI: 10.1177/1059601112461578

Lissak, G. (2018). Adverse physiological and psychological effects of screen time on children and adolescents: Literature review and case study. *Environmental Research, 164*, 149–157. DOI: 10.1016/j.envres.2018.01.015 PMID: 29499467

Li an, D. E. (2025). Online captive: The impact of social media addiction on depression and anxiety—An SEM approach to the mediating role of self-esteem and the moderating effects of age and professional status. *Behavioral Sciences (Basel, Switzerland), 15*(4), 481. Advance online publication. DOI: 10.3390/bs15040481 PMID: 40282102

Livingstone, S. (2004). Media literacy and the challenge of new information and communication technologies. *Communication Review*, *7*(1), 3–14. DOI: 10.1080/10714420490280152

Livingstone, S.. (2017). Children's online risks: Comparative evidence from EU Kids Online and Net Children Go Mobile. *Journal of Cybersecurity*, *3*(2), 1–13. DOI: 10.1093/cybsec/tyw002

Livingstone, S., & Helsper, E. J. (2007). Gradations in digital inclusion: Children, young people and the digital divide. *New Media & Society*, *9*(4), 671–696. DOI: 10.1177/1461444807080335

Livingstone, S., & Stoilova, M. (2020). The 4Cs: Classifying online risks to children. *Communication Research*, *47*(4), 469–485. DOI: 10.1177/0093650218810594

Li, Y., Chen, J., Zhao, M., & Wang, K. (2023). Challenges in Personalized Healthcare with AI: Infrastructure, Privacy, and Trust. *Journal of Biomedical Informatics*, *141*, 104445.

Li, Y., Liu, J., & Ren, J. (2019). Social recommendation model based on user interaction in complex social networks. *PLoS One*, *14*(7), e0218957. DOI: 10.1371/journal.pone.0218957 PMID: 31291288

Li, Z., Mao, R., & Kim, H. (2023). Social anxiety and chatbot use: A mediation model of loneliness and rumination. *Computers in Human Behavior*, *140*, 107577. DOI: 10.1016/j.chb.2022.107577

Loh, K. K., & Kanai, R. (2016). How has the internet reshaped human cognition? *The Neuroscientist*, *22*(5), 506–520. DOI: 10.1177/1073858415595005 PMID: 26170005

Long, D., & Magerko, B. (2020). What is AI literacy? Competencies and design considerations. *Proceedings of the 2020 CHI Conference on Human Factors in Computing Systems,* 1–16. DOI: 10.1145/3313831.3376727

Lo, S. Y., Short, E. S., & Thomaz, A. L. (2020, March). Planning with partner uncertainty modeling for efficient information revealing in teamwork. In *Proceedings of the 2020 ACM/IEEE International Conference on Human-Robot Interaction* (pp. 319-327). DOI: 10.1145/3319502.3374827

Luttrell, R., & Welch, C. (2024). AI-Powered Synthetic Personas: Affecting the Future of Public Relations Campaigns. In *Public Relations and the Rise of AI* (pp. 97-117). Routledge.

Machete, P., & Turpin, M. (2020). "The use of critical thinking to identify fake news: A systematic literature review," in Responsible Design. *Lecture Notes in Computer Science, 12067*, 235–246. DOI: 10.1007/978-3-030-45002-1_20

Macit, H. B., Macit, G., & Güngör, O. (2018). A research on social media addiction and dopamine driven feedback. *Journal of Mehmet Akif Ersoy University Economics and Administrative Sciences Faculty, 5*(3), 882–897. DOI: 10.30798/makuiibf.435845

Madary, M. (2022). The illusion of agency in human–computer interaction. *Neuroethics, 15*(1), 16. DOI: 10.1007/s12152-022-09491-1

Maheswaran, K., Selvakumar, P., Shaikh, M., Shashank, G., Gupta, S., & Manjunath, T. C. (2025). The Evolution of Smart Urban Mobility With Emerging Technologies. In Ponnusamy, S., Assaf, M., Youssef, B., Jeon, G., & Kalyanaraman, S. (Eds.), *Leveraging VANETs and Blockchain Technology for Urban Mobility* (pp. 1–28). IGI Global Scientific Publishing., DOI: 10.4018/979-8-3373-0265-2.ch001

Marengo, D., Montag, C., Sindermann, C., & Elhai, J. D. (2022). Digital media use and psychological well-being: Insights from Instagram. *Computers in Human Behavior Reports, 7*, 100204. DOI: 10.1016/j.chbr.2022.100204

Mark, G., Czerwinski, M., & Iqbal, S. T. (2016). Effects of individual differences in blocking workplace distractions. *Proceedings of the 2016 CHI Conference on Human Factors in Computing Systems,* 6069–6080. DOI: 10.1145/2858036.2858212

Mark, G., Gudith, D., & Klocke, U. (2015). The cost of interrupted work: More speed and stress. *Proceedings of the SIGCHI Conference on Human Factors in Computing Systems,* 107–110. DOI: 10.1145/985692.985715

Markoci, D. (2024). *ANALIZA TURISTIČKE PONUDE NACIONALNOG PARKA PLITVIČKA JEZERA* (Doctoral dissertation, Libertas međunarodno sveučilište).

Marković, S., Popović, G., & Andjelković, L. (2024). Mastering the attention economy: Strategies for competing on digital platforms. *Fusion of Multidisciplinary Research. International Journal (Toronto, Ont.), 5*(1), 568–578.

Marwick, A. E. (2013). *Status Update: Celebrity, Publicity, and Branding in the Social Media Age*. Yale University Press.

Mathur, A., Acar, G., Friedman, M. G., Lucherini, E., Mayer, J., Chetty, M., & Narayanan, A. (2019). Dark patterns at scale: Findings from a crawl of 11K shopping websites. *Proceedings of the ACM on Human-Computer Interaction, 3(CSCW),* 81. DOI: 10.1145/3359183

Mathur, S., Ninan, J., Vuorinen, L., Ke, Y., & Sankaran, S. (2021). An exploratory study of the use of social media to assess benefits realization in transport infrastructure projects. *Project Leadership and Society*, *2*, 100010. DOI: 10.1016/j.plas.2021.100010

Matsakis, L. (2021). Facebook's algorithm: A major threat to society. *MIT Technology Review*. https://www.technologyreview.com

Matthews, A. (2024). Sculpting the social algorithm for radical futurity. *AI & Society*, *39*(1), 75–86. DOI: 10.1007/s00146-023-01760-8

McDaniel, B. T., & Radesky, J. S. (2018). Technoference: Parent distraction with technology and associations with child behavior problems. *Child Development*, *89*(1), 100–109. DOI: 10.1111/cdev.12822 PMID: 28493400

McStay, A. (2018). Emotional AI: The Rise of Empathic Media. *Sage (Atlanta, Ga.)*. Advance online publication. DOI: 10.4135/9781526451293

Mehta, P. B. (2021). Platform governance in India: Lessons from the IT Rules, 2021. *Economic and Political Weekly*, *56*(23), 10–13.

Mei, X., & Ling, H. (2009, September). Robust visual tracking using $\ell$ 1 minimization. In *2009 IEEE 12th international conference on computer vision* (pp. 1436-1443). IEEE.

Mental Healthcare Act, 2017 (India).

Michaud, M., & Colpitts, B. D. (2015). English as a lingua franca: Globalization, ownership, and the diversification of English. *Kwansei Gakuin University Humanities Review*, *20*, 125–131.

Michikyan, M., Subrahmanyam, K., & Dennis, J. (2014). Can you tell who I am? Neuroticism, extraversion, and online self-presentation among young adults. *Computers in Human Behavior*, *33*, 179–183. DOI: 10.1016/j.chb.2014.01.010

Moller, K., Nyberg, T., Tumova, J., & Betz, J. (2025). Pedestrian-Aware Motion Planning for Autonomous Driving in Complex Urban Scenarios. *arXiv preprint arXiv:2504.01409.*

Møller, J., Romero, D. M., Jurgens, D., & Aiello, L. M. (2025). Generative AI and the perception of authenticity in social media conversations. *Nature Human Behaviour*, *9*, 451–460. DOI: 10.1038/s41562-024-01722-4

Molteni, L. (2022). *Impact of nudges on digital well-being for the smartphone* (Doctoral dissertation, Politecnico di Torino).

Montag, C., & Diefenbach, S. (2018). Towards homo digitalis: Important research issues for psychology and the neurosciences at the dawn of the internet of things and the digital society. *Sustainability (Basel)*, *10*(2), 415. DOI: 10.3390/su10020415

Montag, C., Wegmann, E., Sariyska, R., Demetrovics, Z., & Brand, M. (2019). How to overcome taxonomical problems in the study of internet use disorders and what to do with "smartphone addiction"? *Journal of Behavioral Addictions*, *9*(4), 908–914. DOI: 10.1556/2006.8.2019.59 PMID: 31668089

Montag, C., Yang, H., & Elhai, J. D. (2021). On the psychology of TikTok use: A first glimpse from empirical findings. *Frontiers in Public Health*, *9*, 641673. DOI: 10.3389/fpubh.2021.641673 PMID: 33816425

Morales-García, W. C., Sairitupa-Sanchez, L. Z., Morales-García, S. B., & Morales-García, M. (2024, March). Development and validation of a scale for dependence on artificial intelligence in university students. *In Frontiers in Education (Vol. 9, p. 1323898)*. Frontiers Media SA. DOI: 10.3389/feduc.2024.1323898

Murillo-Munoz, M. F., Vazquez-Briseno, M., Cota, C. X. N., & Nieto-Hipólito, J. I. (2018, February). A framework for design and development of persuasive mobile systems. In *2018 International Conference on Electronics, Communications and Computers (CONIELECOMP)* (pp. 59-66). IEEE.DOI: 10.1109/CONIELECOMP.2018.8327176

Mystakidis, S. (2022). Metaverse. *Encyclopedia*, *2*(1), 486–497. DOI: 10.3390/encyclopedia2010031

Nadeem, M. (2025). From Algorithms to Authenticity: Ensuring Ethical Customer Engagement in the Age of Artificial Intelligence. *International Journal of Business and Management*, *20*(2), 13. https://ccsenet.org/journal/index.php/ijbm/issue/view/0/3194. DOI: 10.5539/ijbm.v20n2p13

Nass, C., & Moon, Y. (2000). Machines and mindlessness: Social responses to computers. *The Journal of Social Issues*, *56*(1), 81–103. DOI: 10.1111/0022-4537.00153

Naveed, H. (2022). CHATBOTS AND VIRTUAL ASSISTANTS: THE FUTURE OF CUSTOMER SERVICE. *Computer Science Bulletin*, *5*(01), 15–36.

Nesi, J. (2020). The impact of social media on youth mental health: Challenges and opportunities. *Current Opinion in Psychology*, *36*, 115–120. DOI: 10.1016/j.copsyc.2020.05.005 PMID: 32132255

Nguyen, M. H., Hunsaker, A., & Hargittai, E. (2022). Older adults' online social engagement and social capital: The moderating role of Internet skills. *Information Communication and Society*, *25*(7), 942–958. DOI: 10.1080/1369118X.2020.1804980

Ng, W. (2012). Can we teach digital natives digital literacy? *Computers & Education*, *59*(3), 1065–1078. DOI: 10.1016/j.compedu.2012.04.016

Nikkelen, S. W., Valkenburg, P. M., Huizinga, M., & Bushman, B. J. (2014). Media use and ADHD-related behaviors in children and adolescents: A meta-analysis. *Developmental Psychology*, *50*(9), 2228–2241. DOI: 10.1037/a0037318 PMID: 24999762

Nikken, P., & Schols, M. (2015). How and why parents guide the media use of young children. *Journal of Child and Family Studies*, *24*(11), 3423–3435. DOI: 10.1007/s10826-015-0144-4 PMID: 26472932

Nisha Angeline, M., Selvakumar, P., Gupta, M. K., Nazar, N., Elumalai, D., & Bhattacharya, S. (2025). Emerging Materials for Energy Storage and Environmental Applications. In K. Muduli, B. Moharana, S. Ales, & D. Biswal (Eds.), Using Computational Intelligence for Sustainable Manufacturing of Advanced Materials (pp. 53–72). IGI Global Scientific Publishing. DOI: 10.4018/979-8-3693-7974-5.ch003

Niyato, D., & Hossain, E. (2008). Competitive pricing for spectrum sharing in cognitive radio networks: Dynamic game, inefficiency of nash equilibrium, and collusion. *IEEE Journal on Selected Areas in Communications*, *26*(1), 192–202. DOI: 10.1109/JSAC.2008.080117

Noble, S. U. (2018). *Algorithms of Oppression: How Search Engines Reinforce Racism*. New York University Press. DOI: 10.18574/nyu/9781479833641.001.0001

O'Neil, C. (2016). *Weapons of Math Destruction: How Big Data Increases Inequality and Threatens Democracy*. Crown Publishing.

Oberst, U., Wegmann, E., Stodt, B., Brand, M., & Chamarro, A. (2017). Negative consequences from heavy social networking in adolescents: The mediating role of fear of missing out. *Journal of Adolescence*, *55*(1), 51–60. DOI: 10.1016/j.adolescence.2016.12.008 PMID: 28033503

Odgers, C. L., Jensen, M. R., & Choukas-Bradley, S. (2019). Annual research review: adolescent mental health in the digital age: facts, fears, and future directions. *Journal of Child Psychology and Psychiatry, and Allied Disciplines*, *60*, 254–273. DOI: 10.1111/jcpp.13190 PMID: 31951670

Ojo, S. O., & Afolaranmi, A. O. (2024). The Effects of Artificial Intelligence (AI) on Human Interpersonal Connections. *Lead City Journal of Religions and Intercultural Communication*, *2*(2), 162–174.

Okeke, F., Sobolev, M., Dell, N., & Estrin, D. (2018, September). Good vibrations: can a digital nudge reduce digital overload? In *Proceedings of the 20th international conference on human-computer interaction with mobile devices and services* (pp. 1-12). DOI: 10.1145/3229434.3229463

Oladele, S. (2025). Exploring User Consent Mechanisms in Data-Driven Personalization. https://www.researchgate.net/publication/388508656_Exploring_User_Consent_Mechanisms_in_Data-Driven_Personalization

Olanipekun, S. O.Samson Olufemi Olanipekun. (2025). Computational propaganda and misinformation: AI technologies as tools of media manipulation. *World Journal of Advanced Research and Reviews, 25*(1), 911–923. DOI: 10.30574/wjarr.2025.25.1.0131

Omori, M., Hasegawa, S., Watanabe, T., Fujikake, K., & Miyao, M. (2009). LNCS Computer Science, Springer Virtual and Mixed Reality Lecture Notes in Computer Science, 2009, Volume 5622/2009, 90-96, DOI: . *Lecture Notes in Computer Science, 5622*(2009), 90-96.DOI: 10.1007/978-3-642-02771-0_10

Orben, A., & Przybylski, A. K. (2019). The association between adolescent well-being and digital technology use. *Nature Human Behaviour, 3*(2), 173–182. DOI: 10.1038/s41562-018-0506-1 PMID: 30944443

Panova, T., & Lleras, A. (2016). Avoidance or boredom: Negative mental health outcomes associated with use of mobile phones and social networking sites. *Computers in Human Behavior, 58*, 249–258. DOI: 10.1016/j.chb.2015.12.062

Pardeshi, S., Ovhal, S., Shinde, P., Bansode, M., & Birajdar, A. (2020). A survey on Different Algorithms used in Chatbot. [IRJET]. *International Research Journal of Engineering and Technology, 7*(5), 6092–6098.

Pariser, E. (2011). *The filter bubble: How the new personalized web is changing what we read and how we think*. Penguin.

Park, R. E., Turner, R. H., & Janowitz, M. (1967). *On social control and collective behavior: Selected papers*. No Title.

Parveiz, S., Amjad, A., & Ayub, S. (2023). Fear of missing out (FOMO), social comparison and social media addiction among young adults. [PJAP]. *Pakistan Journal of Applied Psychology, 3*(1), 224–235. DOI: 10.52461/pjap.v3i1.1283

Pasquale, F. (2015). *The Black Box Society: The Secret Algorithms That Control Money and Information*. Harvard University Press. DOI: 10.4159/harvard.9780674736061

Pataranutaporn, P., Liu, R., Finn, E., & Maes, P. (2023). Influencing human–AI interaction by priming beliefs about AI can increase perceived trustworthiness, empathy and effectiveness. *Nature Machine Intelligence*, *5*(10), 1076–1086. DOI: 10.1038/s42256-023-00720-7

Patel, R. K., & Jain, M. (2012). NGS QC Toolkit: A toolkit for quality control of next generation sequencing data. *PLoS One*, *7*(2), e30619. DOI: 10.1371/journal.pone.0030619 PMID: 22312429

Paulus, M. P., Squeglia, L. M., Bagot, K., Jacobus, J., Kuplicki, R., Breslin, F. J., Bodurka, J., Morris, A. S., Thompson, W. K., Bartsch, H., & Tapert, S. F. (2019). Screen media activity and brain structure in youth: Evidence for diverse structural correlation networks from the ABCD study. *NeuroImage*, *185*, 140–153. DOI: 10.1016/j.neuroimage.2018.10.040 PMID: 30339913

Perloff, R. M. (2014). Social media effects on young women's body image concerns: Theoretical perspectives and an agenda for research. *Sex Roles*, *71*(11-12), 363–377. DOI: 10.1007/s11199-014-0384-6

Petronio, S. (2002). *Boundaries of privacy: Dialectics of disclosure*. Suny Press. DOI: 10.1353/book4588

Poláková, P., & Klímová, B. (2019). Mobile technology and Generation Z in the English language classroom—A preliminary study. *Education Sciences*, *9*(3), 203. DOI: 10.3390/educsci9030203

Powers, A., & Kiesler, S. (2006). The advisor robot: Tracing people's mental model from a robot's physical attributes. *Proceedings of the 1st ACM SIGCHI/SIGART Conference on Human-Robot Interaction*, 218–225. DOI: 10.1145/1121241.1121280

Pratt, M. G., & Ashforth, B. E. (2003). Fostering meaningfulness in working and at work. In Cameron, K., Dutton, J. E., & Quinn, R. E. (Eds.), *Positive organizational scholarship: Foundations of a new discipline* (pp. 308–327). Berrett-Koehler.

Premack, D., & Woodruff, G. (1978). Does the chimpanzee have a theory of mind? *Behavioral and Brain Sciences*, *1*(4), 515–526. DOI: 10.1017/S0140525X00076512

Przybylski, A. K., Murayama, K., DeHaan, C. R., & Gladwell, V. (2013). Motivational, emotional, and behavioral correlates of fear of missing out. *Computers in Human Behavior*, *29*(4), 1841–1848. DOI: 10.1016/j.chb.2013.02.014

Purcell, A., Dong, H., Nussberger, A. M., Köbis, N. C., & Jakesch, M. (2023). People judge others more than themselves for using AI in communication. *Scientific Reports*, *13*, 9640. DOI: 10.1038/s41598-023-35955-3

Qi, J. (2024, January). The Impact of Large Language Models on Social Media Communication. In *Proceedings of the 2024 7th International Conference on Software Engineering and Information Management* (pp. 165-170). DOI: 10.1145/3647722.3647749

Radesky, J. S., Schumacher, J., & Zuckerman, B. (2014). Mobile and interactive media use by young children: The good, the bad, and the unknown. *Pediatrics, 135*(1), 1–3. DOI: 10.1542/peds.2014-2251 PMID: 25548323

Radesky, J. S., Weeks, H. M., Ball, R., Schaller, A., Yeo, S., Durnez, J., Tamayo-Rios, M., Epstein, M., Kirkorian, H., Coyne, S., & Barr, R. (2020). Young children's use of smartphones and tablets. *Pediatrics, 146*(1), e20193518. DOI: 10.1542/peds.2019-3518 PMID: 32482771

Raisch, S., & Krakowski, S. (2021). Artificial intelligence and management: The automation–augmentation paradox. *Academy of Management Review, 46*(1), 192–210. DOI: 10.5465/amr.2018.0072

Rakhimovna, A. S. (2025). Cultural and Linguistic Gaps in Contemporary Media Communication. *Spanish Journal of Innovation and Integrity, 38*, 193–197.

Ramkumar, G., Sujatha, V., & Raja, B., TamilSelvi, M., Balaji, A., & Kumar, A. K. (2023, November). An Experiment to Develop an Enhanced Medical Image Security by using Deep Learning Assisted Crypto Policy. In *2023 International Conference on Research Methodologies in Knowledge Management, Artificial Intelligence and Telecommunication Engineering (RMKMATE)* (pp. 1-8). IEEE.

Ravenscraft, E. (25 November, 2021). What is the metaverse, exactly? Wired. Retrieved from: https://www.wired.com/story/what-is-the-metaverse/

Reer, F., Tang, W. Y., & Quandt, T. (2019). Psychosocial well-being and social media engagement: The mediating roles of social comparison orientation and fear of missing out. *New Media & Society, 21*(7), 1486–1505. DOI: 10.1177/1461444818823719

Reeves, B., & Nass, C. (1996). The media equation: How people treat computers, television, and new media like real people and places. Cambridge University Press. The_Media_Equation_How_People_Treat_Comp20161127-17472-1s43e41-libre.pdf

Rempel, J. K., Holmes, J. G., & Zanna, M. P. (1985). Trust in close relationships. *Journal of Personality and Social Psychology, 49*(1), 95–112. https://psycnet.apa.org/doi/10.1037/0022-3514.49.1.95. DOI: 10.1037/0022-3514.49.1.95 PMID: 11474726

Ribble, M., & Miller, T. N. (2013). Educational leadership in an online world: Connecting students to technology responsibly, safely, and ethically. *Phi Delta Kappan, 94*(5), 62–65. DOI: 10.1177/003172171309400514

Ringel, M., & Hirschberg, J. (2002, April). Automated message prioritization: Making voicemail retrieval more efficient. *In CHI'02 Extended Abstracts on Human Factors in Computing Systems* (pp. 592-593). DOI: 10.1145/506443.506499

Roberts, P. (2020). Working smarter with data. Australian Manufacturing Forum. https://www.aumanufacturing.com.au/working-smarter-with-data-ai-gives-agriculture-the-competitive-edge

Rohde, M., Reinecke, L., Pape, B., & Janneck, M. (2004). Community-building with web-based systems–investigating a hybrid community of students. [CSCW]. *Computer Supported Cooperative Work, 13*(5), 471–499. DOI: 10.1007/s10606-004-5066-4

Rosenberg, M. (1965). *Society and the adolescent self-image* (Vol. 11). Princeton university press. DOI: 10.1515/9781400876136

Rosenblat, M. O., Agrawal, A., & Yap, I. (2025). Online Safety Regulations Around. *WORLD (Oakland, Calif.).*

Rosen, L. D., Carrier, L. M., & Cheever, N. A. (2013). Facebook and texting made me do it: Media-induced task-switching while studying. *Computers in Human Behavior, 29*(3), 948–958. DOI: 10.1016/j.chb.2012.12.001

Rosen, L. D., Lim, A. F., Carrier, L. M., & Cheever, N. A. (2011). An empirical examination of the educational impact of text message-induced task switching in the classroom: Educational implications and strategies to enhance learning. *Psicol. Educ., 17*, 163–177. DOI: 10.5093/ed2011v17n2a4

Rothman, D. (2016, October). *A Tsunami of learners called Generation Z.* http://www.mdle.net/Journal/A_Tsunami_of_Learners_Called_Generation_Z.pdf

Sakthivel, M., Jaganathan, A., Mohanraj, M., & Selvakumar, P. Mohit, & Manjunath, T. (2025). Brand Loyalty through AI and Personalisation AI-Generated Content for Financial Marketing. In A. J. Nair, S. Manohar, Y. B. Limbu, & B. A. Huhmann (Eds.), Intersecting Natural Language Processing and FinTech Innovations in Service Marketing (pp. 77–96). IGI Global Scientific Publishing. DOI: 10.4018/979-8-3693-9944-6.ch006

Sarella, S. (2023). Advancements in NLP for Patient-Provider Communication in Telemedicine. *International Journal of Medical Informatics, 173*, 104988.

Schätz, S., Gagrčin, E., Toth, R., & Emmer, M. (2023). Users' perceptions of AI-generated communication in journalism. *Digital Journalism (Abingdon, England)*, *11*(6), 785–802. DOI: 10.1080/21670811.2023.2185951

Schilpzand, P., De Pater, I. E., & Erez, A. (2016). Workplace incivility: A review of the literature and agenda for future research. *Journal of Organizational Behavior*, *37*(S1), S57–S88. DOI: 10.1002/job.1976

Schmidt, P., Biessmann, F., & Teubner, T. (2020). Transparency and trust in artificial intelligence systems. *Journal of Decision Systems*, *29*(4), 260–278. DOI: 10.1080/12460125.2020.1819094

Schneckenberg, D., Roth, S., & Velamuri, V. K. (2023). Deparadoxification and value focus in sharing ventures: Concealing paradoxes in strategic decision-making. *Journal of Business Research*, *162*, 113883. DOI: 10.1016/j.jbusres.2023.113883

Secretary-General, U. N. (2020). *Roadmap for digital cooperation*. https://www.un.org/en/content/digital-cooperation-roadmap/

Sethumadhavan, R. P. P., S., Selvakumar, P., Kadu, S. G., Chandel, P. S., & Gupta, S. (2025). Environmental Sustainability and Employee Participation. In C. Şeker, E. Örücü, & A. Kaya (Eds.), Green Leadership Strategies for Increased Employee Engagement and Performance (pp. 275–298). IGI Global Scientific Publishing. DOI: 10.4018/979-8-3373-2106-6.ch009

Shanmugasundaram, M., & Tamilarasu, A. (2023). The impact of digital technology, social media, and artificial intelligence on cognitive functions: A review. *Frontiers in Cognition*, *2*, 1203077. Advance online publication. DOI: 10.3389/fcogn.2023.1203077

Sheehan, N. (1971, June 13). Vietnam archive: Pentagon study traces 3 decades of growing US involvement. The New York Times,6. https://www.nytimes.com/1971/06/13/archives/vietnamarchive-pentagon-study-traces-3-decades-of-growing-u-s.html

Shum, H. Y., He, X., & Li, D. (2018). From Eliza to XiaoIce: Challenges and opportunities with social chatbots. *Frontiers of Information Technology & Electronic Engineering*, *19*(1), 10–26. DOI: 10.1631/FITEE.1700826

Silver, D., Schrittwieser, K., Simonyan, K., Antonoglou, I., Huang, A., Guez, A., Hubert, T., Baker, L., Lai, M., Bolton, A., Chen, Y., Lillicrap, T., Hui, F., Sifre, L., van den Driessche, G., Graepel, T., & Hassabis, D. (2017). Mastering the game of Go without human knowledge. *Nature*, *550*(7676), 354–359. DOI: 10.1038/nature24270 PMID: 29052630

Singh, V., Singh, A., Jain, D., Kumar, V., & Verma, P. (2018). Patterns affecting structural properties of social networking site 'Twitter'. *International Journal of Business Information Systems*, *27*(4), 411–432. DOI: 10.1504/IJBIS.2018.090286

Smith, C. (2003). *Moral, believing animals: Human personhood and culture*. Oxford University Press. DOI: 10.1093/acprof:oso/9780195162028.001.0001

Socher, R., Pennington, J., Huang, E. H., Ng, A. Y., & Manning, C. D. (2011, July). Semi-supervised recursive autoencoders for predicting sentiment distributions. In *Proceedings of the 2011 conference on empirical methods in natural language processing* (pp. 151-161).

Solove, D. J. (2013). Privacy self-management and the consent dilemma. *Harvard Law Review*, *126*(7), 1880–1903.

Song, Y., Jiang, D., Zhao, X., Huang, X., Xu, Q., Wong, R. C. W., & Yang, Q. (2021, October). Smart meeting: Automatic meeting transcription and summarization for in-person conversations. In *Proceedings of the 29th ACM International Conference on Multimedia* (pp. 2777-2779). DOI: 10.1145/3474085.3478556

Spezialetti, M., Placidi, G., & Rossi, S. (2020). Emotion recognition for human-robot interaction: Recent advances and future perspectives. *Frontiers in Robotics and AI*, *7*, 532279. DOI: 10.3389/frobt.2020.532279 PMID: 33501307

Stanimirović, A. S., Nikolić, M. S., Jović, J. J., Ristić, D. I. I., Ćorać, A. M., Stoimenov, L. V., & Perić, Z. H. (2024). Applying eXplainable AI techniques to interpret machine learning predictive models for the analysis of problematic internet use among adolescents. *Elektronika ir Elektrotechnika*, *30*(2), 63–72. DOI: 10.5755/j02.eie.36316

Stanimirovic, M., Zivkovic, M., Momcilovic, A., Petronijevic, B. S., & Kondic, S. (2024). The role of architecture in the development of smart cities in Serbia. *ZELENA GRADNJA*, *2024*, 323–328. DOI: 10.5937/greenb24046S

Stepanenko, O., & Stupak, O. (2023). The use of GPT Chat among students in Ukrainian universities. *Scientific Journal of Polonia University*, *58*(3), 202–207. DOI: 10.23856/5828

Stiefel, S. (2018). 'The chatbot will see you now': mental health confidentiality concerns in software therapy. *Available at SSRN* 3166640.DOI: 10.2139/ssrn.3166640

Sunstein, C. R. (2017). Nudges that fail. *Behavioural Public Policy*, *1*(1), 4–25. DOI: 10.1017/bpp.2016.3

Suresh, H., & Guttag, J. (2021, October). A framework for understanding sources of harm throughout the machine learning life cycle. In *Proceedings of the 1st ACM Conference on Equity and Access in Algorithms, Mechanisms, and Optimization* (pp. 1-9). DOI: 10.1145/3465416.3483305

Susser, D., Roessler, B., & Nissenbaum, H. (2019). Online manipulation: Hidden influences in a digital world. *Georgetown Law Technology Review*, *4*(1), 1–45.

Susser, D., Roessler, B., & Nissenbaum, H. (2019). Technology, autonomy, and manipulation. *Internet Policy Review*, *8*(2), 1–22. DOI: 10.14763/2019.2.1410

Syvertsen, T., & Enli, G. (2019). Digital detox: Media resistance and the promise of authenticity. *Convergence (London)*, *26*(5–6), 1269–1283. DOI: 10.1177/1354856519847325

Taherdoost, H., & Madanchian, M. (2023). Artificial intelligence and sentiment analysis: A review in competitive research. *Computers*, *12*(2), 37. DOI: 10.3390/computers12020037

Talmatchi, M. L. (2025). THE INFLUENCE OF ARTIFICIAL INTELLIGENCE ON COMMUNICATION. *Scientific Bulletin-Nicolae Balcescu Land Forces Academy*, *30*(1), 115–124. DOI: 10.2478/bsaft-2025-0014

Tang, D., Qin, B., & Liu, T. (2015, September). Document modeling with gated recurrent neural network for sentiment classification. *In Proceedings of the 2015 conference on empirical methods in natural language processing* (pp. 1422-1432). DOI: 10.18653/v1/D15-1167

Tanwar, R., Gupta, N., & Tyagi, S. (2019). Ensuring Security and Privacy of Electronic Health Records in AI-Based Systems. *IEEE Transactions on Industrial Informatics*, *15*(6), 3274–3282.

Tausczik, Y. R., & Pennebaker, J. W. (2013, April). Improving teamwork using real-time language feedback. *In Proceedings of the SIGCHI conference on human factors in computing systems* (pp. 459-468). DOI: 10.1145/2470654.2470720

Taylor, M., & Chen, A. (2024). "It gets me": Emotional resonance and algorithmic intimacy on TikTok. *New Media & Society*. Advance online publication. DOI: 10.1177/14614448241218 73

Taylor, M., & Choi, J. (2024). Algorithmic feedback loops and emotional dependency: A longitudinal study. *Journal of Computer-Mediated Communication*, *29*(2), 145–165. DOI: 10.1093/jcmc/zmae001

Termann, S. (2025). The Dopamine Collapse Hypothesis: Bridging Behavioral Macroeconomics and Neuroscience. *Available at SSRN* 5168672.

Thapa, S., & Adhikari, S. (2023). ChatGPT, bard, and large language models for biomedical research: Opportunities and pitfalls. *Annals of Biomedical Engineering*, *51*(12), 2647–2651. DOI: 10.1007/s10439-023-03284-0 PMID: 37328703

Third, A., Bellerose, D., Dawkins, U., Keltie, E., & Pihl, K. (2019). *Children's rights in the digital age: A download from children around the world.* UNICEF Office of Research.

Thirunagalingam, A., & Selvakumar, P. (2025). Application of Automation and Robotics in the Oil and Gas Industry. In Abdullayev, V., & Khang, A. (Eds.), *Revolutionizing AI and Robotics in the Oil and Gas Industry* (pp. 229–244). IGI Global Scientific Publishing., DOI: 10.4018/979-8-3693-8156-4.ch011

Timmermans, E., Hermans, A. M., & Opree, S. J. (2021). Gone with the wind: Exploring mobile daters' ghosting experiences. *Journal of Social and Personal Relationships*, *38*(2), 783–801. DOI: 10.1177/0265407520970287

Tourkochoriti, I. (2023). The digital services act and the EU as the global regulator of the internet. *Chi. J. Int'l L.*, *24*, 129.

Trier, M., Kundisch, D., Beverungen, D., Müller, O., Schryen, G., Mirbabaie, M., & Trang, S. (2023). Digital responsibility: A multilevel framework for responsible digitalization. *Business & Information Systems Engineering*, *65*(4), 463–474. DOI: 10.1007/s12599-023-00822-x

Tufekci, Z. (2015). Algorithmic harms beyond Facebook and Google: Emergent challenges of computational agency. *Colorado Technology Law Journal*, *13*(1), 203–218.

Turkle, S. (2015). *Reclaiming Conversation: The Power of Talk in a Digital Age*. Penguin Press.

Turkle, S. (2017). *Alone Together: Why We Expect More from Technology and Less from Each Other*. Basic Books.

Twenge, J. M., & Campbell, W. K. (2018). Associations between screen time and lower psychological well-being among children and adolescents: Evidence from a population-based study. *Preventive Medicine Reports*, *12*, 271–283. DOI: 10.1016/j.pmedr.2018.10.003 PMID: 30406005

Uhls, Y. T., Ellison, N. B., & Subrahmanyam, K. (2014). Benefits and costs of social media in adolescence. *Pediatrics, 140*(Supplement 2), S67–S70. DOI: 10.1542/peds.2016-1758E PMID: 29093035

Uhls, Y. T., Michikyan, M., Morris, J., Garcia, D., Small, G. W., Zgourou, E., & Greenfield, P. M. (2014). Five days at outdoor education camp without screens improves preteen skills with nonverbal emotion cues. *Computers in Human Behavior, 39*, 387–392. DOI: 10.1016/j.chb.2014.05.036

Upadhyaya, A. N., Debnath, P., Rani, P., Selvakumar, P., Manjunath, T. C., & Bhattacharya, S. (2025). AI-Based Disaster Prediction and Early Warning Systems. In Mobo, F. (Ed.), *AI and Emerging Technologies for Emergency Response and Smart Cities* (pp. 55–74). IGI Global Scientific Publishing., DOI: 10.4018/979-8-3693-9770-1.ch003

Vaidyam, A. N., Wisniewski, H., Halamka, J. D., Kashavan, M. S., & Torous, J. B. (2019). Chatbots and conversational agents in mental health: A review of the psychiatric landscape. *Canadian Journal of Psychiatry, 64*(7), 456–464. DOI: 10.1177/0706743719828977 PMID: 30897957

Vallor, S. (2015). Moral deskilling and upskilling in a new machine age: Reflections on the ambiguous future of character. *Philosophy & Technology, 28*(1), 107–124. DOI: 10.1007/s13347-014-0156-9

Van Deursen, A., & Van Dijk, J. (2011). Internet skills performance tests: Are people ready for eHealth? *Journal of Medical Internet Research, 13*(2), e35. DOI: 10.2196/jmir.1581 PMID: 21531690

Van Eck, N. J., & Waltman, L. (2010). Software survey: VOSviewer, a computer program for bibliometric mapping. *Scientometrics, 84*(2), 523–538. DOI: 10.1007/s11192-009-0146-3 PMID: 20585380

Van Velthoven, M. H., Powell, J., & Powell, G. (2018). Problematic smartphone use: Digital approaches to an emerging public health problem. *Digital Health, 4*, 2055207618759167. DOI: 10.1177/2055207618759167 PMID: 31463071

Vaswani, A., Shazeer, N., Parmar, N., Uszkoreit, J., Jones, L., Gomez, A. N., . . . Polosukhin, I. (2017). Attention is all you need. *Advances in Neural Information Processing Systems (NeurIPS), 30,* 5998–6008. DOI: 10.48550/arXiv.1706.03762

Vogel, E. A., Rose, J. P., Roberts, L. R., & Eckles, K. (2014). Social comparison, social media, and self-esteem. *Psychology of Popular Media Culture, 3*(4), 206–222. DOI: 10.1037/ppm0000047

Voigt, P., & Von dem Bussche, A. (2017). *The EU General Data Protection Regulation (GDPR): A Practical Guide*. Springer., DOI: 10.1007/978-3-319-57959-7

Volkow, N. D., Koob, G. F., & McLellan, A. T. (2016). Neurobiologic advances from the brain disease model of addiction. *The New England Journal of Medicine*, *374*(4), 363–371. DOI: 10.1056/NEJMra1511480 PMID: 26816013

Walsh, T., Levy, N., Bell, G., Elliott, A., Maclaurin, J., Mareels, I., & Wood, Fiona. (2019). The effective and ethical development of artificial intelligence. ACOLA. https://acola.org/wp-content/uploads/2019/07/hs4_artificial-intelligence-report.pdf

Walther, J. B. (1996). Computer-mediated communication: Impersonal, interpersonal, and hyper personal interaction. *Communication Research*, *23*(1), 3–43. DOI: 10.1177/009365096023001001

Wang, J., Du, H., Niyato, D., Kang, J., Xiong, Z., Rajan, D., Mao, S., & Shen, X. (2024). A unified framework for guiding generative AI with wireless perception in resource constrained mobile edge networks. *IEEE Transactions on Mobile Computing*, *23*(11), 10344–10360. DOI: 10.1109/TMC.2024.3377226

Ward, A. F., Duke, K., Gneezy, A., & Bos, M. W. (2017). Brain drain: The mere presence of one's own smartphone reduces available cognitive capacity. *Journal of the Association for Consumer Research*, *2*(2), 140–154. DOI: 10.1086/691462

Webster, C., & Ivanov, S. (2020). Robotics, artificial intelligence, and the evolving nature of work. In George, B., & Paul, J. (Eds.), *Digital Transformation in Business and Society*. Palgrave Macmillan. DOI: 10.1007/978-3-030-08277-2_8

Weinstein, A. (2022). Lawsuit blames TikTok for girl's death. *The Washington Post*. https://www.washingtonpost.com

Weizenbaum, J. (1966). ELIZA—A computer program for the study of natural language communication between man and machine. *Communications of the ACM*, *9*(1), 36–45. DOI: 10.1145/365153.365168

Whyte, J. (2007). *Virtual reality and the built environment*. Routledge., DOI: 10.4324/9780080520667

Willcutt, E. G. (2012). The prevalence of DSM-IV attention-deficit/hyperactivity disorder: A meta-analytic review. *Neurotherapeutics; the Journal of the American Society for Experimental NeuroTherapeutics*, *9*(3), 490–499. DOI: 10.1007/s13311-012-0135-8 PMID: 22976615

Williams, J. (2018). *Stand Out of Our Light: Freedom and Resistance in the Attention Economy*. Cambridge University Press., DOI: 10.1017/9781108453004

Williams, J. R. (2019). The use of online social networking sites to nurture and cultivate bonding social capital: A systematic review of the literature from 1997 to 2018. *New Media & Society*, *21*(11-12), 2710–2729. DOI: 10.1177/1461444819858749

Wilmer, H. H., Sherman, L. E., & Chein, J. M. (2017). Smartphones and cognition: A review of research exploring the links between mobile technology habits and cognitive functioning. *Frontiers in Psychology*, *8*, 605. DOI: 10.3389/fpsyg.2017.00605 PMID: 28487665

Wolpaw, J. R. (2007, October). Brain-computer interfaces (BCIs) for communication and control. In *Proceedings of the 9th international ACM SIGACCESS conference on Computers and accessibility* (pp. 1-2). DOI: 10.1145/1296843.1296845

Woolfitt, Z. (2015). The effective use of video in higher education. *Lectoraat Teaching. Learning and Technology Inholland University of Applied Sciences*, *1*(1), 1–49.

World Health Organization (WHO). (2018). *International Classification of Diseases 11th Revision (ICD-11): Gaming Disorder.* https://www.who.int/news-room/q-a-detail/gaming-disorder

World Health Organization. (2018). *Gaming disorder*. https://www.who.int/news/item/28-05-2019

Wu, C., Liu, Y., Wang, J., & Yao, Q. (2024). Explainable AI and user agency: Improving recommender system transparency. *Information Processing & Management*, *61*(2), 102065. DOI: 10.1016/j.ipm.2023.102065

Xia, H., Chen, J., Qiu, Y., Liu, P., & Liu, Z. (2025). The impact of human–Chatbot interaction on human–human interaction: A substitution or complementary effect. *International Journal of Human-Computer Interaction*, *41*(2), 848–860. DOI: 10.1080/10447318.2024.2305985

Xu, M., Du, H., Niyato, D., Kang, J., Xiong, Z., Mao, S., Han, Z., Jamalipour, A., Kim, D. I., Shen, X., Leung, V. C. M., & Poor, H. V. (2024). Unleashing the power of edge-cloud generative AI in mobile networks: A survey of AIGC services. *IEEE Communications Surveys and Tutorials*, *26*(2), 1127–1170. DOI: 10.1109/COMST.2024.3353265

Yang, X., Liao, T., Wang, Y., Ren, L., & Zeng, J. (2024). The association between digital addiction and interpersonal relationships: A systematic review and meta-analysis. *Clinical Psychology Review*, *102501*, 102501. Advance online publication. DOI: 10.1016/j.cpr.2024.102501 PMID: 39265317

Yen, C. F., Chou, W. J., Liu, T. L., Yang, P., & Hu, H. F. (2014). The association of Internet addiction symptoms with anxiety, depression and self-esteem among adolescents with attention-deficit/hyperactivity disorder. *Comprehensive Psychiatry, 55*(7), 1601–1608. DOI: 10.1016/j.comppsych.2014.05.025 PMID: 25015304

Yeung, K. (2018). Algorithmic regulation: A critical interrogation. *Regulation & Governance, 12*(4), 505–523. DOI: 10.1111/rego.12158

Ye, X. (2025). Dark patterns and addictive designs. *Weizenbaum Journal of the Digital Society, 5*(3). DOI: 10.34669/wi.wjds/5.3.2

Yildirim, C., & Correia, A. P. (2015). Exploring the dimensions of nomophobia: Development and validation of a self-reported questionnaire. *Computers in Human Behavior, 49*, 130–137. DOI: 10.1016/j.chb.2015.02.059

Yoon, H., Lee, J., Wu, C., & Koh, J. (2024). Designing user-centered recommendation algorithms: The role of transparency and interactivity. *Behaviour & Information Technology, 43*(1), 57–75. DOI: 10.1080/0144929X.2023.2187320

Young, K. S. (2017a). Cognitive behavioral therapy for internet addiction. In Montag, C., & Reuter, M. (Eds.), *Internet Addiction: Neuroscientific Approaches and Therapeutical Interventions* (pp. 193–204). Springer., DOI: 10.1007/978-3-319-46276-9_11

Young, K. S. (2017b). The evolution of internet addiction disorder. In Montag, C., & Reuter, M. (Eds.), *Internet Addiction* (pp. 3–17). Springer., DOI: 10.1007/978-3-319-46276-9_1

Young, K. S., & Brand, M. (2017). Merging theoretical models and therapy approaches in the context of internet gaming disorder: A personal perspective. *Frontiers in Psychology, 8*, 1853. DOI: 10.3389/fpsyg.2017.01853 PMID: 29104555

Yuan, K., Qin, W., Wang, G., Zeng, F., Zhao, L., Yang, X., Liu, P., Liu, J., Sun, J., von Deneen, K. M., Gong, Q., Liu, Y., & Tian, J. (2011). Microstructure abnormalities in adolescents with internet addiction disorder. *PLoS One, 6*(6), e20708. DOI: 10.1371/journal.pone.0020708 PMID: 21677775

Yuan, X., Cheng, C., & Duan, Y. (2024). Affective human-chatbot interaction and emotional fulfillment. *Journal of Artificial Intelligence Research, 77*, 125–146. DOI: 10.1613/jair.1.14090

Zawacki-Richter, O., Marín, V. I., Bond, M., & Gouverneur, F. (2019). Systematic review of research on artificial intelligence applications in higher education – where are the educators? *International Journal of Educational Technology in Higher Education, 16*(1), 39. DOI: 10.1186/s41239-019-0171-0

Zeng, J., Chan, C. H., & Fu, K. W. (2021). The anatomy of the Facebook algorithm: An exploratory study of its impact on news dissemination. *New Media & Society*, *23*(5), 1088–1109. DOI: 10.1177/1461444820902108

Zhai, C., Wibowo, S., & Li, L. D. (2024). The effects of over-reliance on AI dialogue systems on students' cognitive abilities: A systematic review. *Smart Learning Environments*, *11*(1), 28. DOI: 10.1186/s40561-024-00316-7

Zhou, L., & Cheng, Q. (2024). ChatGPT and cognitive offloading in education: An I-PACE model approach. *Education and Information Technologies*, *29*(3), 1583–1601. DOI: 10.1007/s10639-024-12231-w

Zhou, L., Gao, J., Li, D., & Shum, H.-Y. (2018). The design and implementation of XiaoIce, an empathetic social chatbot. *Computational Linguistics*, *46*(1), 53–93. DOI: 10.1162/coli_a_00368

Zhou, L., Paul, S., Demirkan, H., Yuan, L., Spohrer, J., Zhou, M., & Basu, J. (2021). Intelligence augmentation: Towards building human-machine symbiotic relationship. *AIS Transactions on Human-Computer Interaction*, *13*(2), 243–264. DOI: 10.17705/1thci.00149

Zhou, Y., Lin, F. C., Du, Y. S., Qin, L. D., Zhao, Z. M., Xu, J. R., & Lei, H. (2011). Gray matter abnormalities in Internet addiction: A voxel-based morphometry study. *European Journal of Radiology*, *79*(1), 92–95. DOI: 10.1016/j.ejrad.2009.10.025 PMID: 19926237

Ziegler, D. A., Anguera, J. A., Gallen, C. L., Hsu, W.-Y., Wais, P. E., & Gazzaley, A. (2022). Leveraging technology to personalize cognitive enhancement methods in aging. *Nature Aging*, *2*(6), 475–483. DOI: 10.1038/s43587-022-00237-5 PMID: 35873177

Zuboff, S. (2019). *The age of surveillance capitalism: The fight for a human future at the new frontier of power*. PublicAffairs.

Zuboff, S. (2019). *The Age of Surveillance Capitalism: The Fight for a Human Future at the New Frontier of Power*. PublicAffairs.

# About the Contributors

**Mohd Noorulfakhri Yaacob** holds a Doctor of Philosophy (PhD) in Communication and Information Technology from Universiti Malaysia Perlis (UniMAP), awarded in 2021. He is currently a Senior Lecturer at Universiti Malaysia Perlis, where he contributes to the Faculty of Business and Communication. His areas of expertise include keystroke dynamics, soft biometrics, cybersecurity, and system development. Dr. Mohd Noorulfakhri has made significant academic contributions through his research and publications. He has authored numerous journal articles and conference papers, focusing on topics such as biometric authentication, feature extraction in keystroke dynamics, and cybersecurity risk management. His work has been published in reputable journals, including the Journal of Physics: Conference Series, Annals of Emerging Technologies in Computing (AETiC), and the International Journal of Business and Technology Management. His research emphasizes the integration of soft biometrics with keystroke dynamics to enhance user verification systems and cybersecurity measures. In addition to his academic achievements, Dr. Mohd Noorulfakhri has extensive professional experience in system analysis and development. He has led various projects, including the development of ICT systems for the Malaysian Ministry of Higher Education and UniMAP, such as the SUKIPT Information Technology System and the UniMAP E-Promosi System. His expertise extends to data center management, database operations, and the integration of advanced technologies like RFID and biometric systems. Dr. Mohd Noorulfakhri has also been recognized for his innovative contributions, receiving a Silver Medal at the Innovative Research, Invention, and Application Exhibition (I-RIA) 2019 for his work on a user verification system based on keystroke typing rhythm. He is a certified professional in various fields, holding credentials such as Professional Technologist (Ts.), Microsoft Certified Technology Specialist (MCTS), and EC-Council Certified Security Specialist (ECSS). With a strong commitment to advancing research and technology, Dr. Mohd Noorulfakhri continues to contribute to the fields of cybersecurity, biometrics, and information technology, inspiring students and professionals alike.

**Syed Zulkarnain Syed Idrus** holds a Ph.D. in Computer Science and Applications with a specialization in Computer Security from Université de Caen Basse-Normandie (UniCAEN), France, awarded in 2015. He is currently an Associate Professor at Universiti Malaysia Perlis (UniMAP), Malaysia, where he also serves as the Postgraduate Programme Chairperson (Research Mode) in the Communication Department, Faculty of Business & Communication. Dr. Syed Zulkarnain has made significant contributions to the fields of biometrics, keystroke dynamics, pattern recognition, and cybersecurity. His academic achievements include over 33 international refereed journal articles, 185 conference papers, and 5 books/book chapters. He has supervised 19 Ph.D. and 20 Master's students and has been actively involved in numerous international collaborations and research grants. Dr. Syed Zulkarnain has also received multiple awards for research excellence and innovation, including the UniMAP Research Excellence Award and international accolades for his contributions to biometrics and cybersecurity. His work has been widely cited, with an h-index of 19 on Scopus and 22 on Google Scholar, reflecting his impact in the academic community.

**Wan Nor Ashiqin Binti Wan Ali** holds a Doctor of Philosophy (PhD) in Instructional Multimedia from Universiti Sains Malaysia (USM), awarded in 2023. She is currently a Senior Lecturer (DS52) at the Faculty of Business and Communication, Universiti Malaysia Perlis (UniMAP). Her areas of specialization include Information Technology, Instructional Multimedia, Computational Thinking, and Educational Technology. Dr. Wan Nor Ashiqin has made significant contributions to academia through her research and publications. She has authored numerous journal articles indexed in Scopus, Web of Science, and MyCite, focusing on topics such as multimedia learning, computational thinking, and digital video courseware. Her work bridges the fields of cognitive multimedia learning and technology-enhanced education, with a particular emphasis on addressing cognitive load issues among digital natives. She has also contributed to several book chapters and co-authored books on web application development and human development. In addition to her research, Dr. Wan Nor Ashiqin has been actively involved in academic leadership and professional activities. She has served as a technical reviewer, editorial committee member, and internal examiner for various academic journals and conferences. Her dedication to teaching is evident in her supervision of undergraduate projects and her innovative approaches to integrating technology into education. Dr. Wan Nor Ashiqin has received multiple awards and recognitions for her work, including gold and silver medals for her innovative projects in instructional multimedia and cybersecurity. Her research has been supported by government and university grants, furthering advancements in areas such as biometric systems and IPv6 security. With a strong commitment to academic excellence and innovation, Dr. Wan Nor Ashiqin continues to contribute to the fields of educational technology and multimedia learning, inspiring students and researchers alike.

**Wan Ahmad Jaafar Bin Wan Yahaya** holds a Doctor of Philosophy (PhD) in Instructional Multimedia from the University of Leeds, United Kingdom, awarded in 2001. He is currently the Director of the Centre for Instructional Technology and Multimedia at Universiti Sains Malaysia (USM). His areas of specialization include Instructional Multimedia, ICT in Education, and Persuasive Technology. Professor Dr. Wan Ahmad Jaafar has made significant contributions to academia and research, particularly in the fields of multimedia learning, persuasive technology, and educational innovation. Over his career, he has authored numerous journal articles indexed in Scopus, Web of Science, and other reputable databases, as well as several books and book chapters. His research has focused on the development of innovative multimedia applications, including persuasive multimedia for education, virtual reality courseware, and game-based learning interventions. He has also been actively involved in the design and evaluation of digital tools to enhance teaching and learning, particularly in the context of higher education and school settings. In addition to his research, Professor Dr. Wan Ahmad Jaafar has held various academic leadership roles, including serving as the President of the Malaysian Educational Technology Association (META) from 2020 to 2022. He has also been a keynote speaker at numerous international conferences, sharing his expertise on topics such as metaverse-based learning, online education, and digital competencies for educators. His work has been recognized with multiple awards, including gold medals for innovative projects in instructional multimedia and game-based learning. Professor Dr. Wan Ahmad Jaafar has supervised numerous postgraduate students, including PhD and Master's candidates, and has contributed to the development of academic programs and curricula in instructional technology. His dedication to advancing educational technology and multimedia learning continues to inspire students, educators, and researchers worldwide.

**Christophe Rosenberger** obtained his PhD in Information Technology from the University of Rennes 1 in 1999. His PhD thesis work was undertaken at ENSSAT in Lannion between 1996 and 1999 in the field of hyperspectral image segmentation. He joined the ENSI de Bourges school of engineering in Bourges (known now as INSA Centre Val de Loire) as associate professor in 2000. In 2007, he joined the ENSICAEN school of engineering in Caen as full professor. He is actually director of the GREYC research lab composed of 180 members. He belongs to the SAFE

(Security, Architecture, Forensics, biomEtrics) research group in the GREYC research lab. His current work focuses in the domain of cybersecurity, in particular research activities in biometrics (keystroke dynamics, soft biometrics, evaluation of biometric systems, fingerprint quality assessment...) and digital forensics. He has authored or co-authored over 200 publications among 16 book chapters, 47 international journals and 5 patents (5 WO, 5 EP, 5 FR, 2 US, 1 PT).

***

**Rahmath Nisha**, driven by her passion for teaching, transitioned into academia, drawing on her background as an Engineer specializing in Electronics and Communication. Her academic achievements include ranking as a Gold Medalist in her MBA (HR and Hospital Management) from Saveetha University, where she was also recognized as the Best Outgoing Student. Rahmath Nisha's aspiration is to equip students with industry-ready skills through real-time teaching methods, thereby bridging the gap between academic knowledge and practical application in the workplace.

**A.K. Subramani** is a distinguished academic with a PhD in Business Administration from Manonmaniam Sundaranar University, Tirunelveli, India. With 18 years of teaching experience, he has made significant contributions to the field of human resource management and organisational behaviour. He has an impressive publication record with 80 articles in international journals, including two papers in the ABDC-A category, eight in the ABDC-B category, three in the ABDC-C category, 30 in Scopus-indexed journals, and eight in Web of Science journals. He has served as a resource person for various training workshops on SPSS and AMOS software packages

**Gayathri A.R.** holds an undergraduate degree in Optometry (B.Optom) and is currently pursuing her MBA with a specialization in Hospital and Human Resource Management. With a strong foundation in eye care and clinical practice, combined with managerial training, she brings a well-rounded and interdisciplinary perspective to the healthcare sector. Gayathri is deeply interested in enhancing patient care systems through efficient hospital administration. Her core strengths lie in healthcare analytics, communication, and team coordination. She is passionate about bridging clinical expertise with management practices to deliver impactful solutions that improve healthcare delivery and organizational performance.

**Tiara Afifah**, dedicated researcher specializing in Artificial Intelligence and emerging technologies, with a focus on advancing theoretical foundations and practical applications through scholarly investigation and interdisciplinary collaboration.

**N. Mari Anand** has a rich experience of 10 year in the field of teaching and expertise in the field of Marketing and Human Resource Management. Currently he is working as Faculty Member, Department of Business Studies, University of Technology & Applied Sciences, Salalah, Sultanate of Oman. He is also a Member in Research Advisory Committee at VELS Institute of Science, Technology & Advanced Studies, Chennai. To his credit he has published 27 articles in Scopus and UGC Listed Journals. He has guided 63 UG and 22 PG projects. He served as Member of Board of Studies for Business Administration and Member for University Examination Board of SRM-IST. The author is an Editorial Board Member for International Journal of Advance Research in Commerce Management and Finance (IJARCMF). The author has organized various International Conferences and International Conclave during his tenure. The author was an ISO Convener and served as IQAC coordinator & Exam Cell convener. He is also an External Academic Auditor and Chief Examiner for various institutions. He is an active Member in Federation of Indian Chamber of Commerce and Industries (FICCI) & Madras Management Association (MMA).

**Nilesh Anute** is an Associate Professor at Sri Balaji University, Pune, where he brings a wealth of academic and industry experience to the field of management education. With a strong background in research and teaching, Dr. Anute has contributed significantly to the development of students through innovative teaching methods, mentorship, and scholarly work. His areas of expertise include marketing, strategic management, and business analytics. Known for his commitment to academic excellence and continuous learning, Dr. Anute actively participates in conferences, publishes in reputed journals, and engages in consultancy projects that bridge the gap between theory and practice.

**Rama Krishna B** is a dedicated academician serving in the Department of CSE (Data Science) at CVR College of Engineering, Hyderabad, Telangana. With a strong passion for teaching and research, Dr. Rama Krishna focuses on advancing knowledge in the field of data science and its emerging applications. His contributions reflect a commitment to fostering innovation and analytical thinking among students, preparing them to meet the challenges of the evolving technology landscape. Through his expertise and guidance, Dr. Rama Krishna continues to play a vital role in shaping the academic and professional growth of future engineers.

**Abhijeet Das** is a distinguished academic affiliated with the Department of Civil Engineering at C.V. Raman Global University (CGU), located in Bhubaneswar,

Odisha, India. With his expertise and commitment to the field of civil engineering, Dr. Das plays a vital role in advancing both academic instruction and research within the department. Situated in the Khordha district of Odisha, CGU provides a dynamic environment for innovation and education, where Dr. Das contributes significantly through his scholarly work, mentorship, and dedication to developing future engineers. His contributions reflect a deep commitment to excellence in engineering education and regional development.

**Puspita Dash** a highly qualified proficiency with cumulative teaching experience of around 12 years in an educational institution. To merge my enthusiasm and talent for learning and teaching with adult vocational students in order to develop their professional skills and attitudes

**Madhanraj G** is a B.Tech graduate in Information Technology from Sri Manakula Vinayagar Engineering College, Tamil Nadu, India. His research interests include Artificial Intelligence, Natural Language Processing, and Virtual Healthcare Systems. He has worked on multiple academic projects involving machine learning, computer vision, and generative AI, including a Virtual Voice Health Assistant using LLMs and Google APIs. He is passionate about developing innovative software solutions that enhance real-world applications.

**Shivnath Ghosh** is a Professor and Head of the Department of Computer Science and Engineering at Brainware University. With 20 years of academic experience, he has made significant contributions to research and development. He has published over 50 research papers, holds 7 patents, authored 12 books, and contributed to 24 book chapters. Currently, he is guiding 6 Ph.D. research scholars, with two having already been awarded their Ph.D. under his supervision

**Namita Vyas Joshi** is Director & Dean, School of Law & Legal Affairs at Noida International University, with over two decades of academic, research, and administrative excellence. A Ph.D. in Law, she has guided doctoral scholars, edited reputed journals, and published widely in Scopus-indexed and UGC-CARE journals. A recipient of multiple national and international awards, she is committed to fostering ethical legal education, innovation, and social justice in the evolving legal landscape.

**M. R. Arun** completed his BE, ME and PhD from Anna University, Chennai. He completed PG Diploma (PGDEEM) from Annamalai University, M.Sc. Counselling Psychology from TNOU University, M.A. Public Administration from Madras University and B.Lib.Sc. from Alagappa University. He is in the teaching profession for the past 17 years, published around 101 papers in Journals, Patents and

Conferences. Active participant crossing more than 150 events and internationally networked through various Professional bodies. He is skilled and technically proficient in various simulation software associated to Research in Engineering. He organized and coordinated around 15 events in working institution. Authored 12 Books, 15 Book Chapters and he has been technically integrated in various international journals as an Editorial Board Member and Reviewer. His area of interest includes Video Processing, Remote Automation, Wireless Communication, Quantum Computing, Machine Learning & Artificial Intelligence.

**T.C. Manjunath** was born on 6th February 1967. He did his B.E. from RV College of Engg. in 1989 (B'lore Univ), M.E. in Robotics & Automation from Govt.'s LD College of Engg., (Gujarat Univ., Ahmedabad) in 1992 with FCD-First Rank & PhD in Systems & Control Engg. from IIT Bombay in the year 2007, got best research scholar award for the entire IITB. He is currently working as the Dean Research (R & D) and as Professor in Dept. of Computer Science & Engg. with specialization in IoT, Cyber Security, Blockchain Technology in Rajarajeswari College of Engineering, Bengaluru, Karnataka. He has got a teaching (academic), research & administrative experience of more than 35+ years (10 years as Principal & 8 years as HoD, 1 year as Dean Research & rest as faculty) and has published more than 1500+ research papers in various national & international journals & conferences, with 175+ patents, 100+ book-chapters, 25 awards, 100s of Keynote talks and also published 25 text books in various field of science, engineering & technology, completed projects worth Rs. 9 Crores till date & guided 10 PhD scholars in VTU. He is a member of 30 Professional Society Chapters and is a fellow of IE, IETE, AMIEE, Sr. Member of IEEE and a chartered engineer.

**T.C. Manjunath** was born on 6th February 1967. He did his B.E. from RV College of Engg. in 1989 (B'lore Univ), M.E. in Robotics & Automation from Govt.'s LD College of Engg., (Gujarat Univ., Ahmedabad) in 1992 with FCD-First Rank & PhD in Systems & Control Engg. from IIT Bombay in the year 2007, got best research scholar award for the entire IITB. He is currently working as the Dean Research (R & D) and as Professor in Dept. of Computer Science & Engg. with specialization in IoT, Cyber Security, Blockchain Technology in Rajarajeswari College of Engineering, Bengaluru, Karnataka. He has got a teaching (academic), research & administrative experience of more than 35+ years (10 years as Principal & 8 years as HoD, 1 year as Dean Research & rest as faculty) and has published more than 1500+ research papers in various national & international journals & conferences, with 175+ patents, 100+ book-chapters, 25 awards, 100s of Keynote talks and also published 25 text books in various field of science, engineering & technology, completed projects worth Rs. 9 Crores till date & guided 10 PhD scholars in VTU. He is a member of 30 Professional Society Chapters and is a fellow of IE, IETE, AMIEE, Sr. Member of IEEE and a chartered engineer.

**P. Selvakumar** is currently an Associate Professor in the Department of Science and Humanities at Nehru Institute of Technology, Coimbatore, Tamil Nadu, India. Prior to joining Nehru Institute of Technology, he held positions as an Assistant Professor in the Department of Science and Humanities various engineering colleges in Coimbatore, Tamil Nadu, India, spanning from 2011 to 2023. Dr.P. Selvakumar's academic and research interests lie primarily in the field of phytochemistry. He has made significant contributions to his field, with an impressive record that includes 30 journal publications, 12 patents, and 20 conference papers. Additionally, he has organized 5 seminars and conferences, further demonstrating his commitment to academic and scientific exchange. Throughout his career, Dr. P.Selvakumar has been recognized for his dedication and excellence in teaching, having been honored with several awards, including the Best Teacher Awards. He holds a prominent position in the academic community, contributing actively to research.

**Deepika Paira** is an accomplished Assistant Professor of Law, currently pursuing her doctoral research in Criminal Law from Vel Tech Rangarajan Dr. Sagunthala R&D Institute of Science and Technology, Avadi, Chennai. She holds an LL.B. from Law Centre-I, Delhi University, and an LL.M. in Constitutional Law from Amity School of Law. With over five years of teaching experience, she has also practiced litigation, offering her a comprehensive understanding of both academic and practical aspects of law. Deepika Paira specializes in Constitutional Law and Criminal Law, and is known for her insightful teaching methodology. She has published numerous research papers in UGC CARE-listed journals and Scopus-indexed publications. Her active participation in Faculty Development Programs, as well as her engagement in national and international workshops, seminars, and conferences, reflects her commitment to continuous learning and academic excellence. Deepika Paira is a dedicated legal educator and researcher, contributing significantly to the field of law.

**R. Durai Pandian** is a Professor of Finance & Accounting at Saveetha School of Management, Saveetha University, Chennai. He previously served as Professor & Head (Research) at Garden City University (2019–2022) and held a similar role at PES University, Bangalore (2007–2019). Beginning his academic career in 2000, he held positions at Karunya University after initial industry experience in the hotel sector. With 26 years in teaching and research, he holds degrees in Commerce, an MBA from Manipal University, and a Ph.D. from Alagappa Institute of Management. A UGC Junior Research Fellow, he also completed an FDPM at IIM-A. Dr. Pandian has published over 55 research papers, led academic initiatives, and mentored Ph.D. scholars. His interests include history and sustainable agriculture, especially organic farming.

**Shrikant Ratley** is a seasoned academician and administrator with over 24 years of experience in management education and corporate training. Currently serving as Associate Professor at Marwadi University, Rajkot, he has held leadership roles as HOD, SAC Head, and FDC Head. A Ph.D. in Management, Dr. Ratley has published extensively in SCOPUS and ABDC-indexed journals, guided research scholars, and organized national conferences and industry-academia collaborations fostering student development and institutional excellence.

**S. Jyothirmaye Reddy** is a seasoned academician with 24 years of experience in the field of Human Resource Management. She is currently serving in the Faculty of Management Studies at Marwadi University, Rajkot, Gujarat. Dr. Reddy has a strong research background, with 26 published articles in reputed journals including Scopus, Web of Science, and ABDC (Category B & C) as well as other peer-reviewed publications. She has actively participated in numerous national and international conferences, presenting her research work and contributing to academic discourse. In addition to her teaching and research pursuits, she is presently supervising four PhD scholars, further demonstrating her commitment to academic excellence and research mentorship.

**Binastya Anggara Sekti** has been a lecturer at the Faculty of Computer Science, Esa Unggul University, Jakarta, since 2016. He is actively involved in the Artificial Intelligence and Information Security Study Group. He holds a Bachelor's degree in Informatics Engineering from the Bandung Institute of Technology and a Master’s degree in Information Systems Management from Trisakti University, Jakarta. Prior to entering academia, he accumulated over 25 years of professional experience as an IT practitioner in various companies across Jakarta. His work focused on developing data centers for internet service providers and delivering IT solutions for the manufacturing and oil & gas sectors. His research interests include artificial intelligence, cybersecurity, and the development of IT infrastructure.

**Aditi Sharma** is currently working as Assistant Professor Amity University, Jharkhand in the Department of Psychology. She has a Masters degree in Psychology from University of Delhi & a Post graduate diploma in Counseling Psychology. She is also pursuing her PhD in Psychology. Earlier she was a trainer in the European Union funded project ERASMUS+ wherein mentally subnormal adolescents were sensitized to main stream society in Romania, Spain & Turkey. She has worked with XISS as a Trainer for acing personal & professional competencies. She has also been working in the field of capacity building, Counseling & Stress Management for Women at the Namkum Probation Home & students at Kishor Nagar Boys Home. Her area of research interest is in the connection between physical & mental health. She has attended and presented papers in many national and international conferences. She has published 10 Book chapters and 6 research papers in APA certified journal. Her most recent paper has been published in a Scopus indexed journal titled "Impact of Yoga on the Psycho-physical well being of Individuals in COVID-19 times & after."

**Rakshit Sharma** is a final-year law student at Amity University, Noida, India with a dual degree in Business Management and Law (BBA-LLB). Passionate about Intellectual Property Law, Legal Tech, and Commercial Law, working to improve legal awareness and access. Contributor to international legal blogs and journals. Currently exploring research in AI, IP, and digital regulation.

**Farhana Wahidiyah** is an undergraduate student at the Faculty of Computer Science, Esa Unggul University, Indonesia. She has a strong interest in digital communication, media psychology, and the impact of digital addiction on mental health. Currently, she is involved in academic writing projects focused on digital literacy and emotional well-being in the digital age.

# Index

## A



## B



## C



## D

www.ingramcontent.com/pod-product-compliance
Lightning Source LLC
LaVergne TN
LVHW081531300926
849161LV00006B/1382